Preliminary Performance-Based Analyses Relevant to Dose-Based Performance Measures for a Proposed Geologic Repository at Yucca Mountain

I0438912

Center for Nuclear Waste Regulatory Analyses

U.S. Nuclear Regulatory Commission
Office of Nuclear Material Safety and Safeguards
Washington, DC 20555-0001

AVAILABILITY OF REFERENCE MATERIALS
IN NRC PUBLICATIONS

Preliminary Performance-Based Analyses Relevant to Dose-Based Performance Measures for a Proposed Geologic Repository at Yucca Mountain

Manuscript Completed: August 1999
Date Published: October 2001

Edited by
T. J. McCartin, M. P. Lee

Division of Waste Management
Office of Nuclear Material Safety and Safeguards
U.S. Nuclear Regulatory Commission
Washington, DC 20555-0001

Center for Nuclear Waste Regulatory Analyses
6220 Culebra Road
San Antonio, TX 78228-5155

NUREG-1538 has been reproduced from
the best available copy.

For sale by the Superintendent of Documents, U.S. Government Printing Office
Internet: bookstore.gpo.gov   Phone: (202) 512-1800   Fax: (202) 512-2250
Mail: Stop SSOP, Washington, DC 20402-0001

ISBN 0-16-050978-5

ABSTRACT

The National Academy of Sciences' (NAS') Committee on Technical Bases for Yucca Mountain (Nevada) Standards recommended that standards for the disposal of high-level radioactive waste (HLW) at Yucca Mountain should: (1) set a limit on the risk to individuals; (2) use the critical group approach, as defined by the International Commission on Radiological Protection; (3) define the critical group using present knowledge and cautious, reasonable assumptions; (4) use a time period for conducting compliance assessment that includes the period of greatest risk; and (5) use a stylized calculation to assess whether the repository's performance would be substantially degraded as a consequence of a postulated intrusion. The staff and its technical assistance contractor—the Center for Nuclear Waste Regulatory Analyses—have undertaken a series of focused technical analyses to better understand the NAS recommendations and their implementation within the U.S. Nuclear Regulatory Commission's HLW performance assessment program. Overall, the staff believes that it will be able to integrate a dose-based approach into its regulatory framework and supporting guidance. The staff was able to: (1) tentatively identify characteristics for two potential receptor groups—"farming" and "residential" (non-farming)—using information for lifestyles and water-use practices presently occurring in the Yucca Mountain area and in other, similar, environments; (2) ascertain the potential for reducing radionuclide concentrations in ground water caused by dispersive transport processes (reduction of 1 to 75 times) and borehole mixing in a pumping water well (reduction of 1 to 50 times); (3) describe an approach to implement a dose calculation for the residential [mean dose of 30 millirem (mrem)] and farming (mean dose of 10 mrem) receptor groups; (4) describe an approach to implement a dose calculation for direct disruption of the repository from volcanic activity (probability weighted dose of about 1 mrem); (5) describe an approach to a stylized calculation for human intrusion; and (6) evaluate the time dependence of radiological hazard of HLW by comparison with naturally concentrated uranium in an ore body (after 10,000 years the relative radiological hazard of HLW has decreased by 99.9 percent and is within less than an order of magnitude of the hazard of the hypothetical ore body).

CONTENTS

1. Introduction 1–1

M.P. Lee/NMSS; J.P. Kotra/NMSS; and T.J. McCartin/NMSS

2. Considerations in the Definition of a Receptor Group 2–1

*M.P. Lee/NMSS; G.W. Wittmeyer/CNWRA; N.M. Coleman/NMSS; and
R.B. Codell/NMSS*

*G.W. Wittmeyer/CNWRA; M.P. Miklas/CNWRA; R.V. Klar/CNWRA;
D. Williams[1]; and D. Balin[2]*

---

[1]Independent consultant from Oakland, California.

[2]Independent consultant from San Antonio, Texas.

CONTENTS continued

[3]Now with the Sandia National Laboratories (Albuquerque, New Mexico).
[4]Independent consultant from El Paso, Texas.

CONTENTS continued

CONTENTS continued

FIGURES

---

[5] Now with the Los Alamos National Laboratory (Los Alamos, New Mexico).

[6] Now with the Department of Mechanical Engineering at the University of Texas (San Antonio).

FIGURES continued

FIGURES continued

FIGURES continued

TABLES

TABLES continued

APPENDICES

---

[1]Now retired.

[2]Independent consultant from Oakland, California.

[3]Independent consultant from San Antonio, Texas.

EXECUTIVE SUMMARY

1. INTRODUCTION

In 1992, Congress directed the U.S. Environmental Protection Agency (EPA), at Section 801 of the Energy Policy Act of 1992 (EnPA), Public Law 102–486, to contract with the National Academy of Sciences (NAS) to advise EPA on the appropriate technical basis for public health and safety standards governing the proposed geologic repository at Yucca Mountain, Nevada. On August 1, 1995, the NAS Committee on Technical Bases for Yucca Mountain Standards issued its report, *Technical Bases for Yucca Mountain Standards.* In its report, the NAS recommended: (a) the standard should set a limit on the risk to individuals; (b) the critical group approach, as defined by the International Commission on Radiological Protection, should be adopted; (c) the critical group should be defined using present knowledge, and cautious and reasonable assumptions; (d) the compliance assessment should be conducted over a timeframe that includes the period of greatest risk; and (e) a stylized calculation should be used to assess whether the repository's performance would be substantially degraded as a consequence of a postulated intrusion.

The NAS recommended an approach for evaluating the performance of a geologic repository, that is significantly different from previous evaluations performed as part of the high-level waste (HLW) performance assessment program at the U.S. Nuclear Regulatory Commission (NRC). In this NUREG, the staff and its technical assistance contractor—the Center for Nuclear Waste Regulatory Analyses—have undertaken a series of focused technical analyses, to better understand the NAS recommendations and their implementation within NRC's HLW program (e.g., modifications and enhancements to NRC's total-system performance assessment computer code). These analyses focused on: (a) evaluation of lifestyles and water-use practices to be used for identification of potential receptor groups; (b) estimation of receptor doses from the ground-water pathway; (c) evaluation of the consequences from an assumed intrusion scenario; (d) evaluation of the risk for low-probability events; and (e) evaluation of the relative radiological hazard of HLW over time.

2. IDENTIFICATION OF HYPOTHETICAL RECEPTOR GROUPS

The staff examined a range of land and water-use practices occurring in the Yucca Mountain area and in other, similar, environments, as part of the process of establishing reasonable bounds on estimates of these practices. Current use of ground water in the Yucca Mountain area is affected by both physiographic factors and institutional controls. Because the climate is arid to semi-arid, agriculture is restricted to areas where the depth to water is shallow enough to make irrigation economically feasible (i.e., Amargosa Desert, Pahrump, and Oasis Valleys). Agriculture also tends to be confined to areas where the relief is gentle enough to make center-pivot or furrow irrigation methods practical and where the soil conditions are suitable, such as near the distal margin of alluvial fan deposits. North of U.S. Highway 95, much of the land comprising the Nevada Test Site (including Yucca Mountain) is controlled by either the U.S. Department of Energy, the U.S. Bureau of Reclamation, or the U.S. Air Force, which has precluded agricultural development and ranching. Although the withdrawal of this land from private development may have affected land-use patterns, the great depth to ground water and limitations to soil irrigability, throughout the controlled area, suggest that farming is not economically feasible with current technology. Assuming current technology, future agricultural development will most likely continue to be centered in the Amargosa Desert area.

Data from Arizona, southern Nevada, New Mexico, and the Trans-Pecos region of Texas were examined to provide additional insights on the use of ground water from depths greater than the depths that currently exist in the Amargosa Desert area. The data indicate that ground water is pumped from aquifers in arid to semi-arid regions, where the depth to water is as great as that in Jackass Flats to the east of Yucca Mountain. Of 115 wells that pump from aquifers with depths to water equal to or greater than 240 meters; only 2 (1.7 percent) are used for irrigation; 38 (33 percent) are used to supply stock water; and 63 (54.8 percent) are used for public and domestic water supply. Based on local practices in Amargosa Valley and on data gathered in the well survey, it appears that pumping ground water for irrigation from depths greater than 240 meters is a rare practice (1.7 percent). However, data from the water well survey does suggest that existing communities will construct wells that pump from great depths to water if more easily exploited water supplies are insufficient or unreliable. Although current lifestyles in the Yucca Mountain area do not support the idea that very small communities (25 to 100 persons) or individual homeowners will construct wells to pump fresh water from great depths, the survey data do suggest that a residential-type receptor group would be more likely to withdraw ground water from greater depths than a farming-type receptor group. However, the residential receptor group would also be expected to withdraw significantly less water than the farming receptor group.

For the purposes of this NUREG, the staff identified and considered the characteristics for two potential (hypothetical) receptor groups—"farming" and "residential" (non-farming)—in the Yucca Mountain area.

- *"Farming" Receptor Group: Because of topographic, meteorologic, pedologic, and hydrologic considerations, this hypothetical receptor group is a farming community located in an topographically closed basin at a distance no closer than 20 kilometers to the site. The farming community is able to obtain its water from relatively shallow wells located in near-surface, local alluvial aquifers (i.e., generally 30 to 100 meters deep). This is an important consideration*

because development and operating costs for such wells are, in large measure, related to the depth of the water table. Thus, for reasons of practicality, this hypothetical receptor group would establish its irrigation wells in areas where the water table is near the surface. The exposure pathways considered for the hypothetical farming receptor group include ingestion (of contaminated water, crops, and animal products); inhalation (from resuspension of contaminated soil); and direct exposure.

- *"Residential" Receptor Group: This hypothetical receptor group is a residential community located on one of the volcanic mesas or mountainous uplands that flank the topographically-closed basins, but may also be located in higher-elevation valleys, which are characterized by thin sequences of unsaturated alluvial sediments. The residential community is located between 5 and 20 kilometers from the site where the depth to the water table ranges from approximately 300 to 100 meters, respectively, at the two locations. Because freshwater demands for a residential community are substantially less than those for a farming community, the residential community could be located closer to the site than a farming community and could obtain its water from wells located in the deeper tuff or carbonate (regional) aquifers found at depths of 300 meters or more. The exposure pathway considered for the hypothetical residential receptor group is the ingestion of contaminated water.*

3. GROUND-WATER PATHWAY

Radionuclides released from a potential repository at Yucca Mountain can be expected to migrate to the water table and be carried downgradient toward discharge areas, most likely at some point in the Amargosa-Death Valley area. Thus, the ground-water pathway is the most likely exposure pathway. Exposure to humans is assumed to occur through the use of well water that is contaminated with radionuclides. Determination of the concentration of radionuclides in well water depends on: (a) the location of the discharge point; (b) the degree of plume dispersion; and

(c) pumping of the well itself. The staff performed a series of analyses to determine the importance of these three factors.

Ground-water flow beneath Yucca Mountain would initially be in volcanic tuff, generally dipping down-gradient toward the Amargosa-Death Valley area. Several tens of kilometers from the proposed repository site, the water table laterally intersects valley-fill alluvial deposits. The areal extent of a radionuclide plume would increase with distance from the repository because of processes of molecular diffusion and mechanical mixing. However, staff analyses indicate that passive ground-water mixing at the Yucca Mountain site is not likely to produce very large dilution factors. In the immediate vicinity of the proposed repository, dilution is limited because of the directional characteristics of the flow and the magnitudes of the Darcy fluxes (i.e., the tendency for contaminant plumes to remain on or close to the water table surface). As the radionuclide plumes travel away from the proposed repository, they have a greater chance of spreading and becoming diluted both laterally and vertically as a result of movement through or around large-scale structural features such as faults. Depending on their hydraulic properties, faults in the tuff aquifer could play a major role in determining the rate and direction of plume spread. At substantial distances, radionuclide plumes traveling through the alluvium are expected to be further mixed with uncontaminated waters, but the dilution at locations such as the Amargosa Desert, is unlikely to increase by many orders of magnitude. However, mixing resulting from well pumping becomes a significant dilution process as natural mixing decreases.

Dose calculations were made for hypothetical farming and residential receptor groups. The hypothetical farming receptor group is assumed to be located 30 kilometers from the proposed repository site and withdraws large amounts of water (30,400 cubic meters per day) to support the water needs of an agricultural community. The hypothetical residential receptor group is assumed to be located 5 kilometers from the proposed repository site and withdraws 3800 cubic meters per year of water to support household uses of water. Thus, the farming receptor group has more borehole dilution and a longer transport path that reduces radionuclide concentrations and delays the time of the peak dose relative to values for the hypothetical residential group. However, the hypothetical farming receptor group is assumed to have more exposure pathways (e.g., ingestion of contaminated water, crops, and animal products) than the hypothetical residential receptor group (exposure pathway from ingesting contaminated water only) which tends to offset differences in doses between the two hypothetical groups .

Although assumptions concerning location and lifestyle were quite different for the two hypothetical receptor groups, conclusions regarding the cause of the estimated peak dose were similar. Peak doses were the result of a relatively small number of long-lived, mobile radionuclides (e.g., technetium-99, neptunium-237, and iodine-129) that are the first radionuclides to arrive at the hypothetical receptor location. Despite the differences in the time of the peaks for the two locations (2500 years for the 5-kilometer location versus 15,000 years for 30-kilometer location), the estimated mean doses were somewhat similar [30 millirem (mrem) for the 5-kilometer location versus 10 mrem for the 30-kilometer location]. It should be noted that dose curves for both locations are a reflection of the conservative assumption that all waste packages fail and release radionuclides at 1000 years.

4. HUMAN INTRUSION

The NAS recommended the use of a stylized calculation to evaluate the resilience of the repository to a postulated intrusion. The objective of this calculation is to determine if an intrusion into the repository would degrade the ability of the repository to comply with the overall performance objective (i.e., individual dose or risk limit for the critical group). Because the probability of such a scenario would be highly speculative, the NAS recommended that the calculation not be included in the overall performance assessment of the site, but considered separately using the same critical group assumptions as the overall performance assessment. The staff evaluated the consequences of human intrusion by considering the following two scenarios: (a) a single borehole intersecting the emplacement drift and damaging the waste package; and (b) a single borehole intersecting the emplacement drift, drilling completely through a waste package, and continuing through the unsaturated zone to the water table.

The mean peak doses from the postulated intrusion scenarios was between 1 to 4 microrems. Based on these analyses, the staff concludes that the consequences of a postulated human intrusion event can be readily evaluated with current performance assessment techniques, and repository performance is not overly sensitive to assumptions regarding the specifics of the intrusion (i.e., borehole diameter, catchment area, and timing of the drilling event).

5.   RISK FROM LOW-PROBABILITY EVENTS

The NAS recommended that individual risk be used for standards for a potential geologic repository at Yucca Mountain. Estimation of risk needs to consider likely pathways for radiological exposure (e.g., ground-water pathway) as well as less likely exposure pathways from low-probability events. Estimation of the individual dose or risk from an extrusive volcanic event is used to provide insights on approaches for estimating individual dose for low-probability events and the relationship, if any, between the time period of the analysis and the dose calculation.

The exposure scenario for an extrusive volcanic (igneous) event consists of four components in the following progression: (i) magma enters the repository and becomes contaminated with spent nuclear fuel particles; (ii) tephra forms from the contaminated magma and is released from the repository; (iii) an eruption column and plume form and transport contaminated tephra to locations

downwind from the event; and (iv) radionuclide-contaminated ash collects on the earth's surface, potentially exposing receptor groups. The expected dose or "average risk" to an individual is a function of the dose and the probability of receiving that dose. In calculating the expected annual dose at a particular time T, the probability that an individual has an exposure at time T is the probability that the event has occurred at any time previous to T (i.e., exposure from a volcanic event occurs during the year of the event and in each subsequent year because of the residual surface contamination). Thus, at 1000 years, there is a 1 chance in 10,000 that a volcanic event has occurred in the initial 1000 years (for the current analysis, it is assumed that a volcanic cone forms within the center of the repository block with an annual probability of 10^{-7}).

The expected annual dose reaches a peak of approximately 1 mrem around 1000 years after repository closure (the expected annual dose is determined by multiplying the consequence or dose times the probability that the dose has occurred). This early peak in the expected annual dose is caused by a rapid decrease in the dose, over the initial 1000 years, from radioactive decay of key radionuclides (e.g., americium-241, which has a radioactive half-life of 432 years, is the largest contributor to peak dose).

6.   RADIOLOGICAL HAZARD OF HLW

The NAS recommended that compliance with HLW standards should be over the time period of maximum risk up to one-million years. The purpose of this recommendation was to focus the analysis of repository performance on the time at which future populations might be at maximum risk. The health hazard of radioactive waste depends on two primary factors: (a) the inherent radiotoxicity of the material; and (b) the accessibility of the material to possible human intake or exposure. To evaluate the health hazard, a comparison is made between the radiological hazard of a geologic repository containing spent nuclear fuel and a hypothetical ore body. The analysis was done for a 100-million-year time period and assumed both the repository and ore body were located in the unsaturated zone at Yucca Mountain.

A primary difference between a geologic repository and the hypothetical ore body referred to in this analysis is that the repository-destined waste has a significant man-made radionuclide inventory as compared with the naturally occurring radionuclides of the ore body. The hazard of the geologic repository and the hypothetical ore body will decrease, over time, at different rates, because of differences in the inventories (e.g., spent nuclear fuel contains significant amounts of short-lived radionuclides that are not present in the ore body).

The relative radiological hazard of the spent fuel repository is initially about 4 orders of magnitude greater than that of the hypothetical ore body. The hazard diminishes most rapidly over the first few hundred to a few thousand years. By 10,000 years the relative hazard will have decreased by 99.9 percent and be within less than an order of magnitude of the hypothetical ore body. A time period of interest, for regulation of a proposed repository, of 10,000 years, would, therefore, focus attention on the time period when the waste has a significant man-made hazard component that is readily discernable from an equivalent hypothetical ore body.

FOREWORD

Since its inception in the mid-1970s, the U.S. Nuclear Regulatory Commission's (NRC's) geologic repository program for the disposal of spent nuclear fuel and other high-level radioactive waste has relied on the evolving science of performance assessment to accomplish several objectives. Accordingly, the staff has sought to develop, maintain, and enhance its performance assessment capability, in the form of Iterative Performance Assessments (IPAs). Experience developing IPAs has enabled the staff to evaluate total-system performance assessments submitted in support of the U.S. Department of Energy's (DOE's) Pre-licensing activities (e.g., site characterization and the forthcoming site suitability determination), and to prepare to review a potential DOE license application and decision on a possible request for construction authorization.

The NRC staff has also relied on its evolving IPA capability during early interactions with the U.S. Environmental Protection Agency (EPA) staff as EPA developed its site-specific radiation protection standards for a potential geologic repository at Yucca Mountain, Nevada, pursuant to the Energy Policy Act of 1992. In light of the 1995 National Academy of Sciences' findings and recommendations for those standards, the NRC staff and its technical assistance contractor — the Center for Nuclear Waste Regulatory Analyses — undertook a limited series of analyses, using its IPA capability to better understand what technical challenges may be faced in implementing and evaluating health-based (dose) performance measures at Yucca Mountain. EPA published its final site-specific radiation standards on June 13, 2001 (66 FR 23074).

Most of the principal analyses described in this NUREG were conducted between 1995 and 1996, with the key results published and made publicly available as short summaries in Sagar (1997), as NUREG/CR−6513.[1] Two additional analyses and one field investigation were subsequently conducted during the period 1996−98.[2] Documentation in support of the completed work was later placed in NRC's Public Document Room (PDR), but did not receive widespread distribution. As a consequence, a decision was made to include this additional documentation in this NUREG, after limited editorial review and modification. Despite the editorial treatment, this additional technical documentation is substantially the same as the original versions found in the PDR. Lastly, the results of two analyses first published in NUREG/CR−6513 (human intrusion and extrusive volcanism) were updated in this NUREG owing to the availability of more recent data and/or newer analytical approaches.

No proprietary or unpublished data sources were used in these analyses − only data currently in the public domain have been cited. The calculations, figures, and conclusions presented herein result from the continuing exercise of the staff capability to review a performance assessment for a potential geologic repository at Yucca Mountain. In this regard, the approaches, assumptions, and conclusion described in this NUREG should in no way be construed to express the views, preferences, or positions of the staff regarding what the eventual form of the site-specific regulatory framework for Yucca Mountain should be.

Finally, more site characterization information now exists than was available at the time these analyses were first conducted and documented. Thus, given the iterative nature of performance assessments, this NUREG serves to document, as a snapshot in time, the staff's capability for reviewing a performance assessment for the proposed Yucca Mountain site. As DOE proceeds with characterizing

---

[1]See Chapter 9, entitled "Activities Related to the Development of the EPA Yucca Mountain Standard."

[2]As noted in text.

the Yucca Mountain site and its environs, the staff expects that additional information will be forthcoming that will contribute to an improved understanding of combined systems and events and processes that are key to repository performance.

ENGLISH/METRIC CONVERSION FACTORS

The preferred system of measurement today is the "Systèm Internationale (SI)," or the metric system. However, for some physical quantities, many scientists and engineers prefer the familiar and continue to use the English system (inch-pound units). With few exceptions, all units of measure cited in this NUREG are usually in the metric system.

The following table provides the appropriate conversion factors to allow the user to switch between the English and SI systems of measure. Not all units nor methods of conversion are shown. Unit abbreviations are shown in parentheses. All conversion factors are approximate.

Multiply Inch-Pound Units	*By*	*To Obtain SI Units*
	Length	
inch (in)	2.54	centimeter (cm)
feet (ft)	0.3048	meter (m)
mile (mi)	1.609	kilometer (km)
	Area	
square mile (mi^2)	2.590	square kilometers (km^2)
acre	4046.873	square meters (m^2)
	0.40468	hectacres
	Flow	
cubic feet per second (ft^3/sec)	0.02832	cubic meters per second (m^3/sec)
U.S. gallons per minute (gal/min)	0.06309	liters per second (L/sec)
	Transmissivity	
foot squared per day (ft^2/day)	0.0929	meter squared per day (m^2/day)
	Temperature	
degree Fahrenheit (°F)	°C = (°F − 32)/1.8	degree Celsius (°C)
	Radiation Dose	
millirem (mrem)	0.01	millisievert (mSv)

ACKNOWLEDGMENTS

The authors and editors gratefully acknowledge the many contributions made by other Nuclear Material Safety and Safeguards (NMSS), Nuclear Regulatory Research, General Counsel (OGC), and the Center for Nuclear Waste Regulatory Analyses (CNWRA) management and staff, which have been incorporated into the text of this NUREG. In this regard, thanks are also owed the following staff for their thoughtful review comments and suggestions on various sections of this NUREG:

A. Armstrong/CNWRA
N. Jensen/OGC
K. McConnell/NMSS
B. Sagar/CNWRA
M. Weber/NMSS
J. Winterle/CNWRA

Special thanks are also due to Ellen Kraus, who provided editorial guidance.

The authors and editors are especially appreciate the conversations and assistance (including limited review comments, in some instances) provided generously by the following individuals: T. Gallagher and C. Hickenbottom, of the State of Nevada Division of Water Resources/Department of Conservation and Natural Resources, for information and data on water use in Nye County, Nevada; D.A. Singer and J.H. DeYoung, Jr., of the U.S. Geological Survey (Menlo Park, California, and Reston, Virginia, respectively), for information on issues related to natural resources and exploratory drilling; R.L. Kimble, of Science Applications International Corporations, Inc. (Las Vegas), for information and data on the socioeconomics of the Yucca Mountain area; and T.D. Mayer, of the U.S. Fish and Wildlife Service (Portland, Oregon) for information on the regional hydrology of southern Amargosa Valley.

Finally, thanks are also due to Beth St. George, of the U.S. Fish and Wildlife Service, for information on the Ash Meadows National Wildlife Refuge, and K.G. Garey, of Amargosa Valley, for his views on farming and ranching in Amargosa and Pahrump Valleys, Nevada.

The views expressed in this report are those of the contributing authors and editors, not those of the individuals representing the aforementioned organizations.

ACRONYMS AND ABBREVIATIONS

AEC	Atomic Energy Commission
AEM	analytical element methods
AFB	Air Force Base
CA	California
°C	degrees Celsius
CCDF	complementary cumulative distribution function
CNWRA	Center for Nuclear Waste Regulatory Analyses (in San Antonio, Texas)
CRMP	Community Radiation Monitoring Program
DCFs	dose conversion factors
DOE	U.S. Department of Energy
EnPA	Energy Policy Act of 1992
EPA	U.S. Environmental Protection Agency
ET	evapotranspiration
°F	degrees Fahrenheit
GTCC	greater than class-C (radioactive waste)
GWSI	Ground-Water Site Inventory
HLW	high-level radioactive wastes (including spent nuclear fuel)
ICRP	International Commission on Radiation Protection
IPA	iterative performance assessment
MPC	multi purpose canister
msl	mean sea level
MTU	metric ton (equivalent) of uranium
NAS	National Academy of Sciences
NMSS	Office of Nuclear Material Safety and Safeguards
NRC	U.S. Nuclear Regulatory Commission
NTS	Nevada Test Site
NV	Nevada
NWPA	Nuclear Waste Policy Act of 1982, as amended
OGC	Office of the General Counsel
OCRWM	Office of Civilian Radioactive Waste Management
PDR	public document room
RES	Office of Nuclear Regulatory Research
SCP	site characterization plan
SNF	spent nuclear fuel
TDNs	total digestible nutrients
TEDE	total effective dose equivalent
TSPA	total system performance assessment
U.S.	United States
USGS	U.S. Geological Survey
UTM	Universal Transverse Mercator

1–D	one-dimensional
2–D	two-dimensional
3–D	three-dimensional

1. INTRODUCTION

In August 1995, the National Academy of Sciences (NAS) issued its findings and recommendations on a revised environmental standard for the disposal of high-level radioactive waste (HLW)[1] specific to Yucca Mountain, Nevada (National Research Council, 1995). Important differences exist between these findings and recommendations and prior U.S. Environmental Protection Agency (EPA) standards for HLW, as well as the existing U.S. Nuclear Regulatory Commission's (NRC's) geologic disposal regulations at 10 CFR Part 60 (NRC, 1983 and 1986). NRC has used its Iterative Performance Assessment (IPA) capability to evaluate the NAS findings and recommendations and has identified a number of key issues relevant to the implementation of dose-based performance measures at Yucca Mountain. The staff and its technical assistance contractor, the Center for Nuclear Waste Regulatory Analyses, have thus undertaken a series of focused technical analyses, described in this NUREG, to better understand these issues.

1.1 Background

Since the late 1970s, EPA has been engaged in setting standards to protect the public and environment from the potential hazards associated with the geologic disposal of HLW. Pursuant to its legislative authority and responsibilities, EPA issued its HLW standards in the form of 40 CFR Part 191, in September 1985 (see EPA, 1985; 50 *FR* 38066). However, in July 1987, the U.S. Court of Appeals for the First Circuit in Boston vacated Subpart B of the HLW standards and remanded the rule to EPA for further consideration (see EPA, 1993; 58 *FR* 7924).[2]

After the 1987 court decision, EPA attempted to revise its environmental standards (see U.S. General Accounting Office, 1993). However, before EPA could complete its work, Congress enacted the Energy Policy Act of 1992 (EnPA—Public Law 102–486). Through EnPA, Congress directed EPA to promulgate new environmental standards specific to a potential geologic repository for HLW at Yucca Mountain. EnPA stipulates that EPA's new standards are to be based on, and consistent with, the NAS findings and recommendations. After the final standards are promulgated, NRC is required by EnPA to modify its regulations to be consistent with the new EPA standards.

Section 801(a)(2) of EnPA directed the NAS to provide EPA with recommendations on the following issues:

- Whether health-based standards based on doses to individual members of the public from releases to the accessible environment ... will provide a reasonable standard for protection of the health and safety of the general public?

- Whether it is reasonable to assume that a system of post-closure oversight of the repository can be developed, based on active institutional controls, that will prevent an unreasonable risk of breaching the repository's engineered or geologic barriers or increasing the exposure of individual members of the public to radiation beyond allowable limits?

- Whether it is possible to make scientifically supportable predictions of the probability that the repository's engineered or geologic barriers will be breached as a result of human intrusion, over a period of 10,000 years?

The previously applicable EPA environmental standards and the current NRC implementing regulations are found, respectively, at 40 CFR Part 191 (EPA, 1985) and Part 60 (NRC, 1983 and 1986). These regulations are somewhat different from proposals for a *health-based*

---

[1]As used in this document, HLW includes spent nuclear fuel (SNF) and transuranic wastes, unless otherwise specifically stated.

[2]Principal among these was Subpart B, the individual and ground water protection requirements. The Court requested further notice and comment on these provisions as well as their inter-relationship to the Safe Drinking Water Act. In October 1992, the Waste Isolation Pilot Project (WIPP) Land Withdrawal Act (WIPP LWA—Public Law 102–579) was enacted which reinstated all of Part 191 except for those provisions that were the subject of the remand by the First Circuit. Moreover, the WIPP LWA also required issuance of new standards to address those that were the subject of the judicial remand and exempted the Yucca Mountain site from the Part 191 standards. Final disposal standards in 40 CFR Part 191 were issued in December 1993.

standard only (e.g., limiting individual dose or risk), as suggested by the EnPA. Previously, Part 191 had established *containment requirements* that limited the releases of radioactive material to the accessible environment, weighted by a factor approximately proportional to radiotoxicity, and integrated over a period of time (a span of 10,000 years is the current regulatory requirement) after permanent closure of the geologic repository. For its part, Part 60 incorporates Part 191 as the overall performance requirement for a geologic repository. The requirements in 10 CFR 60.112 had set an overall system performance objective that amounted to meeting EPA's containment requirements, whereas certain other sections (10 CFR 60.113) set forth additional subsystem performance objectives.[3]

Forthcoming revisions to both EPA's site-specific standards and NRC's conforming regulations notwithstanding, NRC regulations will continue to require compliance with applicable EPA environmental standards as the overall system performance objective for the repository and that demonstration of compliance with that objective will continue to necessitate a quantitative performance assessment to estimate post-closure performance of the repository system (see Kotra *et al.*, 1998).

1.2 Regulatory Considerations for Dose-Based Performance Measures

As noted above, the NAS has published its findings and recommendations for site-specific environmental standards for Yucca Mountain (see National Research Council, 1995). Among the NAS findings and recommendations was a key recommendation that the revised standards limit individual risk to a member of the public. Specifically, the NAS has recommended that the level of

protection provided by new environmental standards for Yucca Mountain should be comparable to that level of risk that may be acceptable to society at large (*Op cit.*, pp. 47–57), given that society currently tolerates certain *involuntary* risks [e.g., in the range of 10^{-5} to 10^{-6} per year—see Smith (1995, p. B–2) and NAS (1995, p. 50)]. To demonstrate that a geologic repository can be designed to provide such protection, the NAS recommended that assessments of individual risks be conducted for specific target populations, in the Yucca Mountain vicinity, using the approach specified by the International Commission on Radiological Protection (ICRP) (1985)—(e.g., "critical groups"—see Smith, 1995).[4] As EPA considers this particular recommendation, the staff have been exploring how its existing performance assessment review capability, to be used to evaluate DOE's demonstration of compliance with NRC's regulations, might be revised to accommodate such an exposure scenario.

Many of the considerations for a dose-based model are similar to those required for other models used in performance assessments. For example, an assessment of dose will be a function of both the calculation methodology itself (i.e., the calculation of an annual individual dose for an adult male) and certain modeling assumptions (e.g., exposure scenario)—although the two may be hard to distinguish at times [see Neel ("Dose-Assessment Module") in Wescott *et al.* (1995)]. Some of the issues that may need to be considered and treated in a dose-based calculation include the following:

- *Who is exposed (and where are they located)?*

- *What is the time period of concern?*

- *What are the exposure pathways?*

For the purposes of the United States' (U.S.') waste management program, answers to these questions have not been decided, although the

---

[3]At their time of inclusion in Part 60, these subsystem performance objectives were expected to support NRC's ability to find, with reasonable assurance, that the EPA standards would be met. In developing a Yucca Mountain-specific disposal regulation, the NAS asked NRC to reconsider the role of numerical subsystem performance objectives. In its findings and recommendations, the NAS indicated the potential for such requirements to lead to the sub-optimization of repository design (National Research Council, 1995; p. 126).

[4]The ICRP defines risk to a critical group in terms of dose. The term "dose" generically refers to the quantity of radiation absorbed by body organs or tissue. NRC defines "dose" for its regulatory purposes at 10 CFR Part 20. In its recommendations, the NAS adapts the ICRP terminology to its proposed risk-based framework.

NAS made recommendations relevant to many of them. It is expected that answers to most, if not all, all of these will be developed as EPA and NRC promulgate their respective standards and regulations, consistent with the NAS findings and recommendations. However, anticipating that some type of dose-based standard might be adopted in the future, the staff has begun to evaluate the mechanics of implementing such an approach in its performance assessment program and thus provide some insights into the issues cited above.

1.3 Approach and Content of this NUREG

The staff have begun to evaluate how to implement a dose-based HLW standard as part of its overall IPA effort. The staff's earlier in-house efforts to date have been documented in LaPlante *et al.* (1995); Manteufel and Baca (1995); Neel ("Dose-Assessment Module"), in Wescott *et al.* (1995); and Mohanty and McCartin (2000). The analyses described in this NUREG are a continuation of these efforts.[5]

In assessing the NAS findings and recommendations, the staff (with the support of its technical assistance contractor—see the last appendix of this NUREG) undertook a series of short-duration analyses, beginning in 1995. The areas selected for *initial* study by the staff were as follows:

- *Potential Receptor Groups:* The NAS recommended that the dose calculations be performed for specific populations, using the "critical group approach" specified by the ICRP. Based on the staff's earlier work, the most likely exposure scenario for a receptor population in the Yucca Mountain vicinity would be through some ground-water/ food-ingestion pathway [see Neel ("Dose-Assessment Module") in Wescott *et al.* (1995)]. In the first series of analyses, described in Section 2, the staff applied the tenants of the ICRP "critical group

approach" to better understand the lifestyle and habits of existing communities in the Yucca Mountain area.

The staff was able to identify two hypothetical (potential) receptor groups based on a review of information on population demographics and water availability (e.g., drilling practices) of current residents in the Yucca Mountain area. As an expansion of this analysis, the staff also performed a regional evaluation of deep well drilling practices in the arid southwest U.S., to better understand how some communities exploit fresh-water resources found in deep (non-alluvial) aquifers.

- *Ground-Water Pathway:* The calculation of peak dose and the definition of the site-specific critical group requires consideration of the behavior of the radionuclide contaminant plume as it migrates away from the geologic repository. In Section 3, the staff conducted a preliminary simulation of radionuclide dilution in the saturated zone beneath Yucca Mountain, and analyzed the role of dilution/mixing caused by a pumping water well.

As noted above, the NAS recommended that the compliance period should include the time when greatest risk occurs. Consistent with this NAS recommendation, the staff undertook an analysis to calculate peak dose. Specifically, the staff was interested in determining: (a) the difficulty of performing the calculation, itself, given NRC's existing IPA capability; (b) which radionuclides contribute significantly to peak dose; and (c) the relative importance of site-specific assumptions and parameters in dose-based calculations of the ground-water pathway.

- *Human Intrusion:* The NAS study commented that it is not possible to make scientifically supportable predictions of the probability that engineered or geologic barriers will be breached over

---

[5]Initial results from some of the analyses described in this NUREG were first documented in 1996 and later published in 1997, in NUREG/CR–6513 (Sagar, 1997).

the next 10,000 years. Therefore, the NAS recommended that human intrusion should not be included in a probabilistic performance assessment. Instead, the NAS recommended that a consequence analysis of an assumed, stylized human intrusion scenario should be required and that the resulting risk should not exceed the limit adopted for undisturbed performance. The staff's analysis in Section 4 examines the feasibility of performing such a calculation.

- *Disruptive Events:* The NAS recommendation for a risk calculation conducted over the timeframe of greatest risk has implications for the treatment of disruptive events in a performance assessment. Evaluation of certain disruptive events can affect dose estimates by raising the significance of alternative exposure pathways (e.g., inhalation and direct pathways from the release of radionuclides via extrusive volcanism). Additionally, long compliance periods increase the likelihood that low-probability events will occur during the time period of regulatory interest. Section 5 presents the staff analysis of a volcanic scenario, to better understand parameters and assumptions associated with estimating dose from an extrusive volcanic event, and the effect of the timeframe of the analysis on the evaluation of low-probability events.

- *Hazards Comparison Over Time:* As noted earlier, one of the NAS' recommendations was that the assessment of compliance with the HLW standard should be conducted over a timeframe that includes the period when greatest risk occurs. In Section 6, the staff did a comparative analysis, over time, of the relative radiological hazard between a geologic repository containing only SNF, and a hypothetical uranium ore body containing only naturally occurring radionuclides.

These particular topic areas were selected for study because they: (a) would likely provide *preliminary* insights into the NAS recommendations; and (b) would focus on the *major* implementation issues that the staff would need to consider as it continues to modify and enhance its IPA capability.

Finally, it should be noted that as part of the Commission's *Strategic Plan and Rebaselining Initiative*, the Commission directed the staff to, among other things, pursue the development of site-specific regulations for the disposal of HLW at Yucca Mountain, consistent with the findings and recommendations of the NAS (see Kotra *et al.*, 1998). Because revision to the Commission's geologic disposal regulations is currently underway, at this time, the approaches, assumptions, and conclusion described in this report should in no way be construed to express the views, preferences, or positions of the staff regarding what the eventual form of the site-specific regulation should be.

1.4 References

International Commission on Radiological Protection, "Radiological Protection Principles for the Disposal of Solid Radioactive Waste," Pergamon Press, Oxford, 1985. [ICRP Publication 46.]

Kotra, J. P., *et al.*, "Strategy for Development of NRC Regulations for the Proposed Repository at Yucca Mountain, Nevada," in American Nuclear Society, *High-Level Radioactive Waste Management: Proceedings of the Eighth International Conference, May 11– 14, 1998, Las Vegas, Nevada*, pp. 361–363 [1998].

LaPlante, P.A., S.J. Maheras, and M.S. Jarzemba, "Initial Analysis of Selected Site-Specific Dose Assessment Parameters and Exposure Pathways Applicable to a Groundwater Release Scenario at Yucca Mountain," San Antonio, Texas, Center for Nuclear Waste Regulatory Analyses [CNWRA], CNWRA 95–018, September 1995. [Prepared for NRC.]

Mantueufel, R.D., and R.G. Baca, "Iterative Performance Assessment Phase 3: Status of Activities," San Antonio, Texas, Center for

Nuclear Waste Regulatory Analyses, CNWRA 95–007, April 1995.

Mohanty, S., and T.J. McCartin (coordinators), "NRC Sensitivity and Uncertainty Analyses for a Proposed HLW Repository at Yucca Mountain, Nevada, Using TPA [Computer Code Version] 3.1—Volume 1: Conceptual Models and Data," U.S. Nuclear Regulatory Commission, NUREG–1668, February 2001.

National Research Council, "Technical Bases for Yucca Mountain Standards," Washington, D.C., National Academy Press, Commission on Geosciences, Environment, and Resources, July 1995.

Sagar, B. (ed.), "NRC High-Level Radioactive Waste Program Annual Progress Report: Fiscal Year 1996," U.S. Nuclear Regulatory Commission, NUREG/CR–6513, No. 1, January 1997. [Prepared by the Center for Nuclear Waste Regulatory Analyses.]

Smith, G.M., "Compilation and Analysis of Information on Critical Groups (Draft)," Oxfordshire, United Kingdom, Intera Information Technologies, August 1995. [Prepared for the Electric Power Research Institute.]

U.S. Environmental Protection Agency, "Environmental Standards for the Management of Spent Nuclear Fuel, High-Level and Transuranic Wastes [Final Rule]," *Federal Register,* vol. 50, no. 182, September 19, 1985, pp. 38066–38089.

U.S. Environmental Protection Agency, "Environmental Radiation Protection Standards for the Management and Disposal of Spent Nuclear Fuel, High-Level and Transuranic Radioactive Wastes [Proposed Rule]," *Federal Register*, vol. 58, no. 26, February 10, 1993, pp. 7924–7936.

U.S. General Accounting Office, "EPA's Development of Radiation Protection Standards," Washington, D.C., GAO/RCED–93–126, June 3, 1993.

U.S. Nuclear Regulatory Commission, "Disposal of High-Level Radioactive Wastes in Geologic Repositories [Final Rule]," *Federal Register*, vol. 48, no. 120, June 21, 1983, pp. 28194–28229.

U.S. Nuclear Regulatory Commission, "Disposal of High-Level Radioactive Wastes in Geologic Repositories [Conforming Amendments]," *Federal Register*, vol. 51, no. 118, June 19, 1986, pp. 22286–22301.

Wescott, R.G., *et al.* (eds.), "NRC Iterative Performance Assessment Phase 2: Development of Capabilities for Review of a Performance Assessment for a High-Level Waste Repository," U.S. Nuclear Regulatory Commission, NUREG–1464, October 1995.

2. CONSIDERATIONS IN THE DEFINITION OF A RECEPTOR GROUP

In its 1995 findings and recommendations, the NAS proposed that dose calculations be performed, for specific populations, to avoid unlimited speculation about the behavior of future human society. Specifically, in performing the requisite calculations, the NAS recommended consideration of the local biosphere, using the "critical group approach" specified by the ICRP and employing "cautious but reasonable assumptions." The ICRP has generally defined the critical group to be a relatively homogenous group of people whose location and habits are such that they are representative of those individuals expected to receive the highest doses as a result of radionuclide releases.[1]

With this guidance in mind, the initial step in defining a critical group is to identify a set of receptor groups from which those individuals expected to receive the highest dose would be thus designated as the "critical group." Staff initially identified the following types of information that might provide informed judgments on what factors might have influenced the location and behavior of the current population in the greater Yucca Mountain area:

- Distribution and characteristics of existing communities in the Yucca Mountain area.

- Regional geography and climate of southern Nevada.

- Surface and subsurface geohydrology.

- Current sources of water supply for existing communities, focusing on water well properties and water use patterns.

- Relative costs of drilling and pumping freshwater from shallow and deep wells.

Following a review of the aforementioned, the staff prepared analyses for the following two population groups:

---

[1]See ICRP (1977, 1985).

- *Current residents in the area:* Section 2.1 presents information on lifestyles, habits, and locations of possible receptor groups in the Yucca Mountain area.

- *Other southwest communities:* Section 2.2 describes ground-water and land-use practices in other arid communities located in Arizona, Nevada, New Mexico, and Texas.

Finally, Section 2.3 presents the definitions for the hypothetical receptor groups used in the analyses described elsewhere in this NUREG for calculations of individual dose.

2.1 Current Lifestyles and Water-Use Practices in the Yucca Mountain Area

2.1.1 Introduction

Yucca Mountain has been proposed as a deep geologic repository for HLW because, in part, of the regional hydrogeologic regime. Moisture fluxes within the 700-meter thick unsaturated zone at Yucca Mountain are generally believed to be small, because of the region's arid climate and the low permeability of the tuff units comprising the mountain. Low moisture fluxes may reduce the rate of waste package corrosion, subsequent dissolution of the exposed waste form, and transport of radionuclides to the accessible environments. However, it is likely, given time, that some water will eventually contact the waste form and transport dissolved radionuclides out of the waste package. Radionuclides not sorbed by the zeolitic bedded tuffs that underlie the repository [e.g., technetium (Tc), iodine (I), neptunium (Np)], or diffused from fluid-conducting fractures into the rock matrix within welded tuff units, will enter the water table, which, based on current engineering designs, lies 250 to 300 meters below the repository. Hydrogeologic studies (Czarnecki and Waddell, 1984; TRW Environmental Safety Systems, Inc., 1995a) indicate that radionuclides that enter the saturated zone beneath Yucca Mountain will generally flow (down-gradient) to the south-southeast into western Jackass Flats within the welded tuff aquifer and then south-southwest into the Amargosa Desert, where the water table lies within an alluvial aquifer. Accordingly, the staff believes that it is appropriate to examine the range of land- and water-use practices occurring in the Yucca Mountain area and in other, similar, environments, as part of the process of establishing reasonable bounds on estimates of land- and water-use practices of potential receptor groups.

2.1.2 Approach

Based on the staff's earlier work, the most likely exposure scenario for a specific population in the Yucca Mountain vicinity would be through the ground-water/food-ingestion pathway [see Neel ("Dose-Assessment Module") in Wescott *et al.* (1995)]. In the staff's view, based on information previously reviewed (DOE, 1986, 1988, and 1996), definition of a receptor group for the Yucca Mountain region will likely be based in large part on the group's accessibility to ground water. Thus, consistent with the ICRP's guidance, the staff has undertaken a limited review of some types of site-specific information that, in whole or in part, might aid in definition of hypothetical receptor groups in the Yucca Mountain area.

2.1.2.1 Local Population[2] and Lifestyles

Yucca Mountain is located in Nye County, which is in southern Nevada and is approximately 160 kilometers northwest of Las Vegas. The proposed repository site straddles the southeastern boundary of the Nellis Air Force Base (AFB) bombing range, and land administered by the Bureau of Land Management (BLM). NTS is generally located on lands managed by the U.S. Department of Energy (DOE) and BLM, whereas the extreme northern portions of NTS lie within,

---

[2]Population information for portions of Clark (Nevada—NV) and Inyo (California—CA) Counties was provided because these counties share the same ground-water basin and are believed to have lifestyles similar to those of residents of southern Nye County.

or abut, the Nellis AFB Range. Most if not all NTS property (3500 square kilometers) has been withdrawn from the public domain for about a half century. [NTS was created in 1951 by the then Atomic Energy Commission (AEC) from the pre-existing Nellis AFB (established 1941) and the Desert National Wildlife Refuge (established 1935).]

Physiographically, the area is considered to be part of the Basin and Range Province that is characterized by topographically-closed (intermontane) basins separated by ranges, hills, and mesas, with internal drainage into the basins. Within the Basin and Range, mountain ranges trend north-northeast; however the trend of these features is generally north-northwest in the Yucca Mountain area. The basin floors range in altitude from 600 to 1400 meters mean sea level (msl); the mountains reach altitudes of up to 3700 meters. Basins are filled with alluvial fan deposits and account for about 50 percent of the exposed geology in the study area, whereas the mountain ranges—principally volcanic and carbonate sequences—account for the remainder (Thordarson and Robinson, 1971; p. 14). See Figure 2–1. Most major population centers in the study area occur in the basins (valleys). See Figure 2–2.

NTS lies within the most arid part of Nevada, which is the most arid State in the conterminous U.S. (Geraghty *et al.*, 1973; Plate 3)—the present climate in the NTS area is classified as a mid-latitude desert. Temperatures range from about 13 degrees Celsius (°C) in January to over 49°C in July. The annual precipitation is less than 15 centimeters—the precipitation is usually lower in the basins and higher in the ranges, hills, and mesas. The major agricultural crop in the area is alfalfa. Certain meteorologic/geographic conditions (e.g., altitude, length of growing season, the "rain-shadow" effect, accessibility to water, soil types) control the extent and type of the agriculture in this portion of the State (see summary in Appendix A) and, therefore, have limited

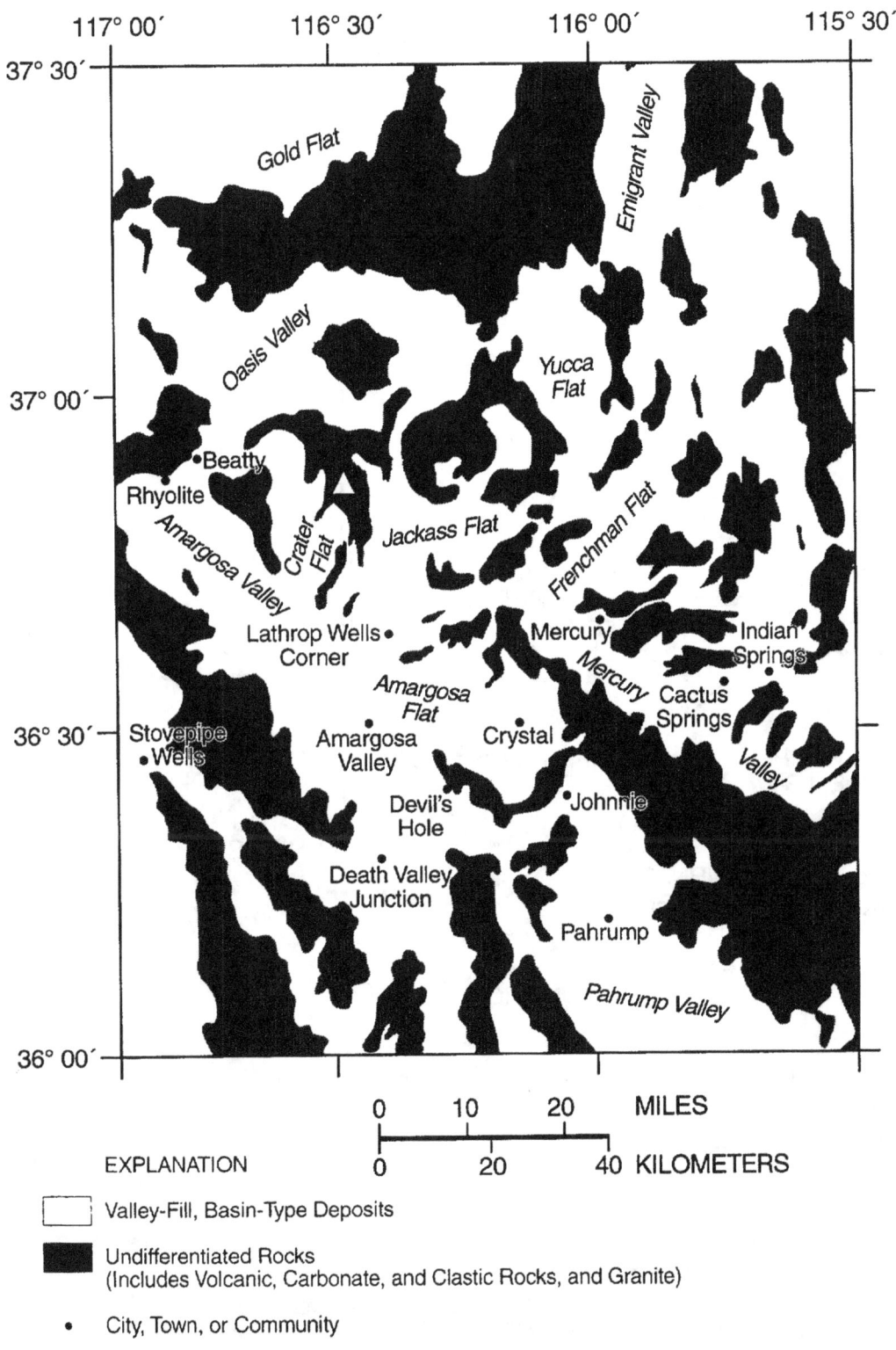

Figure 2–1. **Simplified geologic map of the Yucca Mountain area.** Adopted from Laczniak *et al.* (1996, pp. 3, 9). Thordarson and Robinson (1971, p. 14) estimate that 50 percent of the rocks outcropping within 160 kilometers of the Yucca Mountain area are valley-fill deposits and have the highest density of wells. The mesas and ranges are undifferentiated rocks (principally volcanic rocks and carbonates) which account for about 45 percent of the outcrop area within 160 kilometers of the site.

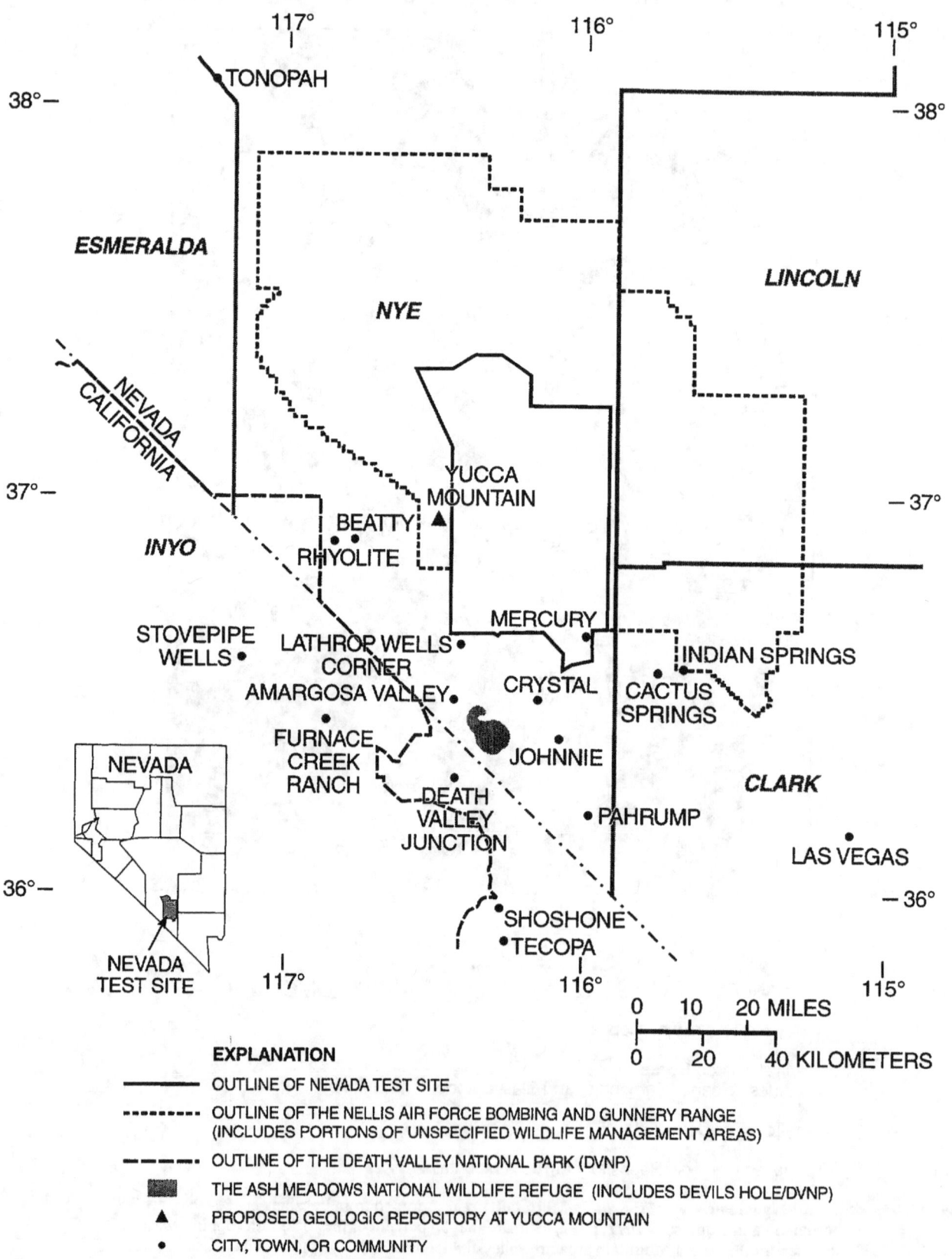

EXPLANATION

——————— OUTLINE OF NEVADA TEST SITE

- - - - - - - - OUTLINE OF THE NELLIS AIR FORCE BOMBING AND GUNNERY RANGE
(INCLUDES PORTIONS OF UNSPECIFIED WILDLIFE MANAGEMENT AREAS)

— — — — — OUTLINE OF THE DEATH VALLEY NATIONAL PARK (DVNP)

▨ THE ASH MEADOWS NATIONAL WILDLIFE REFUGE (INCLUDES DEVILS HOLE/DVNP)

▲ PROPOSED GEOLOGIC REPOSITORY AT YUCCA MOUNTAIN

• CITY, TOWN, OR COMMUNITY

Figure 2–2.   Index Map of the Yucca Mountain Area

agriculture to about 3 percent of the county,[3] and thus the size of the local population engaged in this activity. In the past, the size of the population in the area has been most influenced by the level of activity at the three largest local employers—NTS, Nellis AFB (Clark County), and the Town of Beatty. However, over the past decade, tourism and leisure, together, have fast become a major industry in the State, particularly in the Las Vegas area (Clark County), and many local residents now earn a living in this growing area of the economy.

Information on the population of Nye County (and adjacent Clark and Inyo Counties) is available principally from the Bureau of the Census (U.S. Department of Commerce, 1994b). Nye County is largely rural (less than 1 person per square kilometer) and occupies approximately 16 percent of the State (in terms of area). Based on population estimates listed in Table 2–1a, Nye County currently accounts for about 1.5 percent of the State's population. (By contrast, Inyo County contains less than 0.1 percent of California's population.) Most of the population throughout the area is uneven and confined to discrete rural locations. Several locations have populations in excess of 1000 people; however, many communities are in fact collections of isolated farms and ranches, mining settlements, or commercial (trade) centers. Table 2–1b shows the principal communities in the study area. Approximately 13,000 people live within 100 kilometers of the site. About 70 percent of the local population live in five major communities—the Amargosa Desert area, Beatty, Indian Springs, Lathrop Wells, and Pahrump. (This number increases to 90 percent when Tonopah is included.) A significant percentage of the local population may be transient—reportedly ranging from 20 to 25 percent (DOE, 1986; p. 3–102). As discussed below, most if not all these

communities acquire their water supply from the Death Valley ground-water system.

2.1.2.2 History of Inhabitation of the Amargosa Desert Region and the Ash Meadows Area[4]

In the arid Southwest and elsewhere, Native Americans and settlers have historically chosen to establish camps, homesteads, outposts, and eventually permanent communities where there are reliable water supplies. In southern Nevada, for example, to the south of Yucca Mountain, the springs in Ash Meadows have provided fresh water for agriculture, ranching, and domestic purposes.

The grasslands of Ash Meadows, framed by the leather-leaf ash trees, provided a lush oasis in the otherwise sere Mojave Desert. Prior to the great western migration, Southern Paiute and Shoshone Native Americans camped at the spring waters while foraging and hunting in the highlands of Ash Meadows (McCracken, 1992). Explorers, gold prospectors (California-bound forty-niners), and settlers subsequently sought out and used the Ash Meadows spring waters. Eventually, these pioneers cultivated alfalfa hay to support small cattle operations and grew various truck crops—including potatoes, tomatoes, melons, apples, pears, peaches, and more recently pistachios.

In earlier days, baths were routinely taken by some in Devil's Hole and more than one pioneers' child enjoyed fishing in Ash Meadows springs for "minews" (or minnows that were probably one of several species of Desert pupfish) and feeding them to their cats (*Op cit.*). Nonetheless, before the early 1950s, there were never great numbers of permanent inhabitants in either Ash Meadows or the Amargosa Desert area.

Although local soils are not rich, on average, the presence of exploitable ground water resources, coupled with a long, hot growing

---

[3]In 1987, the Bureau of Census reported that 136 farms were operating on about 150,000 hectares in Nye County (U.S. Department of Commerce, 1994b; p. 169). Over the past 10 years, there has been about a 10 percent reduction (from about 162,000 hectares in 1978) in the amount of county acreage dedicated to agriculture.

[4]For editorial reasons, this discussion, which originally appeared in Witmeyer *et al.* (1996), and now repeated in Section 2.2, has been placed in this section of the NUREG. For additional discussion of the history of this area, the reader is referred to Appendices A and B.

Table 2-1. Comparative 1990 Population Information on California, Nevada, and the Yucca Mountain Area

a. Comparison of Populations in Clark and Nye Counties (Nevada) and Inyo County (California)

County/State	1990 Population Estimation [a]	Area (km²)	Population Density (per km²)
Clark County	741,459	20,489	36
Nye County	17,781	47,000	< 1
(All Nevada)	(1,201,833)	(284,396)	(4)
Inyo County	18,281	26,397	< 1
(All California)	(29,760,021)	(403,968)	(74)

b. Population Centers in the Yucca Mountain Area

Community	1990 Population Estimation [a]	Distance From Yucca Mountain (km)
Amargosa Desert area (NV) [b]	2300 [c]	20-70
Ash Meadows (NV)	[b]	55
Beatty (NV)	1623	29
Cactus Springs (NV)	[d]	72
Crystal (NV)	[d]	41
Death Valley Junction (CA)	15 [e]	60
Furnace Creek Ranch (CA)	800 [f]	56
Indian Springs (NV)	1164 [g]	75
Johnnie (NV)	[d]	58
Lathrop Wells Corner (NV)	30 [b]	23
Mercury (NV)	300 [c, h]	45
Pahrump (NV)	7424	82
Rhyolite (NV)	[d]	35
Stovepipe Wells (CA)	[d]	67
Shoshone (CA)	140 [f]	112
Tonopah (NV)	3616	145
Tecopa (NV)	200 [f]	125

[a] 1990 Bureau of Census estimates (U.S. Department of Commerce, 1994a) unless otherwise noted.

[b] Includes the Communities of Ash Meadows, Amargosa Farms, Amargosa Valley, and Lathrop Wells.

[c] DOE (1986, p. 3-75) estimate.

[d] Not believed to be occupied by permanent residents.

[e] U.S. Geological Survey (USGS) (1970) citing Bureau of Census estimates.

[f] Semi-permanent residents. Population increases by an additional 2000 during the tourist season. DOE (1988, p. 3-120) estimates.

[g] Could be as high as 8400 if Indian Springs AFB personnel are included.

[h] About 3000 personnel are currently employed at NTS (see TRW Environmental Safety Systems, Inc., 1995a; p. 4-3).

season, ultimately allowed permanent inhabitation of this otherwise inhospitable portion of Nevada. Farming has generally produced a wide variety of fruits, vegetables, and alfalfa hay (see Table A–1 in Appendix A), but not in quantities or diversity to be judged truly sufficient. Consequently, permanent inhabitation has been tenuous in the region. Mineral production (specialized clays and borax) and rail transportation (the *Tonopah and Tidewater,* and the *Las Vegas and Tonopah* railroads—see Appendix B) were early catalysts to the continuing human presence before establishment of NTS and Nellis AFB. Numerous jobs and local development of habitations and associated amenities that NTS generated in the early 1950s have continued through the 1990s.

NTS employment opportunities encouraged an increase in the population of the Amargosa Desert area. The community of *Amargosa Valley*[5] (as specified by tax boundaries established by the Nye County Board of Commissioners), includes about 1300 square kilometers with a population of 909 for an average of about 0.7 persons/square kilometer. The low average population per square kilometer in Amargosa Valley is because most of the tax district is uninhabited except for the area of Amargosa Valley known as *Amargosa Farms.* There are approximately 60 industrial/ commercial establishments supported by about 350 housing units averaging 2.6 individuals per unit (TRW Environmental Safety Systems, Inc., 1995b).

In 1994, housing units in the community of Amargosa Valley increased from 352 to 365—attributed to single-family units. This represented a 3.7 percent increase in annual growth, with an attendant population growth of about 33 (assuming 2.5 individuals per new house). Additionally, Amargosa Valley now

has a school with about 150 children enrolled and present on a normal school day.

There is a relatively new dairy at the southern end of Amargosa Desert Valley. Locally grown alfalfa hay provides about 10 percent of the fodder for the dairy herd. In 1994, 2376 dairy cows were reported at the Amargosa Valley operation and over 2.4 square kilometers nearby were planted in alfalfa, yielding about 2500 metric tons of alfalfa hay in 1994 (TRW Environmental Safety Systems, Inc., 1995a; pp. A–21–A–22).

Currently, the nearest private water well to the proposed geologic repository at Yucca Mountain can be found at the *Cind-R-Lite* mining facility, at the Lathrop Wells volcanic cinder cone, about 10 kilometers north of the Amargosa Farms area. Recent information suggests that only two employees work at the facility (TRW Environmental Safety Systems, Inc., 1995a; p. 4–4), and it is not clear whether water is used solely for processing cinders or for human consumption as well. The next nearest non-NTS commercial activity where ground water is pumped is at the junction of U.S. Highway 95 and Nevada State Highway 373 at the site known as *Lathrop Wells.* At least four individuals reside there continuously and others live there during the weekdays. Additionally, there is a 91-unit recreational vehicle park that was completed in late 1995. At present, the Lathrop Wells location does not include families with children. The nearest area with a concentration of families with children is found about 32 kilometers to the south of Yucca Mountain near the school and community center at Amargosa Farm Road (known as *Amargosa Farms—Op cit.,* p. 3–3).

Today, Ash Meadows has been classified as a National Wildlife Refuge and commercial development is prohibited. In 1980, Preferred Equities of Pahrump (Nevada) purchased about 68.9 square kilometers in Ash Meadows and moved forward with plans to subdivide its holdings there, anticipating eventual development of 33,600 residential lots and a community population of 50,000 (McCracken, 1992; p. 96). On learning of the plans, environmental activists took legal action to

---

[5]Elsewhere in this NUREG, the terms "Amargosa Valley" and "Amargosa Farms area" were used to refer collectively to the set of communities of Ash Meadows, Amargosa Farms, Amargosa Valley, and Lathrop Wells, which all generally lie within the Amargosa Valley hydrographic basin. However, in this section of the NUREG, the term "Amargosa Farms" refers to the southern portion of the Amargosa Valley bounded approximately by the California-Nevada border, Nevada State Highway 373, and Amargosa Farm Road because residences and farming activities in the valley are concentrated in this triangular parcel of land.

block further development. Eventually, the Nature Conservancy purchased 51 square kilometers of land and water rights owned by Preferred Equities in Ash Meadows. In 1984, the U.S. Fish and Wildlife Service purchased the Conservancy's Ash Meadows interests and established the Ash Meadows National Wildlife Refuge, to conserve threatened and endangered species found there, to promote all native wildlife, and to provide the public with recreational opportunities that would not threaten the wildlife. (It should be stressed that current knowledge of the regional ground-water flow system in the Yucca Mountain area suggests that water discharging at Ash Meadows from the Paleozoic carbonate aquifer is part of the Ash Meadows ground-water basin, whereas ground water, flowing beneath Yucca Mountain, being pumped in the Amargosa Farms region, is from the Alkali Flat-Furnace Creek Ranch ground-water basin. Hence, it is unlikely that radionuclides that reach the saturated zone beneath the proposed repository would be discharged at Ash Meadows.)

2.1.2.3 Ground-Water Availability[6]

There are no perennial or intermittent streams in or near the immediate Yucca Mountain area; however, short reaches of the Amargosa River near Beatty (NV) and south of Amargosa Farms to Shoshone (CA) are perennial to intermittent. The only major occurrences of surface water are the concentrations of springs found in Oasis Valley, Ash Meadows, the Amargosa Desert, Death Valley, and NTS.

There are many ephemeral stream channels present in the area, including those associated with the drainage systems of Fortymile Wash and the Amargosa River. Runoff occurs irregularly, in response to both summer convective storms and winter frontal storms, with stream discharge rates varying greatly in

magnitude. For example, the estimated discharge for the 100-year flood along Fortymile Wash, just below its confluence with Drillhole Wash, is 340 cubic meters/second (DOE, 1988; p. 3–21). Data on rainfall, runoff, and evaporation are inadequate to determine rainfall-runoff-recharge relationships (*Op cit.*, p. 3–9).

Because there are no substantial sources of surface water supply, most water used in the area is ground water. Yucca Mountain lies within the Death Valley ground-water flow system, which is composed of a series of topographically-closed basins that are hydraulically connected at depth by the highly-conductive Paleozoic carbonate aquifer. Tertiary- and Quaternary-age alluvium and playa lake deposits fill the basins, and locally overlie Tertiary-age volcanic rocks or Paleozoic-age carbonate, clastic, and metamorphic rocks. The flow system originates primarily from the infiltration of precipitation in the mountainous areas through the alluvium to fracture and joint sets or solution cavities in the Paleozoic carbonate rocks that underlie the basins and intervening highlands (Figure 2–3). Ground-water flow is to the south and west from the respective basins toward the regional topographic depression at Death Valley or smaller depressions in Sarcobatus Flats, Oasis Valley, Ash Meadows, and the Amargosa Desert (Thomas, 1964; p. 308).

Although about 30 individual hydrographic basins comprise the Death Valley ground-water system, the system itself can generally be divided into three major ground-water basins: (a) Oasis Valley; (b) Ash Meadows; and (c) Alkali Flat-Furnace Creek Ranch (see Figure 2–4). The Oasis Valley ground-water basin discharges in a series of springs that are forced to the surface by a region of low-permeability rocks down-gradient of Beatty. The Ash Meadows ground-water basin comprises the eastern half of the Death Valley System and discharges along a 14-kilometer spring line formed by the juxtaposition of low-permeability Tertiary-age lake deposits on the western downthrown side of a north-trending normal fault, against the

---

[6]Numerous investigations of the geohydrology of the Yucca Mountain region have been conducted. The results of these investigations have been summarized in various site characterization studies. To name a few, these studies include DOE (1986, 1988); Carr and Yount (1988); Bedinger *et al.* (1989); the National Research Council (1992); Wittmeyer and Turner (1995); and Laczniak *et al.* (1996).

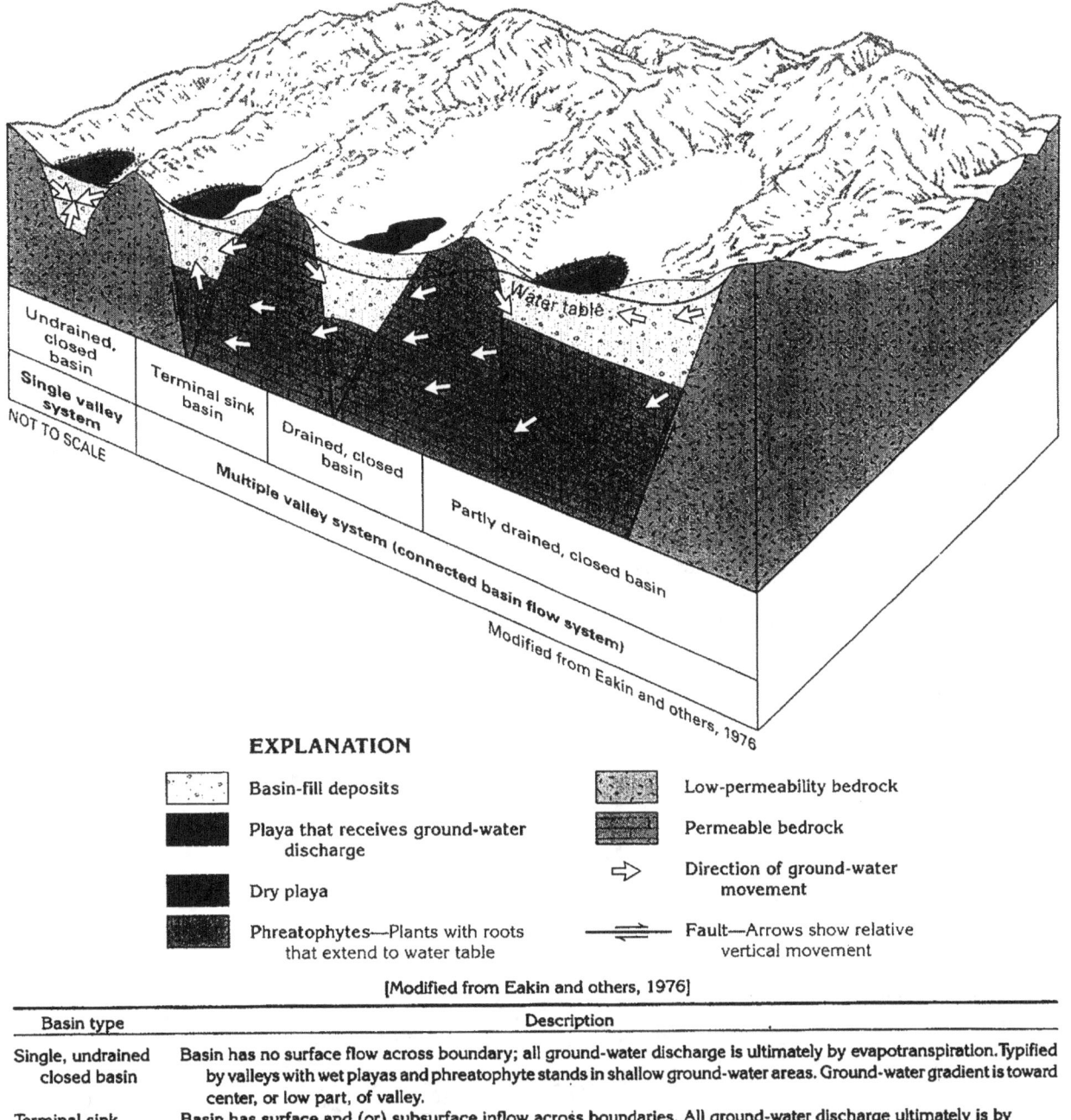

EXPLANATION

Basin-fill deposits		Low-permeability bedrock	
Playa that receives ground-water discharge		Permeable bedrock	
Dry playa		Direction of ground-water movement	
Phreatophytes—Plants with roots that extend to water table		Fault—Arrows show relative vertical movement	

[Modified from Eakin and others, 1976]

Basin type	Description
Single, undrained closed basin	Basin has no surface flow across boundary; all ground-water discharge is ultimately by evapotranspiration. Typified by valleys with wet playas and phreatophyte stands in shallow ground-water areas. Ground-water gradient is toward center, or low part, of valley.
Terminal sink basin	Basin has surface and (or) subsurface inflow across boundaries. All ground-water discharge ultimately is by evapotranspiration. Most sinks have playas that are large in proportion to the size of the area. Valley can contain a large volume of saline ground water.
Drained, closed basin	Basin has no surface flow across boundary. Almost all ground-water discharge is by subsurface outflow; the deep water table prevents evapotranspiration.
Partly drained, closed basin	Basin has no surface inflow or outflow. Valley has moist playa and stand of phreatophytes. Area of ground-water discharge can be small in comparison to undrained basins of similar size. Ground-water gradients may indicate subsurface outflow, if wells are strategically located.
Connected basin flow system	Basin system has surface and (or) subsurface outflow and (or) inflow that links several individual basins. Ground water discharges to playas and (or) springs or streams. Surface inflow and outflow is by ephemeral and perennial streams.

Figure 2–3. **Simplified geologic cross-section of the basins within the Yucca Mountain area.** Cross-section is representative of the relationships depicted by the simplified geologic map shown in Figure 2–1. Basin types are differentiated on the basis of differences in ground-water flow. Taken from Planert and Willaims (1995, p. B7) citing Eakin *et al.* (1976).

NUREG–1538

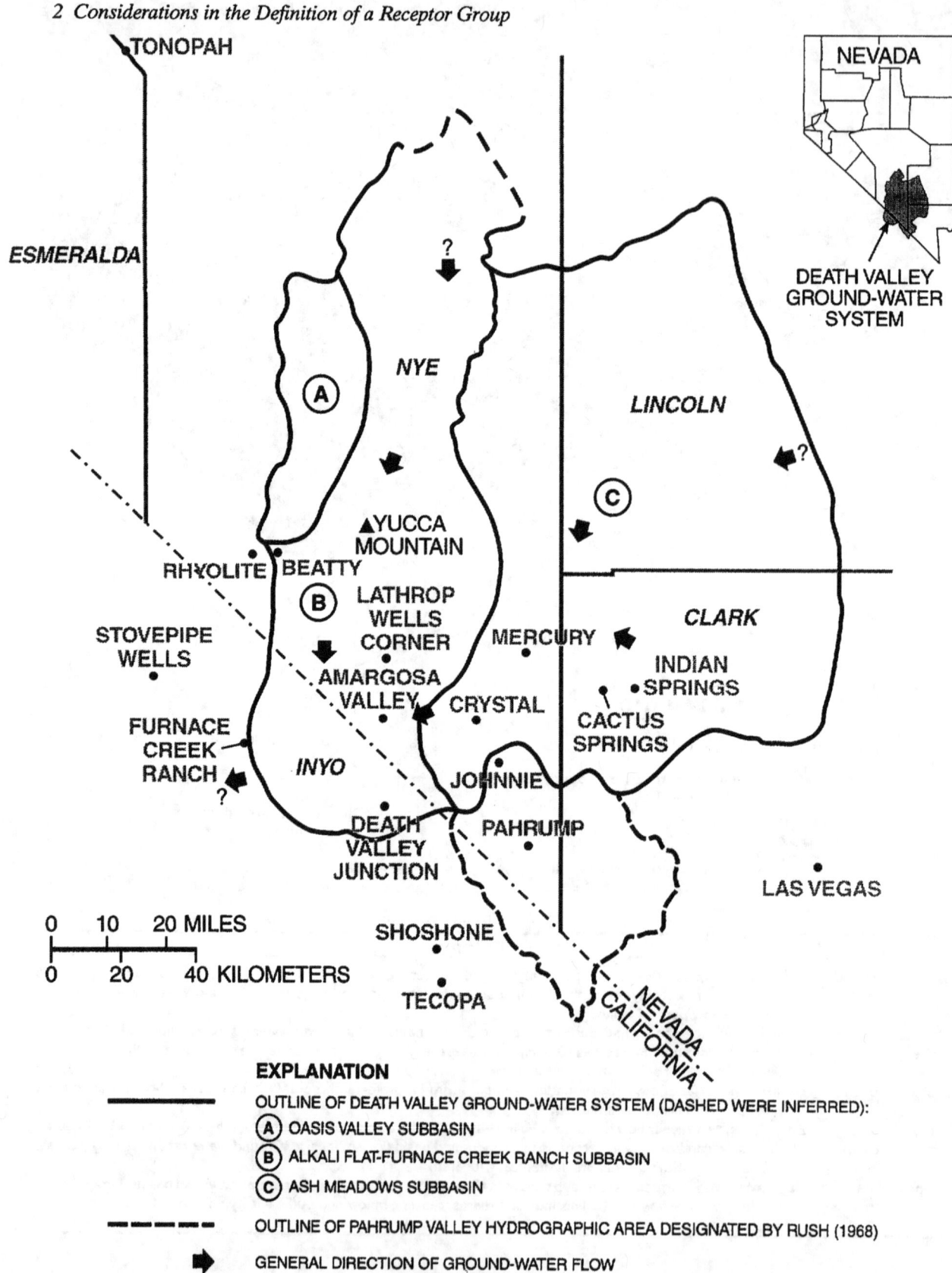

Figure 2–4.   Ground-water sub-basins in the Yucca Mountain area. Taken from Rush (1968) and DOE (1998, p. 3–3), citing Rush (1970); Blankennagel and Weir (1973); Winograd and Thordarson (1975); Dudley and Larson (1976); Waddell (1982); and Waddell *et al.* (1984).

high-permeability Paleozoic carbonate aquifer. Yucca Mountain lies within the Alkali Flat-Furnace Creek Ranch basin, which is recharged in the uplands of Pahute Mesa and discharges by evapotranspiration (ET) at Franklin Lake Playa (*aka* Alkali Flat) and through a series of springs in the Furnace Creek Ranch area of Death Valley. In general, the regional ground-water flow patterns do not coincide with topographic basins.

The regional hydrostratigraphic units within the Alkali Flat-Furnace Creek Ranch basin are: (a) the valley fill aquifer; (b) volcanic rock aquifers and aquitards; (c) upper carbonate aquifer, which occurs primarily in the Yucca Flat area; (d) upper clastic aquitard; (e) lower carbonate aquifer; and (f) the lower clastic aquitard (see Winograd and Thordarson, 1975). Yucca Mountain and the Pahute Mesa uplands consist of layered volcanic rocks of Tertiary age. In the vicinity of Yucca Mountain, the water table occurs within these volcanic rocks, including perched ground water. Deeper within the volcanic rocks, flow conditions may be confined or semi-confined. A much deeper, confined system exists within the lower carbonate aquifer that underlies the volcanic rocks. The uppermost aquifer underlying the proposed geologic repository footprint is principally a tuff aquifer and occurs at great depth [e.g., 380 to 860 meters—see Wittwer *et al.* (1995, p. 24)]. This aquifer becomes much shallower to the south where it is believed to laterally intersect alluvial fan basins. In the Amargosa Desert and Pahrump Valley areas, the depth to the water table in the alluvial aquifer is reported to be no more than 30 meters (USGS, 1977; pp. 61–62), although local variations in water table depth do exist. Overall, the relative elevation of the ground-water surface in the area is influenced by geologic structure and stratigraphy, individual aquifer properties, proximity to recharge and discharge areas, and the extent of previous and current development (i.e., pumping).

Schoff and Moore (1964, p. 45) noted that the ground water from NTS is a relatively small contributor to the total discharge in the Amargosa Desert—no more than 7½ percent

[citing the water chemistry work of Eakin *et al.* (1963, pp. 2–24)]. The remaining ground water used in the Amargosa Desert area apparently comes from a combination of interbasin flows as well as upwelling from the deep Paleozoic carbonate aquifer, as suggested by geochemical signatures and observed vertical gradients in the region (see Winograd and Thordarson, 1975). There also may be areas of local recharge from mountain runoff into the alluvial-fan deposits, as occurs in other alluvial basins.

Regionally, the alluvial fan and lower carbonate aquifers are the most important sources of ground water; the welded tuff aquifer is only locally important in Jackass Flats. Local and regional ground-water flow is controlled largely by the major structural features of the site as well as the hydro-stratigraphy. Fracture flow is predominant within the carbonate sedimentary rocks and welded tuff and lava flow volcanic sequences. Matrix flow is assumed to be predominant within the bedded, non-welded tuff and alluvial fan aquifers. The rates of flow can be quite variable, depending on the types of aquifers present, the degree of fracturing and secondary solution features within the carbonate aquifers, and the hydraulic gradients present in a given area. For example, the quantity of water moving through the Paleozoic carbonate aquifer beneath Yucca Flat is estimated at about 0.013 cubic meters/second, whereas the quantity of water moving beneath Pahute Mesa (volcanic aquifer) is estimated at about 0.31 cubic meters/second (Corchary and Dinwiddie, 1974, p. 25). Estimates for the valley-fill aquifers in the area can be twice as much (see Eakin *et al.*; 1976, pp. G-32–G-33).

Most recharge to the Alkali Flat-Furnace Creek Ranch subbasin is thought to occur in areas of higher elevation and correspondingly higher precipitation, located north of Yucca Mountain. A major proportion of recharge occurs in the winter and spring because of lower temperatures and ET rates. Recharge rates in lower elevation areas of the Amargosa Desert are unknown but are estimated to be very small. Czarnecki (1985) estimated the average areal recharge to be 0.7 millimeters/

year for a zone of precipitation that includes Yucca Mountain.[7]

There is a general lack of hydraulic property data in the region, although some field data exist in the vicinity of Yucca Mountain, NTS, and elsewhere. Available hydraulic property data are summarized in Bedinger *et al.* (1985, Table 1; p. A18). Regionally, Winograd and Thordarson (1975) have estimated average flow rates to range from 2 to 201 meters/year. The most transmissive unit in the region is the lower carbonate aquifer, which has transmissivity values as large as 10,000 square meters/ day. All other aquifers have transmissivities that are more than an order of magnitude smaller (DOE, 1988; p. 3−68). Transmissivity for the valley-fill aquifer ranges from about 10 to 400 square meters/day.

2.1.2.4 Water Supply and Consumption

One factor that can aid in characterizing receptor groups is the manner in which they acquire their water supply. Almost all water used in Nye County is provided through either public or private wells, although some springs meet (limited) local needs. Some smaller communities, individual residences, and businesses rely entirely on private (commercial) water suppliers (see DOE, 1988; pp. 3-118−3-119). Only a few communities (Beatty, Mercury, Tonopah, and portions of Pahrump) have centralized public water systems (DOE, 1986; p. 3−75).

DOE previously published information on water consumption in the Yucca Mountain

area in the following: the *1986 Environmental Assessment; the 1988 Site Characterization Plan* (SCP); and, most recently, in the 1996 *Final Environmental Impact Statement (EIS) for the Nevada Test Site and Off-Site Locations in the State of Nevada* (see, respectively, DOE, 1986, 1988, and 1996). Using limited consumption data for only 5216 Nye County residents, DOE estimated that the per-capita consumption of water county-wide was 2473 cubic meters/day per 1000 people (DOE, 1986; p. 3−74).[8] Extrapolating this figure to the 1990 population produces a consumption rate estimate of approximately 43,972 cubic meters/ day county-wide. DOE also provided information on estimated water consumption for selected communities in the Yucca Mountain area (see Table 2−2). This information was first reported in the *Environmental Assessment* (DOE, 1986; p. 3−75) and subsequently updated in the *SCP* (DOE, 1988; p. 3−135) and the *Final NTS EIS* (DOE, 1996; p. 4−132).

Table 2−2. Estimated Level of Water Consumption for Selected Communities in the Yucca Mountain Area. From DOE (1988, p. 3−315).

Community	Estimated Water Consumption (m^3/day)
Amargosa Valley	6000
Ash Meadows[a]	150
Beatty	3000
Crystal[a]	230
Death Valley Junction	64
Indian Springs[a]	3000
Indian Springs AFB[a]	1500
Johnnie[a]	26
Mercury[a]	1100
Pahrump[a]	9400
Rhyolite	11

[a] Not within Alkali Flat-Furnace Creek Ranch groundwater basin.

---

[7]Other theories about regional flow in the subbasin were presented and documented by Czarnecki (1987, 1989) and Czarnecki and Wilson (1989). The previously accepted conceptual model of the regional ground-water system assumed that flow beneath the central Amargosa Desert ultimately discharges from two major areas: Furnace Creek Ranch and Franklin Lake Playa. In the baseline model of Czarnecki (1985), zero recharge was assumed to be occurring over most of the subregion south of Yucca Mountain. New data were obtained by Czarnecki (1989) which led to an alternate conceptual model of subregional flow. Potentiometric data were obtained from mining property boreholes in the Greenwater Range (between Death Valley and the Amargosa Desert). These data show a water-table altitude in that area of about 875 meters, providing evidence of significant groundwater recharge and the probable presence of a ground-water flow divide beneath this range. The data suggest that flow divides beneath the Greenwater and Funeral Mountains may isolate the water table aquifer in the Amargosa Desert area from the flow system in Death Valley.

[8]Estimate based on consumption rate of 12,900 cubic meters/day per 5216 persons.

In general, water quality throughout the area is adequate for personal consumption, stock and agricultural purposes except for areas in the southern Amargosa Desert where evaporites from lacustrine deposits cause the ground water to have total dissolved solids concentrations in excess of 10,000 parts/million (Winograd and Thordarson, 1974). As can be seen in Figure 2–5 (see end plate), there are small clusters of wells near the communities of Amargosa Valley and Death Valley Junction, located at highway crossroads. Until recently, some ground water was used for processing specialty clays and zeolites mined from lacustrine deposits in southern Amargosa Desert and in Ash Meadows. Agricultural development is currently confined to the southern Amargosa Desert area where depths to water range from 10 to 40 meters (Kilroy, 1991) and the topography is suitable for center pivot irrigation.

It should be noted that since 1973, irrigation pumping in the Ash Meadows area has been controlled to prevent the lowering of ground-water levels in Devils Hole and subsequent threats to the long-term survival of a unique species of desert pupfish [*Cyprionodon diabolis*—see Dudley and Larson (1976)]. As noted earlier, in 1984, the Ash Meadows National Wildlife Refuge was established to protect flora and fauna unique to the area. The U.S. Supreme Court has subsequently ruled that maintenance of water levels in Devils Hole has precedence over other water uses in the area (Also see Appendix A).

2.1.2.5 Water Well Surveys[9]

The arid, desert-like climate in the Yucca Mountain area results in few sources of surface water supply although there have proven to be extensive ground-water resources in this portion of the Basin and Range. To better understand how the ground-water resources have been used in the past, the staff reviewed previously published information on water well surveys.

The USGS performed one of the first comprehensive surveys of ground-water availability (as well as ground-water use) in the Yucca Mountain area in 1971 (see Thordarson and Robinson, 1971). To assist AEC officials in assessing damage claims to water wells and springs possibly resulting from nuclear explosions, the USGS reviewed published and unpublished geologic and ground-water data within a 161-kilometer radius of NTS. The census covered 81,367 square kilometers in portions of six counties in southern California and Nevada. The types of information collected for the census included aquifer type, water-table depth, yield, and end-use. This census identified 6032 water wells (and 754 springs and seeps). Most of the wells (98 percent) were located in alluvial fan deposits. In addition to being the most extensive surficial geology in the region, alluvial basins are usually the most accessible topographically (occupying physiographic low terrain) and have the highest water-yielding capacity of the aquifer types identified [see Bedinger *et al.* (1989; Figure 1, p. A1)].

To a lesser extent, water wells are also reported in carbonate and volcanic rocks, but these aquifers generally tend to have lower water yields in the study area. Almost 54 percent of the wells were reported to be less than 60-meters deep; almost 84 percent were reported at depths less than 150-meters deep. Of the wells identified, 60 percent were reported to yield at least 380 liters/minute. In terms of end use, most of the wells in the study area were reported to be used for domestic purposes (56 percent); followed by irrigation (17 percent); municipal and commercial (6 percent each); and stock supply (2 percent). (Nine percent of the wells in the 1971 study area were reportedly no longer in use.) In a 1988 survey of wells in the Amargosa Desert area, for purposes of characterization of the Yucca Mountain site, DOE reported that 50 percent of the wells in the area (199 of 397) were used for domestic use and 41 percent (164 of 397) were used for agricultural irrigation (see DOE, 1988; p. 3–119).

---

[9]Because of time and resource limitations, not all available sources of ground-water information were examined. For example, the Nevada State Engineer's Office of Division of Water Resources (in Carson City) has extensive information on current ground-water availability and use, including pumping inventories by hydrographic basin. Some of this information was studied for the purposes of the analyses described in Sections 2.2 and 3.3.

The greatest depths to water in wells currently being pumped to supply agricultural or domestic needs in the immediate Yucca Mountain region occur in the community of Amargosa Valley where depths to water range from 100 to 120 meters. Well J−13 in Jackass Flats on NTS pumps water from a depth of 280 meters to supply drilling and tunneling operations for the Yucca Mountain Project; however, this may be considered an exceptional practice for this region. Depth to water increases monotonically from approximately 100 to more than 300 meters along a trajectory extending from the community of Amargosa Valley in the south and terminating in the north approximately 10 kilometers from the perimeter drift of the proposed Yucca Mountain repository (see Figure 2−5).

2.1.2.6 Water Well Properties

There are about 170 boreholes at NTS (Fernandez, 1991)[10] but only a few are reported to be pumped periodically to obtain hydrologic information. In its 1988 SCP, DOE provided information on depth to the water table and production statistics for selected wells at NTS (Table 2−3). Some of these data were updated in 1993 (Table 2−4). Two of the wells (J−12 and J−13) are approximately 7 kilometers southeast of the Yucca Mountain site and have been used regularly during site characterization and provide water to NTS facilities (see Tables 2−5 and 2−6). Czarnecki (1992) simulated water level declines in the Yucca Mountain area in response to future ground-water withdrawals from these wells. This work is important because it represents a 10-year forecast of how future ground-water levels will be affected by human activities (as discussed later in Section 3.2 of this NUREG). This work also supported a DOE request to the State of Nevada for a permit to pump up to 5.7×10^{-3} cubic meters/second from J−13, for the purposes of characterization work.

Eight different pumping scenarios were analyzed, using a transient version of

Czarnecki's 1985 model and various combinations of withdrawal rates. Four of the scenarios involved pumping from a single well, whereas both wells were pumped in the other four scenarios. For each withdrawal rate, simulations were made with aquifer-specific yields[11] set at 0.001, 0.005, and 0.01. Czarnecki (1992) considered a specific yield of 0.01 to be the value that is best supported by available data. The most extreme scenario represented the combined maximum pumping capacities from both wells (8.771×10^{-2} cubic meters/second) and assumed an aquifer specific yield of 0.001. This resulted in a drawdown of over 12.2 meters at both wells J−12 and J−13 at the end of the 10-year period. Under the same pumping conditions, and assuming a specific yield of 0.01, simulated drawdowns at J−13 and J−12 were about 3.0 meters and varied from 1.8 to 2.4 meters at the Yucca Mountain site. The simulated drawdown for the anticipated withdrawal rate of 5.7×10^{-3} cubic meters/second from well J−13 (based on a 10-year pumping period and a specific yield of 0.01) was 0.29 meters at J−13. The drawdown at the Yucca Mountain site would be about 0.2 meters. If one of the scenarios analyzed by Czarnecki (1992) is representative of actual ground-water withdrawals during site characterization, it can be used to test how well the regional model represents the flow system.

2.1.2.7 Ground-Water Utilization (End-Use)

Another criterion that might be used to aid in the identification of potential receptor groups in the Yucca Mountain area is the manner in which ground-water supplies are used locally. Although most of the wells in the study area are used for municipal, domestic, or ranching (livestock) needs, by volume (end-use), most ground water in southern Nevada (excluding Las Vegas) is applied chiefly to agricultural irrigation and mining (Solley *et al.*, 1993).

Since the early 1980s, the State Engineer has maintained ground-water pumping records that also reveal how ground water is being

---

[10]Fernandez, J.A., "Overall Approach and Performance Calculations [Strategies to Seal Shafts, Ramps, and Underground Openings]," Unpublished Presentation by the Sandia National Laboratories to the U.S. Technical Review Board/Panel on Structural Geology and Geoengineering, Seattle, Washington, November 12−13, 1991.

[11]Volume of water an unconfined aquifer releases from storage per unit surface area of aquifer per unit decline in the water table.

Well	Aquifer Type	Pumping Rate (L/min)	Total Withdrawals In 1985 (m³)
Table 2–3. Water Well Production for Selected NTS Wells. Adopted from DOE (1988, pp. 3–120, 3–124).			
Alkali Flat-Furnace Creek Subbasin			
8	Tuff	1500	241,000
19	Tuff	1360	433,200
U20a–2	Tuff	1290	76,400
Ash Meadows Subbasin			
UE–1t	Not reported	1020	21,200
2	Carbonate (?)	625	78,100
A	Alluvial	610	148,300
5b	alluvial	910	231,300
5c	Alluvial	1230	231,300
UE–5c	Not reported	1320	16,400
C	Carbonate (?)	1020	99,000
C–1	Carbonate (?)	1060	99,000
4	Not reported	2460	158,300
UE–15d	Not reported	1020	not reported
UE–16d	Tuff	734	59,100
Army Well–1	Carbonate (?)	2010	192,900

Table 2–4. Summary of 1993 Water Well and Discharge Information for NTS. Adopted from DOE (1996, p. 4–133), unless otherwise noted.

Well	Aquifer Type	Well Depth (m)	Static Water Level (m)	Pump Depth Setting (m)	Yield (m³/min)	Annual Pumping [a] (10⁶ m³)
Army Well 1	Carbonate	593.14	210.31	289.86	2.01	0.4178
Well 5C	Alluvial	361.80	211.23	238.96	1.23	0.2393
Well 5B	Alluvial	274.32	208.48	---	1.02	0.1126
Well 4	Alluvial	450.80	286.82	387.40	2.46	0.2856
Well 4a	Volcanic	---	---	---	---	0.4172
Well C	Carbonate	518.46	470.61	473.35	1.02	0.2390
Well C1	Carbonate	520.29	471.83	484.94	1.06	0.0357
Well 8	Volcanic	1673.35	327.05	374.29	1.51	0.1185
UE–16D	Carbonate	914.40	230.12	330.10	0.73	0.1813
UE–15d [b, c]	Volcanic	5940	203.6	505.7	---	0
J–12	Volcanic	347.17	225.25	250.55	3.09	0.0945
J–13	Volcanic	1063.14	283.16	350.82	2.57	0.1584
UE–5c [d]	Alluvial	---	---	---	---	0.0278
UE–19c [b]	Volcanic	---	---	---	---	0.0269
UE–20a [d]	Volcanic	---	---	---	---	0.1058
					TOTAL	2.4606

a Well yields calculated from controlled pump tests are typically within one order of magnitude of well drillers' estimates.

b Well no longer in use.

c Claassen (1973, pp. 104–105).

d Construction well water.

Table 2−5. **Summary of Pumping Test Data for Wells J−12 and J−13 (in the Topopah Spring Member of the Paintbrush Tuff), during the Period 1960−69.**
Adopted from DOE (1988, p. 3−226) citing Claassen (1973).

Well	Distance From Site (km)	Depth to Aquifer (m)	Specific Capacity [$(m^3/d)/m$]	Pumping Rate (m^3/d)
J−12	12	180−347.2	220−2800	2000−4500
J−13	8	207.3−449.6	310−540	2800−3800

Table 2−6. **Water Production from Wells J−12 and J−13, during the Period 1983−85.**
Adopted from DOE (1988, p. 3−226) citing Witherill (1986).

Well	Production (m^3)		
	1983	1984	1985
J−12	96,460	98,700	94,900
J−13	159,500	152,700	143,100

 NUREG−1538

used within the respective hydrographic basins. In the Amargosa Desert and Pahrump Valley hydrographic basins, the pumping inventories are shown in Table 2−7. For example, during the 1985−95 period, this table shows that in the Amargosa Desert hydrographic basin, irrigation averaged about 78 percent of the pumping inventory, followed by mining/industrial usage—about 21 percent. Domestic/quasi-municipal usage has accounted for little more than 1 percent of the ground-water pumping during this period. By contrast, in the Pahrump Valley hydrographic basin, irrigation averaged only about 69 percent of the pumping inventory for the same period of time, followed by mixed public/commercial usage by Central Nevada [Water] Utilities—about 22 percent. Domestic/quasi-municipal usage from other sources of ground-water supply has accounted for about 10 percent of the pumping inventory during this period. A little less than 4 percent of the ground-water pumping inventory in the Pahrump Valley hydrographic basin during this period can be attributed to the Champion Golf Course.

2.1.2.8 Well Costs

The costs of producing (e.g., extracting) the water could provide an additional criterion for distinguishing between potential receptor groups in the Yucca Mountain area. Inasmuch as the water table below NTS usually occurs at great depth (see DOE, 1988; pp. 3−157 − 3−159), extraction and operating costs could be prohibitive for certain scenarios, thereby creating disincentives to agricultural, residential, or even commercial development at particular locations within the site. Because of its accessibility (e.g., depth), there is an economic argument that the costs of drilling, developing, and pumping ground water from the (deep) carbonate ground-water resource within (below) the site are higher in comparison with the costs of using (shallow) alluvial ground-water resources found beyond NTS boundaries. For example, pumping costs will tend to increase because of the additional electricity needed to lift the water from the greater depths, even when the price of electricity drops or remains constant (see Schefter, 1984).

Previously, the State Engineers Office (State of Nevada, 1982; p. 11) made the following estimates with regard to the development (and production) of new ground-water resources in southern Nevada, which tend to support this argument:

Aquifer Type	Yield (gpm)	Capital Cost Per Well (1982 Dollars)	Total Production Cost (Dollars/Acre-foot)
Alluvial	300− 2500	$85,000− $500,000	$25−$30
Carbonate	< 5000	$2,000,000	$115

(In Section 2.2 of this NUREG, an analysis was undertaken that evaluated the capital costs of deep well construction in semi-arid portions of the U.S. outside of the Yucca Mountain area.[12] The cost estimates developed are believed to be generally consistent with the State's 1982 cited figures.)

Additional economic information about the marginal (preferred) use of ground water, as a resource (see Science Applications International Corporation, 1991; and Frederick *et al.*, 1996), may provide further insights in defining potential receptor groups.

2.1.3 Other Issues Related to Near-Term Ground-Water Use

Over the past decade, Nevada has experienced about a 50 percent increase in population.[13] This high rate of growth has led to concerns about the general availability of water and in particular, the potential for overdrafting of regional ground-water systems. Surface water has been fully appropriated for many years and most priority water rights in the major river basins were established well before 1900 (Moody *et al.*, 1986; p. 328). The principal

---

[12]Arizona, Nevada, New Mexico, and the Trans-Pecos region of Texas.

[13]Nye County has had one of the highest population growth rates in the State (115 percent), followed by Clark County (82 percent), and the City of Las Vegas (79.5 percent). During the 1980−92 period, Las Vegas was the second fastest growing municipality in the conterminous U.S. (U.S. Department of Commerce, 1994b; p. xxvii).

Table 2–7. Ground-Water Pumping Inventories in the Amargosa Desert and Pahrump Valley Hydrographic Basins, During the Period 1985–95. Based on data from the State Engineers Office cited in Buqo (1997, pp. 29, 34).

Category	Inventoried Pumping by Year ($10^6 m^3$)										
	1995	1994	1993	1992	1991	1990	1989	1988	1987	1986	1885
Amargosa Desert Hydrographic Basin											
Irrigation [a]	15.2	12.3	10.7	7.1	6.1	6.1	1.9	3.7	7	8.1	10
Mining/Industrial [b]	3.2	3.1	3.1	2.8	1.3	3.4	2.7	1.2	0.37	0.7	1.7
Quasi-Municipal/Domestic	0.123	0.123	0.123	0.123	0.123	0.154	0.154	0.154	0.154	0.154	0.28
Commercial	0.012	0.012	0.012	0.012	0.012	0.012	0.012	0.012	0.012	0.012	0.025
TOTAL	18.54	15.54	13.94	10.04	7.54	9.67	4.77	5.07	7.54	8.97	12.01
Pahrump Valley Hydrographic Basin											
Irrigation	17.5	21.1	17.3	20.1	23.8	19	18.3	17.9	18.3	19	23.6
Quasi-Municipal/Domestic	6.8	6	5.2	4.6	4.1	3.7	3.7	3.4	2.3	2.1	1.9
Central Nevada [Water] Utilities [c]	3.4	2.2	1.9	1.8	1.3	1.6	1.3	1.5	1.6	1.4	1.5
Commercial [d]	1.5	1.5	1.5	1.5	1.5	1.5	1.5	1.5	1.5	1.5	1.5
TOTAL	29.2	30.8	25.9	28	30.7	25.8	24.8	24.3	23.7	24	28.5

a Includes unpermitted irrigation.
b Includes pumping inventories from the St. Joe Bullfrog, American Borate, and IMV Floridin mining/mineral processing operations.
c A publicly owned water utility. Inventory likely to include commercial and domestic consumption not listed elsewhere in this table.
d Pumping for the Champion Golf Course.

source of water for the greater Las Vegas area is an allocation from the Colorado River (vis-a-vis the *Colorado River Compact*—see California Department of Water Resources, 1998; pp. 9-28–9-29), which accounts for about half of the State's allocation (Moody *et al.*, 1986; p. 323). However, this allocation is finite and is believed to be insufficient to meet the region's growing needs beyond the end of the century (Water Resources Management, Inc., 1992). It is believed, therefore, that there will be growing pressure to develop the available regional ground-water resources, including those in southern Nye County (see Basse, 1990).

Ground-water use in many southern Nye County communities (e.g., Amargosa Desert, Pahrump Valley, Indian Springs, Oasis Valley) is already over-appropriated and there are restrictions in place to protect the affected aquifers (see DOE, 1988; pp. 134–135; and Appendix A, this NUREG). Consequently, as is the case in much of the arid southwestern U.S. (see Reisner, 1993), it is not clear whether there will be sufficient water resources to support additional development in southern Nevada. Information about the ground-water resources is incomplete and appears to be limited to the first 100 meters for the alluvial ground-water reservoirs (Eakin *et al.*, 1976); information about the consolidated rock-reservoirs (e.g., carbonates and volcanics) is believed to be even more incomplete. Complicating these matters are the complexities associated with developing realistic estimates of the water budgets (recharge, discharge, ET) for the respective hydrographic basins in the area (see D'Agnese *et al.*, 1997; pp. 43–56). For these reasons, it is reasonable to assume that finite ground-water resources and expanding needs in areas like Las Vegas will cause continued ground-water mining and overdrafts in the region (Coleman, 1993).

2.1.4 Summary

Current use of ground water in the Yucca Mountain area is affected by both physiographic factors and institutional controls. Because the climate is arid to semi-

arid, agriculture is restricted to areas where the depth to water is shallow enough to make irrigation economically feasible (i.e., Amargosa Desert, Pahrump, and Oasis Valleys). Agriculture also tends to be confined to areas where the relief is gentle enough to make center-pivot or furrow irrigation methods technically feasible and where the soil texture is suitable, such as near the distal margin of alluvial fan deposits. North of Highway 95 much of the land in the vicinity of Yucca Mountain is controlled by either the NTS, the U.S. Bureau of Reclamation, or the U.S. Air Force, which has precluded potential development. Although the withdrawal of this land from private development may have affected land use patterns, the great depth to ground water and limitations to soil irrigability,[14] throughout the controlled area, suggests that farming would not be economically feasible with current technology.

As noted in Appendix A, none of the residents in this area appears to be living a "subsistence" lifestyle. No resident is understood to subsist solely off the food produced from his/her garden or ranch. Most residents still purchase the majority of their food stuffs at local grocery stores and use the locally grown produce/meat-poultry to supplement their diets. Most, if not all residents therefore appear to need "infrastructure" to subsist and run their households—bottled gas to cook their meals; roads to get to work and to town (to purchase food and to obtain services); and in particular, electricity to pump water from their wells.

Present water use in the Amargosa Valley area is much greater than what could be sustained by the in-flow of ground water coming into the Alkali Flat-Furnace Creek Ranch

---

[14]In this regard, it is noted that the soil classification system in Nevada is based on both judgments of the feasibility of performing initial site improvements such as drainage, removing stones, leveling, ripping hardpan (i.e., caliché), or removing soluble salts and alkali, and on continuing site limitations for use requiring special management, such as the control of salt build-up (State of Nevada, 1974). Most of the soils in the Yucca Mountain area are gravelly and coarse-textured with low inherent fertility and low waterholding capacity. Consequently, they have been classified as having properties that "...preclude their use for irrigated agriculture..." or "...have severe limitations that reduce [the] choice of crops or require special conservation practices or both...." (*Op cit.*)

ground-water basin underlying Yucca Mountain. Ground water from NTS is believed to be a relatively small contributor to the total discharge in the Amargosa Desert area—no more than 7½ percent. The remaining ground water used in the Amargosa Desert area apparently comes from a combination of interbasin flows as well as upwelling from the deep Paleozoic carbonate aquifer, as suggested by geochemical signatures and observed vertical gradients in the region. There also may be areas of local recharge from mountain runoff into the alluvial-fan deposits, as occurs in other alluvial basins in Death Valley. It is reasonable to assume, therefore, that under a hypothetical farming-type receptor group scenario (30-kilometer location), based on current water use, all (incoming) ground water entering the basin would be taken up by the irrigation wells pumping in the area.

Based on current technology, agricultural activity will most likely continue to be limited to the Amargosa Desert vicinity. Geochemical facies in various wells in the region show that the ground water is highly heterogeneous, depending on such factors as the location, screened well depth, and pumping (see Wittmeyer and Turner, 1995). There is reason to believe, therefore, that there is only limited mixing between Alkali Flat-Furnace Creek Ranch ground waters and those from the other hydrologic basins in the Death Valley ground-water system (see Figure 2–2). The net effect of this absence of mixing, under natural conditions, is to suggest that radionuclide concentrations may vary greatly from irrigation well to irrigation well.

As regards the use of specific criteria for the selection of a potential critical group in the Yucca Mountain area, the staff has the following observations based on the aforementioned review:

- Information on current lifestyles—existing population distribution, employment centers, agricultural/ranching practices—is useful in limiting speculation on potential receptor groups.

- The availability and accessibility to ground water—such as aquifer source type and depth-to-aquifer—are useful parameters to consider in the selection of potential receptor groups.

- Farming in the area is highly influenced by unique geographic and meteorologic factors that were not considered to any significant extent in this review. This or similar types of information may be used to further define the attributes of receptor groups for the Yucca Mountain area.

2.1.5 References

Basse, B., "Water Resources in Southern Nevada," Denver, Colorado, Adrian Brown Consultants, Inc., 1990. [Prepared for the CNWRA.]

Bedinger, M.S., W.H. Langer, and J.E. Reed, "Synthesis of Hydraulic Properties of Rocks in the Basin and Range Province, Southwestern United States," U.S. Geological Survey Water Supply Paper 2310, 1985.

Bedinger, M.S., *et al.*, "Studies of Geology and Hydrology in the Basin and Range Province, Southwestern United States, for Isolation of High-Level Radioactive Waste—Basis for Characterization and Evaluation," U.S. Geological Survey Professional Paper 1370–A, 1989.

Blankennagel, R.K., and J.E. Weir, Jr., "Geohydrology of the Eastern Part of Pahute Mesa, Nevada Test Site, Nye County, Nevada," U.S. Geological Survey Professional Paper 712–B, 1973.

Buqo, T.S., "Baseline Water Supply and Demand Evaluation of Southern Nye County, Nevada," Blue Diamond, Nevada, [1997]. [Independent consultants' report prepared for the Nye County Nuclear Waste Repository Office (Nye County, Nevada)].

California Department of Water Resources, "California Water Plan Update," Sacramento, Department of Water Resources Bulletin 160–98, 2 vols., November 1998.

Carr, M.D. and J.C. Yount (eds.), "Geologic and Hydrologic Investigations of a Potential

Nuclear Waste Disposal Site at Yucca Mountain, Southern Nevada," U.S. Geological Survey Bulletin 1790, 1988.

Claassen, H.C., "Water Quality and Physical Characteristics of Nevada Test Site Water Supply Wells," Lakewood, Colorado, U.S. Geological Survey, USGS–474–158 [NTS–242], 1973. [Non-serial report prepared for the AEC.]

Coleman, N.M., "Groundwater Impacts of Foreseeable Human Activities on a HLW Repository," in American Nuclear Society/ American Society of Civil Engineers, *Proceedings of the Fourth Annual International Conference: High-Level Radioactive Waste Management*, April 26–30, 1993, Las Vegas, Nevada, 1:261–264 [1993].

Corchary, G.S., and G.A. Dinwiddie, "Field Trip to [the] Nevada Test Site," Denver, Colorado, U.S. Geological Survey [1974]. [NTS field guide with limited distribution prepared for the AEC.]

Czarnecki, J.B., "Simulated Effects of Increased Recharge on the Ground-Water Flow System of Yucca Mountain and Vicinity, Nevada-California," U.S. Geological Survey, Water Resources Investigations, WRI–84–4344, 1985.

Czarnecki, J.B., "Should the Furnace Creek Ranch-Franklin Lake Playa Ground-Water Subbasin Simply Be the Franklin Lake Playa Ground-Water Subbasin? [Abstract]," *EOS Transactions*, American Geophysical Union, 68:1292 [1987].

Czarnecki, J.B., "Characterization of the Subregional Ground-Water Flow System at Yucca Mountain and Vicinity, Nevada-California," *Radioactive Waste Management and the Nuclear Fuel Cycle*, 13:51–61 [1989].

Czarnecki, J.B., "Simulated Water-Level Declines Caused by Withdrawals from Wells J–13 and J–12 Near Yucca Mountain, Nevada," U.S. Geological Survey, Open-File Report 91–478, 1992.

Czarnecki, J.B. and R.K. Waddell, "Finite-Element Simulation of Ground-Water Flow in the Vicinity of Yucca Mountain, Nevada-California," U.S. Geological Survey, Water-Resources Investigations Report, WRI–84–4349, 1984.

Czarnecki, J.B. and W.E. Wilson, "Site Characterization and Conceptual Models of the Regional Ground-Water Flow System, Yucca Mountain and Vicinity, Nevada-California [Abstract]," in Post, R.G. (ed.), *Waste Management '89: Proceedings of the Symposium on Waste Management*, February 26-March 2, 1989, Tucson, Arizona, 1:473 [1989].

D'Agnese, F.A., *et al.*, "Hydrogeologic Evaluation and Numerical Simulation of the Death Valley Regional Ground-water Flow System, Nevada and California, Using Geoscientific Information Systems," U.S. Geological Survey, Open-File Report 96–4300, 1997.

Dudley, W.W., Jr., and J.D. Larson, "Effect of Irrigation on Desert Pupfish Habitats in Ash Meadows, Nye County, Nevada," U.S. Geological Survey Professional Paper 927, 1976.

Eakin, T.E., S.L. Schoff, and P. Cohen, "Regional Hydrology of a Part of Southern Nevada," U.S. Geological Survey, Trace Elements Investigations Report TEI–833, 1963. [Prepared for the AEC.]

Eakin, T.E., D. Price, and J.R. Harrill, "Summary Appraisals of the Nation's Ground-Water Resources," U.S. Geological Survey Professional Paper 813–G, 1976.

Frederick, K.D., J. Vandenberg, and T. Hanson, "Economic Values of Freshwater in the United States," Washington, D.C., Resources for the Future Discussion Paper 97–03, October 1996. [Prepared for the Electric Power Research Institute.]

Geraghty, J.J., *et al.*, "Water Atlas of the United States," Port Washington, New York, Water Information Center, 1973.

International Commission on Radiological Protection, "Recommendations of the ICRP,"

Annals of the ICRP, Vol. 1, No. 3 [1977]. [ICRP Publication 26]

International Commission on Radiological Protection, "Radiological Protection Principles for the Disposal of Solid Radioactive Waste," Pergamon Press, Oxford, 1985. [ICRP Publication 46.]

Kilroy, K.C., "Ground-Water Conditions in Amargosa Desert, Nevada-California, 1952–87," U.S. Geological Survey, Water-Resources Investigations Report 89–4101, 1991.

Laczniak, R.J., *et al.*, "Summary of Hydrogeologic Controls on Ground-Water Flow at the Nevada Test Site, Nye County, Nevada," U.S. Geological Survey, Water-Resources Investigations Report 96–4109, 1996.

McCracken, R.D., *A History of Amargosa Valley, Nevada*, Tonopah, Nevada, Nye County Press, 1992.

Moody, D.W., *et al.* (compilers), "Nevada" in "National Water Summary 1985—Hydrologic Events and Surface-Water Resources," U.S. Geological Survey, Water-Supply Paper 2300, 1986.

National Research Council, "Ground Water at Yucca Mountain: How High Can It Rise?— Final Report of the Panel on Coupled Hydrologic Tectonic/Hydrothermal Systems at Yucca Mountain: Board on Radioactive Waste Management; Commission on Geosciences, Environment, and Resources," Washington, D.C., National Academy Press, April 1992.

Planert, M., and J.S. Williams, "Ground Water Atlas of the United States. Segment 1: California, Nevada," U.S. Geological Survey, Hydrologic Investigations Atlas 730–B, 1995.

Reisner, M., *Cadillac Desert—The American West and Its Disappearing Water*, New York, Penguin Books, 1986. [Revised 1993.]

Rush, F.E., "Index Map of Hydrographic Areas," Carson City, Division of Water Resources/Department of Conservation and Natural Resources, Information Series Report 6, 1968.

Rush, F.E., "Regional Ground-Water Systems in the Nevada Test Site Area, Nye, Lincoln, and Clark Counties, Nevada," Carson City, Division of Water Resources/Department of Conservation and Natural Resources, Water Resources Reconnaissance Series Report 54, 1970.

Schefter, J.E., "Declining Ground-Water Levels and Increasing Pumping Costs: Floyd County, Texas—A Case Study," in "National Water Summary 1984—Hydrologic Events, Selected Water Quality Trends, and Ground-Water Resources," U.S. Geological Survey, Water-Supply Paper 2275, 1984.

Schoff, S.L. and J.E. Moore, "Chemistry and Movement of Ground Water, Nevada Test Site," U.S. Geological Survey, Trace Elements Investigations Report TEI–838, 1964. [Prepared for the AEC.]

Science Applications International Corporation, Inc., "Water Resource Assessment of Yucca Mountain, Nevada," Las Vegas, Nevada, U.S. Department of Energy, Study Plan 8.3.1.9.2.2, Revision 0, June 1991. [Prepared for DOE's Office of Civilian Radioactive Waste Management (OCRWM).]

Solley, W.B., R.R. Pierce, and H.A. Perlman, "Estimated Water Use in the United States in 1990," U.S. Geological Survey Circular 1081, 1993.

State of Nevada and University of Nevada of Nevada [Reno], "Water for Nevada: Report 8. Forecasts for the Future—Agriculture," Carson City, Division of Water Resources/ Department of Conservation and Resources and Division and Agricultural and Resource Economics/Max C. Fleischmann College of Agriculture, January 1974. [Contains a separate map plate entitled "Irrigability Classification of Soils," (dated 1973) that shows the distribution of soil irrigability classes within the state and provides a legend describing the soils.]

Thomas, H.E., "Water Resources," in Nevada Bureau of Mines, "Mineral and Water

Resources of Nevada," University of Nevada (Reno), Mackay School of Mines, Bulletin 65, 1964. [Prepared in cooperation with the USGS. Reprinted 1974.]

TRW Environmental Safety Systems, Inc., "Yucca Mountain Site Characterization Project: Summary of Socioeconomic Data Analyses Conducted in Support of Radiological Monitoring Program during Calendar Year 1994," Las Vegas, Nevada, Science Applications International Corporation, Inc., Document No. DE-AC01-91RW00134, June 1995a. [Prepared for OCRWM. The most recent update is dated June 1998, but was not considered in this analysis]

TRW Environmental Safety Systems Inc., "Total System Performance Assessment—1995: An Evaluation of the Potential Yucca Mountain Repository," Las Vegas, Nevada, Document No. B00000000-01717-2200-00136 (Rev. 01), November 1995b.

Thordarson, W. and B.P. Robinson, "Wells and Springs in California and Nevada within 100 Miles of the Point 37 Deg. 15 Min. N., 116 Deg. 25 Min. W., on Nevada Test Site," U.S. Geological Survey, USGS-474-85, 1971. [Prepared for the AEC.]

U.S. Department of Commerce, "County and City Data Book—1994 (12th edition)," Economics and Statistics Administration/ Bureau of Census, 1994a.

U.S. Department of Commerce, "1992 Census of Agriculture: State and County Data [for California and Nevada]," Economics and Statistics Administration/Bureau of Census, Volume 1, Geographic Area Series, 1994b.

U.S. Department of Energy, "Environmental Assessment: Yucca Mountain Site, Nevada Research and Development Area, Nevada—Volume I," Office of Civilian Radioactive Waste Management, Nevada, DOE/RW-0073, May 1986.

U.S. Department of Energy, "Site Characterization Plan, Yucca Mountain Site, Nevada Research and Development Area, Nevada," Office of Civilian Radioactive Waste Management, Nevada, DOE/RW-0199, 9 vols., December 1988.

U.S. Department of Energy, "Final Environmental Impact Statement for the Nevada Test Site and Off-Site Locations in the State of Nevada," Nevada Operations Office, DOE/EIS 0243, 3 vols. (and appendices), August 1996.

U.S. Geological Survey, "The National Atlas of the United States," Washington, D.C., 1970.

U.S. Geological Survey, "Ground-Water Levels in the United States—1971-74: Southwestern States," Washington, D.C., Water Supply Paper 2162, 1977.

Waddell, R.K., "Two-Dimensional, Steady-State Model of Ground-Water Flow, Nevada Test Site and Vicinity, Nevada-California," U.S. Geological Survey, Water-Resources Investigations Report 82-4085, 1982.

Waddell, R.K., J.H. Robison, and R.K. Blankennagel, "Hydrology of Yucca Mountain and Vicinity, Nevada-California—Investigative Results Through Mid-1983," U.S. Geological Survey, Water-Resources Investigations Report 84-4267, 1984.

Water Resources Management, Inc. [WRMI], "WRMI Process—Water Supply Planning for the Las Vegas Region," Columbia, Maryland, May 1992. [Prepared for the Las Vegas Valley Water District.]

Wescott, R.G., *et al.* (eds.), "NRC Iterative Performance Assessment Phase 2: Development of Capabilities for Review of a Performance Assessment for a High-Level Waste Repository," U.S. Nuclear Regulatory Commission, NUREG-1464, October 1995.

Winograd, I.J. and W. Thordarson, "Hydrogeologic and Hydrochemical Framework, South-Central Great Basin, Nevada-California, with Special Reference to the Nevada Test Site (Hydrology of Nuclear Test Sites)," U.S. Geological Survey, Professional Paper 712-C, 1975.

Witherill, J.V., U.S. Department of Energy/ Nevada Test Site, untitled letter to M.D.

Tuebner, Science Applications International Corporation [General Subject: Water Supply Information for the Nuclear Test Site"], June 4, 1986.

Wittmeyer, G.W. and D.R. Turner, "Conceptual and Mathematical Models of the Death Valley Regional Groundwater Flow System," San Antonio, Texas, Center for Nuclear Waste Regulatory Analyses, CNWRA 95–109, September 1995.

Wittmeyer, G.W., *et al.*, "Use of Groundwater in the Arid and Semi-Arid Western United States: Implications for [the] Yucca Mountain Area," San Antonio, Texas, Center for Nuclear Waste Regulatory Analyses, letter report, August 1996.

Wittwer, C., *et al.*, "Preliminary Development of the LBL/USGS Three-Dimensional Site-Scale Model of Yucca Mountain, Nevada," Berkeley, California, Lawrence Berkeley Laboratory, LBL–37356/UC–814, June 1995. [Prepared for DOE.]

2.2 Use of Ground Water in the Arid and Semi-Arid Western United States: Possible Implications for the Yucca Mountain Area[15]

2.2.1 Introduction

Assessment of water and land-use practices in the arid to semi-arid western U.S. can be used to help define a hypothetical receptor group for the Yucca Mountain area. Unlike Section 2.1 of this NUREG, which examined water- and land-use practices in the area immediately around the proposed repository, this section examines such practices on a broader, state-wide scale, to determine what additional inferences, if any, may be made. Inasmuch as most of the land in the immediate Yucca Mountain area was withdrawn from private sector development, it is difficult to determine

if current water- and land-use practices are solely the result of obvious topographic, hydrogeologic, climatologic, and pedologic factors, or the result of certain institutional factors, such as the establishment of NTS and Nellis AFB. To evaluate the type of water use practices that might have existed in the vicinity of Yucca Mountain in the absence of NTS and Nellis AFB, the staff have conducted a review of water- and land-use practices from similar arid regions for comparison with the Yucca Mountain area.

2.2.2 Scope of Study and Methods of Analysis

The scope of this study has been limited to gathering data from Arizona, New Mexico, southern Nevada, and the Trans-Pecos region of west Texas on ground-water utilization practices *potentially* relevant to the Yucca Mountain area. The climate of this region of the southwestern U.S. generally ranges from arid to semi-arid, except in higher elevations, where orogenic effects result in a more humid, temperate climate. Based on the *Köppen-Geiger* climate classification scheme,[16] the climate at Yucca Mountain is arid. Hence, certain water-use practices, such as pumping ground water for cattle grazed on marginal, semi-arid lands, should perhaps not be extrapolated to the immediate Yucca Mountain area.

The tables and maps in this analysis present data on wells with water levels deeper than 150 meters. The basic data were obtained from the *Ground-Water Site Inventory* (GWSI) database for Arizona, New Mexico, and Nevada. (GWSI is part of the *National Water*

---

[15]This analysis was first published as Wittmeyer *et al.* (1996). Although it can be found in NRC's Public Document Room (PDR), Wittmeyer *et al.* has not received wide-spread distribution thus far and as a consequence, a decision was made to include it in this NUREG. However, for the purposes of publication in this format, it has undergone a limited editorial review. Despite this review, the analysis is substantially the same as the earlier version placed in the PDR.

[16]In the Köppen-Geiger system of climate classification, the annual precipitation boundary between humid and arid/ semi-arid precipitation/climate regimes is determined for places where winter is the wet season (like Yucca Mountain vicinity) by the following equation:

$$R(Humid/Sub\text{-}humid\ boundary) = .44\ (T - 32)$$

where R is the average annual boundary precipitation in inches and T is the average annual temperature, in Fahrenheit degrees (°F).

For Yucca Mountain which has an average annual temperature of about 61° F (or 16° C), the boundary between a humid and sub-humid climate would be 12.8 inches (325 millimeters) precipitation annually.

continued on next page

Information System developed and maintained by the USGS.) Because the data for each State were obtained from that State's USGS Water Resources Division Office, the format and content of the data varied somewhat. Data for Texas were obtained directly from the Texas Water Development Board. Additional water well and depth-to-water data were obtained from various reports prepared by State and Federal agencies. Anecdotal information about the occurrence of wells with great depths to water was obtained during telephone conversations with USGS personnel, ground-water supply consultants, and local well drillers.

Although the majority of wells studied have depths to the water table ranging from 150 to 240 meters, other locations in the arid U.S. pump ground water from depths greater than 240 meters. Because of the higher capital (i.e., developmental) and operating costs, the practice of pumping water from these "very deep wells" is less common, and is generally due to site-specific conditions and local water supply needs. Nonetheless, because it is possible (but not necessarily practical) to construct deep water wells in the NTS area, as a matter of background, the staff has evaluated these very deep well pumping practices. This evaluation can be found in Appendix C

2.2.3 Exploitation of Deep Ground Water

Outside of a few, very deep (greater than 240 meters) wells drilled on NTS to supply water

to remote locations, and several wells that supply water to mining operations in Crater Flat (e.g., Sterling Mine) and the Greenwater Range (U.S. Borax), most domestic and agricultural wells in the Yucca Mountain area are located where the water table is from 10- to 100-meters deep. This is in accord with the assumption that water wells tend to be drilled where the depth to water is shallowest, to limit development and production costs. Clearly, the occurrence of valuable mineral deposits may make the construction of a 500-meter-deep well economically feasible for a mining company, whereas a farmer might be unwilling to expend funds on such a well to irrigate alfalfa. The extremes to which a commercial enterprise will go to secure a water supply depends wholly on the marginal value that a unit of water has in producing a commodity, such as an ounce of gold or a bale of alfalfa. At the Sterling Mine, which is on the eastern flank of Bare Mountain at an altitude of approximately 1150 meters, water is currently trucked in from borehole VH−2 in Crater Flat to supply heap leach operations. For this case, it is evident that the cost of transporting water a distance of some 8 kilometers is less than pumping expenses in conjunction with the amortized cost of constructing a well at the mine. It must be noted that VH−2 was constructed as part of the Yucca Mountain site characterization program, before being ceded to the Sterling Mine, so costs borne by the mining company do not reflect actual costs of borehole construction.

Because water used to supply basic human needs tends to have a higher marginal utility than water used for mining and agriculture, domestic (household) users are more willing to pay for water than nonagricultural, commercial, and industrial users, who in turn have a greater willingness to pay for water than agricultural users (Science Applications International Corporation, 1991). Although domestic users tend to be willing to pay for water, they generally use far less water than industrial and agricultural users. Based on this pattern of consumptive behavior alone, one would expect domestic water use to predominate where water is expensive and agricultural use to predominate where water is

---

16 *continued*

The boundary in the Köeppen-Geiger climate classification between semi-arid and arid climates is one-half the precipitation value obtained for the humid/sub-humid boundary. The formula is

$$R(Semi\text{-}arid/Arid\ boundary) = .22\ (T - 32)$$

Thus, the precipitation boundary for an arid climate classification at Yucca Mountain would be 6.4 inches (163 millimeters) annually.

The approximate average annual precipitation at Yucca Mountain is 5.9 inches (150 millimeters). Yucca Mountain classifies as an arid climate according to the Köeppen-Geiger climate classification scheme because its precipitation is below 6.4 inches, the boundary between arid/semi-arid climates at sites that have winter-dominated precipitation and an average annual temperature of 16° F.

inexpensive. Of course other physiographic factors influence the development of a region: (a) climate and native vegetation; (b) topography; and (c) soil fertility. For this study, it is assumed the two primary factors affecting ground-water use are depth to the water table and climate. Depth to ground water directly affects the cost of obtaining fresh water, whereas climate influences agricultural practices.

Current well drilling and pump technology allows water to be pumped from extreme depths (in excess of 1000 meters); however, its potability and, thus, suitability for watering stock or irrigating cropland, generally decreases with depth. The power that must be delivered to a pump is proportional to the product of pump discharge and total lift, whereas the capital cost of a well depends on the rated power of the motor and capacity of the pump; diameter, length, and composition of the casing and well screen; and the method used to drill the well. As an illustration of pumping costs, consider two cases: (a) a domestic well that annually supplies 617 cubic meters (0.5 acre-feet—about 150 gallons/person per day for a household of 3 persons) of water to a home from a depth of 30 meters; and (b) an agricultural well used to supply 1.52 meters of water to 64.7 hectares of cropland during the growing season, from a depth of 7.6 meters. Assuming a composite well efficiency of 60 percent, annual operating expenses (excluding maintenance and amortized capital costs) for the domestic well, based on electricity costs of 100 mil/kWh would be $8.40.[17] Assuming 60 percent well efficiency and electricity costs of 100 mil/kWh, annual operating expenses for the agricultural well would be $3391.04. If the pump lift for both the domestic and agricultural wells were increased to 240 meters, annual energy costs

---

[17][Volume Pumped (617 m^3) $\times$ Pump Lift (30 m) $\times$ Unit Weight of Water (9800 N/m^3)] $\div$ [Efficiency (60 percent—0.60)] $\div$ [Conversion from Joules to Kilowatt-hours (3.6$\times$10^6 J/kWh) $\times$ Unit Cost of Electricity (0.10 Dollars/kWh)] = $8.40.

would rise to $67.20 and $32,553.98, respectively. This example illustrates the effect of depth to water on variable pumping expenses and highlights the costs of irrigating cropland where the depth to water is large.

2.2.3.1 Exploitation of Deep Ground Water in Arizona

Records for 1172 wells with depths to water equal to or greater than 150 meters were obtained from the GWSI database for Arizona. A general breakdown of these occurrences by depth to water and, where known, use of water, is given in Table 2−8. Note that the entries in the *Total Column* exceed the row total because some well records have no entry under the water use data field. The locations of water wells in Arizona with depths to water equal to greater than 150 meters are shown in Figure 2−6.

Many of the wells with depths to water from 150 to 180 meters are in the major agricultural areas of Pinal County and southern Maricopa County; however, these depths to water reflect extensive ground-water overdraft that occurred over the past 30 to 60 years, rather than natural pre-development hydrogeologic conditions. Since agricultural development began, water levels have declined 137 meters in the Stansfield Basin in western Pinal County, 128 meters southeast of Chandler, and more than 61 meters in the Eloy Basin in central Pinal County (Anderson, 1995). These depths to water do not reflect pre-development conditions; hence it was believed that water use practices in these areas could not be used to infer water-use practices that would have prevailed in the absence of current governmental controls in the relatively undeveloped welded tuff of the immediate Yucca Mountain vicinity. Therefore, analysis of the data instead focused on the occurrence of clusters of wells with depths to water in excess of 240 meters. Table 2−9 indicates the percentage of wells in a specified depth to water range that are used for a given purpose.

Table 2–8. Use of Water in Wells with Depth to Water Greater than 150 Meters, in Arizona

Depth to Water (m)	Specified Use						Unused	Total	Total with Specified Use
	Irrigation	Public	Stock	Industrial	Domestic	Commercial			
150 – 180	282[a]	76[b]	50	5	80	0	184	717	493
180 – 210	110[a]	29[c]	28[d]	4	26	1	51	262	198
210 – 240	25[e]	11	12	5	13	0	22	96	66
240 – 270	2	7	4	3	4	0	4	31	20
270 – 300	0	6	3	0	2	0	5	17	11
300 – 330	0	3	1	0	1	0	2	8	5
330 – 360	0	3	2	0	3	0	1	9	8
360 – 390	0	6	0	0	1	0	3	10	7
390 – 420	0	2	1	0	1	0	4	8	4
420 – 450	0	3	1	0	0	0	1	5	4
450 – 480	0	2	0	0	1	0	1	4	3
> 480	0	1	0	0	0	0	2	5	3
TOTALS	419	149	102	17	132	1	280	1172	822

a Primarily Pinal, Maricopa, and La Paz Counties.
b Phoenix and Chandler areas.
c Tucson, Casa Grande, Chandler, Phoenix, Flagstaff, and Kingman areas.
d Casa Grande area.
e Cave Creek Carefree area.

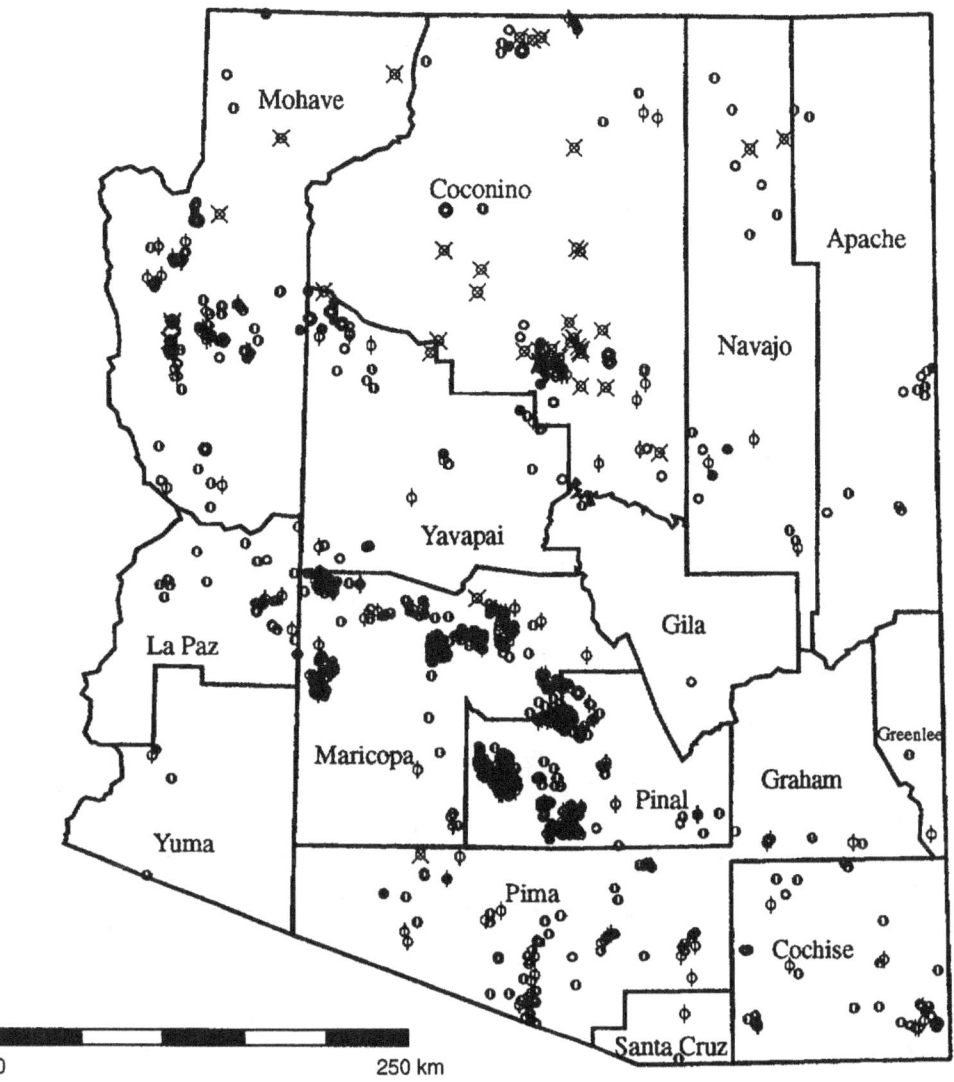

Figure 2−6. Locations of water wells in Arizona with depths to water greater than or equal to 150 meters.

Table 2–9 clearly shows that as the depth to water increases, the percentage of wells used for agriculture decreases, whereas the percentage of wells used for public supply, stock water, and domestic supply increases. This pattern in part reflects the higher value placed on water for drinking—and hygiene—uses that consume very little water compared with irrigated agriculture. For wells with depths to water in excess of 240 meters, public and domestic use accounts for 65 percent, stock water for 19 percent, and irrigation use for 3 percent. Of the 97 wells in Arizona with depths to water greater than 240 meters, 53 are located north of the 35th parallel and east of the 113th meridian on the highlands of the Colorado Plateau; 29 are north of the 35th parallel and west of the 113th meridian in the transition zone between the Colorado Plateau and eastern Mojave Desert; and the remaining 15 wells are scattered throughout a wide area south of the 35th parallel. Table 2–10, which gives a breakdown of wells with depth to water in excess of 240 meters as a function of land-surface elevation, indicates that 63 percent of these wells are located in regions where the elevation exceeds 1500 meters. For approximately 40 of these 97 deep wells, detailed descriptions of locations and climatologic and topographic conditions are presented in Section C–1 of Appendix C.

2.2.3.2 Exploitation of Deep Ground Water in Nevada

Records for 58 wells with depths to water equal to or greater than 150 meters were obtained from the USGS GWSI database for Nevada. Of the 58 wells, 49 lie in the southern half of Nevada, within the counties of Nye (4 wells); Lincoln (6 wells); and Clark (38 wells); and one well in these data is in Death Valley National Monument, Inyo County, California. Of the 16 wells in Nevada with depths to water equal to or greater than 240 meters, 13 are in the southern Nevada counties of Nye (1 well); Lincoln (5 wells); and Clark (7 wells). A general breakdown by water use for all 58 deep wells in Nevada is listed in Table 2–11. The locations of water wells in Nevada with depths to water in excess of 150 meters are

shown in Figure 2–7. Detailed descriptions of water wells with depths to water equal to or greater than 240 meters are given in Section C–2 of Appendix C. In the alluvial aquifer in the Amargosa Farms region, there is presently an estimated to be about a 40 percent ground-water overdraft (DOE, 1988; p. 3–121).

2.2.3.3 Exploitation of Deep Ground Water in New Mexico

Records for 94 wells with depths to water equal to or greater than 150 meters were obtained from the USGS GWSI database for New Mexico. Additional data on water wells were extracted from Orr (1987). Of the 94 wells, 83 are located in the northwestern quadrant of New Mexico in the counties of San Juan, Rio Arriba, Taos, McKinley, Sandoval, Santa Fe, Cibola, and Bernalillo. Elevations in this region range from 1500 meters msl near Four Corners and along the Rio Grande River, near Albuquerque, to 4011 meters msl at Wheeler Peak in the Sangre de Cristo Mountains. Although no references on the climate of northwestern New Mexico were available at the time this report was prepared, it is estimated the climate varies from cool semi-arid at the lower elevations to cool humid at the higher elevations. This wide range in climatic conditions is typical of so-called highland climates where enclosed valleys, plateaus, and exposed peaks in a highland region are very different climatically (Trewartha, 1954). A general breakdown by water use for all 94 deep wells in New Mexico is listed in Table 2–12. The locations of water wells in New Mexico with depths to water in excess of 150 meters are shown in Figure 2–8.

Twenty-seven of these 34 wells occur in clusters in the northwestern quadrant of New Mexico in McKinley, Cibola, Sandoval, and Bernalillo Counties. Because the data received from the USGS for New Mexico did not include well head elevation in the well records, a table similar to Table 2–10 for Arizona was not prepared. Detailed descriptions of wells with depths to water equal or greater than 240 meters are given in Section C–3 of Appendix C.

Table 2–9. Percentage Water Use for Wells in Arizona						
Depth to Water (m)	**Specified Use (percent)**					
	Irrigation	*Public*	*Stock*	*Industrial*	*Domestic*	*Commercial*
150 – 180	57	15	10	1	16	0
180 – 210	56	15	14	2	15	1
210 – 240	38	17	18	8	20	0
240 – 270	10	35	20	15	20	0
270 – 300	0	55	27	0	18	0
300 – 330	0	60	20	0	20	0
330 – 360	0	38	25	0	38	0
360 – 390	0	86	0	0	14	0
390 – 420	0	50	25	0	25	0
420 – 450	0	75	25	0	0	0
450 – 480	0	66	0	0	33	0
> 480	0	100	0	0	0	0
> 240	3	52	19	3	13	0

Table 2–10. Arizona Wells with Depth to Water in Excess of 240 Meters as a Function of Well Head Elevation	
Land Surface Elevation (m)	**Number of Wells**
0 – 300	1
300 – 600	5
600 – 900	12
900 – 1200	9
1200 – 1500	9
1500 – 1800	21
1800 – 2100	27
2100 – 2400	13

NUREG–1538

Table 2-11. Use of Water in Wells with Depth to Water Greater than 150 Meters, in Nevada

Depth to Water (m)	Number of Wells by Specified Use								Total with Specified Use
	Irrigation	Public	Stock	Industrial	Domestic	Commercial	Unused	Total	
150 – 180	1	3	2	1	4	0	6	21	11
180 – 210	0	0	3	2	5	0	6	16	10
210 – 240	0	0	1	0	2	0	2	5	3
240 – 270	0	0	3	0	1	0	7	12	4
270 – 300	0	0	1	0	0	0	2	3	1
300 – 420	0	0	0	0	0	0	1	1	0
TOTALS	1	3	10	3	12	0	24	58	29

Table 2-12. Use of Water in Wells with Depth to Water Greater than 150 Meters, in New Mexico

Depth to Water (m)	Number of Wells by Specified Use								Total with Specified Use
	Irrigation	Public	Stock	Industrial	Domestic	Commercial	Unused	Total	
150 – 180	1	9	2	2	0	0	6	22	14
180 – 210	1	7	3	2	0	1	6	20	14
210 – 240	0	4	4	1	0	0	8	18	9
240 – 270	0	1	1	3	1	2	4	12	8
270 – 300	0	2	5	0	0	1[a]	2	11	8
300 – 330	0	1	1	0	1	0	6	9	3
330 – 360	0	1	0	0	0	0	0	1	1
360 – 480	0	0	0	1	0	0	0	1	1
> 480	0	0	0	1	0	0	0	1	1
TOTALS	2	25	16	9	2	4	32	94	58

a Institutional water use.

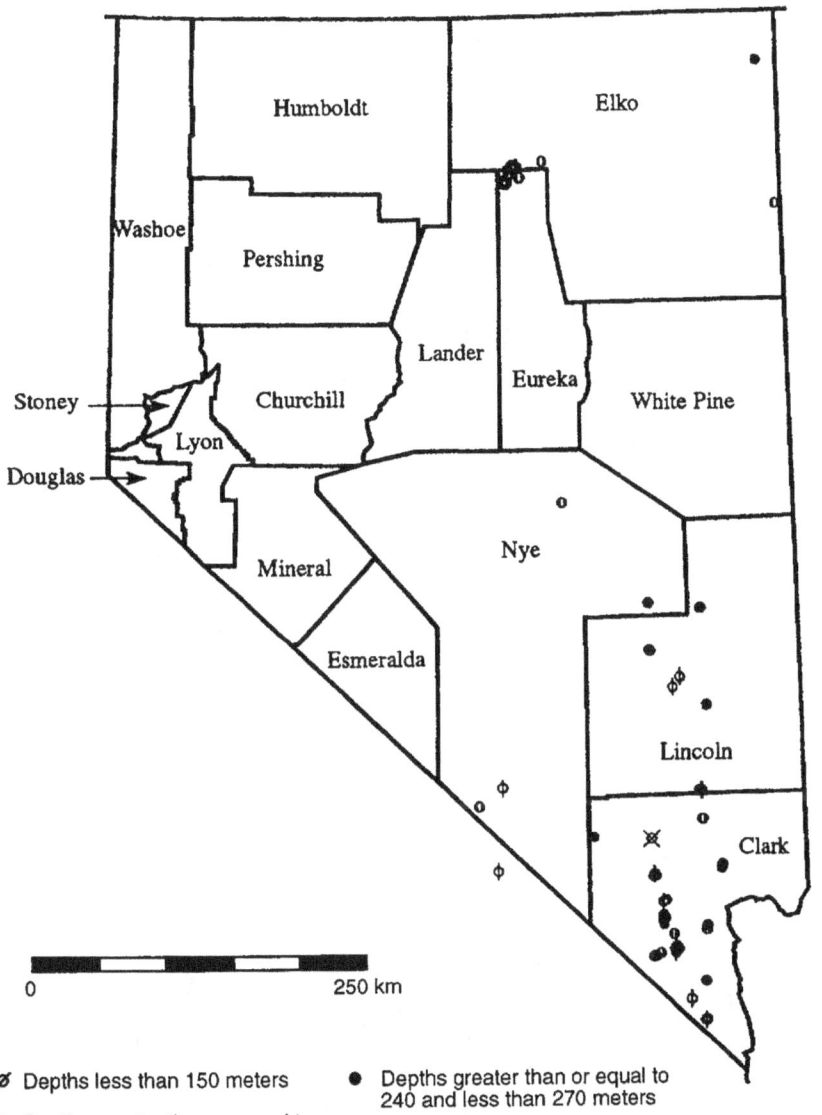

Figure 2—7. Locations of water wells in Nevada with depths to water greater than or equal to 150 meters.

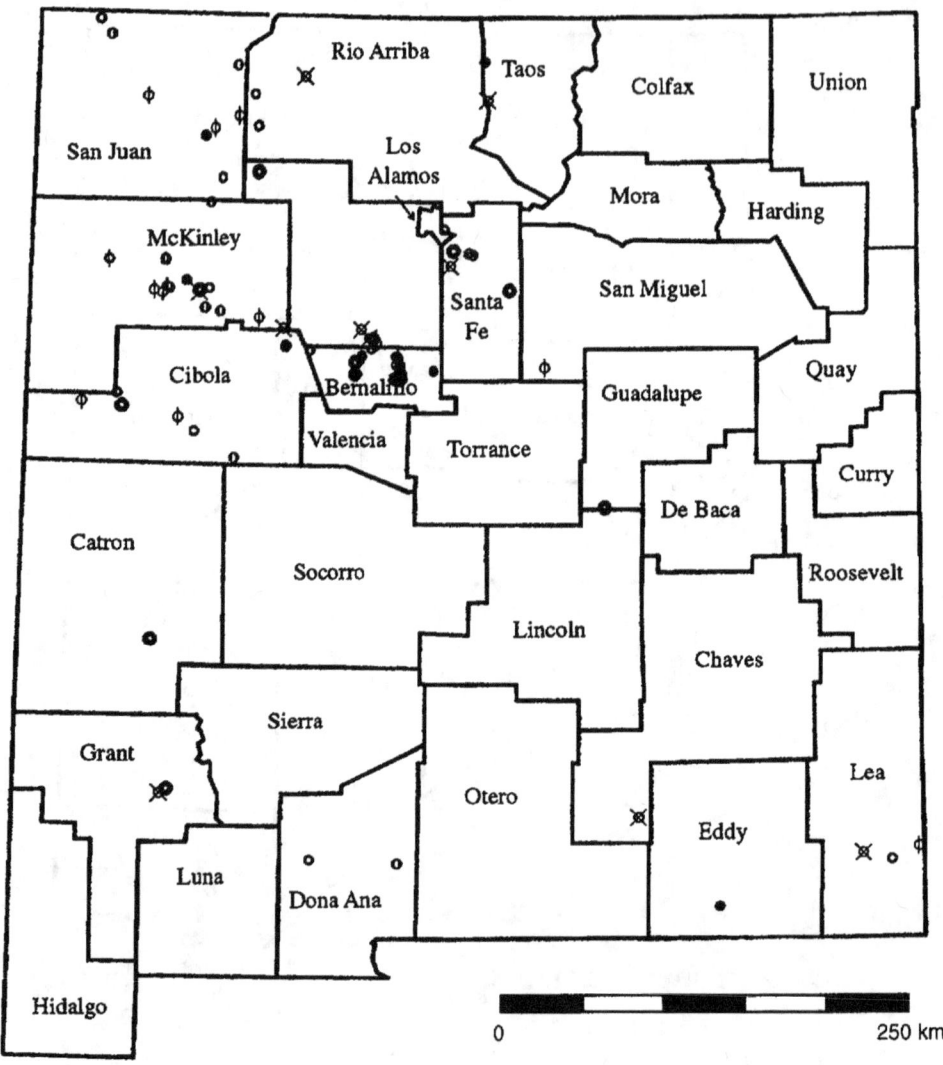

Ø Depths less than 150 meters

o Depths greater than or equal to 150 and less than 180 meters

φ Depths greater than or equal to 180 and less than 210 meters

o Depths greater than or equal to 210 and less than 240 meters

● Depths greater than or equal to 240 and less than 270 meters

⊙ Depths greater than or equal to 270 and less than 300 meters

⊠ Depths greater than or equal to 300 meters

Figure 2–8.   Locations of water wells in New Mexico with depths to water greater than or equal to 150 meters.

2.2.3.4 Exploitation of Deep Ground Water in Texas

Records for 220 wells with depths to water equal to or greater than 150 meters were obtained from the Texas Water Development Board water well database. Additional data for the Trans-Pecos region were extracted from Rees (1987). Of the 220 wells, 168 are located in the Trans-Pecos (area in Texas west of the Pecos River) and in the adjoining counties of Upton, Crockett, and Val Verde, immediately to the east of the Pecos River. The Trans-Pecos region as a whole is arid to semi-arid, with mean annual precipitation of approximately 30 centimeters, although there are isolated mountain ranges where precipitation may exceed 40 centimeters/year, such as the Chisos Mountains, where average annual precipitation at the Chisos Basin is 42.4 centimeters/year (Bomar, 1983). The remaining 52 wells are located in the Llano Estacado and Panhandle regions of the High Western Plains great physiographic province, where mean annual precipitation is 45 centimeters (*Op cit*) and the climate is semi-arid steppe. General exploitations by water use of all 220 wells and the 168 wells in the Trans-Pecos region are listed in Tables 2–13 and 2–14, respectively.

The locations of water wells in the Trans-Pecos region of Texas are shown in Figure 2–9. Well construction practices for low-discharge, high-lift stock and domestic wells used in the Trans-Pecos region and New Mexico may have implications for water use within 10 kilometers of the proposed repository where depths to water exceed 240 meters. Typical stock and domestic wells only need to be capable of pumping 1.26×10^{-4} to 3.79×10^{-4} cubic meters/second. For example, the Pate Altuda Ranch near Alpine (Brewster County), Texas, has three wells that each pump 1.26×10^{-4} cubic meters/second from depths to water of 335, 396, and 430 meters.[18] One of the Pate Altuda wells is pumped with a 3.7-kilowatt (5-horse power) submersible pump, whereas the other two use pump jacks.[19] (Pump jacks

or sucker rods are commonly used to extract heavy oils from reservoirs that have de-pressurized; however, using pump jacks for deep water wells is uncommon in most of the U.S.) According to local drillers in Brewster County, pump jacks are regularly used for high-lift, low-discharge water wells. Because several of the deep water wells in the Trans-Pecos region were originally drilled as oil or gas tests, the use of pump jacks may reflect the drillers' experience with, and preference for, oilfield technology, rather than a decision based on economic or technical considerations. Windmills are also used for high-lift, low-discharge wells in the Trans-Pecos region. A typical windmill may employ a 6-meter *Aermotor turbine* mounted on a 18-meter-high tower.[20]

2.2.3.5 Estimated Well Construction Costs in the Yucca Mountain and Amargosa Desert Areas

As illustrated in Section 2.2.3, pumping costs vary in direct proportion to the depth to water. Capital costs of a well depend on the total borehole depth, well diameter, and rated capacity of the pump. A detailed well construction cost study was conducted to estimate capital costs for four wells typical of the Yucca Mountain and Amargosa Desert regions. Wells 1 and 2 are based on the actual design of Wells J–13 and J–12, respectively (Young, 1972). Well 3 is based on a generic design for a well that would be used to supply water to a quarter-section, center-pivot irrigation plot in the Amargosa Farms area. Well 4 is based on a generic design of a well used to supply domestic or public water to the community of Amargosa Valley. Detailed construction and completion costs are shown for each of these four wells in Appendix D,[21] which will be referred to in the following section.

---

[18]Personal communication, W. Skinner, Independent Well Driller (Alpine, Texas), July 1996.

[19]*Ibid.*

[20]*Ibid.*

[21]Most drilling engineers in the U.S. still prefer the use of inch-pound units (the so-called English system), when describing water well characteristics. Therefore, for ease of comparison with existing engineering practice, in this regard, the English system has been used in this section. Conversion factors can be found in the front of this NUREG. Also, all cost estimates are in 1996 dollars.

Table 2–13. Use of Water in Wells with Depth to Water Greater than 150 Meters, in Texas

Depth to Water (m)	Number of Wells by Specified Use								Total with Specified Use
	Irrigation	Public	Stock	Industrial	Domestic	Commercial	Unused	Total	
150 – 180	9	6	38	4	11	1	17	87	69
180 – 210	2	3	20	6	8	0	14	53	39
210 – 240	0	0	9	4	3	0	7	24	23
240 – 270	0	0	7	5	2	0	4	19	14
270 – 300	0	3	4	2	1	0	8	18	10
300 – 330	0	0	1	2	1	0	2	6	4
330 – 360	0	0	2	0	1	0	1	4	3
360 – 390	0	0	0	4	0	0	1	5	4
390 – 420	0	0	0	1	0	0	0	1	1
420 – 450	0	0	0	0	0	0	0	0	0
450 – 480	0	0	0	0	1	0	0	1	1
>480	1	0	1	0	0	0	0	2	2
TOTALS	12	12	82	28	28	1	54	220	163

Table 2–14. Use of Water in Wells with Depth to Water Greater than 150 Meters, in the Trans-Pecos Region of Texas

Depth to Water (m)	Number of Wells by Specified Use							Total	Total with Specified Use
	Irrigation	Public	Stock	Industrial	Domestic	Commercial	Unused		
150 – 180	0	3	36	0	11	1	13	64	51
180 – 210	0	2	20	5	8	0	11	46	35
210 – 240	0	0	9	0	3	0	7	20	19
240 – 270	0	0	7	0	2	0	3	13	9
270 – 300	0	3	4	2	1	0	8	14	10
300 – 330	0	0	1	1	1	0	2	5	3
330 – 360	0	0	2	0	1	0	1	4	4
> 360	0	0	1	0	1	0	0	2	2
TOTALS	0	8	80	8	28	1	45	168	133

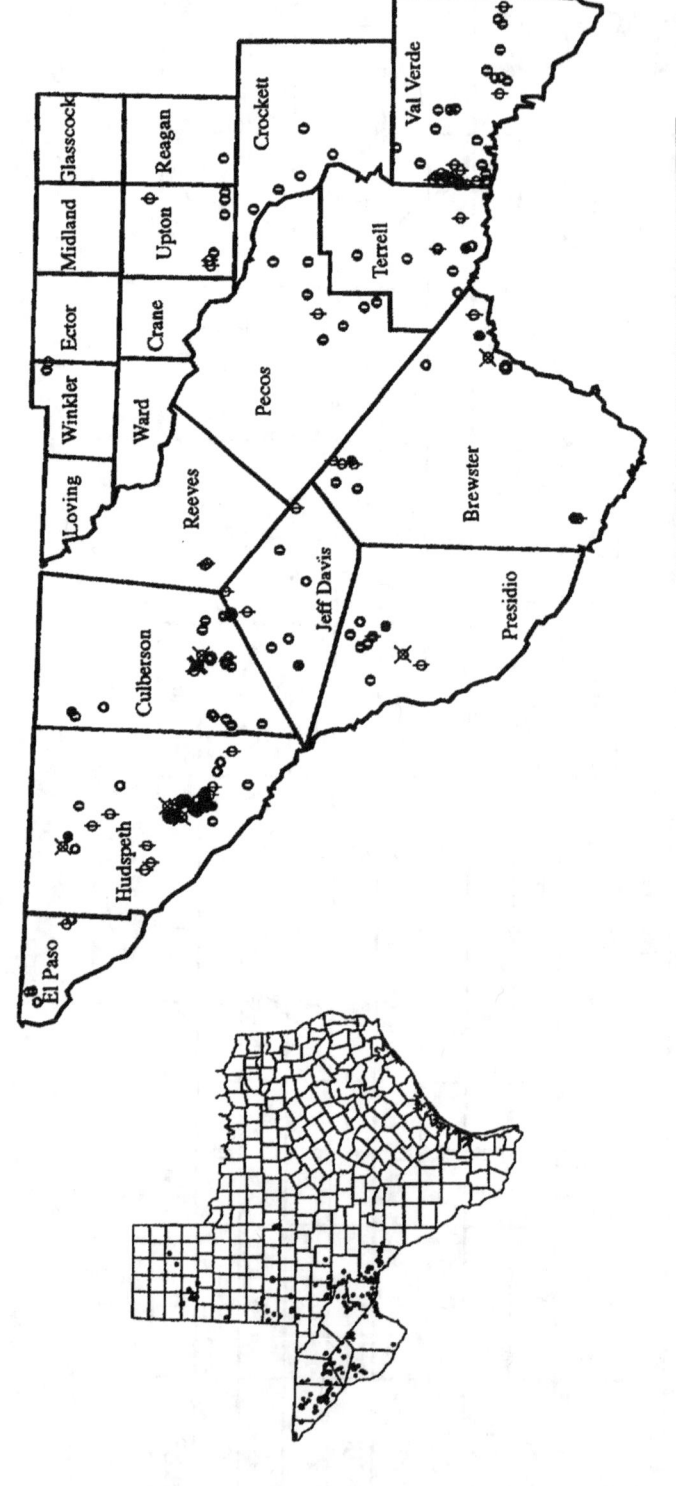

Figure 2–9. Locations of water wells in the Trans-Pecos region of Texas with depths of water greater than or equal to 150 meters.

Using current construction practices, the total cost of installing a well similar to J–13 (Well 1) is $1,117,670. This large expenditure is primarily caused by the great depth of Well J–13 (1066 meters/3500 feet), directly reflected in the costs of drilling, casing, screening, and installing the gravel pack (Table D–1). Because J–12 (Well 2) is only 274 meters (900 feet) deep, its estimated cost is $229,145 (Table D–2). The generic Amargosa Farms irrigation well (Well 3), which is 97 meters deep, pumps from a depth of 30 meters and has a rated pump capacity of approximately 0.15 cubic meters/second (2400 gallons/minute) and costs $167,745 (Table D–3). The Amargosa Valley domestic well (Well 4), which has a total depth of 183 meters (600 feet), a depth to water of 91 meters (300 feet), and a rated pump capacity of only 0.00063 cubic meters/second (10 gallons/minute) costs $161,470 (Table D–4).[22,23] Examples of unit and total pumping costs for each of the four archetypal Yucca Mountain and Amargosa Desert region wells are illustrated in Table 2–15.

Construction methods used for water wells in the Trans-Pecos region of Texas and in New Mexico suggest that the installation of a small-diameter, high-lift, low-capacity domestic well powered by either a pump jack or a windmill is possible for the area near Yucca Mountain, where the depth to water is approximately 300 meters. Such a well may be economically feasible for drinking water only. Construction cost estimates for such a well, pumped by a submersible turbine, are shown in Table D–5. As shown in Table D–6, substituting an appropriately-sized windmill costs approximately $10,000 more than the submersible, although unit pumping costs for the windmill would be minimal. A comparable pump jack would probably cost somewhat less than the submersible.

---

[22]Estimated construction costs are based on an informal bid received from a commercial water well drilling company unfamiliar with local hydrogeology and local well construction practices. The staff believe that actual construction costs for a well with the specifications listed in Appendix D may be substantially less.

[23]Well 4 is designed to supply a small community of 40 persons, assuming daily per capita water use of 0.57 cubic meters (150 gallons) and a pump utilization capacity of 50 percent.

2.2.4 Summary

Data from Arizona, southern Nevada, New Mexico, and the Trans-Pecos region of Texas indicate that ground water is pumped from aquifers in arid to semi-arid regions, where the depth to water is as great as that in Jackass Flats to the east of Yucca Mountain. Table 2–16 lists the number of wells with depths to water greater than 240 meters by State and type of water use. Of 115 wells that pump from aquifers with depths to water equal to or greater than 240 meters, only 2 (1.7 percent) are used for irrigation, 38 (33 percent) are used to supply stock water, and 63 (54.8 percent) are used for public and domestic water supply. Based on local practices in Amargosa Valley and on the data gathered in the well survey, it appears that pumping ground water for irrigation from depths greater than 240 meters is a rare practice (1.7 percent).

There is evidence that small ranching operations existed in the portions of the Yucca Mountain area prior to establishment of the NTS (see Table B–1 in Appendix B). Although there are the remains of a corral at Cane Spring, which lies approximately 30 kilometers east of Yucca Mountain at an elevation of 1241 meters msl, most relict corrals are located near Captain Jack, Tippipah, White Rock, and Topopah springs, which lie approximately 40 kilometers north-northeast of Yucca Mountain at elevations ranging from 1530 to 1737 meters msl. Although not unequivocal, the historic data appear to suggest that cattle from these ranches were grazed on Timber Mountain, Pahute Mesa, and Rainier Mesa, where the mean annual precipitation of 320 millimeters (Wang *et al.*, 1993) is sufficient to support grasslands suitable for grazing. Although feral burros in Crater Flat west of Yucca Mountain are apparently able to sustain themselves on the meager grasses that grow in the much dryer lowlands of Jackass and Crater Flats, it seems unlikely that less hardy cattle could find sufficient forage in the immediate vicinity of Yucca Mountain.

Table 2–15. **Unit Water Costs for Four Yucca Mountain–Amargosa Desert Area Wells**

	Well 1	*Well 2*	*Well 3*	*Well 4*
Unit Pumping Cost ($/m^3) [a]	0.128	0.102	0.0136	0.0413
Annual Consumption (m^3)	622,000[b]	622,000[b]	771,000[c]	8300[d]
Amortized Capital Cost ($) [e]	117,687	24,127	17,669	17,012
Unit Amortized Capital Cost ($/m^3)	0.189	0.0387	0.0229	2.05
Total Unit Cost ($/m^3)	0.317	0.141	0.0365	2.091
TOTAL ANNUAL COST [f] ($)	197,174	87,515	28,141	17,355

a   Following this conversion: Volume Pumped (617 m^3) $\times$ Pump Lift (30 m) $\times$ Unit Weight of Water (9800 N/m^3) $\div$ Efficiency (0.60) $\div$ Conversion from Joules to Kilowatt-hours (3.6 10^6 J/kWh) $\times$ Unit Cost of Electricity (0.10 Dollars/kWh) = $8.40.

b   Population of 3000, daily per-capita water use 0.57 m^3.

c   Alfalfa Farm, 1.52 m of water per season, on 50.7 ha.

d   Population of 40, daily per-capita water use 0.57 m^3.

e   Economic lifetime of 30 years with an interest rate of 10 percent.

f   Does not include distribution and maintenance costs.

Table 2–16. **Use of Water in Wells with Depth to Water Greater than 240 Meters, in Arizona, Southern Nevada, New Mexico, and the Trans-Pecos Region of Texas**

State/ Region	*Number of Wells by Specified Use*						
	Irrigation	*Public*	*Stock*	*Industrial*	*Domestic*	*Commercial*	*Total*
Arizona	2	33	12	3	13	0	63
Nevada	0	0	4	0	1	0	5
New Mexico	0	5	7	4	2	2	20
Trans-Pecos Texas	0	3	15	3	6	0	27
TOTALS (Percent Total)	2 (1.7)	41 (35.7)	38 (33.0)	10 (8.7)	22 (19.1)	2 (1.7)	115

Data from the water well survey suggest that existing communities will construct wells that pump from great depths to water if more easily exploited water supplies are insufficient or unreliable. Note that approximately one-third of the public supply wells listed earlier in Table 2–16 are found in the Flagstaff (Arizona) area, which originally relied on water pumped from shallow water table aquifers. Although current practices in the Yucca Mountain area do not support the idea that very small communities (25 to 100 persons) or individual homeowners will construct wells to pump fresh water from great depths (Appendix A), the survey data do suggest that a residential receptor group would be more likely to withdraw ground water from greater depths than a farming receptor group. However, the residential receptor group would also be expected to withdraw significantly less water that the farming receptor group.

2.2.5   References

Anderson, T.W., "Summary of the Southwest Alluvial Basins, Regional Aquifer-Systems Analysis, South-Central Arizona and Parts of Adjacent States," U.S. Geological Survey Professional Paper 1406–A, 1995.

Bomar, G.W., *Texas Weather,* Austin, University of Texas Press, 1983.

Orr, B.R., "Water Resources of the Zuni Tribal Lands, McKinley and Cibola Counties, New Mexico," U.S. Geological Survey Water Supply Paper 2227, 1987.

Rees, R.W., "Records of Wells, Water Levels, Pumpage, and Chemical Analyses from Selected Wells in Parts of the Trans-Pecos Region, Texas," Austin, Texas, Texas Water Development Board Report 301, 1987.

Science Applications International Corporation, "Water Resource Assessment of Yucca Mountain, Nevada (Study Plan for Study 8.3.1.9.2.2), "Las Vegas, Nevada, Revision 0, June 1991. [Prepared for OCRWM.]

Trewartha, G.T., *An Introduction to Climate,* New York, McGraw-Hill Book Company, Inc., 1954.

U.S. Department of Energy, "Chapter 3, Hydrology" in "Site Characterization Plan, Yucca Mountain Site, Nevada Research and Development Area, Nevada," Office of Civilian Radioactive Waste Management, DOE/RW–0199, Vol. II, Part A, December 1988.

Wang, J.S.Y., *et al.*, "Geohydrologic Data and Models of Rainier Mesa and Their Implications to Yucca Mountain", in American Nuclear Society/American Society of Civil Engineers, *Proceedings of the Fourth Annual International Conference: High-Level Radioactive Waste Management, April 26–30, 1993, Las Vegas, Nevada,* 2:675– 681 [1993].

Wittmeyer, G.W., *et al.*, "Use of Groundwater in the Arid and Semi-Arid Western United States: Implications for [the] Yucca Mountain Area," San Antonio, Texas, Center for Nuclear Waste Regulatory Analyses, letter report, August 1996.

Young, R.A., "Water Supply for the Nuclear Rocket Development Station at the U.S. Atomic Energy Commission's Nevada Test Site," U.S. Geological Survey Water-Supply Paper 1938, 1972.

2.3 Definition of Hypothetical Receptor Groups Used in this NUREG

2.3.1 Receptor Group Characteristics

As discussed earlier, an ICRP-type critical group is to be based on consideration of current population locations and lifestyles. Based on the information reviewed and summarized in Sections 2.1 and 2.2 (as well as Appendices A through D), as possible measures of these parameters, the staff identified characteristics for two potential hypothetical receptor groups—"farming" and "residential" (non-farming) in the Yucca Mountain area:

- *"Farming" Receptor Group: Because of topographic, meteorologic, pedologic, and hydrologic considerations, this hypothetical receptor group is a farming community located in an topographically-closed basin at a distance no closer than 20 kilometers to the site. The farming community is able to obtain its water from relatively shallow wells located in near-surface, local alluvial aquifers (i.e., generally 30 to 100 meters deep) in so-called "discharge zones" (Mifflin, 1968). This is an important consideration because development and operating costs for such wells are, in large measure, related to the depth of the water table. Thus, for reasons of practicality (and cost), this hypothetical receptor group would establish its irrigation wells in areas where the water table is near the surface. The exposure pathways considered for the farming hypothetical receptor group include ingestion (of contaminated water, crops, and animal products); inhalation (from resuspension of contaminated soil); and direct exposure.*

- *"Residential" Receptor Group: This hypothetical receptor group is a residential community located on one of the volcanic mesas or mountainous uplands that flank the topographically-closed basins, but may also be located in higher-elevation valleys, which are characterized by thin sequences of unsaturated alluvial sediments. The residential community is located between 5 and 20 kilometers from the site where the depth to the water table ranges from approximately 300 to 100 meters, respectively, at the two locations. Because freshwater demands for a residential community are substantially less than those for a farming community, the residential community could be located closer to the site than a farming community and could obtain its water from wells located in the deeper tuff or carbonate (regional) aquifers found at depths of 300 meters or more.[24] The exposure pathway considered for the hypothetical residential receptor group is the ingestion of contaminated water.*

2.3.2 Limitations to the NUREG Definition

The two hypothetical receptor groups described in this analysis were identified for the purpose of supporting the analyses described elsewhere in this NUREG. Not all potential sources of information were examined. Other information that might be useful to examine would include:

- Socio-economic information on current lifestyles (habits) and population density within the Yucca Mountain area, such as the type currently being collected by DOE [e.g., Black *et al.* (1995) and University of Nevada (1997)].

- Information on the pedogenic classification and distribution of soils was not evaluated. This type of information has been previously collected by the Soil Conservation Service (U.S. Department of Agriculture) and the State Engineers Office, and may be useful in identifying the location of potential receptor groups. If a farming scenario is contemplated, a determination will need to be made whether there were suitable conditions at a particular site (such as those in some portions of the central Amargosa Desert area), sufficient to support agriculture. A

preliminary review of published soil information (State of Nevada/University of Nevada, 1974) already suggests that a significant percentage of the land in the greater Yucca Mountain area have limitations to their irrigability. (Also see Appendix A.) This type of information, in conjunction with other types of practical information related to farming— topography/slope; extent of and depth to the "hardpan;" crop types; length of growing season; number of freeze-free days; altitude; and the like—may also be useful to evaluate.

Finally, the staff has not attempted to speculate on what type of activities might take place at NTS if the site were opened to private development, at this time.[25] DOE recently evaluated alternative land-use issues at NTS in its *Final Environmental Impact Statement for the Nevada Test Site and Off-Site Locations in the State of Nevada* (DOE, 1996). However, because there is pre-existing contamination at the site, ground-water availability and quality have been noted to figure prominently in possible alternative (non-nuclear) land-use decisions (*Op cit.*, pp. 4-106–4-135). Although there are environmental restoration programs currently in place at NTS, there are no plans to open the site to public or private development at this time.

2.3.3 References

Black, S.C., W.M. Glines, and Y.E. Townsend (eds.), "U.S. Department of Energy Nevada Operations Office Annual Site Environmental Report—1994," Las Vegas, Nevada, Reynolds Electrical & Engineering Co., Inc., Document No. DE–AC08–94NV11432, September 1995. [Prepared for OCRWM.]

Mifflin, M.D., "Delineation of Ground-Water Flow Systems in Nevada," Las Vegas, Desert Research Institute Technical Report Series H–W, 1968.

U.S. Department of Energy, "Final Environmental Impact Statement for the

---

[24]It should also be noted that shallow wells may also not practicable at this location because the alluvial sediments constitute "recharge zones" (Mifflin, 1968) that drain into basins found at lower elevations, and thus have little ground water in storage.

[25]The staff performed a limited examination of lifestyle and water-use practices within the current boundaries of the NTS before its withdraw from public use. This evaluation can be found in Appendix B.

Nevada Test Site and Off-Site Locations in the State of Nevada," Nevada Operations Office, DOE/EIS 0243, 3 vols. (and appendices), August 1996.

University of Nevada, "Identifying and Characterizing the Critical Group: Results of a Pilot Study of Amargosa Valley," Las Vegas, Nevada, Cannon Center for Survey Research, 1997. [Preliminary data/ results of the survey were made by D.A. Swanson (DOE) in an unpublished presentation entitled "The 'Biosphere' Food Survey," during a *DOE/NRC*

Technical Exchange on Total-System Performance Assessments held in Las Vegas, Nevada, on November 6, 1997.]

State of Nevada and University of Nevada of Nevada [Reno], "Water for Nevada: Report 8. Forecasts for the Future—Agriculture," Carson City, Division of Water Resources/ Department of Conservation and Resources and Division and Agricultural and Resource Economics/Max C. Fleischmann College of Agriculture, January 1974.

3. GROUND-WATER PATHWAY ANALYSES[1]

Based on the staff's earlier work, the most likely exposure scenario for a receptor population in the Yucca Mountain vicinity would be exposure at some point down-gradient from the site, through a ground-water/food-ingestion pathway. When evaluating this type of exposure scenario, the following types of questions come to mind:

- *How and where would radionuclides travel in the aquifer?*

- *What are the potential concentrations of radionulides in ground water used by possible receptor groups?*

- *What is the estimation of risk (dose) to possible receptor groups over long time periods?*

To address these concerns, the staff undertook a series of analyses, in this section of the NUREG, that evaluated dose from a ground-water exposure pathway. These analyses addressed the following:

Radionuclide Dilution: During transport in the saturated zone, from an area immediately beneath Yucca Mountain, to two hypothetical receptor group locations (farmer and residential). See Section 3.1.

Well Head Dilution/Mixing: Of radionuclides in ground water, caused by a pumping water well. See Section 3.2.

Peak Dose: For two hypothetical receptor groups (farmer and residential) to determine when the greatest risk occurs. See Section 3.3.

3.1 Analysis of Radionuclide Dilution in Ground Water

3.1.1 Introduction

Because of its importance to determining dose, dilution of radionuclides in ground water

is likely to be a central issue in future performance assessments of the Yucca Mountain site. For example, if mixing of a contaminant stream with ground-water flow in the tuff aquifer dilutes the concentration by a factor of 100, then the dose (and associated radiologic risk) would be reduced by the same factor (assuming no dilution effects from water well pumping). Dilution of radionuclides released into the ground water occurs as a result of fluid mixing along the flow path between the source point(s) and the location of the potential receptor group(s). Mixing a dissolved contaminant (i.e., hydrodynamic dispersion) is, in general, strongly related to variations in both the magnitude of the fluid velocity and flow direction. These variations are principally caused by small- and large-scale heterogeneities in the geologic media (Waldrop *et al.*, 1985; Gelhar, 1993; Fetter, 1993). Large-scale features, such as faults, may in some instances induce flow variations and thereby enhance natural mixing, whereas in other cases, they may produce highly channelized flow with limited mixing.

In this scoping analysis, ground-water flow and transport models were used to study dilution characteristics of the proposed repository site for two basic purposes:

- To gain insight into site-specific factors that may affect ground-water mixing and attendant dilution of dissolved radionuclides in the Yucca Mountain area; and

- To determine if there are any methodology issues that may impact implementation of a dose-based standard, as proposed by the NAS (National Research Council, 1995).

The analysis presented herein was limited to evaluation of concentration variations during passive transport considering only a few variations in the assumed hydraulic properties and boundary conditions. In addition, the geohydrologic system was treated as an equivalent porous continuum, and no attempt was made to account for flow and transport

---

[1]The figures and tables shown in this section present the results from the demonstration of the continuing staff capability to review a total-system performance assessment (TSPA). These figures and tables, like the demonstration, are limited by the use of simplifying assumptions and sparse data.

through discrete fractures or to include matrix diffusion effects. Additionally, mixing induced by water well pumping was not considered in this analysis; the dilution effects from well pumping are addressed in Section 3.2. Because of the simplifications made and incompleteness of site characterization, the calculations presented in this section should not be viewed as an evaluation of regulatory compliance with existing or future HLW disposal standards.

3.1.2 Analysis

To assess ground-water dilution and its dependence on the hydrogeologic characteristics of the Yucca Mountain setting, a series of two-dimensional (2-D) computer simulations of ground-water flow and radionuclide transport were performed. Computer models were applied to compute four quantities: (a) hydraulic head distributions; (b) flow paths; (c) particle travel times; and (d) radionuclide plume distributions. Dilution of ^{99}Tc was modeled because it is important to dose and reflects the dilution behavior of important radionuclides with relatively large inventories, long half-lives, and non-sorbing characteristics. Numerical calculations and graphical display of these four quantities were used to gain insight into the nature of the hydrogeologic processes that may control the degree of dilution at the Yucca Mountain site. Although available field data for the Yucca Mountain site are used, this scoping analysis did not consider uncertainties associated with the conceptualizations of ground-water flow or the spatial variability of hydraulic properties.

Two computer codes were used in performing the scoping analysis: *MAGNUM–2D*, a saturated flow model (England *et al.*, 1985) and *CHAINT*, a multi-component transport model (Kline *et al.*, 1985). Hydraulic head distributions simulated with the *MAGNUM–2D* code were post-processed to provide visualizations of the flow paths (i.e., streamlines) and particle travel times.

Dilution factors[2] calculated with the *CHAINT* code were contoured to depict plume spreading and dilution patterns. First, a 2–D representation of planar flow from the proposed repository site down-gradient to the Amargosa Desert (i.e., the potential location of a farmer/rancher for a hypothetical receptor group, as proposed for this analysis in Section 2.3) was considered to assess the extent of hydrodynamic dispersion that may occur as the hypothetical ^{99}Tc plumes move through relatively long and heterogeneous flow paths. A second 2–D representation of a vertical cross-section through the proposed repository site was also considered. The purpose of this case was to examine mixing processes immediately beneath the site that may occur as a result of channelized flow through the complex geometry of the hydrostratigraphic units and fault zones. Of particular interest was the extent to which structures such as fracture zones and faults control flow patterns, mixing, and dilution.

3.1.2.1 Conceptual Models of Ground-Water Flow

Conceptualizations of lateral and vertical flow used in this scoping analysis drew largely on information from previous DOE modeling studies (Czarnecki and Waddell, 1984; Wilson *et al.*, 1994) and existing field data. The lateral flow model consisted of a 580-square-kilometer flow tube extending from the repository site south to the Amargosa Desert area. The vertical flow model approximates the cross-section through the repository from borehole USW H–5 and extending through USW H–4; this cross-section, which encompasses about 3 square kilometers, is especially relevant because it appears to be aligned with the general direction of ground-water flow beneath the proposed repository site. Both the lateral and vertical flow conceptual models are defined in terms of:

- Geometry of the hydrostratigraphic units;

---

[2]Dilution factor refers to the ratio of an initial concentration and a later concentration (e.g., ratio of concentration in the saturated zone directly below the repository footprint and the concentration in the saturated zone 20 kilometers down-gradient from the site).

- Contrasting values of saturated hydraulic conductivity;

- Variability of effective porosity;

- Location of distinct fault zones; and

- Hydraulic head gradient and flow boundary conditions.

The specific aspects of the two conceptual models are summarized in the following sections.

3.1.2.1.1 Conceptual Model of Lateral Flow in the Yucca Mountain Region

In developing a 2–D lateral flow model, computer simulation results previously published by the USGS (Czarnecki and Waddell, 1984) were examined and used. Czarnecki and Waddell applied a vertically integrated, steady-state model to simulate the regional flow system. These authors present a plot of the ground-water flux vectors that were computed from the hydraulic head field [see Plate 2 in Czarnecki and Waddell (1984)]. A subdomain of the Czarnecki and Waddell regional flow model was selected by tracing selected streamlines west and east of the proposed repository. Locations of the upper and lower boundaries of this streamtube were taken coincident with head contours of 800 meters and 675 meters, respectively, as estimated from available field measurements. The streamtube, which is shown in Figure 3–1, was divided into seven distinct material types or zones; each of these zones is designated by a number (see circled numbers). Boundaries for the seven zones (designated by dashed lines) were determined by inspecting available hydrostratigraphic cross-sections (Gillson *et al.*, 1995; Roberson *et al.*, 1995) and hydraulic head contours.

Estimates of the horizontal hydraulic conductivities K_{xx} and K_{yy} were obtained by a manual calibration procedure in which the hydraulic conductivities of the seven zones were adjusted until the *MAGNUM–2D* code produced a reasonable fit with measured hydraulic heads (Robison, 1984; and Ervin *et al.*, 1993). These initial estimates were

subsequently checked and adjusted using an autocalibration algorithm that employed an indirect inverse procedure based on either maximum likelihood or statistically robust *M*-estimator theory to estimate model parameters (Wittmeyer, 1990; Wittmeyer and Neuman, 1992; and Carrera and Neuman, 1986a,b,c). Within the selected flow domain (see Figure 3–1), there were 146 locations at which estimates of hydraulic head data were available. Of these measurements, 22 were in the general vicinity of Yucca Mountain; 5 just west of the community of Lathrop Wells; and the remaining 119 in the greater Amargosa Desert. Within each of the seven zones, the hydraulic conductivity was assumed uniform and isotropic.

Because the lateral flow model used two Dirichlet and two no-flow boundary conditions, the values of hydraulic conductivity in the seven major zones are not uniquely identifiable in the absence of prior estimates of either areal flux or hydraulic conductivity (Carrera and Neuman, 1986b). Inasmuch as areal recharge within this region is minimal, fixing at least one hydraulic conductivity value was judged the best option. Accordingly, Zone 1, located at the southern end of the streamtube model, was assigned a fixed hydraulic conductivity value of 1.7×10^{-5} meters/second, consistent with the estimate of Czarnecki (1985). To assess the fit between predicted and observed values, the hydraulic head residual was calculated for each well location. The head residuals ranged from -38.4 to 62.3 meters, with an average head residual of 1.4 meters and an average absolute head residual of 6.3 meters. The head residual value is equal to the head value predicted by the streamtube model minus the measured head value. An improved fit could have been achieved by increasing the number of zones; however, the selected zonation was considered adequate for this 2–D scoping analysis. The seven zones and assumed hydraulic properties are summarized in Table 3–1.

After completing the calibration of the flow model, an additional zone representing the Bow Ridge fault was added to the conceptual

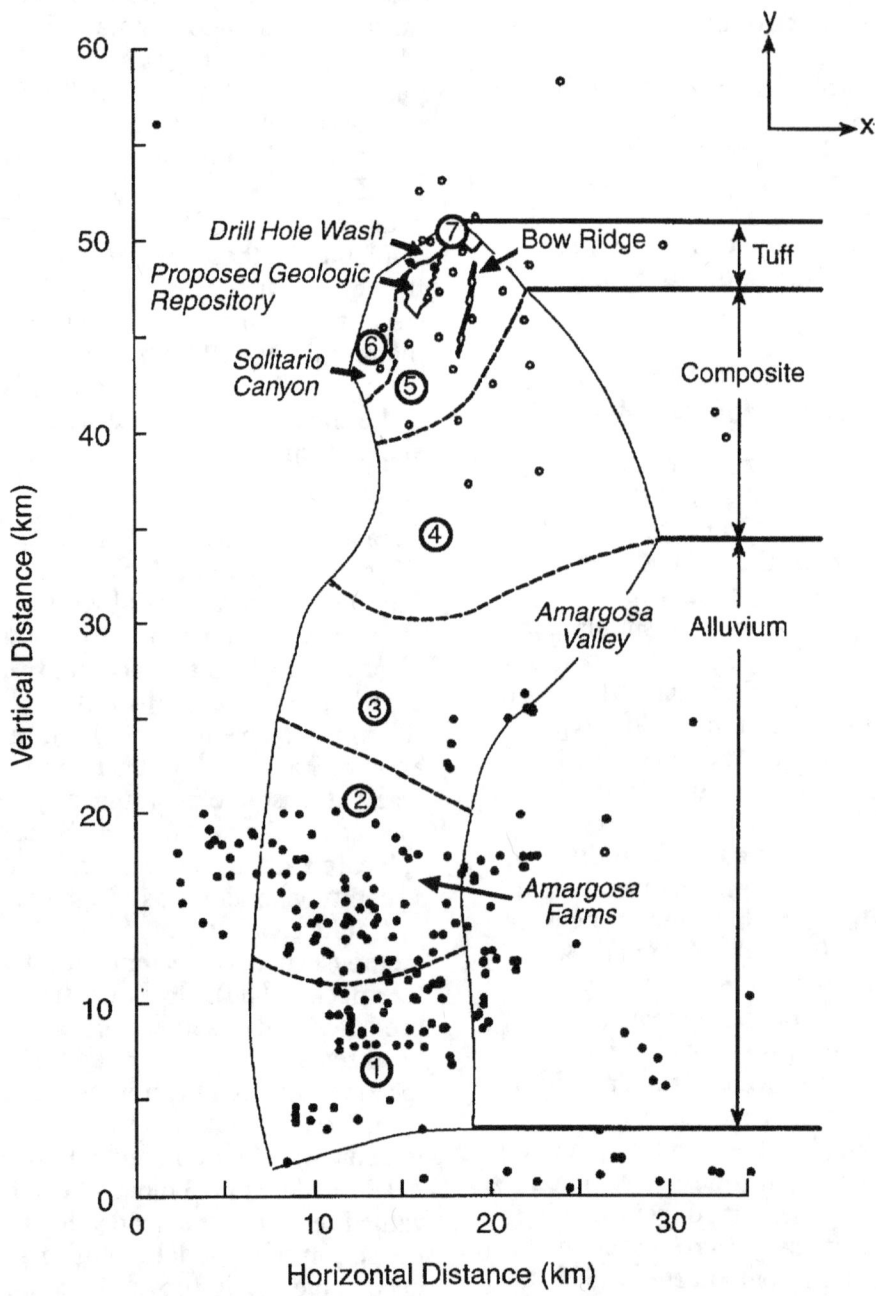

Figure 3–1. **Location of lateral flow model, material zones (circled numbers), well locations, and location of the proposed repository footprint.** The symbol ● designates a private water well location whereas the symbol ○ designates a DOE water well location.

Table 3–1. Estimates of Hydraulic Conductivities Computed Using Autocalibration Technique		
Zone	*Hydraulic Conductivity (m/sec)*	
	K_{xx}	K_{yy}
1 – Alluvium	1.7×10^{-5}	1.7×10^{-5}
2 – Alluvium	8.6×10^{-6}	8.6×10^{-6}
3 – Alluvium	4.5×10^{-6}	4.5×10^{-6}
4 – Composite (Alluvium/Tuff)	1.7×10^{-5}	1.7×10^{-5}
5 – Tuff Aquifer	1.1×10^{-5}	1.1×10^{-5}
6 – Solitario Canyon	7.4×10^{-7}	7.4×10^{-7}
7 – Drill Hole Wash	2.0×10^{-9}	2.0×10^{-9}

model, with hydraulic properties assigned to represent two contrasting cases:

- Preferential flow along the fault and partial barrier to flow across the fault (i.e., K_{xx} and K_{yy} set to 10^{-7} and 10^{-5} meters/second, respectively); and

- Barrier to ground-water flow (i.e., K_{xx} and K_{yy} set to 10^{-8} meters/second).

These two cases produced distinct flow paths, particle travel times, and plume dilution patterns in the vicinity of the proposed repository.

In addition to the hydraulic conductivities discussed previously, calculation of ground-water velocity and plume dilution required estimates of "effective porosity" (i.e., the portion of the total porosity participating in the transmission of water). At the time this analysis was performed, there are no field data for effective porosities of the tuff formations or the alluvium at the Yucca Mountain site. Fracture porosity, estimated using the cubic law (Snow, 1969) and observed fracture porosities, is one surrogate for effective porosity. Erickson and Waddell (1985) estimated fracture porosities of productive zones in the tuff aquifer to range from about 10^{-4} to 10^{-3}; this range was estimated using transmissivity data for fracture zones from borehole USW H–4. In an unconfined system,

the specific yield is another surrogate parameter for effective porosity (Domenico and Schwartz, 1990). The USGS obtained specific yield data for the tuff aquifer (Geldon, 1995) in boreholes east of the proposed repository site and for the alluvium (Walker and Eakin, 1963) in the vicinity of the Amargosa Desert. In the calculations presented, the specific yield data were used to provide representative estimates of effective porosity ϕ.

The C-Well Complex (Geldon, 1995) of boreholes (i.e., UE-25c #1, UE-25c #2, and UE-25c #3), located on the east flank of the Yucca Mountain site, penetrates the saturated Calico Hills aquifer, Upper Prow Pass confining unit, the Prow Pass-Upper Bullfrog aquifer, the Middle Bullfrog confining unit, the Bullfrog aquifer, the Lower Bullfrog confining unit, and the Tram aquifer. Geldon analyzed two well interference tests conducted in the Calico Hills and Prow Pass-Upper Bullfrog aquifers using the Neuman-type curve method (1975) for an unconfined, anisotropic aquifer. Type curve analysis of heads measured in UE-25c #1 with pumping in UE-25C #2 indicated that the specific yield for the unconfined Calico Hills aquifer is 0.003 (*Op cit.*). The Prow Pass- Upper Bullfrog aquifer may either be confined or unconfined in UE-25C #1. If unconfined, the Prow Pass-Upper Bullfrog aquifer has a specific yield of 0.004(*Op cit.*). For a field test where

UE-25c #3 was pumped with heads monitored in UE-25c #2, the specific yield for the composite column was estimated to be 0.07 (*Op cit.*). Thus, for those portions of the planar flow model in which the upper 100 to 300 meters of the saturated zone are ontained in the fractured volcanics, effective porosity was assumed to be bounded by $0.003 \leq \phi \leq 0.07$.

For the remaining zones of the model domain, effective porosities for the alluvium were inferred from specific yield estimates made by Walker and Eakin (1963). These authors estimated the average specific yield to be 0.17 from textural descriptions from drillers' logs for 57 wells in the Amargosa Desert. Walker and Eakin also noted that the variation in physical conditions throughout the Amargosa Desert would suggest that the specific yield ranges from about 0.10 to 0.20. Accordingly, the effective porosity for these portions of the flow domain model was assumed to be bounded by $0.10 \leq \phi \leq 0.20$. It is important to acknowledge that the effective porosities of alluvium can be much larger than 0.20—e.g., 0.30 to 0.40 (Freeze and Cherry, 1979; Domenico and Schwartz, 1990)]. The significance of this observation is that larger values of effective porosities result in longer particle travel times.

3.1.2.1.2 Conceptual Model for Vertical Flow beneath the Yucca Mountain Site

To develop a 2−D representation of flow in the tuff aquifer beneath the proposed repository site, the geologic cross-section developed by the USGS (Scott and Bonk, 1984) was used (see Figure 3−2). This cross-section clearly illustrates the heterogeneous nature and complex geometry of the strata beneath Yucca Mountain, which are expected to influence mixing and dilution. The cross- section depicts the slightly east-dipping hydrostratigraphic units of the tuff aquifer, as well as the Ghost Dance and Bow Ridge fault zones. To simplify the generation of the computational grid, various secondary faults in this cross-section were not explicitly modeled. This northwest to southeast cross-section, which passes through

boreholes USW H−5 and USW H−4, is particularly relevant because it is oriented along the principal direction of ground-water flow and through the center of the proposed repository site.

The location of the upper boundary of the conceptual model was obtained by interpolation of available borehole data. Both the upper and lower boundaries of the model domain were treated as no-flow boundaries. The hydraulic heads at the inflow and outflow boundaries were set to impose an average hydraulic gradient of 3.4×10^{-3}. This gradient was estimated from the steady-state hydraulic head field calculated for the planar flow model. The hydraulic conductivities assigned to the individual hydrostratigraphic units were largely drawn from the field data for borehole USW H−4 presented in Whitfield *et al.* (1985). A hydraulic conductivity profile for USW H−5 was not available because the field test results were apparently too difficult to interpret (Robison and Craig, 1991) possibly because of the hydraulic influence of high-angle fractures near the borehole. The effective porosities assigned to the units were consistent with those used in the planar flow model.

The hydraulic conductivity profile measured in borehole USW H−4 (Whitfield *et al.*, 1985) was used to assign properties to individual hydrostratigraphic units. Whitfield *et al.*, report pump test data for 19 individual hydrostratigraphic units. For simplicity, certain adjacent flow zones with similar hydraulic conductivities were lumped together. This produced a simpler hydrostratigraphic model consisting of 11 major zones. To account for anisotropic characteristics of these strata, an anisotropy ratio (i.e., ratio of vertical hydraulic conductivity K_{zz} to the horizontal hydraulic conductivity K_{xx}) of 1 to 5 was assumed. This assumption had the effect of emphasizing channelized flow along the hydrostratigraphic units. The Bow Ridge fault was represented as an anisotropic feature in the conceptual model. The hydraulic conductivity values assumed for the hydrostratigraphic model are summarized in Table 3−2.

Figure 3–2. **Vertical cross-section through boreholes USW H–5 and USW H–4 (Scott and Bonk, 1984).**

Symbol	Unit
QTac	Alluvium and Colluvium
Tmrn	Ranier Mesa Member of Timber Mountain Tuff, nonwelded
Tpcw	Tiva Canyon Member of Paintbrush Tuff, welded
Tptw	Topopah Spring Member of Paintbrush Tuff, welded
Tcbw	Bullfrog Member, welded
Tctw	Tram Member, welded
BF	Zone of west-dipping strata containing abundant breccia and faults
Tcpw	Brow Pass Member of Crater Flat Tuff, welded
n	Nonwelded tuff

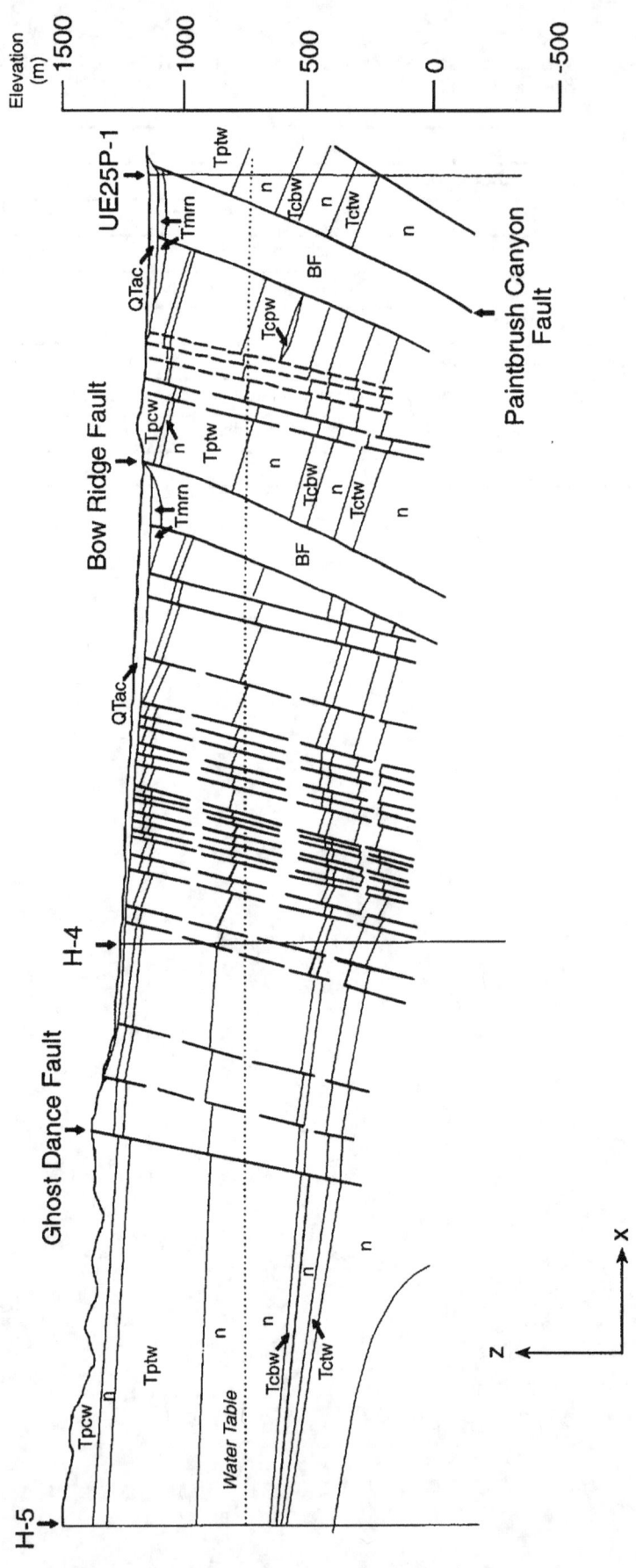

Figure 3–2. continued

Table 3–2. Assumed Hydraulic Conductivities for the Vertical Cross-Section Model, Based on Data Presented by Whitfield *et al.* (1985). Abbreviations are for stratigraphic units depicted in Figure 3–7.

Zone	Hydraulic Conductivity (m/sec)	
	K_{xx}	K_{yy}
1 – Calico Hills (CH)	1.0×10^{-6}	2.0×10^{-7}
2 – Prow Pass #1 (PP1)	1.0×10^{-5}	2.0×10^{-6}
3 – Prow Pass #2 (PP2)	2.0×10^{-6}	4.0×10^{-7}
4 – Bull Frog #1 (BF1)	2.0×10^{-5}	4.0×10^{-6}
5 – Bull Frog/Tram (BF/TR)	4.0×10^{-6}	8.0×10^{-7}
6 – Tram #1 (TR1)	2.0×10^{-5}	4.0×10^{-6}
7 – Tram #2 (TR2)	2.0×10^{-6}	4.0×10^{-7}
8 – Tram #3 (TR3)	2.0×10^{-5}	4.0×10^{-6}
9 – Tram #4 (TR4)	1.0×10^{-6}	2.0×10^{-7}
10 – Lithic Ridge #1 (LR1)	2.0×10^{-5}	4.0×10^{-6}
11 – Lithic Ridge #2 (LR2)	2.0×10^{-6}	4.0×10^{-7}
12 – Bow Ridge Fault	1.0×10^{-7}	5.0×10^{-7}

3.1.2.2 Computer Simulations for Lateral Flow Model

Steady-state representations of the potentiometric field for the lateral flow model were generated for two cases in which the Bow Ridge fault was treated as a preferential flow pathway and a flow barrier. The hydraulic head fields calculated (with the *MAGNUM–2D* computer code) for both cases were post-processed to obtain head contours, flow vectors, Darcy fluxes, streamlines, and cumulative particle travel times. Flow paths, for particles released at locations along a line tangential to the lower boundary of the proposed repository footprint, were plotted to provide a visualization of ground-water flow patterns. Along each flow path (or streamline), the particle travel time was calculated and summed to give an indication of the impact of velocity variations.

The formation and movement of hypothetical ^{99}Tc plumes were computed (with the *CHAINT* computer code) for 10^4 years using a longitudinal mass dispersivity α_L of 200

meters and transverse mass dispersivity α_T of 10 meters. The longitudinal dispersivity value was selected by examining dispersivity data plotted in Gelhar (1993), which displays the relation between α_L and the scale of observation; the selected value is about one-fifth of that used by DOE (Wilson *et al.*, 1994) in radionuclide transport simulations for the proposed repository site. The transverse dispersivity was computed as $\alpha_T = \alpha_L /20$, following Fetter (1993).

A relatively fine grid, consisting of more than 6000 elements, was used to represent the flow domain. This fine grid was used to minimize numerical dispersion. The following sections present and interpret the significance of subregional flow path and particle travel time, and plumes and dilution factors.

3.1.2.2.1 Hydraulic Heads, Flow Vectors, and Darcy Fluxes

Patterns of subregional ground-water flow are determined by the combined effects of the hydraulic boundary conditions, geometry of flow domain, contrasts in hydraulic properties, and structural features such as fault zones. Some of these effects are illustrated in the contour plot of the hydraulic head field shown in Figure 3–3; the dashed and heavy solid lines designate the material zone boundaries within the flow domain. In both cases (the preferential flow case and the barrier to flow case, for properties of the Bow Ridge fault), the hydraulic heads exhibit large gradients to the west (Solitario Canyon) and north (Drill Hole Wash) of the repository and then transition to more gradual variations in the tuff (Zone 5), composite (Zone 4), and alluvial regions (Zones 1, 2, and 3). In comparing the head fields for the two cases, the hydraulic characteristics assigned to the Bow Ridge fault only appear to have local and relatively small effects.

Flow vector plots for the two cases are shown in Figure 3–4, along with the tabulated ranges for the Darcy fluxes; note that the flux magnitude is indicated by the arrow length. The principal differences in calculated results are confined to a small region between the proposed repository and Bow Ridge fault. For the preferential flow pathway case, ground-water flow occurs along and through the fault. In contrast, the flow barrier case shows that flow is routed around the fault. Particularly noteworthy was the fact that between the two cases the range of flux magnitudes was not substantially different, except in the Bow Ridge fault zone where differences were expected. Also presented in the figure are the Darcy fluxes (maximum and minimum values) computed for each zone. In the zone below the proposed repository footprint, the calculated fluxes for both cases range from about 0.5 to 1.9 meters/year. The largest flux magnitude is 3.7 meters/year in the tuff aquifer (i.e., Zone 5).

3.1.2.2.2 Pathlines, Particle Travel Times, and Dilution Factors

Flow paths calculated for particles released along the border of the repository provide insight into the subregional flow patterns. As can be seen in Figure 3–5, the streamlines for the preferential flow pathway case refract as

they pass through the Bow Ridge fault whereas, for the flow barrier case, the streamlines flow around the fault. The isopleths (heavy dashed lines) of constant particle travel time (also shown in this figure) add additional detail to the contrasting effects of the fault. These isopleths depict the relative rate of travel of particles moving passively with the ground water. It is clear from these isopleths that patterns of ground-water flow in the vicinity of the fault are quite distinct for the two cases considered. However, these distinct flow patterns appear to have relatively small local effects on lateral mixing and almost no observable influence on the larger-scale transport; this is more clearly shown in the subsequent figure.

The impact of local and subregional flow patterns on contaminant movement is illustrated in the contour plot of ^{99}Tc (see Figure 3–6); the isopleths are quantified in terms of dilution factors instead of radionuclide concentrations. Plume representations for a snapshot in time at 10^4 years after release are shown in the figure. The contour plots suggest that local mixing and dilution in the vicinity of the repository are relatively small—i.e., dilution factors are about 2. Significant in both cases is that predicted dilution factors in the Amargosa Desert area are about the same.

3.1.2.2.3 Computer Simulations for Vertical Flow Model

A steady-state hydraulic head field was generated with the *MAGNUM–2D* computer code, using the boundary conditions and hydraulic properties described previously. The calculated hydraulic head field was contoured as well as post-processed to obtain flow vectors, Darcy fluxes, streamlines, and cumulative particle travel times. Flow paths for particles released at selected locations along the Ghost Dance fault were computed to provide a visualization. Along each flow path, the particle travel time was calculated and summed to give an indication of the influence of velocity variations.

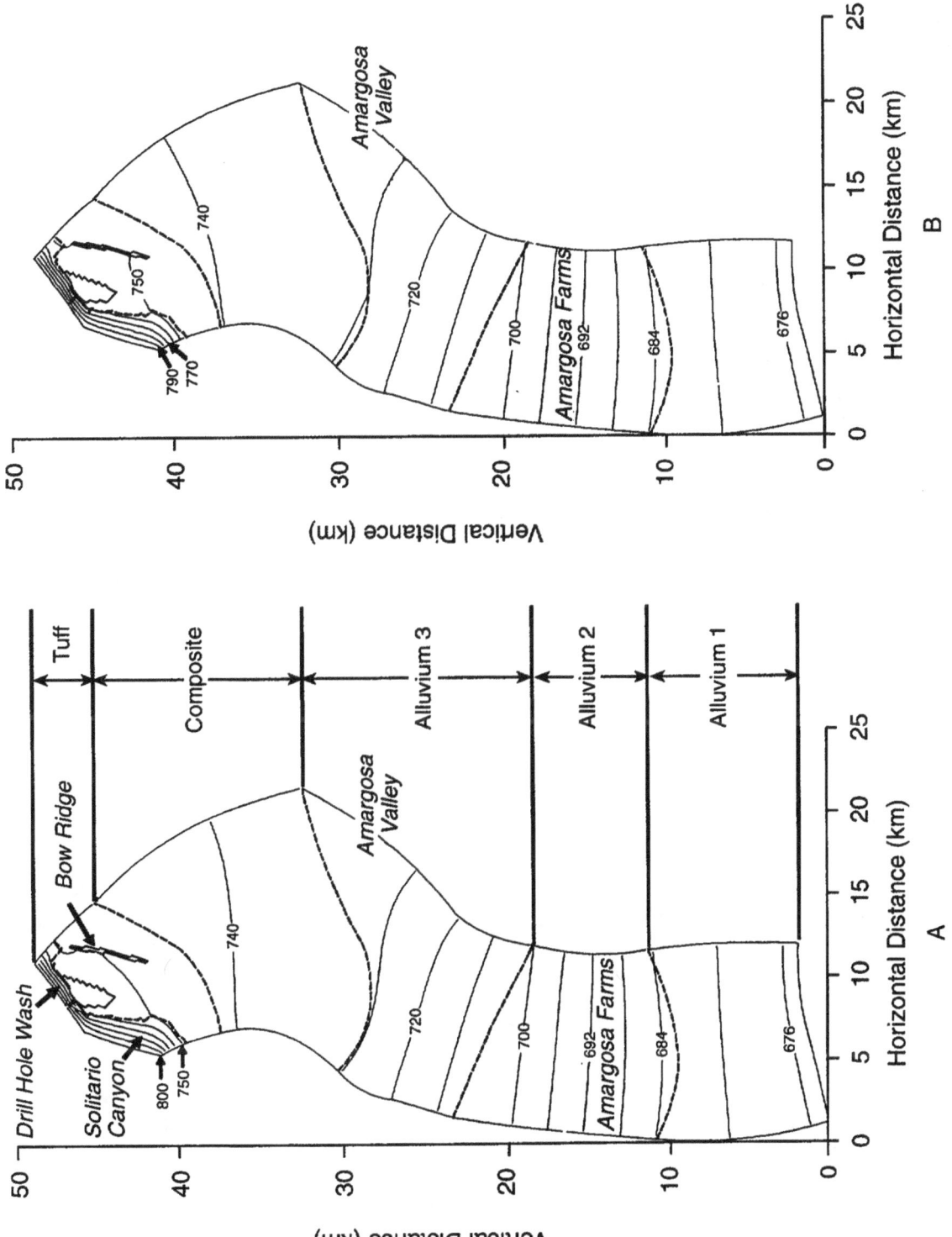

Figure 3–3. Hydraulic head fields for the lateral flow model for two cases, with the Bow Ridge fault assumed to be (a) the preferential flow pathway and (b) the flow barrier.

Figure 3–4. **Darcy flux vector plots for lateral flow model for two cases, with the Bow Ridge fault assumed to be (a) the preferential flow pathway and (b) the flow barrier.** Darcy velocity values are provided in the accompanying table. Material types in table refer to circled numbers in figure.

A—The Preferential Flow Pathway			B—The Flow Barrier		
Material Type	Darcy Velocities (m/yr)		Material Type	Darcy Velocities (m/yr)	
	Minimum	Maximum		Minimum	Maximum
1	0.42	0.68	1	0.41	0.67
2	0.43	0.66	2	0.41	0.65
3	0.022	0.61	3	0.02	0.6
4	0.027	0.8	4	0.023	0.81
5	0.013	3.7	5	0.0085	3.8
6	0.17	2.2	6	0.19	2.3
7	0.00016	0.0055	7	0.0002	0.0056
8	0.48	1.9	8	0.55	1.9
9	0.031	1.8	9	0.0033	0.018

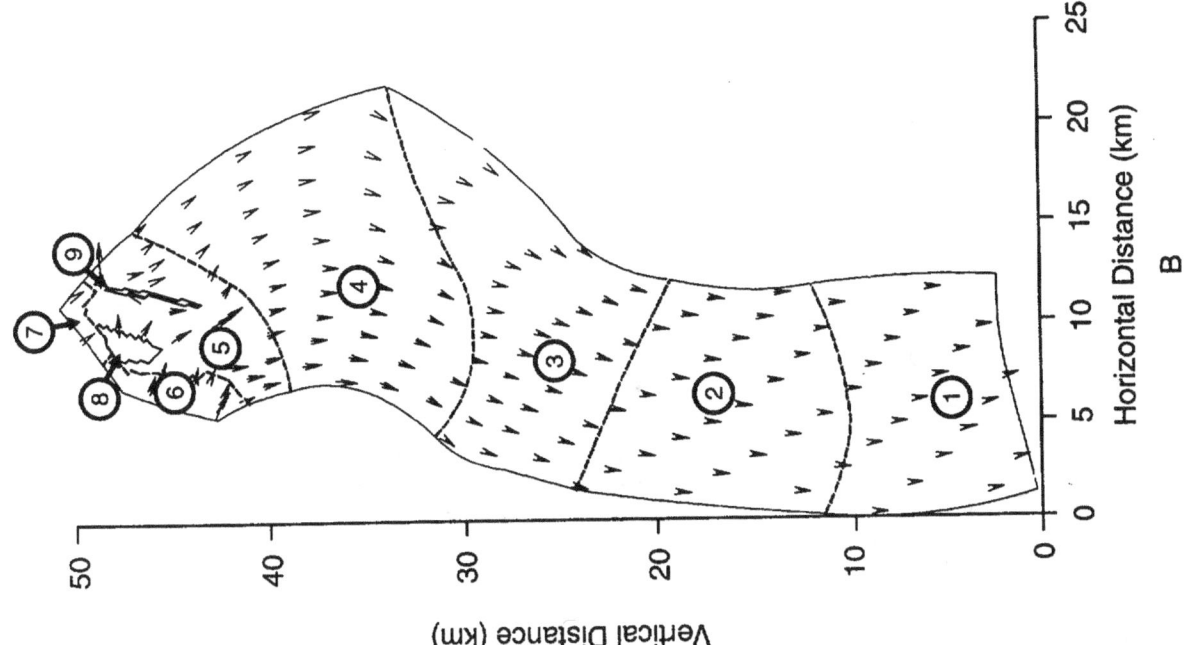

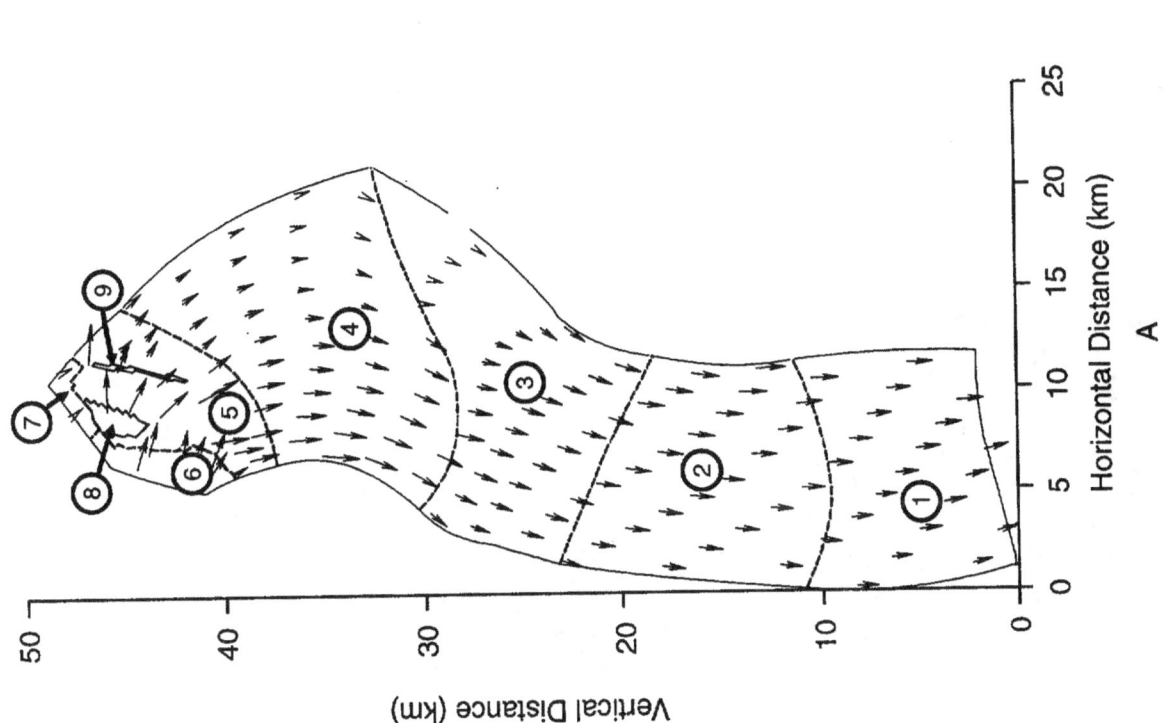

Figure 3–4. continued

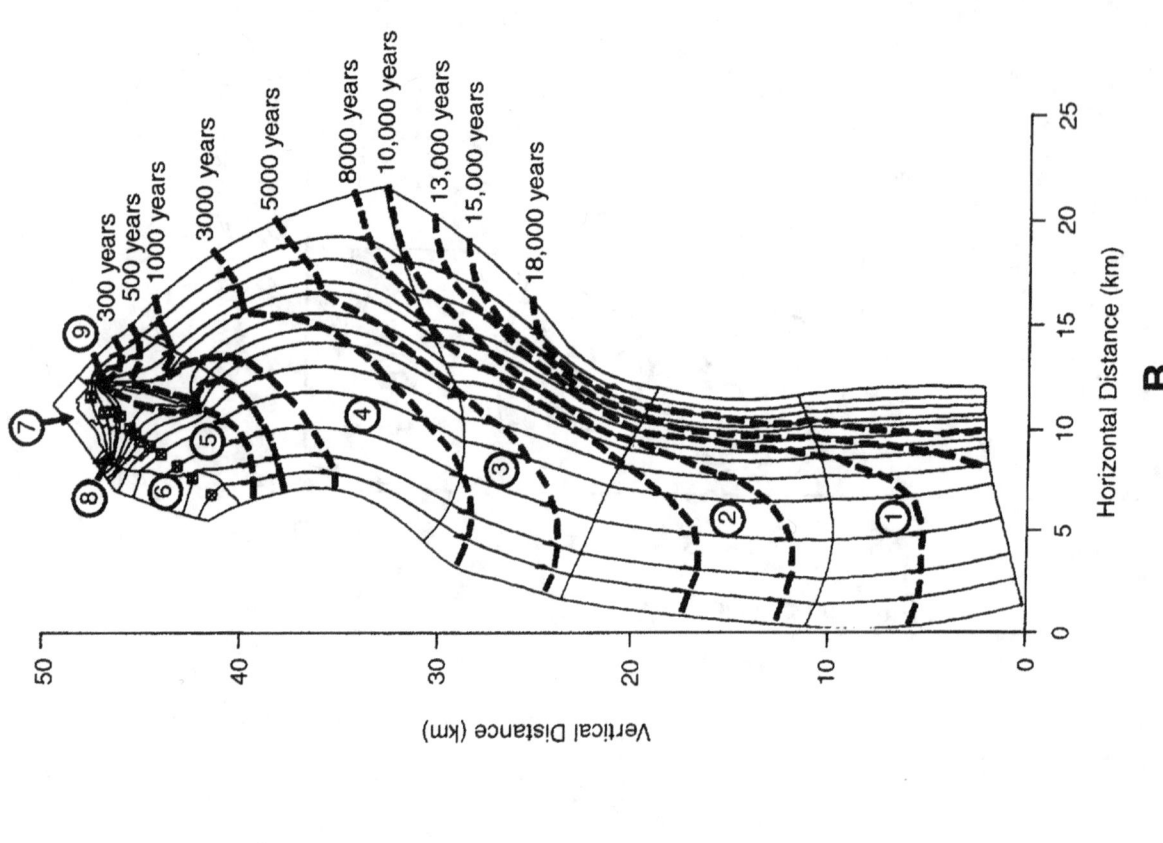

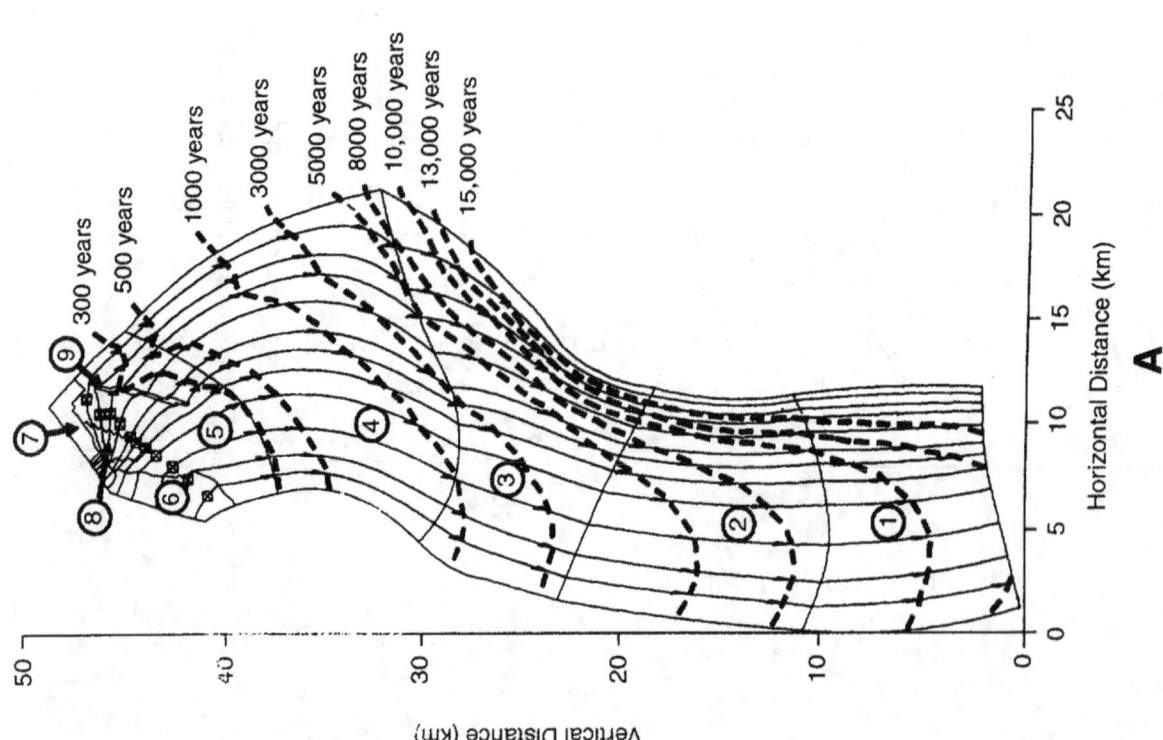

Figure 3–5. Pathlines and particle travel times for lateral flow model for two cases, with the Bow Ridge fault assumed to be (a) the preferential flow pathway and (b) the flow barrier.

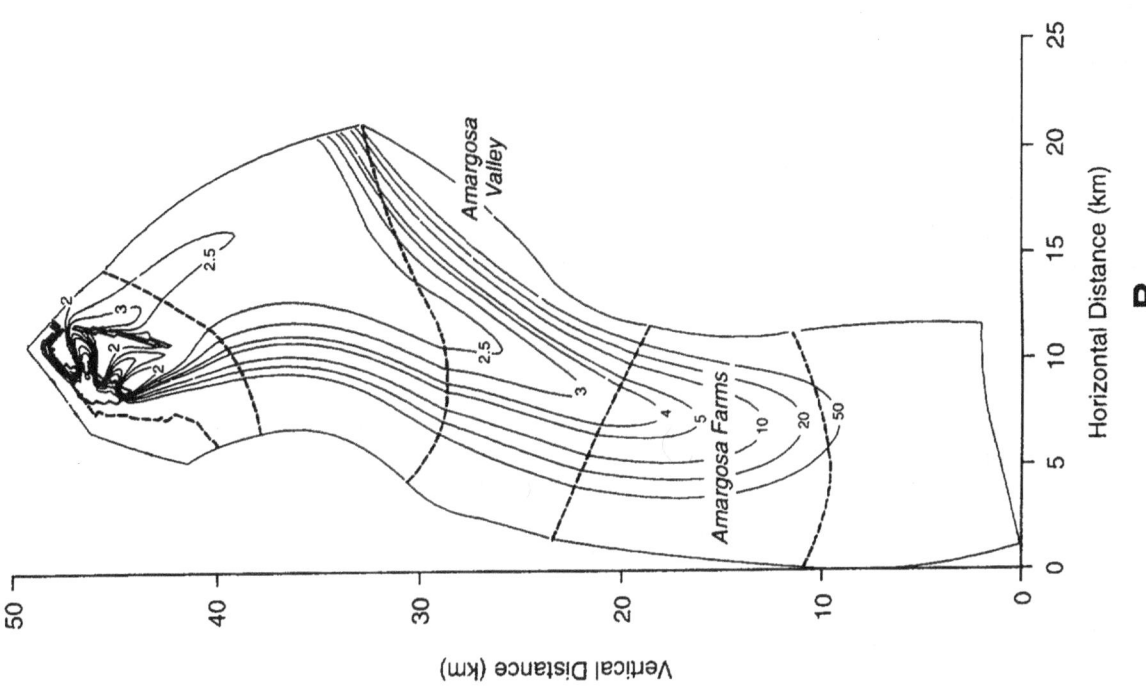

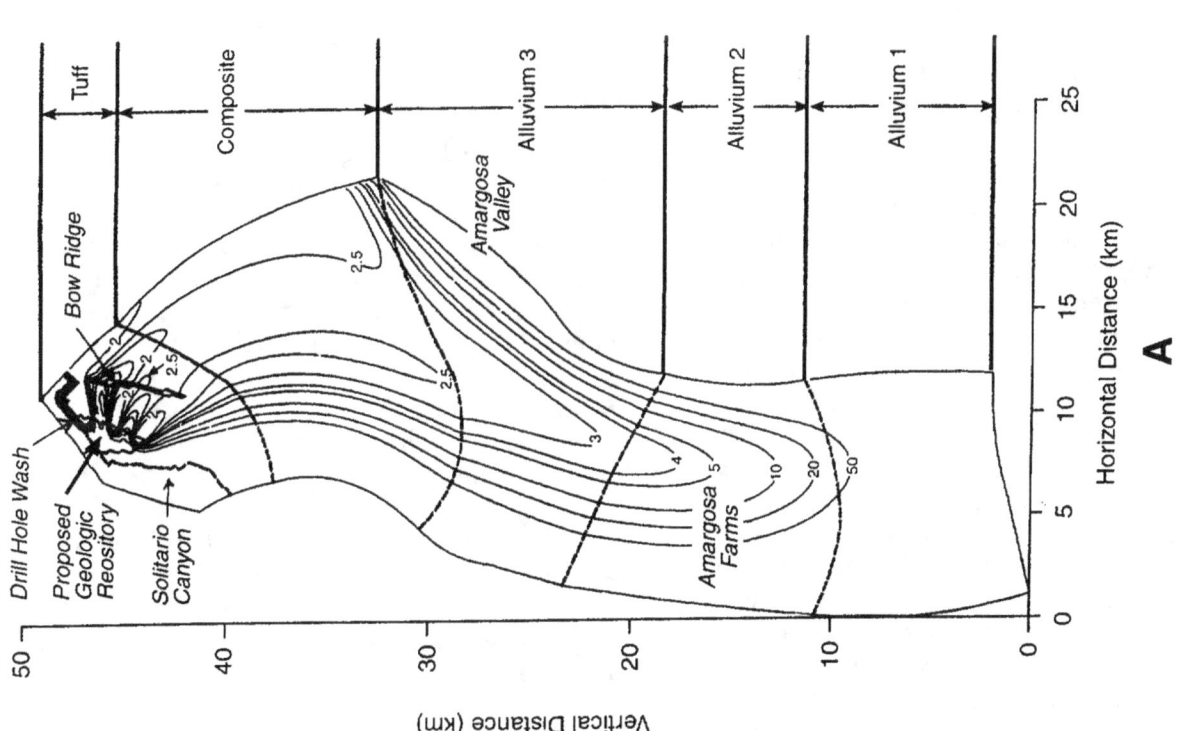

Figure 3–6. Radionuclide plume distributions for lateral flow model for two cases, with Bow Ridge fault assumed to be (a) the preferential flow pathway and (b) the flow barrier. Contour levels are in terms of dilution factors.

The formation and movement of the hypothetical ^{99}Tc plumes were computed with the *CHAINT* computer code, using a longitudinal dispersivity α_L of 30 meters and transverse dispersivity α_T of 3 meters. The mass dispersivities were chosen to be smaller than those used in the lateral flow model because of the shorter length of the flow domain (i.e., smaller scale of observation). The longitudinal dispersivity was chosen to be consistent with the value used in IPA Phase 2 (Wescott *et al.*, 1995) whereas the transverse dispersivity was taken as $\alpha_T = \alpha_L /10$; a slightly larger transverse-to-longitudinal-dispersivity ratio was assumed, to reduce gridding requirements.

A relatively fine grid, consisting of more than 8000 elements, was used to represent the flow domain. This fine grid was used to minimize numerical dispersion. The following sections present and interpret the significance of: (a) local flow path and particle travel times; and (b) plumes and dilution factors. A range of computer simulations was made for this conceptualization; however, only selected cases are presented.

3.1.2.2.3.1 Hydraulic Heads, Flow Vectors, and Darcy Fluxes

Patterns of vertical ground-water flow in the tuff aquifer are determined by the combined effects of the hydraulic boundary conditions, geometry of the strata (e.g., dipping layers), and the presence of discontinuities associated with fault zones. These effects are illustrated in the contour plot of the hydraulic head field shown in Figure 3–7. Although the boundary conditions are uniform, the contours indicate the head field becomes reoriented. In some locations, the plot suggests that the hydraulic head fields adjusted to move water along the most conductive hydrostratigraphic units. In contrast, the hydraulic head field in the lower permeability units is oriented in such a manner as to gradually move water up, toward more conductive units. Very high local gradients develop in the vicinity of the Bow Ridge fault, indicating that this feature acts as a partial flow barrier.

Additional insights into the vertical flow field were obtained by computing and plotting the velocity vectors (see Figure 3–8). The presence of the Ghost Dance fault appears to have little or no effect on the flow field, whereas the Bow Ridge fault zone produces a distinct downward flow field. Downstream of the Bow Ridge fault, the flow field becomes upward trending, negating the effects of the downward-dipping hydrostratigraphic units. Also presented in Figure 3–8 are the calculated ranges of Darcy fluxes computed for each unit (see accompanying table). In the vicinity of the water table, the maximum fluxes are estimated to be about 1.3 meters/year in the Prow Pass unit and about 1.5 meters/year in the Bullfrog unit. The largest flux (i.e., 2.9 meters/year) occurs in the Lithic Ridge unit located about 500 meters below the water table.

3.1.2.2.3.2 Flow Paths, Particle Travel Times, and Dilution Factors

The flow paths calculated for particles released along the Ghost Dance fault confirm interpretations drawn from flow vectors. As can be seen in Figure 3–9, the streamlines near the water table in the Prow Pass unit are horizontal and then dip down, avoiding flow within the lower-permeability Calico Hills unit. These streamlines dip down, as they cross the Bow Ridge fault zone, but return to levels very near the water-table surface. Also shown in Figure 3–9 are isopleths (heavy dashed lines) of constant particle travel time. These depict the relative rate of particle travel through the ground-water system. It is clear from these isopleths that ground-water movement is highly nonuniform in both the Prow Pass and Bullfrog units. This pattern of flow suggests that contaminants entering the aquifer would be transported primarily along the surface of the water table, with vertical mixing only occurring in areas where there are large changes in flow direction—i.e., the Bow Ridge fault.

The previously inferred trends of contaminant movement are clearly illustrated in the

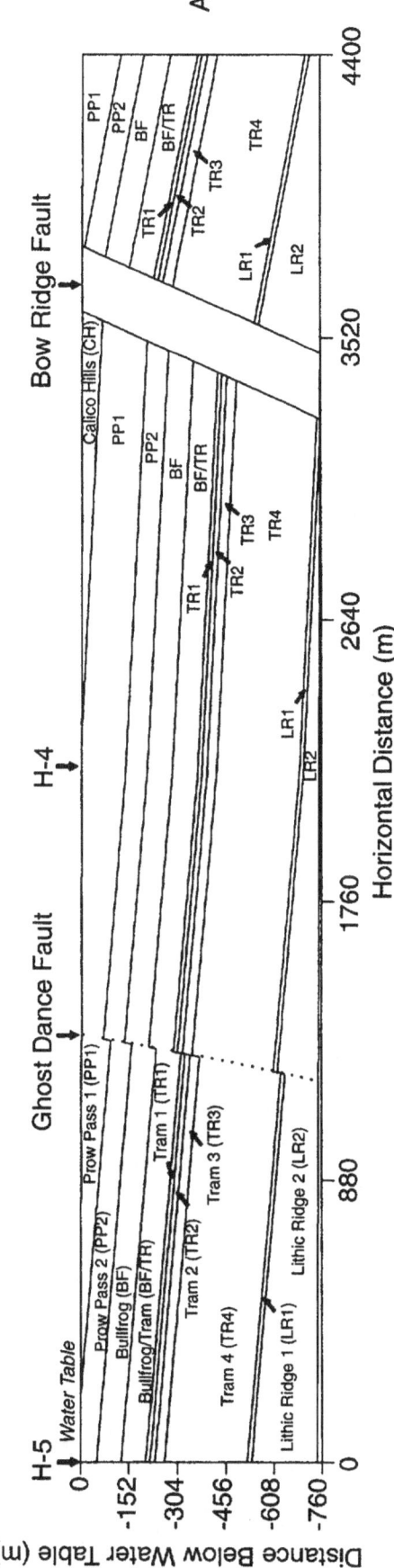

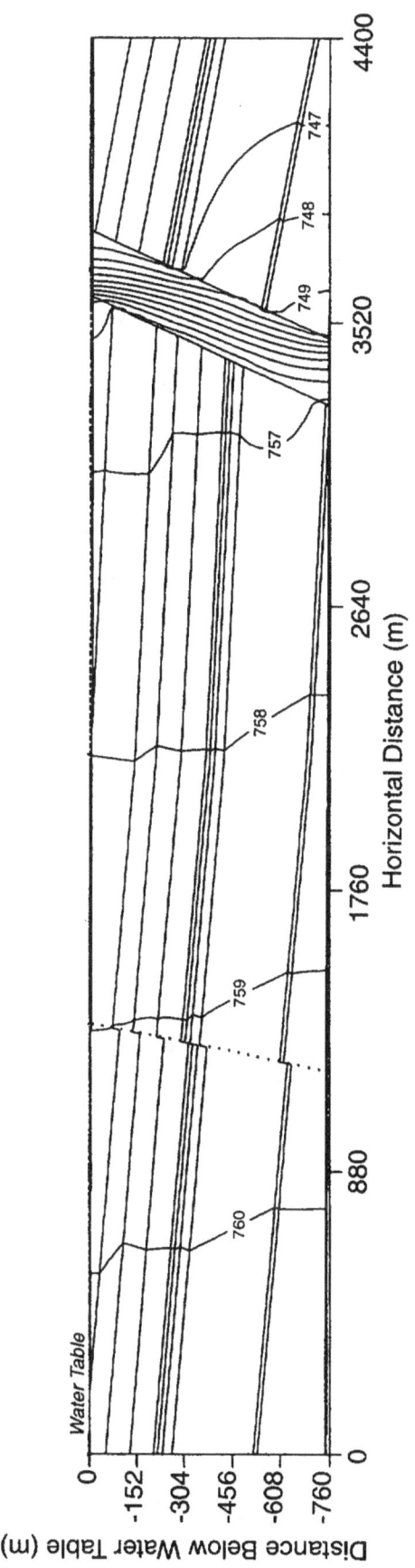

Figure 3–7. **Hydraulic head fields for vertical cross-section model.** Stratigraphic nomenclature taken from Whitfield *et al.* (1985).

Figure 3–8. **Darcy flux vector plots for vertical cross-section flow model.** Darcy velocity values are provided in the accompanying table.

Stratigraphic Unit	Darcy Velocities (m/yr)	
	Minimum	Maximum
Calico Hills	0.03	0.79
Prow Pass 1	0.015	1.3
Prow Pass 2	0.018	0.27
Bullfrog	0.087	1.5
Bullfrog/Tram	0.066	0.38
Tram 1	0.28	1.2
Tram 2	0.029	0.23
Tram 3	0.045	2.2
Tram 4	0.011	0.32
Lithic Ridge 1	0.041	2.9
Lithic Ridge 2	0.027	0.83
Bow Ridge	0.018	0.5

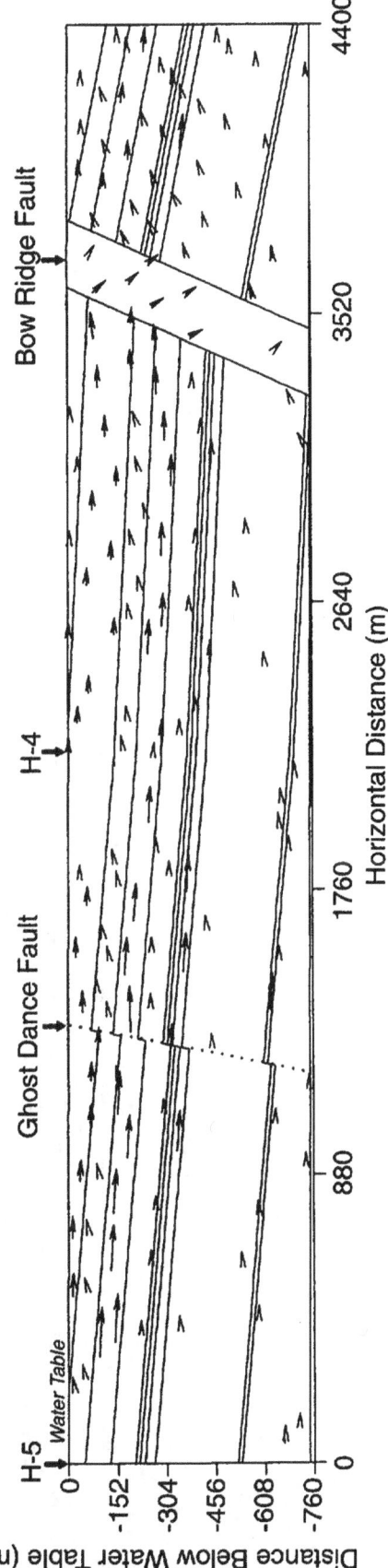

Figure 3 – 8. continued

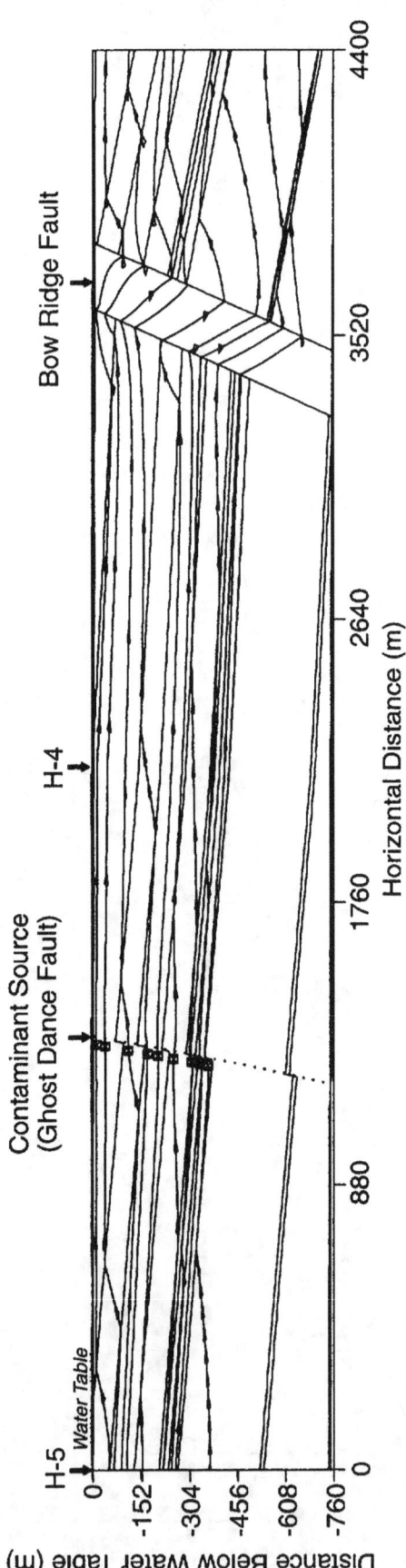

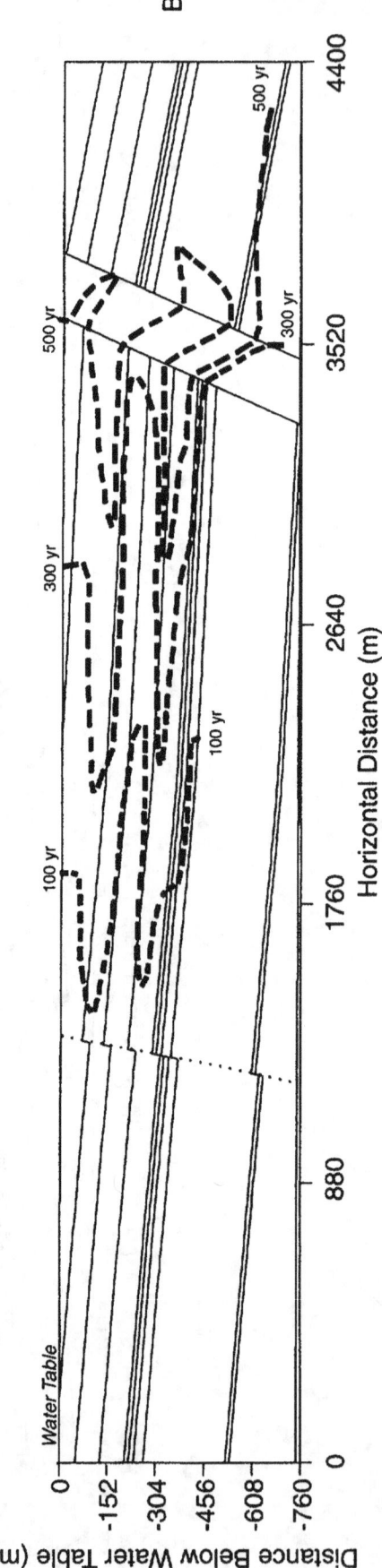

Figure 3–9. Pathlines (a) and particle travel times (b) for vertical cross-section flow model.

contour plot of the ^{99}Tc plume shown in Figure 3–10; the isopleths in this case are expressed in terms of dilution factors. Plume representations for two snapshots in time (i.e., times of 200 and 1000 years after release) are shown in the figure. The computer simulation results suggest there is relatively little local mixing and dilution (i.e., dilution factor of about 2) near the contaminant source. The plot for 1000 years clearly illustrates two important points: (a) the contaminant plumes remain relatively undiluted near the water-table surface; and (b) structural features such as the Bow Ridge fault can indeed produce significant vertical spreading of the contaminant plume.

3.1.3 Assumptions and Limitations

3.1.3.1 Conceptual Models

The reliability of the dilution factor estimates presented here depend, to a very large degree, on the appropriateness of ground-water flow conceptualizations implemented in the numerical models. Much direct and indirect evidence (e.g., hydrostratigraphy, head gradients, and temperature profiles) suggests a relatively complex three-dimensional (3–D) flow system in the tuff aquifer. For example, the general lateral ground-water flow in the tuff aquifer, which appears to primarily occur through interconnected shear fracture zones (Geldon, 1993), can be interrupted by upward flow (or upwelling) in the vicinity of faults—e.g., upward flow along splays of the Solitario Canyon fault (Wilson *et al.*, 1994). In developing conceptual models for this scoping analysis, a number of simplifying assumptions were made regarding:

- Dimensionality of the conceptual model;

- Hydraulic conductivity and mass dispersivity tensors;

- Heterogeneity and spatial variability of hydraulic properties; and

- Hydraulic boundary conditions.

As discussed previously, 2–D conceptual models were adopted to simplify the modeling task. The reduced dimensionality of the conceptual models used in this analysis is significant in that mixing processes in the third dimension are neglected, which results in underestimating the degree of dilution. This limitation may be particularly significant in the lateral flow model, where the plume was assumed to be confined to a 10-meter mixing depth, because of the 2–D assumption. In the actuality, vertical mixing of the plume would occur over the long flow path length (i.e., more than 30 kilometers), dispersing the plume over much greater depths and enhancing dilution. In the case of the vertical flow model, the 2–D assumption is probably less significant because of the short path length of the flow domain.

In the 2–D models, the tensorial nature of hydraulic conductivity and mass dispersivity was simplified by assuming the principal directions were aligned with the coordinate axes. Although this assumption is convenient (i.e., the cross terms of the tensors become zero) and commonly employed, it reduces the ability of the models to capture important directional characteristics of the flow field. These simplifications, however, are typically conservative with respect to dilution, because certain aspects of hydrodynamic dispersion are neglected. Further conservatism was introduced by choosing mass dispersivities (α_L and α_T) which are expected to be on the low side relative to values reported in the literature (Waldrop *et al.*, 1985).

Available site data indicate that the actual ground-water system exhibits much heterogeneity and spatial variability. Hydraulic conductivities of relatively large spatial regions and individual hydrostratigraphic units were assumed uniform in both the lateral and vertical flow models. This assumption of homogeneous regions and strata is consistent with simplifications made in recent DOE 3–D ground-water flow analyses (Wilson *et al.*, 1994; Arnold and Barr, 1996); however, it is significant to analysis of mixing processes (as well as to flow paths and particle travel times). Effects of heterogeneity were indirectly taken into account through the use of mass

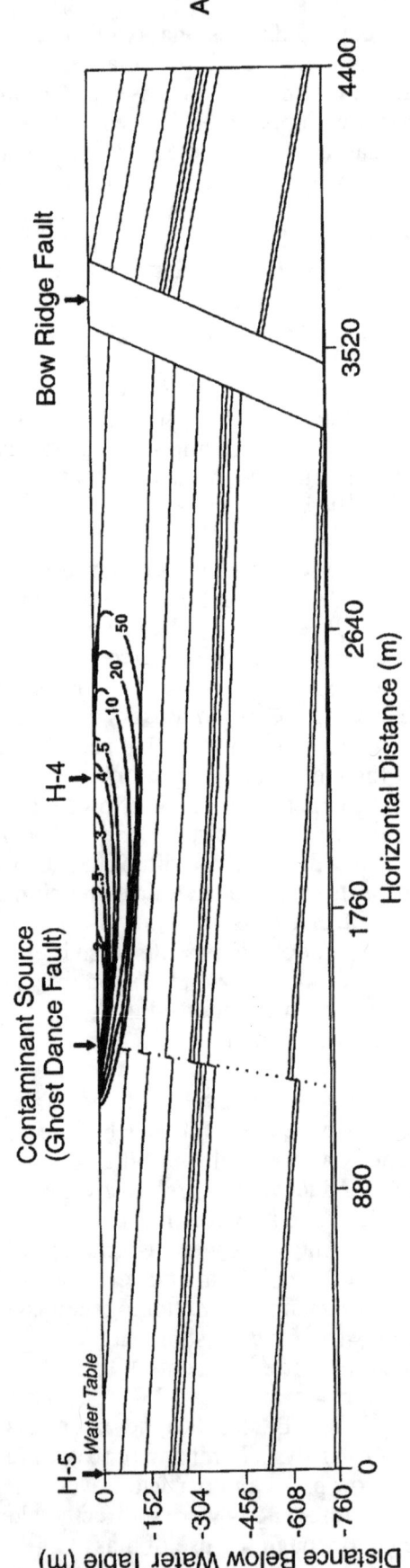

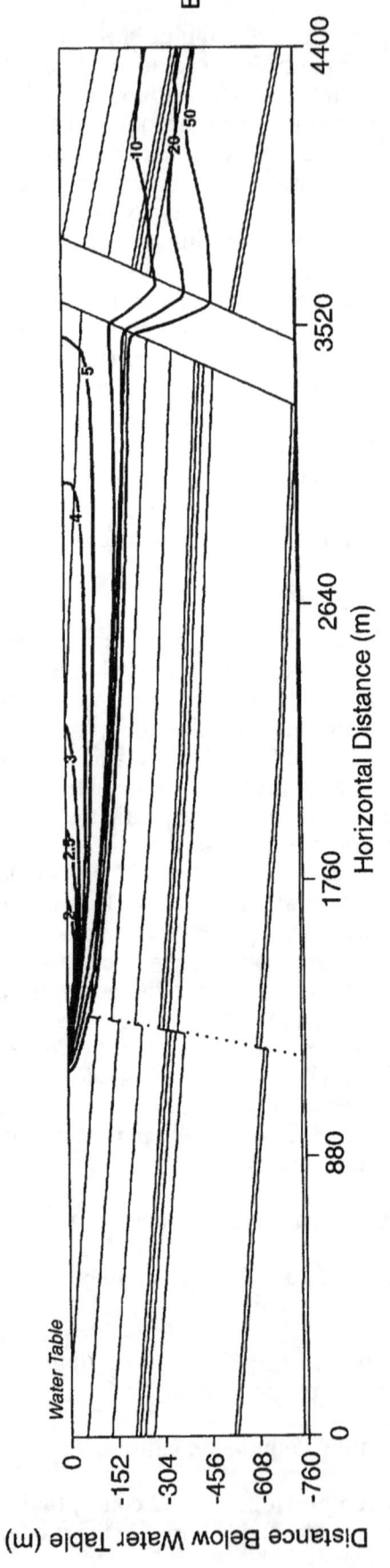

Figure 3–10. Radionuclide plume distributions for vertical cross-section model with contour levels in terms of dilution factors. 200 years after release (a); 1000 years after release (b).

dispersivities, but nevertheless the homogeneity assumption probably leads to an underestimation of dilution.

The current sparsity of data required making certain assumptions regarding the hydraulic boundary conditions for both the lateral and vertical flow models. The hydraulic heads assigned to the inflow and outflow boundaries of the lateral flow model are consistent with field data; however, the side boundaries were assumed to be no-flow boundaries. The no-flow assumption may be tenuous in the vicinity of the Amargosa Desert, where water well pumping probably affects flow patterns as may interbasin transfers. In the case of the vertical flow model, the uniform head profile assigned to the inflow boundary (at USW H−5) is probably not accurate because this is a region of likely upward flow; the true head profile at this boundary probably exhibits distinct vertical gradients. How significantly these types of assumptions affect the dilution effects is uncertain at this time.

One of the fundamental assumptions made is that the hydraulics of the ground-water system can be modeled as an *equivalent porous medium*. This assumption is probably quite defensible for the alluvial aquifer (lower portion of the lateral flow model) but potentially weak for the tuff aquifer (upper portion of lateral flow model). Dual porosity or dual permeability models (National Research Council, 1996) may provide more realistic representations of hydraulic and transport behavior of fracture zones in the tuff formations. For at least one borehole at Yucca Mountain, the dual porosity approach has been shown to yield a better interpretation of pump test data (Moench, 1984).

3.1.3.2 Hydraulic and Transport Properties

At present, there are many published data sets on the hydraulic and transport properties of the unsaturated zone at Yucca Mountain. These data sets—documented in Flint and Flint (1990); Wittwer *et al.* (1995); Rautman *et al.* (1995); Schenker *et al.* (1995); and Flint *et al.* (1996)—have been used in various subsystem performance assessments (i.e.,

Arnold *et al.*, 1995; Ho *et al.*, 1995; Arnold and Barr, 1996) as well as TSPAs (i.e., Wilson *et al.* 1994; TRW Environmental Safety Systems, Inc., 1995). In contrast to the considerable data published for the unsaturated zone, the amount of field data available for the saturated zone is limited, particularly for parameters necessary for dilution calculations. These data are not only limited in amount but also in spatial coverage.

In the conduct of this scoping analysis, past and recent USGS reports on field testing conducted in the tuff aquifer were reviewed to compile necessary data. Other borehole data for the alluvial aquifer were also examined. Particularly important was identifying data for estimation of:

- Hydraulic heads and gradients;
- Hydraulic conductivities;
- Effective porosities; and
- Mass dispersivities.

Most hydraulic head data (from which head gradients may be calculated) available for the Yucca Mountain site are in terms of composite heads (i.e., vertically averaged heads). As such, these data do not provide a means of estimating vertical head gradients. Hydraulic conductivity profiles such as those measured in USW H−4 (Whitfield *et al.*, 1985) provide a good indication of the range of values for the horizontal component K_{xx} of the conductivity tensor. At present, there are no data to estimate the vertical component K_{zz}. There are no field data for effective porosities or mass dispersivities, but the USGS is currently evaluating tracer tests in the C-Well Complex (Geldon, 1995) expected to yield such data. At the subregional scale, there are again composite head data but no known data for hydraulic conductivity, effective porosity, or mass dispersivities.

3.1.3.3 Radionuclide Source Term

The calculation of the radionuclide release from a repository generally requires the application of a detailed source term and release model (Sagar *et al.*, 1992) that takes into account such factors as the engineered barrier design, thermohydrologic conditions, near-field chemistry, and drift-scale flow conditions. For the purposes of this scoping analysis, a simple approach for calculating the ^{99}Tc release to ground water was adopted. In this approach, the release was computed assuming a fractional release rate of 10^{-5}/year, a mixing depth of 10 meters, and 50 percent of the waste packages failed. This simple calculation of the source term assumed no dilution of ^{99}Tc in the unsaturated zone and that the radionuclide instantaneously reached the saturated zone. For the lateral flow case, three separate source locations on the periphery of the repository footprint were assumed for the purpose of creating distinct plumes. For the vertical cross-section model, source locations adjacent to the Ghost Dance fault were assumed; these source zones spanned a distance of about 120 meters on each side of the fault. No uncertainties or parameter variations in the radionuclide source term were examined. These assumptions are significant when interpreting the calculational results.

3.1.4   Summary of Analysis Results

3.1.4.1   Ground-Water Flow Paths and Particle Travel Times

Computer visualizations of flow paths for the two conceptualizations of 2–D ground-water flow provided a preliminary understanding of flow patterns. For example, the simulations of lateral flow in regional ground-water flow systems indicated that, depending on the hydraulic characteristics of faults (such as the Bow Ridge fault), streamlines depict either flow across and along the fault zone or, alternatively, flow completely around it. Such observations are consistent with the hydraulic head field generally orienting itself to move water along the most conductive components of the hydrogeologic system. Similarly, the simulations for the vertical flow conceptual model (based on the cross-section through USW H–5 and USW H–4) suggested that the streamlines in the aquifer beneath the proposed repository generally follow hydrogeologic units with higher hydraulic conductivity. This trend was only altered by

the presence of fault zones that caused refraction and spreading of streamlines.

Particle travel time (t_p) calculations for both the vertical flow and lateral flow models highlighted the sensitivity to location of the particle release point and hydraulic conductivities and effective porosity values. For example, release points on the northeastern boundary of the proposed repository footprint appear to follow the longer flow paths, whereas those on the southern boundary trace out more direct paths with shorter particle travel times. Order-of-magnitude estimates of particle travel times were calculated for the assumed upper bound values (see Section 3.1.2.1.1) for effective porosities:

- Lateral flow model (from edge of the proposed repository to the Amargosa Desert): $t_p - 10^4$ years; and

- Vertical flow model (from Ghost Dance fault to Bow Ridge fault): $t_p - 500$ years.

It is important to note that the calculation of particle travel times is very sensitive to effective porosity ϕ values. For instance, if the lower bound values of ϕ (see Section 3.1.2.1.1) are assumed, the lateral flow model produces particle travel times of about 3000 to 5000 years for a path length of about 30 kilometers (to the Amargosa Desert area); for equivalent ϕ assumptions, the vertical flow model yields particle travel times of about 25 years for a path length of about 3 kilometers.

The relatively short particle travel times in the vertical flow model are consistent with conditions of fracture flow as opposed to matrix flow. The expectation of fracture flow is supported by field data (Geldon, 1993) that indicate the primary ground-water flow in the tuff aquifer occurs in fracture zones (e.g., shear fractures). It is noteworthy to mention that although some field data were used in these calculations, the deterministic analyses presented have not considered parameter uncertainties (e.g., spatial variability of hydraulic properties), flow in discrete fractures, or possible implications of matrix diffusion effects.

3.1.4.2 Ground-Water Fluxes

The ratio of moisture flux through the unsaturated zone (q_{uz}) to the saturated zone ground-water flux (q_{sz}) is a rough indicator of the bulk mixing and dilution that can potentially occur in the aquifer immediately beneath the proposed repository footprint. As shown in TRW Environmental Safety Systems, Inc. (1995), a bulk mass balance can be used to derive an approximate expression for the dilution factor DF:

$$DF = \frac{q_{sz}}{q_{uz}} \, g_f \qquad (3-1)$$

where g_f is a geometric factor computed by dividing the cross-sectional flow area in the aquifer by the effective flow area of the proposed repository footprint. The factor is g_f equals 0.1 assuming a cross-sectional flow area in the aquifer of 40,000 square meters (i.e., a 4 kilometer width and a mixing depth of 10 meters) and an effective flow area of the repository footprint of 410,000 square kilometers (i.e., 10,000 waste packages and a catchment area of 41 square meters/waste package). In NRC's IPA Phase 2 study (Wescott *et al.*, 1995), the maximum unsaturated zone flux values assumed for the current and pluvial climates were 5×10^{-3} and 10^{-2} meters/year, respectively. The flow simulations using the *MAGNUM−2D* computer code indicate ground-water fluxes (below the proposed repository) ranging from about 0.5 to approximately 2.0 meters/year. Using the above equation, a rough estimate of the range of dilution factors yields $5 \leq DF \leq 20$. The lower-bound value is consistent with the more detailed transport calculations.

3.1.5 References

Arnold, B.W., *et al.*, "Unsaturated-Zone Fast-Path Flow Calculations for Yucca Mountain Groundwater Travel Time Analyses (GWTT−94)," Albuquerque, New Mexico, Sandia National Laboratories, SAND95−0857, September 1995. [Prepared for DOE.]

Arnold, B.W., and G.E. Barr, "Numerical Modeling for Saturated-Zone Groundwater Travel Time Analysis at Yucca Mountain," American Nuclear Society/American Society of Civil Engineers, *Proceedings of the Seventh Annual International Conference: High-Level Radioactive Waste Management, April 29− May 3, 1996, Las Vegas, Nevada*, pp. 187−189 [1996].

Czarnecki, J.B., "Simulated Effects of Increased Recharge on the Ground-Water Flow System of Yucca Mountain and Vicinity, Nevada-California," U.S. Geological Survey, Water Resources Investigations, WRI−84−4344, 1985.

Czarnecki, J.B. and R.K. Waddell, "Finite-Element Simulation of Ground-Water Flow in the Vicinity of Yucca Mountain, Nevada-California," U.S. Geological Survey, Water-Resources Investigations Report, WRI−84−4349, 1984.

Carrera, J., and S.P. Neuman, "Estimation of Aquifer Parameters under Transient and Steady-State Conditions: 1. Maximum Likelihood Method Incorporating Prior Information," *Water Resources Research*, 22(2):199−210 [1986a].

Carrera, J., and S.P. Neuman, "Estimation of Aquifer Parameters under Transient and Steady-State Conditions: 2. Uniqueness, Stability, and Solution Algorithms," *Water Resources Research*, 22(2):211−227 [1986b].

Carrera, J., and S.P. Neuman, "Estimation of Aquifer Parameters under Transient and Steady-State Conditions: 3. Application to Synthetic and Field Data," *Water Resources Research*, 22(2):228−242 [1986c].

Domenico, P.A., and F.W. Schwartz, *Physical and Chemical Hydrogeology*, New York, John Wiley and Sons, 1990.

England, R.L., *et al.*, "MAGNUM−2D Computer Code: Users' Guide," Richland, Washington, Rockwell International, RHO−BW−CR−143P, January 1985.

Erickson, J.R., and R.K. Waddell, "Identification and Characterization of Hydrologic Properties of Fractured Tuff Using Hydraulic and Tracer Tests—Test Well USW H−4, Yucca Mountain, Nevada," U.S. Geological Survey, Water-Resources Investigations Report WRI−85−4066, 1985.

Ervin, E.M., R.R. Luckey, and D.J. Burkhard, "Summary of Revised Potentiometric-Surface Map for Yucca Mountain and Vicinity, Nevada," American Nuclear Society/ American Society of Civil Engineers, *Proceedings of the Fourth International Conference: High-Level Radioactive Waste Management, April 26–30, 1993, Las Vegas, Nevada*, 2:1554–1558 [1993].

Fetter, C.W., *Contaminant Hydrogeology*, New York, MacMillan Publishing Company, 1993.

Flint, L.E. and A.L. Flint, "Preliminary Permeability and Water-Retention Data for Nonwelded and Bedded Tuff Samples," U.S. Geological Survey, Open-File Report, USGS/OFR–90–569, 1990.

Flint, L.E., *et al.* "Physical and Hydrologic Properties of Rock Outcrop Samples at Yucca Mountain, Nevada," U.S. Geological Survey, Open-File Report, USGS/OFR–95–280, 1996.

Freeze, R.A. and J.A. Cherry, *Groundwater*, Englewoood Cliffs, New Jersey, Prentice Hall, Inc., 1979.

Geldon, A.L., "Preliminary Hydrogeologic Assessment of Boreholes UE–25c #1, UE–25c #2, and UE–25c #3, Yucca Mountain, Nye County, Nevada," U.S. Geological Survey, Water-Resources Investigations Report, WRI–92–4016, 1993.

Geldon, A.L., "Results and Interpretation of Preliminary Aquifer Tests in Boreholes UE–25c #1, UE–25c #2, and UE–25c #3, Yucca Mountain, Nevada," U.S. Geological Survey, Water-Resources Investigations Report, WRI–94–4177, 1995.

Gelhar, L.W., *Stochastic Subsurface Hydrology*, Englewood Cliffs, New Jersey, Prentice Hall, Inc., 1993.

Gillson, R.G., III, *et al.*, "A Computer Hydrogeologic Model of the Nevada Test Site and Surrounding Region [Abstract]," Geological Society of America, *1995 Annual Meeting: Abstracts with Program, November*

6–9, 1995, New Orleans, Louisiana, p. A–187 [1995].

Ho, C.K., S.J. Altman, and B.W. Arnold, "Alternative Conceptual Models and Codes for Unsaturated Flow in Fractured Tuff: Preliminary Assessments for GWTT–95," Albuquerque, New Mexico, Sandia National Laboratories, SAND95–1546, September 1995. [Prepared for DOE.]

Kline, N.W., R.L. England, and R.G. Baca, "CHAINT Computer Code: Users' Guide," Richland, Washington, Rockwell International, RHO–BW–CR–144P, December 1985.

Moench, A.F., "Double Porosity Models for a Fissured Groundwater Reservoir with Fracture Skin," *Water Resource Research*, 20(7):831–846 [1984].

National Research Council, "Technical Bases for Yucca Mountain Standards," Washington, D.C., National Academy Press, Commission on Geosciences, Environment, and Resources, July 1995.

National Research Council, "Rock Fractures and Fluid Flow—Contemporary Understanding and Applications," Washington, D.C., National Academy Press, U.S. National Committee for Rock Mechanics, 1996.

Neuman, S.P., "Analysis of Pumping Test Data from Anisotropic Unconfined Aquifers Considering Delayed Gravity Response," *Water Resources Research*, 11(2):329–342 [1975].

Rautman, C.A., *et al.*, "Physical and Hydrologic Properties of Rock Outcrop Samples from a Nonwelded Tuff Transition, Yucca Mountain, Nevada," U.S. Geological Survey, Water-Resources Investigation Report, WRI–95–4061, 1995.

Robison, J.H., "Ground-Water-Level Data and Preliminary Potentiometric Surface Map of Yucca Mountain and Vicinity, Nye County, Nevada," U.S. Geological Survey, Water-Resources Investigations Report, WRI–84–4197, 1984.

Robison, J.H., and R.W. Craig, "Geohydrology of Rocks Penetrated by Test Well USW H–S,

Yucca Mountain, Nye Country, Nevada," U.S. Geological Survey, Water-Resources Investigations Report, WRI−88−4168, 1991.

Roberson, K.E., E.H. Price, and S.J. Lawrence, "Simplification of the Geologic Framework of the Nevada Test Site and Surrounding Region for a Hydrogeologic Computer Model," Geological Society of America, *1995 Annual Meeting: Abstracts with Program, November 6−9, 1995, New Orleans, Louisiana,* A−187 [1995].

Sagar, B., *et al.*, "SOTEC: A Source Term Code for High-Level Geologic Repositories— Users' Manual (Version 1.0)," San Antonio, Texas, Center for Nuclear Waste Regulatory Analyses, CNWRA 92−009, July 1992. [Prepared for NRC.]

Schenker, A.R., *et al.*, "Stochastic Hydrogeologic Properties Development for Total-System Performance Assessments," Albuquerque, New Mexico, Sandia National Laboratories, SAND94−0244, September 1995. [Prepared for DOE.]

Scott, R.B. and J. Bonk, "Preliminary Geologic Map of Yucca Mountain, Nye County, Nevada, with Geologic Sections," U.S. Geological Survey, Open File Report 84−494, 1984.

Snow, D.T., "Anisotropic Permeability of Fractured Media," *Water Resources Research,* 5(6):1273−1289 [1996].

TRW Environmental Safety Systems Inc., "Total System Performance Assessment— 1995: An Evaluation of the Potential Yucca Mountain Repository," Las Vegas, Nevada, Document No. B00000000−01717−2200− 00136 (Rev. 01), November 1995.

Waldrop, W.R., *et al.*, "A Review of Field-Scale Physical Solute Transport Processes in Saturated and Unsaturated Porous Media," Palo Alto, California, Electric Power Research Institute, EPRI EA−4190, August 1985. [Prepared by the Tennessee Valley Authority

and the Massachusetts Institute of Technology.]

Walker, G.E., and T.E. Eakin, "Geology and Ground-Water of Amargosa Desert, Nevada-California," Carson City, Nevada, State of Nevada Department of Conservation and Natural Resources, Ground-Water Resources Reconnaissance Series Report 14, 1963.

Wescott, R.G., *et al.* (eds.), "NRC Iterative Performance Assessment Phase 2: Development of Capabilities for Review of a Performance Assessment for a High-Level Waste Repository," U.S. Nuclear Regulatory Commission, NUREG−1464, October 1995.

Whitfield, M.S., *et al.*, "Geohydrology of Rocks Penetrated by Test Well USW H−4, Yucca Mountain, Nye County, Nevada," U.S. Geological Survey, Water-Resources Investigations Report, WRI−85−4030, 1985.

Wilson, M.L., *et al.*, "Total-System Performance Assessment for Yucca Mountain— SNL Second Iteration (TSPA−1993)," Albuquerque, New Mexico, Sandia National Laboratory, SAND93−2675, 2 vols., April 1994.

Wittmeyer, G.W. "Robust Estimation of Parameters in Nonlinear Subsurface Flow Models Using Adjoint State Methods," Tucson, Arizona, University of Arizona, Ph.D. Dissertation, 1990.

Wittmeyer, G.W., and S.P. Neuman, "Monte-Carlo Experiments with Robust Estimation of Aquifer Model Parameters," *Advances in Water Resources,* 14:252 272 [1992].

Wittwer, C., *et al.*, "Preliminary Development of the LBL/USGS Three-Dimensional Site-Scale Model of Yucca Mountain, Nevada," Berkeley, California, Lawrence Berkeley Laboratory, LBL−37356/UC−814, June 1995. [Prepared for DOE.]

3.2 Initial Assessment of Dilution Effects Induced by Water Well Pumping in the Yucca Mountain Region[3]

3.2.1 Introduction

The ground-water flow and transport modeling studies described in Section 3.1 provide estimates of the degree to which radionuclide concentrations may be reduced during passive transport in the saturated zone from the area immediately beneath Yucca Mountain to potential receptor locations. These preliminary studies suggest that radionuclide concentrations at the water table experience relatively little dilution during saturated zone transport. Kessler and McGuire (1996) note that dispersive transport processes are relatively ineffective at reducing contaminant concentrations in a steady-state ground-water flow regime. However, if there are large temporal variations in the magnitude and direction of the ground-water velocity field, then mixing and attendant dilution during transport may be significant (Bellin *et al.*, 1996).

Current conceptual models of the Yucca Mountain saturated ground-water system would suggest that the flow regime in the immediate Yucca Mountain region is relatively unperturbed by fluctuations in the magnitude and location of recharge and discharge. However, increased pumping for irrigated agriculture in the Amargosa Farms area[4] (see Figure 3–11) over the past 30 years may have had some effect on the ground-water flow regime south of Yucca Mountain.

Nonetheless, in this section it is assumed that pumping has no effect on the ground-water flow regime between Yucca Mountain and potential receptor locations. If the primary effect of pumping on the flow regime is enhanced mixing or more rapid transport, the assumption of steady-state flow conditions, if not realistic, is at least conservative from the standpoint of radionuclide dose.

Even if the transient effects of well pumping on *in situ* radionuclide concentrations may be neglected, the radionuclide concentrations of water pumped from a well may differ significantly from *in situ* concentrations. Differences between *in situ* and borehole concentrations arise because a pumped well may capture water from different parts of the contaminant plume and the water in the borehole, therefore, reflects the average concentration of the portions of the radionuclide plume captured by the well. For small, low-discharge pumps extracting water from large, well-mixed plumes, the effects of borehole mixing may be negligible; however, if the plume is small relative to the discharge volume of the pumping, borehole mixing may be significant.

Dilution factors can be defined in a number of ways. Each of the three definitions mentioned in this section are based on a particular approach to addressing dilution. The first approach addresses dilution that results from dispersion of a solute during transport for which the dilution factor is calculated as the ratio of concentration at the source area to that at the receptor location. The second approach addresses dilution from mixing and the corresponding dilution factor is calculated as the mass release rate divided by the largest flux of water into which the solute may be mixed and used by a hypothetical receptor group. The third approach addresses dilution caused by the intersection of the capture zone of a pumping well with the plume configuration at the withdrawal location. In this third case, the dilution factor is calculated as the ratio of the plume area intercepted by the capture area and the entire capture area. The third approach describes borehole

---

[3]This analysis was first published as Fedors and Wittmeyer (1998). Although it can be found in NRC's PDR, Fedors and Wittmeyer has not received wide-spread distribution thus far and as a consequence, a decision was made to include it in this NUREG. However, for the purposes of publication in this format, it has undergone a limited editorial review. Despite this review, the analysis is substantially the same as the earlier version placed in the PDR.

[4]Elsewhere in this NUREG, the terms "Amargosa Valley" and "Amargosa Farms area" were used to refer collectively to the set of communities of Ash Meadows, Amargosa Farms, Amargosa Valley, and Lathrop Wells, which all generally lie within the Amargosa Valley hydrographic basin. However, in this section of the NUREG, the term "Amargosa Farms" refers to the southern portion of the Amargosa Valley bounded approximately by the California-Nevada border, Nevada State Highway 373, and Amargosa Farm Road because residences and farming activities in the valley are concentrated in this triangular parcel of land.

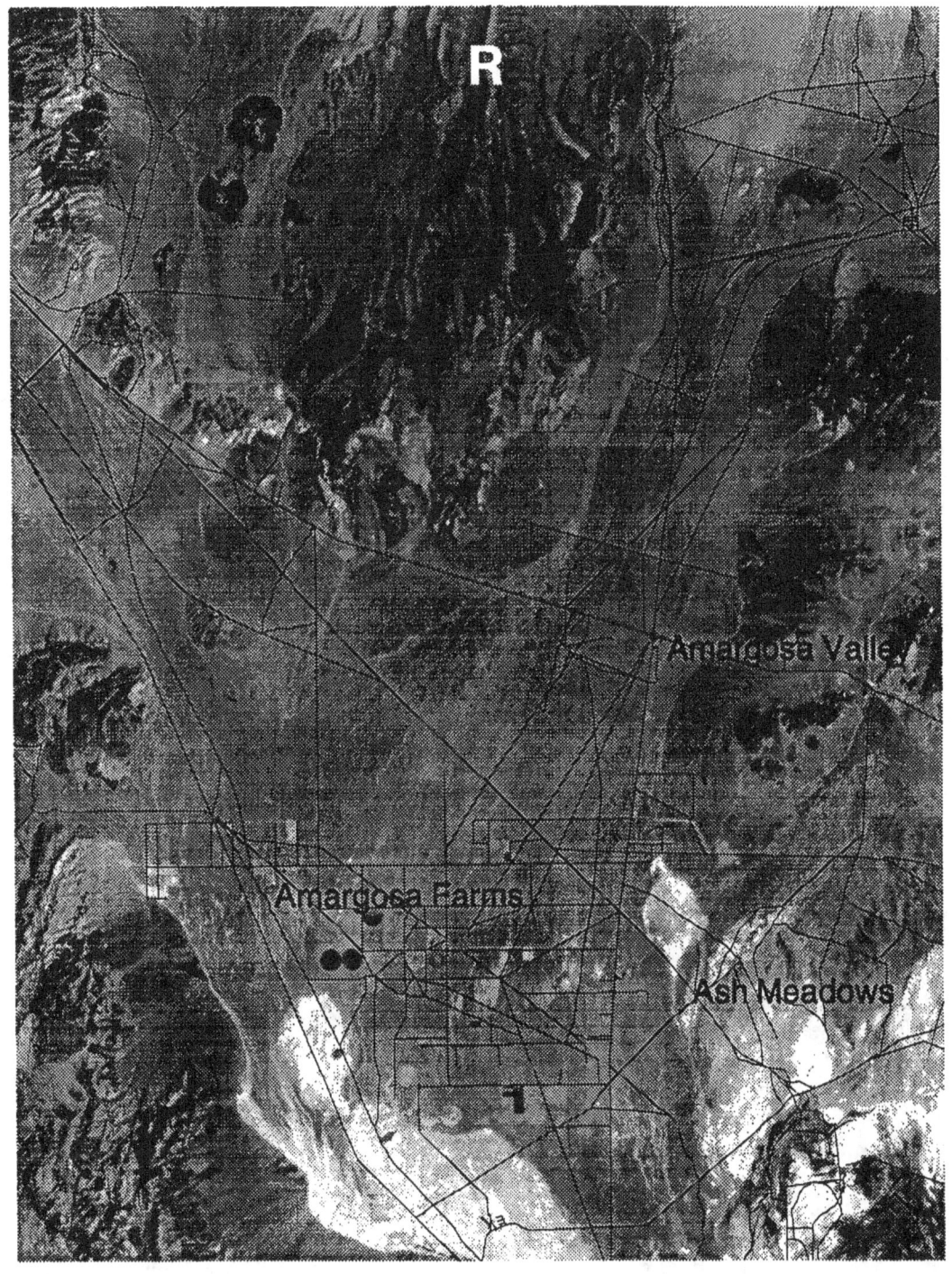

Figure 3 – 11. **Lower Amargosa Desert Region south of the proposed Yucca Mountain repository site (R), including the Amargosa Valley and Amargosa Farms areas.** Scale is 1:250,000.

dilution from the geometric standpoint and it may be linearly combined with the first approach for a total borehole dilution factor. Usage of the first two approaches is described further below.

Kessler and McGuire (1996) and Baca *et al.* (this report)[5] used the first approach to calculate *point dilution factors* (P−DFs) where point refers to concentration at a single point. Under assumptions of steady-state flow, estimated dilution factors, caused by dispersive mixing along the saturated zone transport pathway from the proposed Yucca Mountain repository to locations 20 to 30 kilometers to the south, have ranged from 5 to 50 (Baca *et al.*, this report) and from 4 to 44 (Kessler and McGuire, 1996). In both analyses, the reported dilution factors were determined by solving the advection-dispersion equation. Baca *et al.* contoured the P−DF, while Kessler and McGuire tabulated P−DFs based on centerline concentration. In DOE's TSPA−1993 (Wilson *et al.*, 1994); TSPA−1995 (TRW Environmental Safety Systems, Inc., 1995); and NRC's IPA Phase 2 effort (Wescott *et al.*, 1995), it was assumed that additional dilution occurs at the receptor location because of mixing clean and contaminated water in the borehole and, in the case of TSPA−1995, from mixing of waters from ground-water basins influent to the central region of the Amargosa Desert.

In NRC's ongoing IPA effort (Mohanty and McCartin, 2000), it is assumed that a borehole dilution factor can be estimated using a single well that is pumped at a rate sufficient to supply all water needs for the hypothetical receptor group in question. For example, for 12 quarter- section, center-pivot irrigation plots under cultivation with alfalfa, the equivalent annual well discharge[6] is 9,300,000 cubic meters. If a hypothetical receptor group consists of a residential community of 500 persons located 5 kilometers south of Yucca Mountain, the equivalent annual well

discharge[7] would be 103,700 cubic meters. Borehole dilution factors can be computed directly for a potential receptor group, if the volume of contaminated water captured by the pumping well is known. For example, if, the volume of contaminated water captured by an irrigation well is 930,000 cubic meters, the dilution factor is 10. However, to determine a dose, one must compute the radionuclide concentration in the borehole and, hence, must either know the concentration of radionuclides in the contaminated water or the total mass of radionuclides captured by the well. Inherent in this approach is the assumption that the entire radionuclide plume is captured and that there is no well-to-well variation in the concentration. This analysis addresses the validity of this assumption considering the concept of borehole dilution as well as the distribution of pumping well locations and pumping-rate magnitudes.

3.2.1.1 Geosphere Release Pathways Considered in a TSPA

Farming in the Amargosa Farms area is partially related to the accessibility to well water. The combination of soil conditions and large depths to the water table restrict farming-based population growth to the area immediately south of the community of Amargosa Valley. The water table gradually approaches the land surface toward the southern reaches of the Amargosa Farms area. Based on the IPA Phase 2 analysis [See Neel ("Dose Assessment Module") in Wescott *et al.* (1995)], exposure scenarios are assumed to occur through a combination of drinking water and ingestion of locally-raised produce and livestock. The lengths of the ground-water flow paths from Yucca Mountain to domestic and commercial wells and irrigation wells are approximately 25 and 30 kilometers, respectively.

3.2.1.2 Literature Review

In ground-water hydrology, the term *borehole dilution* is used to describe several phenomena including: (a) contaminant sampling biases resulting from improper monitoring well

---

[5]Described in Section 3.1.

[6](12 plots × 126 acres/plot × 8 feet of water/yr) ÷ (8.107 × 10^{-4} m^3 /acre-ft).

[7](150 gal/person-day) × (500 persons) × (365.25 days/yr) × (3.785 × 10^{-3} m^3 /gal).

construction; (b) the effectiveness of "pump and treat" remediation systems; and (c) capture zone analysis. Borehole dilution is used to explain one to two order-of-magnitude differences in values between concentrations measured in sampling wells and concentrations measured in the aquifer. Borehole dilution is also the name of a procedure used to estimate permeabilities or the seepage velocity in a single well bore through analysis of the dilution rate after release of a solute in the wellbore. Borehole dilution, as used in this scoping analysis, refers to dilution of the resident contaminant concentrations in a wellbore from pumping a well that captures both contaminated and uncontaminated portions of the aquifer.

Six factors that may significantly affect the borehole concentration are: (a) well pumping rate and well distribution in the well field; (b) regional hydraulic gradient; (c) transmissivity; (d) hydrostratigraphy and anisotropy; (e) well penetration depth and length of screen; and (f) vertical and horizontal contaminant plume distribution. Analytical solutions for flow can incorporate the effects of well pumping rates, well design, and regional gradients under certain restrictions for a sensitivity analysis. Complex numerical models are generally required to analyze the effects of heterogeneity in the hydraulic properties and simulate complex plume configurations, especially if 3–D effects are considered to be important. An increase in the spacing of the wells may increase the capture zone horizontally but may decrease the capture zone vertically and may introduce gaps in the capture zone between wells through which contaminants may escape. An increase in the regional hydraulic gradient will act to decrease the capture area. An increase in horizontal to vertical anisotropy will increase the capture zone horizontally but decrease it vertically.

Analytic solutions (Grubb, 1993; Faybishenko *et al.*, 1995; Schafer, 1996) and *analytic element methods*—AEMs (Strack, 1989; Haitjema, 1995) have been published for estimating capture zones for partially penetrating wells in steady-state 3–D flow fields. Sensitivity analyses of effects that include vertical

movement of water or solute in a heterogeneous domain require the use of numerical models. A good illustration of the factors that affect capture zone size and shape is found in Bair and Lahm (1996). Bair and Lahm used a finite difference method to determine the steady-state flow field, and particle tracking, to delineate the size and shape of the capture zone. They determined the magnitude of changes to the capture zone area because of perturbations in the regional gradient, well penetration, pumping rates, well configuration, and degree of hydraulic conductivity anisotropy in the context of an idealized pump and treat design.

Three published articles on numerical simulation of 3–D flow in and around a wellbore contain pertinent information for refined modeling in the vicinity of a single well. Chiang *et al.* (1995) simulated 3–D flow and advective solute transport in the vicinity of a partially penetrating well, to understand the order-of-magnitude difference in contaminant concentrations between well samples and point aquifer samples. The concentration profile in the aquifer was known. The well bore was modeled as separate elements with a permeability in the range of that predicted for laminar flow in a tube. They noted that their transient simulation results asymptotically approached the simple, mass-balance-based result that assumes a flat water table.

Akindunni *et al.* (1995) simulated 3–D flow near a well for various screen and plume positions. They approximated the well using a Neumann boundary condition at the edge of the domain at which the discharge was equally apportioned to the nodes along the screened length of the well. They compared vertically-averaged values of concentration for both the wellbore and the aquifer. In the transient simulations, concentrations differed significantly in the well and aquifer. Concentrations in the wellbore were higher or lower than the vertically averaged aquifer value, depending on the relative position of the plume depth and screened interval. However, over long times, the concentration in the wellbore asymptotically approached the vertically averaged aquifer value. In addition to screen position and plume position, they also investigated the dependence on screen length and anisotropy. Again, initial concentrations differed significantly, but long-time concentrations appeared to approach the vertically averaged aquifer value. As expected, simulations with large anisotropy ratios for hydraulic conductivity exhibited less vertical mixing than the isotropic case.

Reilly *et al.* (1989) also modeled the wellbore as a column of hydraulically connected cells; however, their focus was on wellbore flow in a monitoring well with implications for sampling bias and cross-contamination. In a monitoring well, cross-contamination will act to dilute the plume. Of note was their conclusion that greater than half the aquifer-to-wellbore flow occurred in the top 10 percent of the screened length, whereas greater than half the wellbore-to-aquifer flow occurred in the bottom 10 percent of the screened length. Hence, solute plumes approaching the top of the screened portion will enter the wellbore, whereas plumes approaching the bottom will tend to flow around the well. This finding may be pertinent for a hypothetical farming-type receptor group, when irrigation wells are shut down, but is probably irrelevant during periods of pumping.

3.2.1.3 Methods Used to Conduct this Study

Wellbore design and pumping practices in the Yucca Mountain region may have a significant effect both on the capture of a potential plume and, from another perspective, on the radionuclide concentration of the water pumped from the wells. Existing databases were analyzed to characterize the location, design, and production of wells. An important feature of the wells in the Amargosa Farms area is that they partially penetrate the alluvial aquifer thickness. The first wells encountered in a path of a simulated plume released from the proposed repository site are low-pumping-rate domestic, commercial, and quasi-municipal wells at a distance of approximately 25 kilometers. Large-pumping-rate irrigation wells capable of lowering the water table over several square kilometers are located at a distance of approximately 30 kilometers from Yucca Mountain.

The AEM is used to model 3−D flow in the vicinity of a partially penetrating well. Particle tracking is used to delineate a capture area for different well designs, pumping rates, and regional flow characteristics. The capture area is determined at an up-gradient point from the well location where the flow is essentially one-dimensional (1−D); for example, no longer 3−D. Also, the cross-sectional area of a plume entering the Amargosa Farms area is approximated by using 2−D and 3−D solutions to the advection-dispersion equation. Geometric arguments are used to estimate dilution factors caused by the portion of the plume captured. For dilution factors based on dispersive transport, numerical integration is used to estimate a representative concentration for the portion of the plume captured.

3.2.1.4 Limitations of this Study

The geometric borehole dilution factors reported here account only for borehole dilution from pumping. Dilution caused by mixing with clean water, either underneath the repository footprint or at the northern portion of Fortymile Wash, or from any interbasin transfers, is not included. Dilution factors calculated using different approaches may neither be directly compared nor linearly combined except under certain restrictions. For this scoping analysis, comparison of the streamtubes described in Section 3.1 (ambient dilution) with the geometries of the capture zone and plume configuration are not possible, since they are derived from different phenomena.

Three significant assumptions are used in this scoping analysis, in part because of the paucity of data for the ground water in the alluvial sediments of Amargosa Farms area. Material properties are assumed to be homogeneous and isotropic; the flow field is assumed to be uniform; and steady-state pumping rate and contaminant transport are assumed to represent the effects of borehole dilution. The latter assumption specifically implies that the transient effects of irrigation pumping can be approximated by an annual pumping discharge volume.

3.2.2 Hydrogeology of the Amargosa Desert Region[8]

The Amargosa Desert region is a northwest-trending, triangular-shaped alluvial basin bounded on the north by Bare Mountain, Yucca Mountain, and the Specter Range; on the east by the Resting Spring Range; and on the west by the Funeral Range and Black Mountains. Elevations on the valley floor range from 975-meter msl at the Amargosa River narrows near Beatty and 720 meters msl at the proximal edge of the fan formed by Fortymile Wash, as it discharges from Jackass Flats, to less than 610 meters msl at Franklin Lake playa south of the Amargosa Farms area.

3.2.2.1 Structure and Depositional History

The Amargosa Desert is an alluvial valley that resulted from large-scale block faulting in the Basin and Range Province (Bedinger *et al.*, 1989; Plume, 1996). Sediments deposited in depressions created by Tertiary to Quaternary block faulting can be classified as alluvial fan, lake bed, and fluvial deposits. In general, the coarsest materials (gravels and boulders) were deposited near the mountains, and the finer materials (silts and clays) were deposited in the central part of the basin. The distribution of sediment is generally associated with distance from the mountains. Alluvial fans with steep gradients and coarse sediments flatten and coalesce basinward, interfingering with the lake bed deposits. Within the alluvial fans there is a complex interfingering and interbedding of fine and coarse sediments caused shifting of fluvial processes across the top of the fan. The finer grained, distal portions of the fans merge laterally and interlayer with the lake deposits. The lake bed deposits can include beach sand and gravel lenses, silts and clay layers, and evaporites from playa-type environments. The fluvial deposits of recent times consist of sand and gravel lenses along present or ancestral streams. These exhibit a greater degree of sorting than the alluvial fan deposits.

Repeated upheaval events led to a complex interbedding and interlayering of the proximal and distal facies of the alluvial basin sediments. The repeated upheavals, together with the lateral and down-gradient transitions within the alluvial fan and grading into the lake bed or playa deposits, have strong implications for flow and transport on a basin-wide scale.

The Amargosa Farms area is in the distal portion in terms of sediment facies of an alluvial basin where lowland fans and lake beds would comprise much, but not all, of the stratigraphic section. Geologic lithologies and maps are described in Walker and Eakin (1963); Denny and Drewes (1965); Naff (1973); Swadley and Carr (1980); Swadley (1983); Fischer (1992); and Burchfiel (1966). Recent maps of the central Amargosa Desert region have followed the lithologic characterization of Hoover *et al.* (1981). Local features pertinent to the hydrogeology include the presence of tuffaceous beds (ash fall); limestone horizons; perched water systems (especially where the Funeral Mountain fanglomerates overlie lake sediments); common occurrence of caliché; and cementation of sand and gravel units. The high east-west hydraulic gradient, in the otherwise north-south regional gradient, between Amargosa Farms and Ash Meadows, is thought to be caused by low-permeability lake-bed sediments faulted into juxtaposition with the conductive Paleozoic carbonates of Ash Meadows.

The thickness of the alluvial sediments in the Amargosa Farms area is not well-known. Bedinger *et al.* (1989) report the basin-fill as greater than 1300 meters, possibly as thick as 2000 meters for basins in the Death Valley Region. Oatfield and Czarnecki (1991) used geophysical data to estimate the thickness of the alluvial valley fill sediments in the range 800 to 1100 meters for the Amargosa Farms area. Laczniak *et al.* (1996) infer depths up to 1140 meters on their east-west cross-section across the Amargosa Farms area.

3.2.2.2 Basin-Scale Ground-Water Flow

Hydrographically, Amargosa Desert is part of the Death Valley ground-water flow system, which is a series of topographically-closed

---

[8]Also see Sections 2.1.2.2, 2.1.2.3, and Appendix A.

basins connected at depth by the Paleozoic carbonate aquifer. As noted earlier, the Death Valley ground-water system can be further subdivided into three basins: (a) the Alkali Flat-Furnace Creek Ranch sub-basin; (b) the Ash Meadows sub-basin; and (c) the Oasis Valley sub-basin. Amargosa Farms is in the southern portion of the Alkali Flat-Furnace Creek sub-basin and adjacent to the Ash Meadows sub-basin (DOE, 1988; D'Agnese *et al.*, 1997). The Ash Meadows sub-basin, which drains the eastern and northeastern basins of the Death Valley regional flow system, is not believed to be influent to Alkali Flat-Furnace Creek Ranch sub-basin in the vicinity of the primary agricultural pumping area.

The diverse mix of geochemical signatures in the Amargosa Desert region suggests that the ground water comes from a combination interbasin flow, upwelling from the deep Paleozoic carbonate aquifer, and intrabasin flow from the northwest and from the north (Winograd and Thordarson, 1975). Because of high ET rates for the Amargosa Desert, most of the recharge occurs through the ephemeral stream channels (Osterkamp *et al.*, 1994; Savard, 1995). Since the stream channels in the Amargosa Farms portion of the Amargosa Desert rarely have flow, the recharge estimates of Osterkamp *et al.* are about 0.5 percent of precipitation. Precipitation is generally between 100 and 200 millimeters for the Amargosa River basin (*Op cit.*).

The ground-water contribution from the proposed Yucca Mountain repository area is a small portion of the southward flow along Fortymile Wash. The contribution from the Ash Meadows springs area to the Amargosa Farms area may be minimal. The Ash Meadows springs line and high gradient toward the Amargosa Farms area are a reflection of the hydraulic conductivity contrast across a gravity fault that abuts the carbonates of Ash Meadows on the east side with the confining playa deposits on the west side (Naff, 1973).

3.2.3 Well Construction and Water Use in the Amargosa Farms Area

Four sources of information were used to characterize well construction and water use in the Amargosa Farms area. The well permit database, well drillers' logs, and annual water use estimates were obtained from the State Engineer's Office in the Nevada Division of Water Resources (Bauer and Cartier, 1995; State of Nevada, 1997a,b,c). A fourth source was the GWSI portion of the *National Water Information System* developed and maintained by the USGS (see Mathey, 1989). The well permit tables, well drillers' logs, and annual water use tables are recorded by location using the standard range, township, section, quarter section, and possibly quarter-quarter section coordinate system. The tables are organized by hydrographic basin, with the Amargosa Desert being defined as *Hydrographic Basin 230*. The Amargosa Farms area of the Amargosa Desert includes townships (T.) 15, 16, and 17 south (S.) and ranges (R.) 48 and 49 east (E.), as well as the western half of R. 50 E.

The GWSI database uses both the township-range coordinate system as well as the longitude-latitude coordinate system. The wells in Amargosa Farms and Amargosa Valley are taken as those bounded by 116° 21′ 34″ to 116° 37′ 15″ west longitude and 36° 40′ 10″ to 36° 20′ 53″ north latitude. For graphical purposes, township-range coordinates and latitude and longitude coordinates are converted to Universal Transverse Mercator (UTM) section 11 coordinates using the 1927 North American Datum. The former conversion is made directly to UTM by assuming a well is in the middle of the smallest reported area (e.g., quarter section). The latter conversion is made using a USGS-supplied conversion program.

3.2.3.1 Number and Distribution of Wells

A division of wells into two categories based on water use is made here for the purpose of presentation of separate results for different receptor pathways. Domestic and quasi-municipal wells can be characterized as having low but continuous pumping rates throughout the year. Irrigation wells and commercial and industrial wells constitute the large pumping rate category. Although irrigation wells operate intermittently through the growing season, they are approximated in this study as a continuously pumping well at the annual rate estimated from the annual volume pumped.

There are no municipal wells in the Amargosa Farms area. Instead, quasi-municipal wells and domestic wells support direct human use. In addition, a portion of the irrigation wells (well drillers' logs) and industrial wells (Buqo, 1997) may also supply water for direct human use. Five percent of the total irrigation wells recorded in the well drillers' logs also listed domestic use. Dependent on the State Engineers concurrence, the water use category associated with a permit may be changed at a later date.

At the time this analysis was conducted, there were 508 wells recorded in the State of Nevada's well drillers' logs, which date back to at least 1921. Many of these wells are no longer in operation. The GWSI database contains 224 well records for approximately the same area of central Amargosa Desert. The well permit database contained 185 certificated or permitted water rights entries. The estimated water use tables from the State Engineer tracked as many as 72 entries in one year (1996) and a combined 126 different entries over the span 1983–96. Individual domestic wells are not recorded in the State water use tables, nor were quasi-municipal wells, before 1996 for Hydrographic Basin 230.

The distribution of wells spatially and across water use categories is illustrated in Table 3–3 by township and Figure 3–12 by township and range. DOE (1988) identified nine quasi-municipal wells, five commercial wells, and three industrial wells that were active at the time the SCP was prepared. Changes in water use category may occur on permitted or certificated water rights. A majority (70 percent) of all wells were drilled in T. 16 S., with domestic wells concentrated in T. 16 S. and R. 48–49 E. Locations of sections where

14 or more (up to 40) domestic wells have been drilled, according to the well drillers' logs, are marked in Figure 3–12.

3.2.3.2 Statistical Analysis of Well Construction Practices

The GWSI database (Mathey, 1989) also contains information on well construction. Of the 227 wells from the Amargosa Farms region listed in the database, 188 records included water table depth; 113 included screen positions, and 15 records included specific discharge data. Although 18 wells had multiple screened portions; a majority of the screened portions are closely spaced. This is reflected in the fact that there is only a 2 percent (1-meter) difference between the average of the sum of the screened portions and the average of the length of the combined screened portion. Table 3–4 is a statistical summary of relevant well characteristics. Of note are the averages of 11- and 62-meter depths from the water table to the top and bottom of the screened portions, respectively.

3.2.3.3 Estimation of Water Use

For the Amargosa Desert basin, the State has estimated the perennial yield to be about 30×10^6 cubic meters (Buqo, 1997). Committed water use, which includes both certificated and permitted water use, is over 51×10^6 cubic meters. This situation makes it unlikely that new permits will be granted by the State Engineer. In the past few years, proceedings for water users to demonstrate beneficial use have led to thousands of acre-feet of forfeiture for well permits. These proceedings may have had an impact on the number of water users reported in the basin during the mid-1990s (*Op cit.*, pp. 30–31).

Based on information provided by the State Engineer, on a volume basis, the water pumped in the Amargosa Farms area is predominantly used for irrigation and mining (see Table 2–7). The bulk of the mining-related water use is in the playa area, which lies south of the farming area. The Saint Joe Bullfrog gold mine is also a large-volume water user, as reported in the tables for the

Table 3–3. Distribution of Wells by Water Use Across Townships T. 15 S. Through T. 17 S. Using Well Drillers' Logs. There are 34 log entries classified as other. Figure 3–12 identifies the locations of the townships and ranges.

Township	Domestic	Irrigation	Industrial/ Commercial	Quasi-Municipal
T. 15 S.	12	5	2	1
T. 16 S.	207	120	1	3
T. 17 S.	55	65	1	1

Table 3–4. Statistics for Well Construction Practices and Water Level Positions for Wells Recorded in the GWSI Database in the Amargosa Valley and Amargosa Farms Areas

Well Characteristic	Average	Standard Deviation	Number	Minimum	Maximum
Distance from Water Level to Top of Screen (m)	11	13.0	113	0.00	66.0
Distance from Water Level to Bottom of Screen (m)	62	36.7	113	1.7	219
Distance from Water Level to Screen Centerline (m)	35	23.1	113	1.2	124
Total Screen Length (m)	52	33.2	113	0.9	191
Distance from Top to Bottom of Screens (m)	53	33.1	113	0.9	191
Depth of Well (m)	83	42.6	172	0.9	229
Wellbore Diameter (m)	0.31	0.08	112	0.032	0.41
Specific Discharge (m^2/hr)	32.3	33.4	15	2.34	104

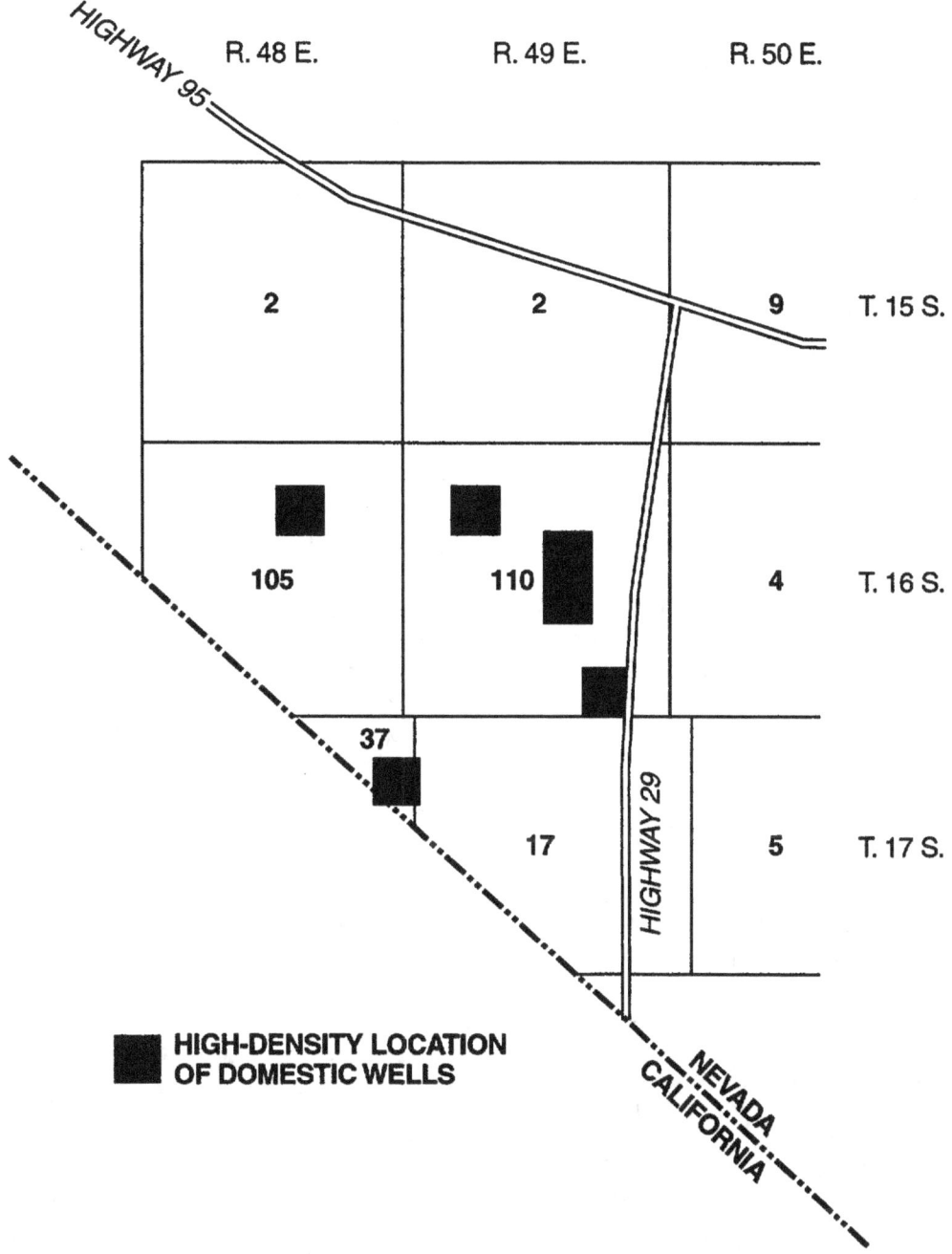

Figure 3–12. **The distribution of domestic and quasi-municipal wells based on Range and Township from well drillers' logs.** The number of wells in each range and township includes those listed for dual usage, domestic, and irrigation. Locations of sections (1 square mile/2.56 square kilometers) with 14 or more domestic wells are highlighted.

Amargosa Desert, but it is not located in the Amargosa Farms region.

Historically, ground-water pumping for irrigation increased significantly in the late 1950s (D'Agnese, 1994; Buqo, 1997). Irrigation use was 3700 cubic meters by 1962, by category, although data for 1984 were not recorded. Table 3—5 is the annual summary of water use, with 1.15×10^5 cubic meters by 1967, and 9×10^6 cubic meters in 1973. Kilroy (1991) reports rapid declines in the water table during the 1970s and less severe declines in the 1980s. The declines are about 6 to 9 meters in three different areas of Amargosa Farms, with the largest being a northeast-trending trough near the Nevada-California border in T. 16 S., R. 48 E. Since 1983, the State Engineer has tabulated water use for individual commercial, mining, irrigation, and quasi-municipal users and summarized annual use by both the Amargosa Desert total and the Amargosa Farms portion total. The annual totals increased significantly from 1993 to 1996, because of large increases in irrigation use, with the largest volume being 16×10^6 cubic meters in 1995.

Individual domestic water use is not recorded in the State Engineers' tables, and individual records for quasi-municipal water users did not start until 1996. Annual estimates were lumped together for the domestic and quasi-municipal/commercial use for each year, although there is some re-categorization occurring in 1996. About 1233 cubic meters (approximately 1 acre-foot) annual usage is assumed for every household, although this may be an over-estimate (Buqo, 1997). [For the purposes of the SCP, DOE used 2482 cubic meters annual consumption (around 1800 gallons/day) citing State Engineer estimates. (See Section A—4 of Appendix A). One acre-foot is about 895 gallons/day or about 3.4 cubic meters/day.]

Individual records for each irrigation user are tabulated (see Appendix E) for the years 1983, and 1985—96, and pertinent summaries are included in Table 3—6. For individual irrigation use, the maximum average daily pumping discharge for any particular user is

3960 cubic meters. The average for all years for an individual irrigation user is 828 cubic meters per day and the range in any particular year is 348 to 1300 cubic meters per day. The number of irrigation users for any year ranged from 15 in 1991 to a high of 55 in 1996. Most of the ground-water pumping occurs in T. 16 S., R. 48—49 E., and T. 17 S., R. 49 E. Figure 3—13 shows the distribution of ground-water pumping for the year 1996 by township and range based on the individual records (no domestic wells are recorded). Figure 3—14 also shows the pumping distribution for 1996 relative to the streamtube model boundaries used in Baca *et al.* (this report). In combination, Figures 3—13 and 3—14 illustrate the fact that large-capacity irrigation wells are generally located to the south of the community of Amargosa Valley where the depth to water is between 10 to 40 meters.

In summary, the typical pumping rates range from 300 to 2000 cubic meters/day for irrigation wells and 3 to 6.8 cubic meters/day for wells supplying water for domestic use. Although the Amargosa Desert hydrographic basin is generally believed to be over-appropriated (Appendix A), actual usage has remained less than 65 percent of the estimated perennial yield. Ground-water pumping in the Amargosa Farms portion of the Amargosa Desert has led to an estimated decline in the water table locally of up to 10 meters (Kilroy, 1991).

3.2.4 3—D Capture Zone Analysis and Plume Delineation

The approach used here to estimate borehole dilution factors in the Amargosa Farms area is to separate them into two components; one, the factor caused by volumetric-flux within a borehole; and two, the factor caused by dispersion during transport. The factor caused by volumetric flux is a comparison of the cross-sectional areas of a capture zone of a pumping well to the intercepted portion of a contaminant plume. In all cases, the areas discussed here refer to the cross-sectional area normal to the principal direction of regional flow. The second component of borehole dilution is the effect caused by dispersion

Table 3–5. Annual Estimates of Water Use by Type (in cubic meters).
Based on data from Mathey (1989).

Year	Irrigation	International Minerals Venture Floridan/American Borate	Domestic	Quasi-Municipal/ Commercial	Amargosa Farms Total	Basin 230 Total
1996	13.60	1.26	0.06	0.25	15.20	30.37
1995	15.20	0.96	0.12	0.01	16.30	32.60
1994	12.30	0.88	0.12	0.01	13.30	26.62
1993	10.68	1.24	0.12	0.01	12.10	24.16
1992	7.05	0.81	0.12	0.01	7.99	15.98
1991	6.09	0.56	0.12	0.01	6.79	13.57
1990	6.11	1.09	0.12	0.01	7.37	14.71
1989	1.90	1.74	0.12	0.01	3.84	7.62
1988	3.67	1.23	0.12	0.01	5.07	10.11
1987	7.03	0.37	0.12	0.01	7.57	15.11
1986	8.09	0.68	0.15	0.01	8.93	17.86
1985	10.45	1.17	0.28	0.03	11.90	23.83
1983	11.23	1.54	0.28	0.03	11.72	24.80

Table 3–6. Summary Statistics of Individual Irrigation Users on an Annual Basis. Based on data from Mathey (1989).

Year	Average (m^3/day)	Number of Users	Minimum (m^3/day)	Maximum (m^3/day)
1996	772	55	3.4	2707
1995	886	51	6.8	2928
1994	771	44	3.4	3960
1993	711	41	3.4	3960
1992	645	30	3.4	3368
1991	1116	15	67.7	3960
1990	645	26	16.9	2675
1989	348	16	16.9	1354
1988	503	20	8.5	2370
1987	900	20	8.5	2912
1986	1300	17	8.5	2928
1985	1134	25	76.9	2928
1983	1083	26	16.9	2116
OVERALL	**828**			

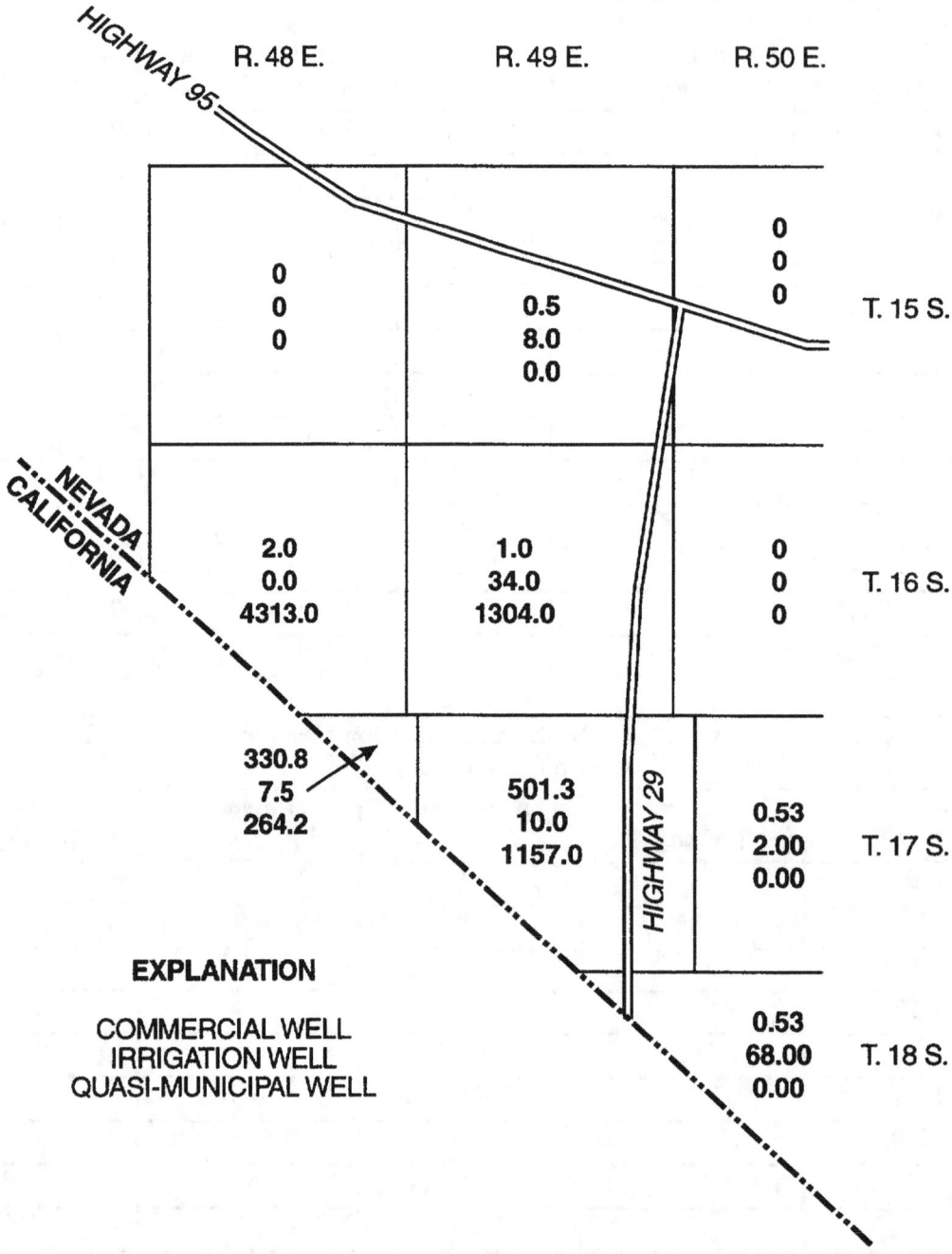

Figure 3–13. Distribution of annual water use (cubic meters) by type and by Range and Township for commercial, irrigation, and quasi-municipal wells for the year 1996.

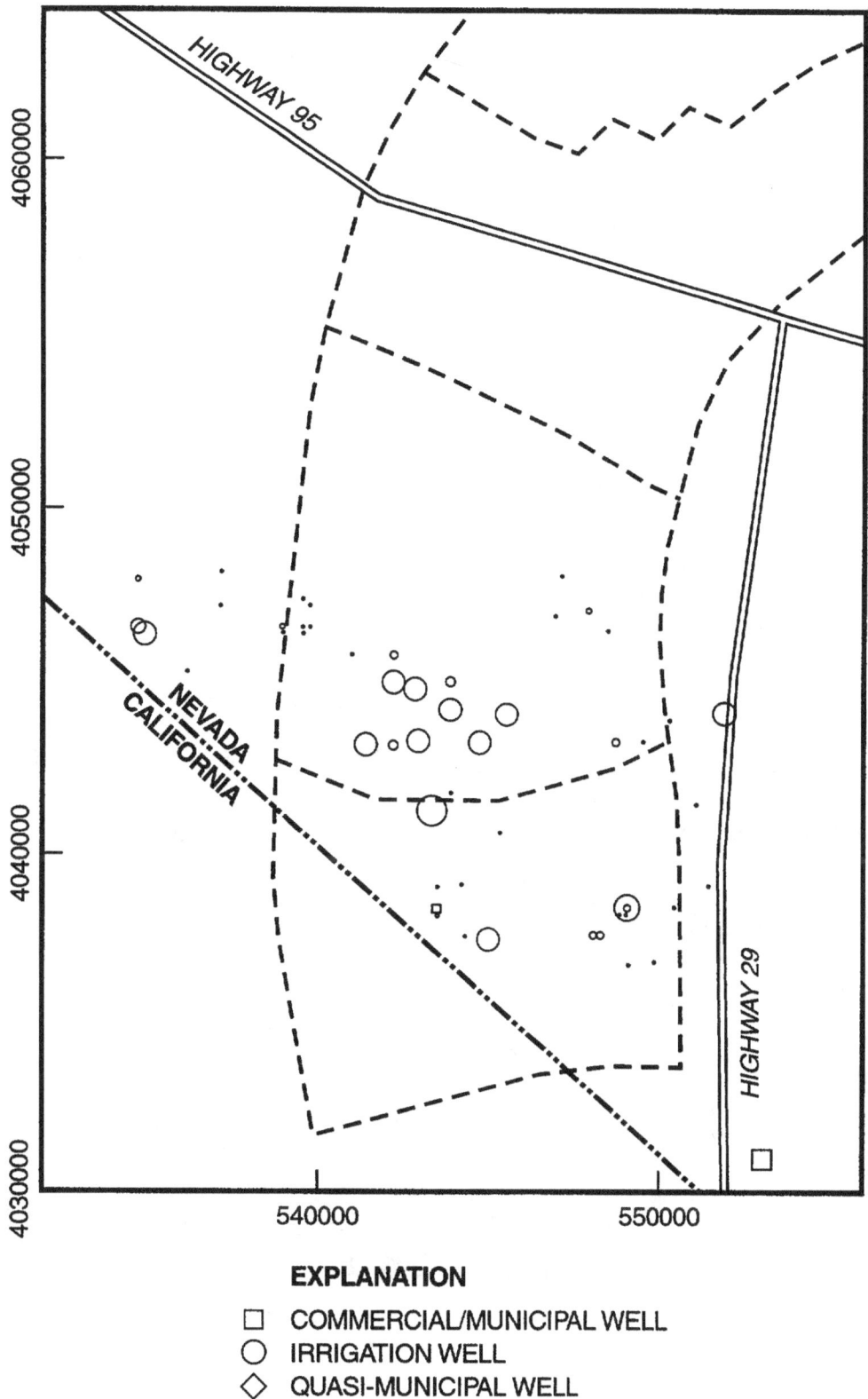

EXPLANATION

□ COMMERCIAL/MUNICIPAL WELL
○ IRRIGATION WELL
◇ QUASI-MUNICIPAL WELL

Figure 3–14. **Distribution of water use by type for the year 1996.** The symbol size for each category is scaled to the magnitude of ground-water pumping volume. Data are from the State of Nevada (1976b) and are converted to UTM Section II coordinates so as to correspond with the streamtube model (dashed lines) of Baca *et al.*(Section 3.1 of this report).

during transport. It is calculated as the ratio of the source concentration to the areal average concentration of the portion of the plume that is captured by a pumping well.

Different configurations for the intersection of the plume and the capture area are possible. For domestic wells, the capture area is generally much smaller than the cross-sectional area of a plume that has undergone transverse spreading caused by macro-dispersion during transport along a 20- to 30-kilometer pathway (Figure 3–15). Hence, there would likely be little borehole dilution even if the well were aligned along the center of the plume, and any borehole dilution that did occur would be caused by vertical gradients in the plume concentration. For a 2–D plume of prescribed thickness, the location of the plume relative to the capture area affects the dilution factor. For irrigation wells, or any high discharge wells, the capture area is generally thicker than the plume. Also, the capture area may be wider or narrower than the contaminant plume, depending on the problem. In all cases, the well is assumed to be in the transverse center of the plume, which is the conservative assumption.

The effects of the regional gradient, transmissivity, pumping rate, and screen position and length on the area of the capture zone can be described in qualitative terms. An increase in transmissivity or the regional gradient will decrease the width of the capture area. An increase in the pumping rate will increase the capture area. An increase in the depth of a partially penetrating well will increase the vertical capture area, but decrease the horizontal capture area. The position and distribution of the plume in relation to the capture zone will control the dilution of the solute in the well bore.

At present, there are few published data for the hydraulic properties, well construction, and pumping in the greater Amargosa Desert area. Moreover, the size, location, and shape of a plume are uncertain and usually must be obtained from large-scale transport modeling. Because of the relative paucity of site-specific data, the focus of this scoping analysis is relating dilution trends to generic well design and plume configuration.

3.2.4.1 Determination of Flow Field and Capture Zone

The ground-water flow simulation program, *GFLOW* (Haitjema, 1995), which is based on AEM, was used to estimate the size and shape of capture zones for individual wells. *GFLOW*

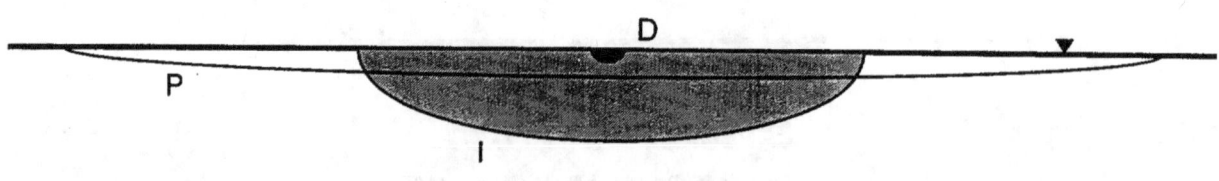

Figure 3–15.   **Relative comparison between cross-sections of contaminant plume (P), irrigation well (I) capture area, and domestic well (D) capture area.**

is designed to simulate partially penetrating wells in a uniform regional gradient. The 3−D effects of the partially penetrating well are superimposed on the 2−D regional flow field. At some distance from the well, the vertical components from pumping become negligible. Forward or backward particle tracking is used in *GFLOW* to determine a capture area at some distant, up-gradient point where vertical flux components become insignificant. This capture area is a vertical plane normal to the direction of regional flow.

3.2.4.1.1   Description of AEM

AEM provides a composite analytic solution that satisfies the differential equation in an unbounded domain. Delineation of streamlines is more precise than with standard numerical methods, since both the head and the velocities are known at every point, rather than solely at computational nodes. Combined 2−D and 3−D modeling is accomplished by superposition of 3−D effects on the general 2−D solution. For example, near a partially penetrating well, a 3−D solution is used. However, at a location sufficiently far from the well, the vertical flow components are negligible and a 2−D approximation to the well may be superimposed on the solution. AEM is not well suited for complex flow problems in which material property heterogeneity is large. The equations for flow in AEM are written in terms of discharge potentials instead of hydraulic head. The discharge potential is defined differently for confined, unconfined, 1−D flow, 2−D flow, or for any analytic element. An advantage of the AEM is that the solution to the equation for flow written in terms of the discharge potential is not dependent on whether the problem domain being solved is confined or unconfined. Once the strength of the potential is known for each analytic element, the head or ground-water discharge may be determined at any point in the flow domain. The solution for the partially penetrating well is based on work by both Muskat and Polubarinova-Kochina (Haitjema, 1995) for the representation of the strength distribution

along a line sink (point sinks along a line) while constraining the discharge to a fixed value.

3.2.4.1.2   Ranges for Parameter Values

Four parameters are varied to test their effects on the capture area, including: (a) pumping rate; (b) well screen position and length; (c) regional gradient; and (d) hydraulic conductivity or transmissivity. The pumping rates range from those typical of domestic wells to those typical of irrigation wells. A reasonable range to use for wells that pump water for domestic use is 1 to 75 cubic meters/day. As noted in Section 3.2.3.3, DOE previously estimated 6.8 cubic meters/day (1800 gallons/day or 2 acre-feet/year) consumption for a single household citing the State Engineer. Buqo's (1997) analysis suggests that this value may have been too high and that a more realistic estimate of use is around 3.4 cubic meters/day (892 gallons/day or 1 acre-foot/year) per household.[9] The high end of the domestic range corresponds to a quasi- municipal well or to multiple domes'-tic wells (10 to 20 family wells) modeled as a single well. For example, the first wells in a potential plume's path are multiple domestic, quasi-municipal, and small commercial wells near the junction of Highways 95 and 29 at

---

[9]Buqo does not explicitly explain how he determined the per capita fresh water consumption for Amargosa Valley. The 1 acre-foot/year per household estimate might be explained by looking to page 31 of his report, where, assuming 2.8 people/household × 319 gallons/day per capita, a value of 892 gallons/day per household or 1 acre-foot/year per household, can be derived. The staff believes that Buqo's estimate of future water consumption was determined following a review of current water use rates for communities in the Amargosa Valley, Beatty, and Pahrump Valley areas. This supposition is based on consideration of the following:

(i) Buqo (*Op cit.*, p. 28) makes reference to the current "assumption" made by the Nevada Division of Water Resources, that domestic water users, including those currently living in the Amargosa Valley area, consume only 1 acre-foot/year per household. The Nevada Division of Water Resources uses the 1 acre-foot/year per household to estimate the domestic and quasi-municipal annual water use for their pumping inventories as reported in the table on page 29 (*Op cit.*); the source data for this table were used in this NUREG. However, it is clear that the numbers in these tables are not tied into population, as only three values appear in the tables from 1983 to 1995 (e.g., 230, 125, and 100 acre-feet).

continued on next page

Amargosa Valley. For irrigation wells, pumping may be as high as 4000 cubic meters/day; however, a more typical large irrigation pumping rate is 2116 cubic meters/day. The average pumping rate from 1983–96 was about 800 cubic meters/day, whereas the lowest was 300 cubic meters/day for any particular year.

The average screened length of the wells in the Amargosa Farms area (top to bottom) is 53 meters; the maximum screen length is 190 meters (Table 3–4). The typical screen position starts 11 meters below the static water level at the time of well construction. Hence, the typical well modeled here will be screened from the water table to 60 meters below the water table.

The range of regional hydraulic gradients considered is 0.001 to 0.01. Bedinger *et al.* (1989) list a value of 0.003 for generic basin fill environments in the Death Valley region. Estimates for the Amargosa Farms area are made from water table maps by Nichols and Akers (1985); DOE (1988); and Kilroy (1991), and fall within the 0.001 to 0.01 range. Most estimates are in the 0.001 to 0.005 range; the 0.01 values are from the east-west gradients immediately south and east of Amargosa Valley and may reflect the abrupt decrease in transmissivity across the northern end of the

---

continued

(ii) Buqo (*Op cit.*, p. 25) estimates the per capita water consumption of Beatty to be 182 gallons/day (0.57 acre-foot/year per household for 2.8 people per household). However, using metered data, actual water consumption in Beatty was reported to be 393 acre-foot/year in 1995 (*Op cit.*, p. 22) instead of the 896 acre-foot/year expected using the DOE estimate of 1800 gallons/day per household (as cited in the SCP). The actual metered amount of 393 acre-foot/year translates to 0.57 acre-foot/year per household.

(iii) Using both metered data and data from other sources, actual per capita water consumption in Pahrump Valley was estimated to be 486 gallons/day per capita (*Op cit.*, p. 37). Buqo notes, but does not properly reference, that this "...value is somewhat higher than the 390 gallons/day per capita water use reported in recent years for Las Vegas...." Nonetheless, in developing this estimate, Buqo does note that "...the higher demand rate in Pahrump Valley reflects in part the disproportionate area of golf courses, tree farms, and parks... relative to the number of residents...." (*Op cit.*).

Finally, using the reported per capita consumption rate of 210 gallons/day in Basse (1990, p. 8; Table 2), for Nye County, multiplied by 2.8 people/household yields 588 gallons/day per household or 0.66 acre-feet/year per household.

---

so-called *Gravity fault*, which has been inferred along the Ash Meadows spring line.

The range of transmissivities reported for basin-fill alluvium in the Death Valley Region is 10 to 400 square meters/day (Winograd and Thordarson, 1975; DOE, 1988; Plume, 1996). Since Amargosa Farms is in the area of sediment facies of lower fans and lowland sediments, rather than the coarser sediments of the upper and middle fan deposits, the saturated hydraulic conductivities should encompass a wide range and be highly heterogeneous relative to other basin-fill. Plume (1996) recently estimated a range of 0.006 to 43 meters/day for saturated hydraulic conductivity, whereas DOE (1988) had earlier reported a range of 0.21 to 2.9 meters/day. The transmissivity (L^2/T) can be expressed as a product of the saturated hydraulic conductivity (L/T) and the saturated thickness (L) of the aquifer.[10] The aquifer thickness is assumed to be 1000 meters for all modeling scenarios.

3.2.4.1.3 Sensitivity Analysis for Capture Zone

The effects of reasonable variations in transmissivity, regional gradient, and pumping rate for all well types are presented in this section. In addition, the effects of screen position and length for domestic wells are presented. Because of their large discharge rates and small degree of well penetration relative to the aquifer thickness, the effects of screen position and length are negligible for irrigation wells. The capture area is determined at an upgradient point from the well location where the flow is essentially 1–D, for example, no longer 3–D. At this upgradient point, the width and thickness are at a maximum for the capture area. A table of the widths and depths of the capture area results is included in Appendix F.

The effect of a partially penetrating well compared with that of a fully penetrating well is shown in Figure 3–16 for a small irrigation well pumping at 300 cubic meters/day. The maximum screen length of 190 meters is marked as maximum on the figure. The

---

[10]L and T refer to physical dimensions of length and time, respectively.

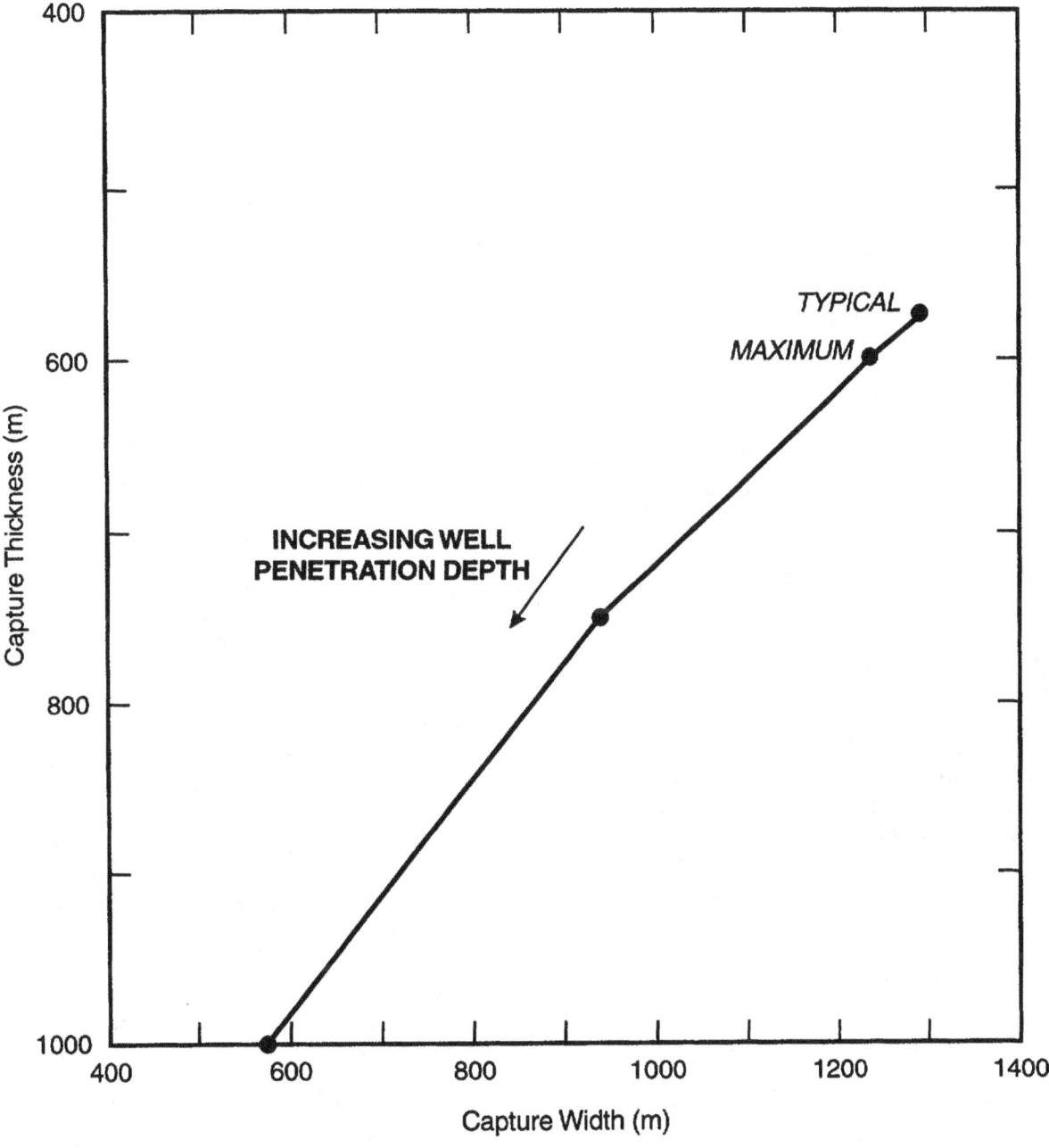

Figure 3-16. **Plot illustrating the effect of well penetration depth (60, 190, 500, and 1000 meters) on a small irrigation well's capture zone width and thickness.** A pumping rate of 300 cubic meters/day and regional gradient of 0.005 are used. The "maximum" denotes the maximum well penetration depth, and "typical" denotes the typical well penetration depth for the Amargosa Farms region.

capture width of the fully penetrating well is about 44 percent of that for the typical partially penetrating well.

Figure 3−17 represents the capture zone width and thickness for combinations of regional gradients and transmissivities for a large pumping rate well of 2116 cubic meters/day. The combination of a regional gradient of 0.001 and transmissivity of 200 square meters/day (the lowest represented here) leads to a capture width of about 5600 meters, which captures nearly the entire width of a streamtube (Baca *et al.*, this report) that brackets the repository. Conversely, a larger gradient (0.005) and higher transmissivity (400 square meters/day) lead to a much smaller capture area, 1800 meters wide by 720 meters deep. A similar trend also occurs for low-discharge, domestic wells (Figure 3−18). Maximum capture areas are created either by the smallest regional gradient (0.001) or the lowest transmissivity (10 square meters/day) for capture thicknesses up to 200 meters. Since the Darcy velocity is a function of the hydraulic conductivity and hydraulic gradient, Figures 3−17 and 3−18 also illustrate the effect of Darcy velocity on capture width and thickness.

The effect of pumping rate on the capture area is presented in Figure 3−19. A gradient of 0.005 and transmissivity of 100 square meters/day are used for all pumping rates. Of significance for borehole dilution is that all wells in the low pump-rate range (less than 75 cubic meters/day) will have capture areas that would be much less than the plume area, based on 3−D advection-dispersion equation modeling.

3.2.4.2 Radionuclide Plume Shape and Location

The potential release and subsequent movement of radionuclides from a potential Yucca Mountain repository is likely to follow a path generally southeast to Fortymile Wash and then continue south-to-southwest toward the Amargosa Valley and Amargosa Farms areas. The shape of the plume at a 30-kilometer distance from the proposed repository, in particular the amount of vertical

dispersion that leads to an increase in the plume thickness, is yet another unknown. Vertical dispersion may be limited by the possible presence of confining horizons (Naff, 1973) in the lake bed facies of the basin-fill sediments.

Given the uncertainty of the plume configuration, two scenarios were analyzed. The first scenario was a plume modeled for 3−D dispersion. The second scenario is a plume for which no vertical dispersion is incorporated. Both scenarios are simulated to a steady-state solution, to assess a wide range of dimensions for the plume when it reachs a well.

Dispersion, adsorption, and radioactive decay of the radionuclides will occur along this transport path. Adsorption and decay depend on the particular radionuclide. However, most of the radionuclides of concern in the far field (e.g., ^{237}Np, ^{129}I, ^{99}Tc) have half-lives greater than 10,000 years. Adsorption also depends on the surface mineralogy of the porous media as well as the chemistry of the ground water. There are no site-specific data for adsorption in terms of distribution coefficients for the valley fill sediments. Considering these points, the conservative approach of neglecting both decay and adsorption is adopted.

To evaluate dilution caused by both vertical and horizontal capture of clean water by a pumping well, an estimate of the shape of a potential plume is needed. Specifically, the configuration of the cross-sectional area perpendicular to the direction of flow is needed. Analytic solutions to the advection-dispersion equation were previously used to describe the plume shape at down-gradient points from the two recent TSPAs conducted for Yucca Mountain (TRW Environmental Safety Systems, Inc., 1995; Kessler and McGuire, 1996). The advection-dispersion equation for 3−D dispersion and 1−D flow is:

$$\frac{\partial C}{\partial t} = D_x \frac{\partial^2 C}{\partial x^2} + D_y \frac{\partial^2 C}{\partial y^2} + D_z \frac{\partial^2 C}{\partial z^2} - V \frac{\partial C}{\partial x}$$

$$(3-2)$$

where C is the concentration, D_x, D_y, and D_z are the dispersion coefficients in the coordinate directions, V is the seepage velocity in the principal direction of flow, and t is time.

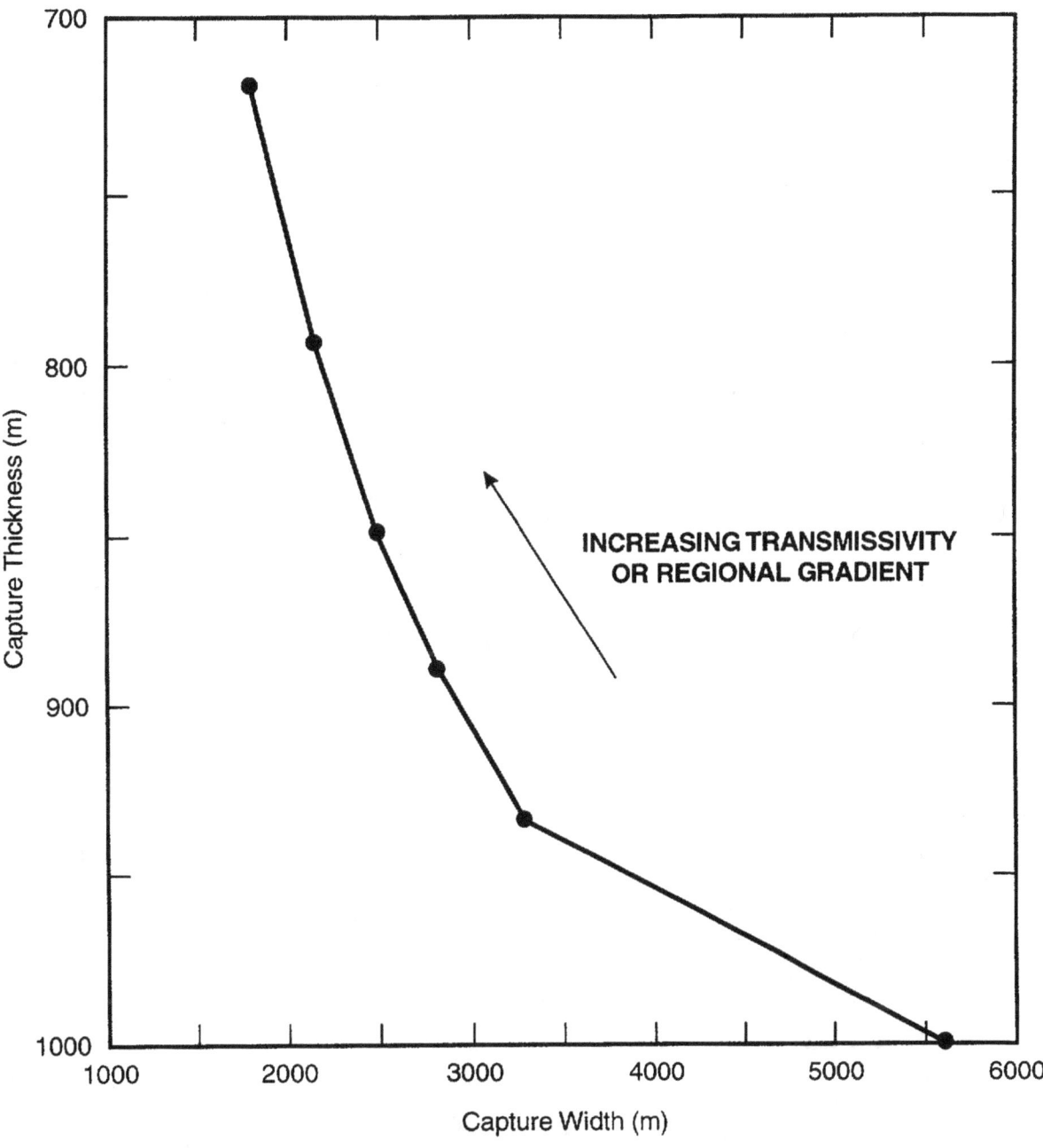

Figure 3–17. Effect of combinations of transmissivity (200, 300, and 400 square meters/day) and hydraulic head gradient (0.001, 0.002, 0.003, and 0.005) on a large irrigation well's capture zone width and thickness. A pumping rate of 300 cubic meters/day is used.

NUREG–1538

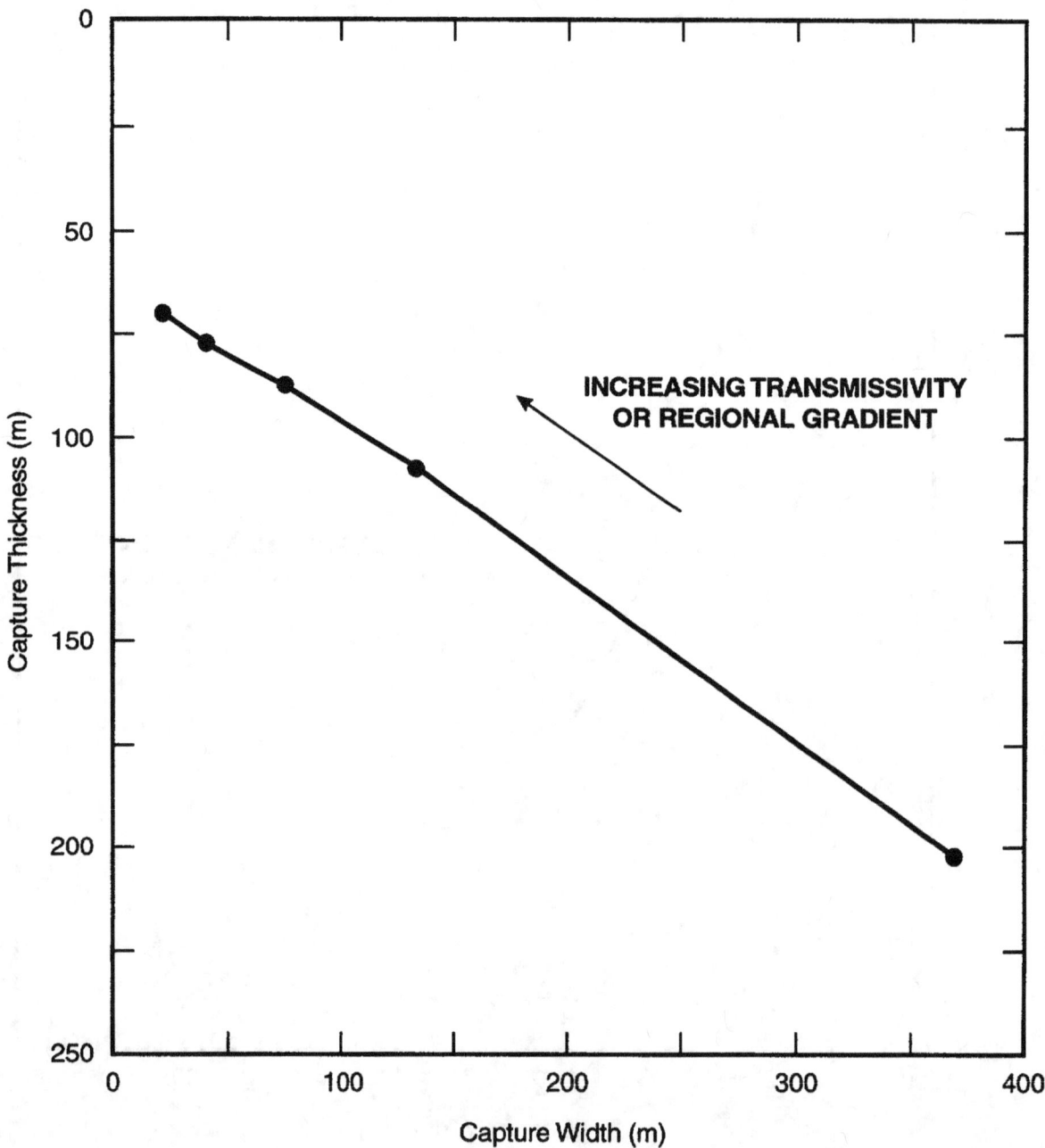

Figure 3–18. **Effect of combinations of transmissivity (50, 100, 200, 300, and 400 square meters/day) and hydraulic head gradient (0.001, 0.0025, 0.005, and 0.01) on a domestic well capture zone's width and thickness.** A pumping rate of 3 cubic meters/day and the screened portion is 60 meters long, starting from the water table.

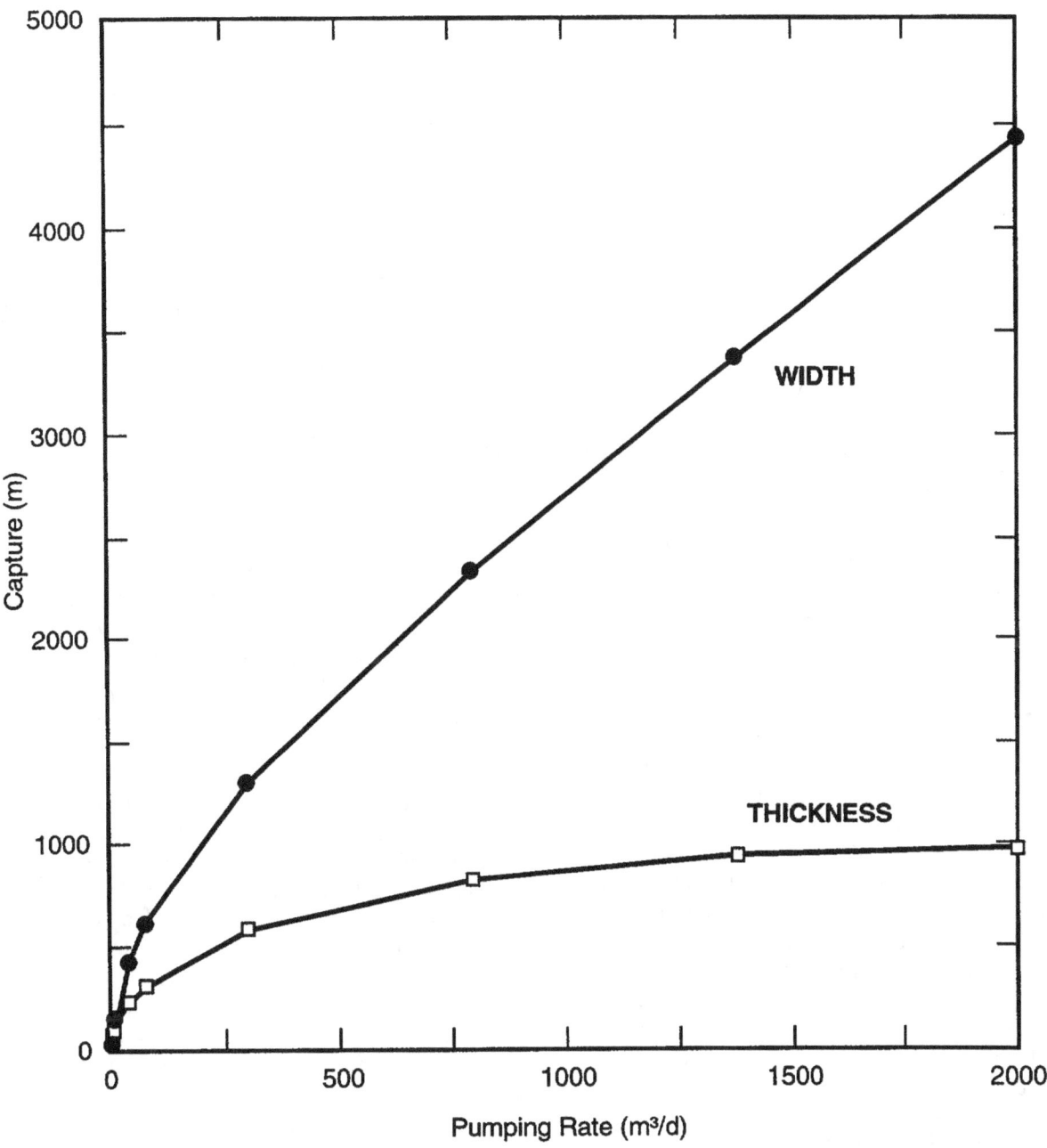

Figure 3–19. **Plot illustrating the effect of pumping rate (range: 1 to 2000 cubic meters/day) on the capture zone's width and thickness.** A transmissivity of 100 square meters/day and regional gradient of 0.005 are used.

3.2.4.2.1   Transport Parameters

The initial source size, seepage velocity, and the dispersivities all control the plume configuration after 30 kilometers of advective-dispersive transport. Kessler and McGuire (1996) noted the inverse relationship between source size and mean concentration reductions. They also found that a doubling of the source thickness led to an increase of 17 percent in the plume width at 25 kilometers. Similarly, a 60-percent increase in the source width led to an increase of 6 percent in the plume width at 25 kilometers. For the purposes of this scoping analysis, the source size will be held constant at 500 by 25 meters for the 3−D dispersion plumes and 500 meters wide for the 2−D dispersion plumes.

Since transport simulations were run to steady state to determine maximum plume dimensions, a reasonable value of the seepage velocity along the flow path from the repository to potential receptor locations is needed. Seepage velocity is related to the Darcy flux by porosity. The Darcy flux for the transport analysis need not be the same as that for the capture zone analysis since the former represents the porous media and hydraulic head gradients from the repository to a potential receptor location approximately 30 kilometers to the south. Seepage velocity for transport was chosen to represent the mean pathway velocity from the tuff through the alluvium. Baca *et al.* (this report) report calculated ranges of Darcy flux of 0.01 to 3.7 meters/year for the saturated tuff aquifer and 0.4 to 0.7 meters/year for the alluvium. Assuming a porosity of 0.3 for the alluvium, the seepage velocity would be in the range of 1.3 to 2.3 meters/year. Kessler and McGuire (1996) used a seepage velocity of 1.76×10^{-6} meters/second (55 meters/year) although it is not clear whether site-specific information— gradient, hydraulic conductivity, porosity—was used to obtain this estimate. The value of 2.4 meters/year used here for seepage velocity is closer to that approximated from the Darcy flux values reported by Baca *et al.*

The value of the concentration at the source is chosen to approximate a mass-release rate of 10 Ci/year, which is taken as an upper bound for mass-release rates, as delineated by the ^{99}Tc example in Mohanty *et al.* (1997). Assuming that dispersion from the constant concentration boundary is negligible, the constant source concentration corresponding to a 10-Ci/year release rate is 1.11×10^{-6} Ci/liter for a source size of 500 by 25 meters and a Darcy velocity corresponding to a seepage velocity of 2.4 meters/year with a porosity of 0.3.

Simulation of 3−D dispersion requires values for the longitudinal, horizontal transverse, and vertical transverse dispersivities. Generally, dispersivities are considered to be scale-dependent (Gelhar *et al.*, 1992). TSPA−1995 (TRW Environmental Safety Systems, Inc., 1995) assumed relatively large transverse dispersivities that resulted in exceptionally large plumes (especially in the vertical direction) and correspondingly large dilution factors (10^3 to 10^5). Kessler and McGuire (1996) recognized that there is a limit to the heterogeneity scale that a plume would encounter, although they nonetheless used a vertical transverse dispersivity equal to the horizontal dispersivity. This seems unlikely in light of the lithologic layering in the alluvial basin sediments that would result in differences between the vertical transverse and horizontal dispersivities. Contaminant plumes generally exhibit limited vertical spreading (Gelhar *et al.*, 1992). Thus, small vertical transverse dispersivities values are likely. In a literature review of measured dispersivity values and ratios, Gelhar *et al.* note that horizontal-to-vertical transverse dispersivity ratios are often 1 to 2 orders of magnitude different. Furthermore, the measured vertical dispersivity values were all reported, in Gelhar *et al.*, to be less than 1 meter, generally, in the range 0.06 to 0.3 meters for scales ranging from 20 meters to 10 kilometers. In addition, the vertical transverse dispersivity values exhibited no scale dependency. The longitudinal and horizontal transverse dispersivity are scale-dependent, with their ratio equal to one order of magnitude. For the constant concentration source, the longitudinal dispersivity and the velocity do not affect the mean plume concentration in steady-state transport. Plume size is controlled by the transverse dispersivities.

In this scoping analysis, the location of the radionuclide source area is the same as that assumed by Kessler and McGuire (1996). A patch source area aligned perpendicular to the flow direction is located 5 to 7 kilometers from the repository, as described in Kessler and McGuire, as opposed to locating the source area at the repository. The conceptual model consists of a release from the repository reaching the 5 to 7 kilometer location from where it is modeled as a patch source, to obtain a plume configuration 15 to 25 kilometers farther along Fortymile Wash toward the Amargosa Farms area. Noting the variations in the flow path lengths; the quasi-municipal and domestic wells are about 20 kilometers from the repository. The majority of irrigation wells are first encountered approximately 25 kilometers from the accessible environment, or 30 kilometers from the repository.

3.2.4.2.2 Plume Dimensions for 3–D Dispersion from Constant Concentration Source

The analytic solution to Equation (3–3) for the constant concentration patch source, as described in Wexler (1992) is:

$$C(x,y,z,t) = \frac{C_0 \, x \, \exp\left[\frac{Vx}{2D_x}\right]}{8\sqrt{\pi D_x}} \int_0^t \tau^{-\frac{3}{2}} \exp\left[-\left(\frac{V^2}{4D_x} + \lambda\right)\tau - \frac{x^2}{4D_x\tau}\right]$$

$$\left[erfc\left(\frac{(Y_1 - y)}{2\sqrt{D_y\tau}}\right) - erfc\left(\frac{Y_2 - y}{2\sqrt{D_y\tau}}\right) \right]$$

$$\left[erfc\left(\frac{(Z_1 - z)}{2\sqrt{D_z\tau}}\right) - erfc\left(\frac{(Z_2 - z)}{2\sqrt{D_z\tau}}\right) \right] d\tau$$

(3–3)

where C_0 is the concentration at the source, τ is a dummy variable of integration for time, λ is the decay coefficient, *exp* is the natural exponential, and *erfc* is the complementary

error function. The dispersion coefficients in the $x, y,$ and z directions are defined as the products of the seepage velocity and the dispersivities in the $x, y,$ and z directions, respectively. This equation is the solution to the 3–D solute transport equation for a vertical patch source aligned normal to the principal direction of flow, where the patch dimensions are defined by $y_2—y_1$ and $z_2—z_1$. The solution to the advection-dispersion equation is valid for a 1–D uniform flow field and 3–D dispersion for a constant concentration source in an aquifer of infinite depth and lateral extent. Adsorption and radioactive decay of the solute are incorporated into the solution, but were not used in this study. Tables 3–7 and 3–8 contrast plume width and thickness for various sets of dispersivity values at 20 and 30 kilometers, respectively, from the repository. The longitudinal dispersivity value is reported in the tables, but its magnitude is not a controlling factor for the results. The plume width and thickness are delineated at a threshold concentration of approximately $C_0 \times 10^{-4}$. The P–DF is also included in Tables 3–7 and 3–8. These values will be used as a reference point for the dispersion-based dilution factors that are estimated later in Section 3.2.4.4. At 30 kilometers, a reduction of the transverse dispersivities by 80 percent leads to almost a 50-percent reduction in plume width and thickness when the ratio of the horizontal and vertical transverse dispersivities is kept at an order of magnitude. The percentages are approximately the same for the 15-kilometers results. Similarly, a 50-percent reduction in the transverse dispersivities leads to almost a 25-percent reduction in plume width and thickness at 30 kilometers.

3.2.4.2.3 Plume Dimensions Neglecting Vertical Dispersion for Constant Concentration Source

From the literature (Bedient *et al.*, 1994), it is evident that existing plumes (caused either by accidental contamination or by deliberate injection of tracers for experimental purposes), are often confined to a thin layer near the water table. Exceptions occur in areas of high infiltration. Thus, the conservative case

Table 3–7. Plume Configuration and Point Dilution Factors at 20 Kilometers from the Proposed Repository (15 Kilometers from Source Area) for a Range of Dispersivity Values. C_c is the centerline concentration. The source area is 25-meters thick by 500-meters wide.

a_x:a_y:a_z (m)	Thickness (m)	Width (m)	P—DF = C_0/C_c
20:2:0.2	330	2200	6
50:5:0.5	480	3100	13
100:20:2	830	5200	48
100:10:1	640	4000	25
100:10:0.1	250	4300	9

Table 3–8. Plume Configuration and Point Dilution Factors at 30 Kilometers from the Proposed Repository (25 Kilometers from Source Area) for a Range of Dispersivity Values

a_x:a_y:a_z (m)	Thickness (m)	Width (m)	P—DF = C_0/C_c
20:2:0.2	410	2600	9
50:5:0.5	580	3700	21
100:20:2	970	5800	80
100:10:1	780	4800	41
100:10:0.1	290	5200	14

is to assume no vertical dispersion so the plume remains the same thickness as the source area, but is dispersed laterally. This conceptual model for plume movement can be modeled using the following solution for 2–D dispersion for a line source of specified width and constant concentration (Wexler, 1992):

$$C(x,y,t) = \frac{C_0 x}{4\sqrt{\pi D_x}} \exp\left(\frac{Vx}{2D_x}\right) \int_0^t \tau^{-\frac{3}{2}} \exp\left[-\left(\frac{V^2}{4D_x} + \lambda\right)\tau - \frac{x^2}{4D_x\tau}\right]$$

$$\left[erfc\left(\frac{(Y_1 - y)}{\left(2\sqrt{D_y\tau}\right)}\right) - erfc\left(\frac{(Y_2 - y)}{\left(2\sqrt{D_y\tau}\right)}\right)\right] d\tau$$

(3–4)

The solution to Equation (3–4) is implemented in Wexler's *STRIPI* computer program. The solution for the line source can be extended to any source thickness. In light of the arguments presented in the previous section, a reasonable selection of sets of dispersivities is 20:2, 50:5, and 100:10 for the longitudinal and transverse directions (Table 3–9). Although these dispersivities are not strictly comparable to the dispersivities used for the 3–D analysis (i.e., no transverse vertical dispersivity for the 2–D analysis), the resulting plume widths were somewhat similar for the 2–D and 3–D analyses. The 2–D analysis, without vertical dispersion, resulted in increases in plume width of 6 to 16 percent at 20 kilometers from the repository, and 10 to 21 percent at 30 kilometers from the proposed repository, compared to plume widths in the 3–D analysis for corresponding dispersivities.

Table 3—9. Plume Configuration in Terms of Width at 20 and 30 Kilometers from the Proposed Repository (15 and 25 Kilometers from the Source Area) and Point Dilution Factors for a Source Area Width of 500 Meters and No Vertical Dispersion

$a_x:a_y$ (m)	Width at 20 Kilometers (m)	P—DF = C_o/C_c at 20 Kilometers	Width at 30 Kilometers (m)	P—DF = C_o/C_c at 30 Kilometers
20:2	2,330	1.5	2860	1.8
50:5	3,410	2.1	4230	2.6
100:10	4,640	2.8	5800	3.6

3.2.4.3 Borehole Dilution Factors Based on Volumetric Flux

Volumetric flux-based borehole dilution factors (F—BDFs) are determined by comparison of the plume and capture zone configurations (Figure 3—15). The ratio of the cross-sectional area of the capture zone to the cross-sectional area of the portion of the plume that intersects the capture area in the plane perpendicular to the principal direction of flow is the dilution factor caused by borehole mixing, based on volumetric flux comparisons. In other words, the F—BDF is the ratio of the capture and the intersection area. No credit is taken for the distribution of the concentration across the plume in the calculation of the F—BDF. All plumes in this section are modeled from a constant concentration source.

Generally, the plumes are wider than the capture zone but not as thick. Four plume scenarios are chosen to represent a range of conditions. The first and second scenarios are 10-meter- and 25-meter-thick plumes for which no vertical dispersion has occurred. The width of the plume depends on the horizontal transverse dispersivity that is used. For domestic wells, it does not matter what horizontal transverse dispersivity is chosen since all plumes are wider than all domestic well capture zones. The third and fourth scenarios incorporate vertical dispersion with dispersivity ratios of 20:2:0.2 and 100:10:0.1. The F—BDFs for the third and fourth scenarios are presented for the high-volume irrigation well pumps.

3.2.4.3.1 Domestic Wells

The plume configuration that results from 3—D dispersion from a constant concentration source (see Tables 3—7 and 3—8) will generally be larger than the capture area of a single domestic well, a closely spaced collection of domestic wells, or a

quasi-municipal well for wells typical of the Amargosa Farms area. Hence, with the assumption of a uniform plume concentration, there will be no borehole dilution. Only for the smallest vertical transverse dispersivity values (less than 0.2) and for the largest pumping volumes from a closely spaced collection of domestic and quasi-municipal wells will there be vertical gradients that are strong enough to capture clean water and provide borehole dilution.

For a typical domestic well that pumps about 6.8 cubic meters/day (1800 gallons/day), the F—BDF decreases from 10 to 4, when the plume thickness increases from 10 to 25 meters at the 30-kilometer distance (Figure 3—20). The difference in the factors increases as the pumping rate increases. The F—BDFs for the 10-meter plume range between 7 and 26 for pumping rates in the range of domestic and quasi-municipal wells. Similarly, the F—BDFs for the 25-meter plume range between 3 and 10.

The position of the screened portion of the well does not have a significant effect on domestic wells for the 25-meter-thick plume until the screened portions are lower than three standard deviations from the average screen position (Figure 3—21). The limited effect of screen position is caused by a

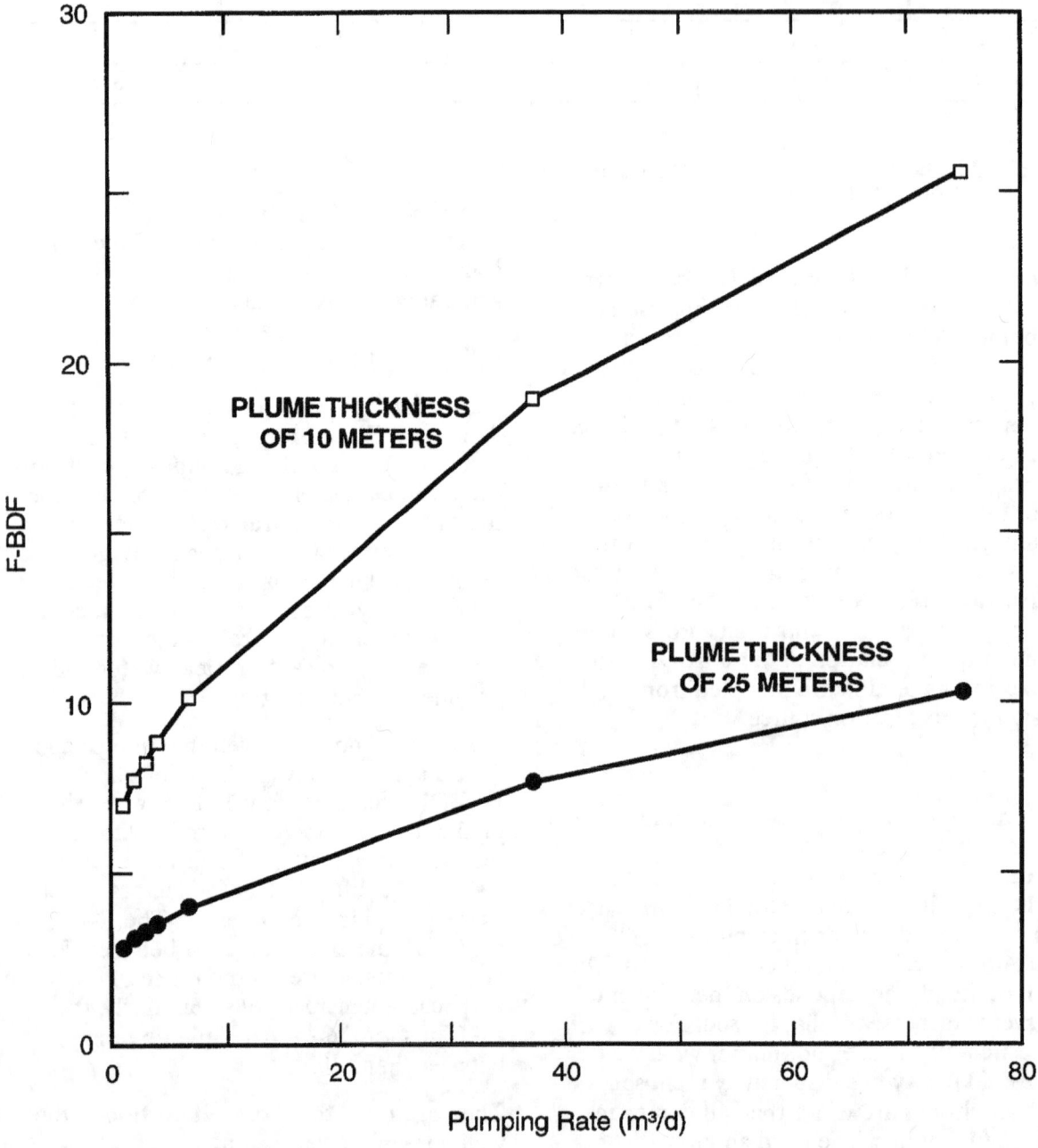

Figure 3–20. **Effect of pumping rate (range: 1 to 75 cubic meters/day) on the flux-based borehole dilution factor for plumes of thickness 10 and 25 meters (no vertical dispersion).** The regional gradient is 0.005 and the transmissivity is 100 square meters/day for all cases.

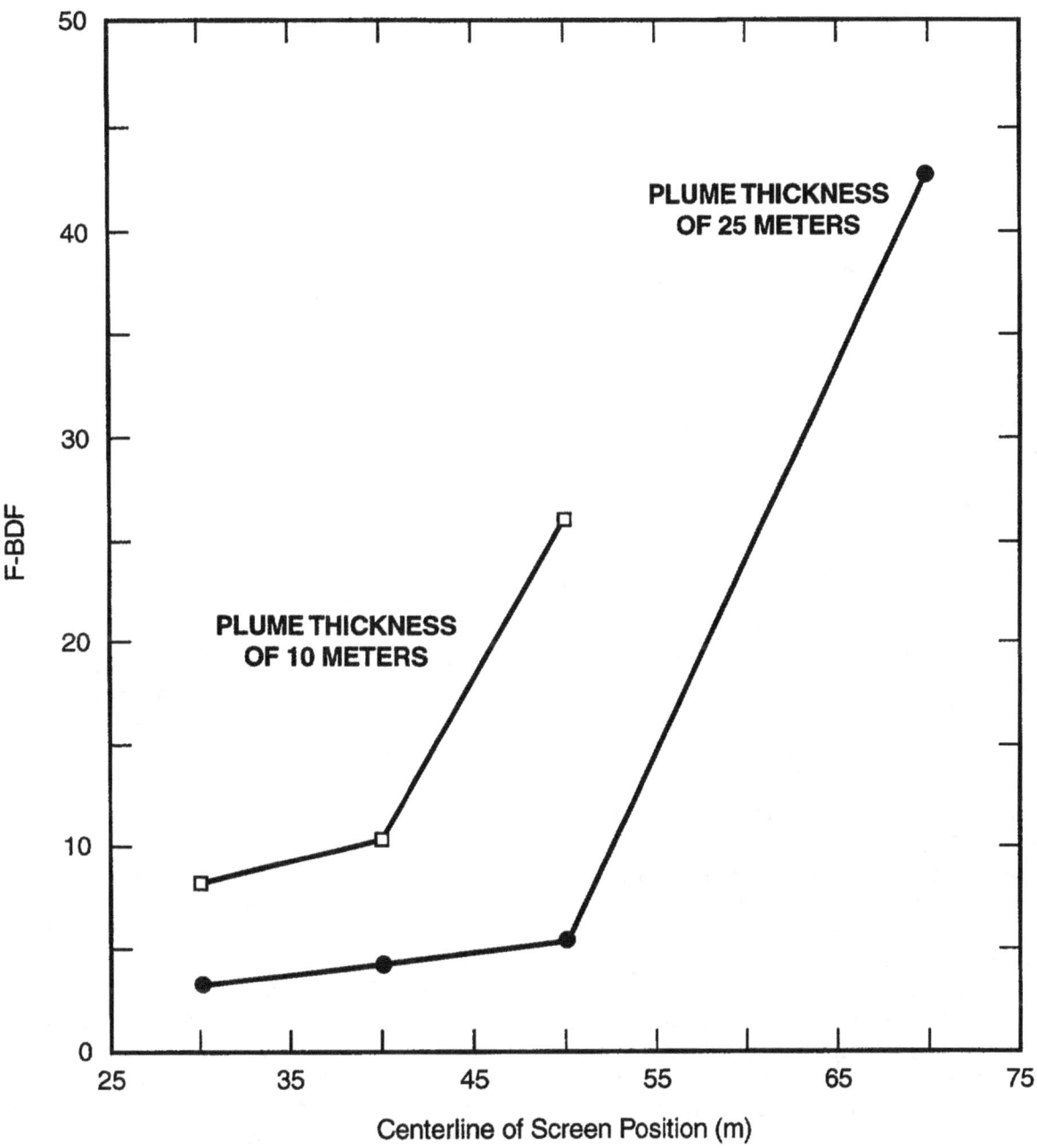

Figure 3–21. **Effect of screen position for domestic-sized wells on the flux-based borehole dilution factor for plumes of thickness 10 and 25 meters (no vertical dispersion).** All screen lengths are 60 meters, the regional gradient is 0.005, and the transmissivity is 100 square meters/day for all cases.

combination of the center of mass of the plume being near the water table, as well as the small impact on the capture area caused by different screen position and lengths. Within about two standard deviations from the average position of the screen, the F−BDFs do not vary by more than a factor of 2. In all scenarios, the plume is assumed to be at the water table. The borehole dilution factors exhibited greater sensitivity to the screen position by a variation of the F−BDF of 8 to 26 for approximately two standard deviations from the average position of the screen.

The effects of transmissivity and regional gradient on F−BDFs, for the 10- and 25-meter-thick plumes with no vertical dispersion, are not significant until the smallest values of transmissivity and gradient are used (Figures 3−22 and 3−23). For transmissivities greater than 50 square meters/day, the F−BDFs are in the range of 7 to 10 for the 10-meter-thick plume and 3 to 4 for the 25-meter-thick plume. A regional gradient of 0.001 leads to a F−BDF of 13 for the plume thickness of 10 meters, whereas for the larger gradients, the F−BDFs range from 7 to 10. The F−BDFs for the 25-meter-thick plume are between 3 and 5 for a regional gradient range of 0.001 to 0.01.

3.2.4.3.2 Irrigation Wells and Plumes with No Vertical Dispersion

The F−BDFs were calculated for irrigation wells using the scenario of a 25-meter-thick plume with no vertical dispersion. In this scenario, the large vertical gradients and deep capture for the wells lead to large amounts of clean water mixing in the borehole with the contaminated water from the plume. Depending on the capture zone width and the plume width, some horizontal mixing of clean and contaminated water may occur. The width of the plume depends on the transverse dispersivity.

Figure 3−24 shows the F−BDFs for a well pumping rate of 300 to 2000 cubic meters/day for plumes using three different dispersivity values. Since the plume width decreases as the dispersivity decreases, the F−BDF increases as the dispersivity decreases. This effect is not

present at the low pumping rates for the particular flow field parameters chosen for this comparison. The F−BDFs range from 19 to 49 for all dispersivity combinations. It must be re-emphasized that the F−BDF only reflects the effects of contaminant concentration reduction in the borehole and not the effects of dispersion on the resident or aquifer contaminant concentrations. This explains the otherwise counter-intuitive observation that, for high capacity wells, the F−BDF increases as the transverse dispersivity decreases.

3.2.4.3.3 Irrigation Wells and Plumes with Vertical Dispersion

The F−BDFs are calculated for irrigation wells using the scenario of a plume where 3−D dispersion from a constant concentration source occurs. The effect of dispersion on the concentration distribution across the plume is not considered here; only its effect on the overall the shape of the plume is considered in the dilution factors. Generally, the capture zones are thicker and narrower than the thin but wide plumes. Depending on the dispersivity values used for the plume and the pumping rate and hydraulic properties used for the capture zone, the capture zones may be wider than the plume. Only for low pumping rates are the plumes thicker than the capture zone; this occurrence leads to no volumetric-based borehole dilution.

Plume shapes using dispersivities of 100:10:0.1 meters and 20:2:0.2 meters are compared to capture areas, to calculate F−BDFs. The plume for the 100:10:0.1-meter scenario is wider but thinner than the plume for the 20:2:0.2-meter scenario. Figures 3−25 to 3−27 show the effects of pumping rate, transmissivity, and regional gradient on the F−BDFs, which generally range from 1 to 5, regardless of dispersivity values used. For the pumping rate (Figure 3−25) and the regional gradient (Figure 3−27) curves, the two dispersivity sets intersect because of the interplay between the thickness of the plume (the 20:2:0.2-meter plume is thicker) and the point where the entire plume is captured (the 100:10:0.1-meter plume is larger in area).

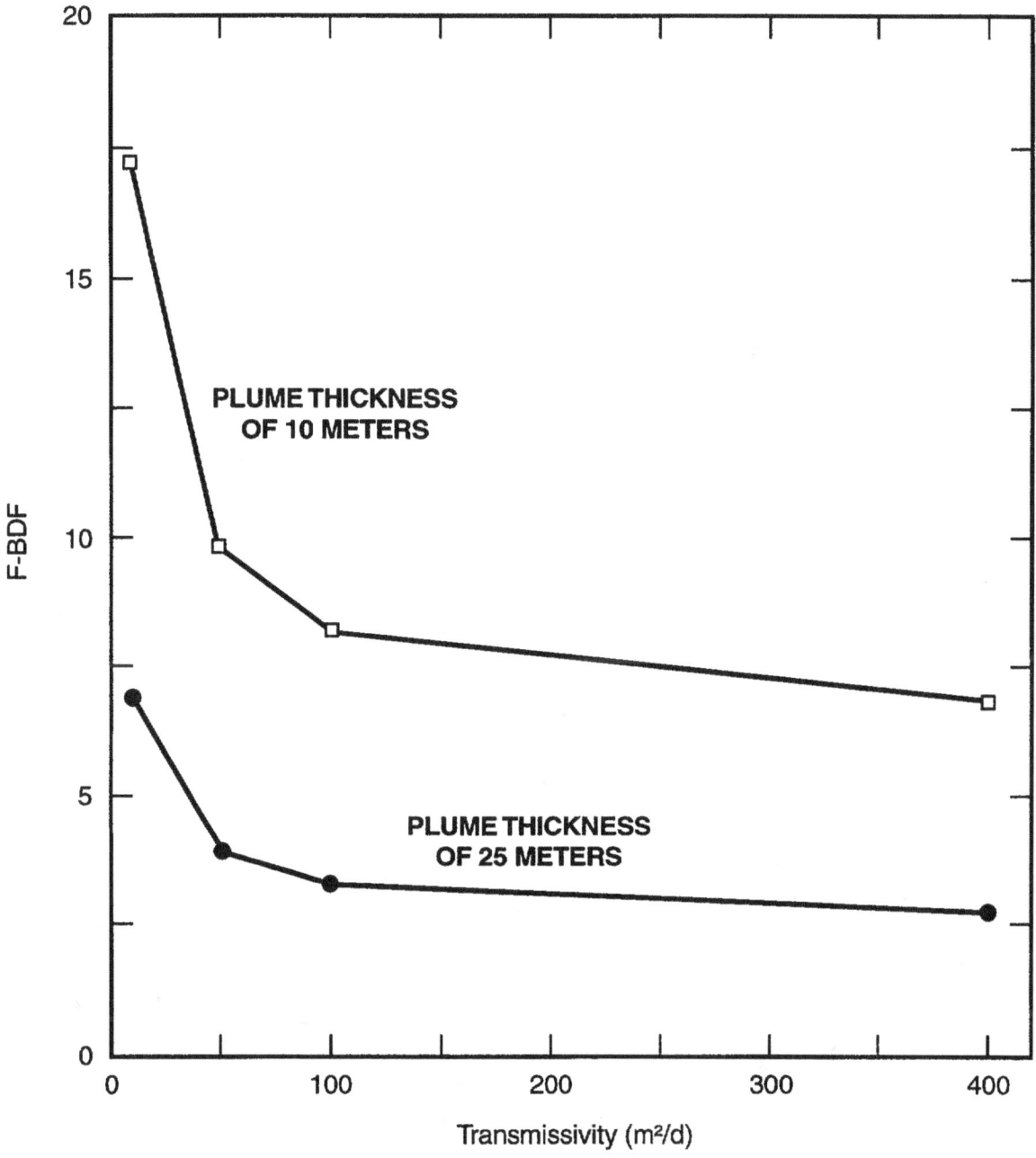

Figure 3–22. **Effect of transmissivity (10, 50, 100, and 400 square meters/day) on the flux-based borehole dilution factor for plumes of thickness 10 and 25 meters (no vertical dispersion).** The regional gradient is 0.005 and the pumping rate is 3 cubic meters/day for all cases.

NUREG–1538

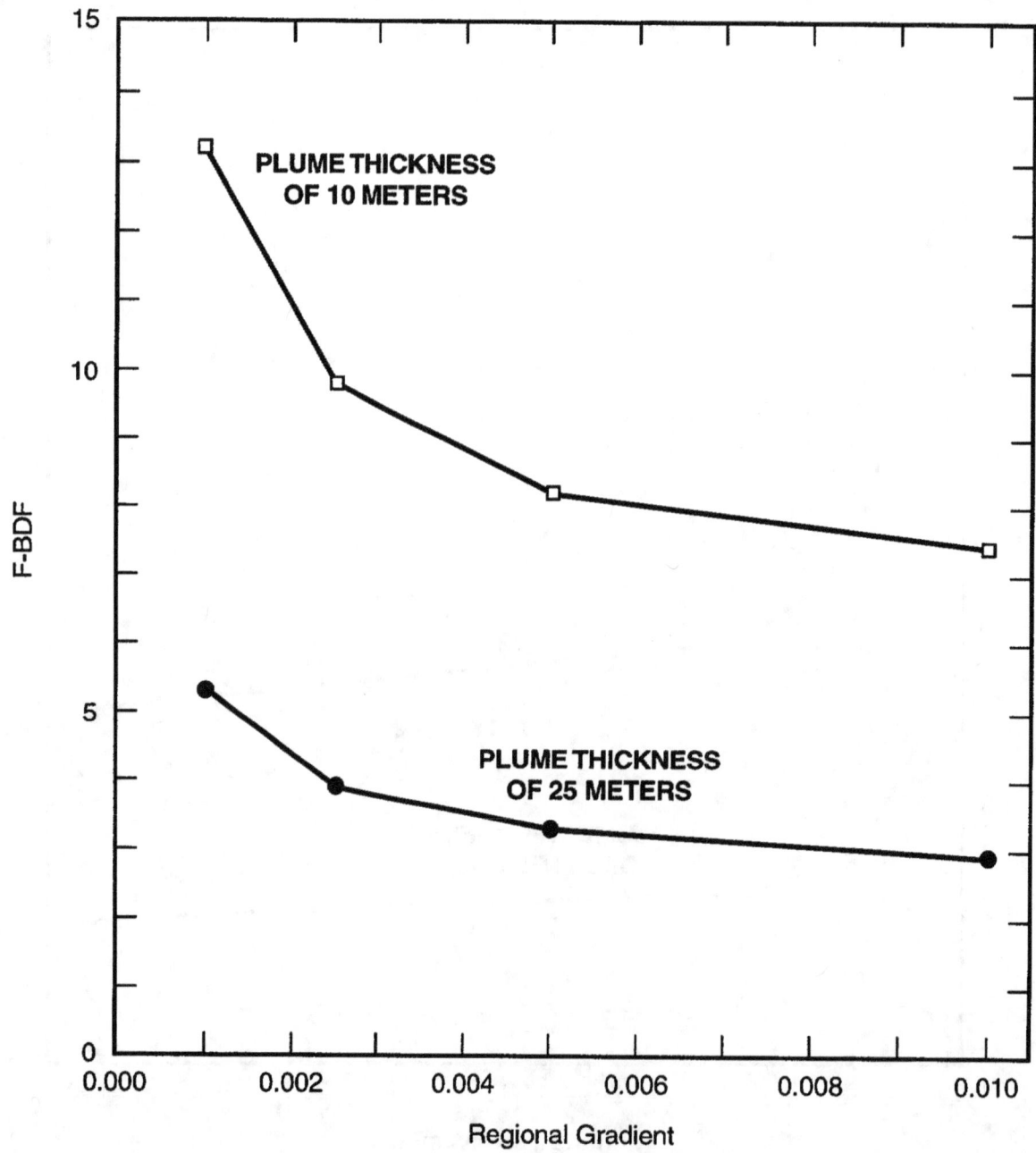

Figure 3–23. Effect of the regional gradient (0.001, 0.0025, 0.005, and 0.01) on the flux-based borehole dilution factor for a domestic-sized well and plumes of thickness 10 and 25 meters (no vertical dispersion). The transmissivity is 100 square meters/day and the pumping rate is 3 cubic meters/day for all cases.

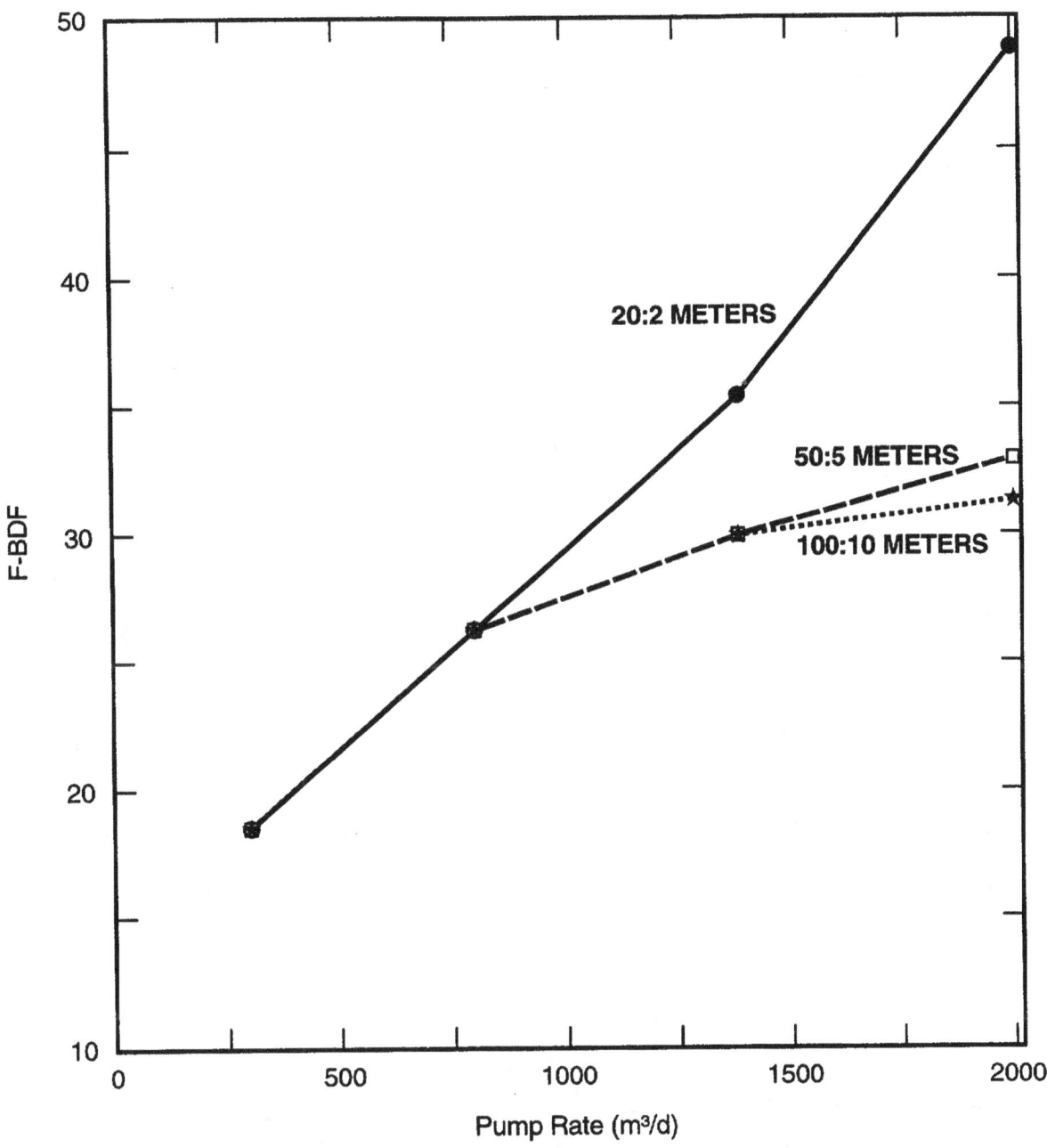

Figure 3—24. **Effect of pumping rate on flux-based borehole dilution factors for irrigation wells and a 25-meter-thick plume with no vertical dispersion.** Three curves are plotted for different sets of dispersivity values.

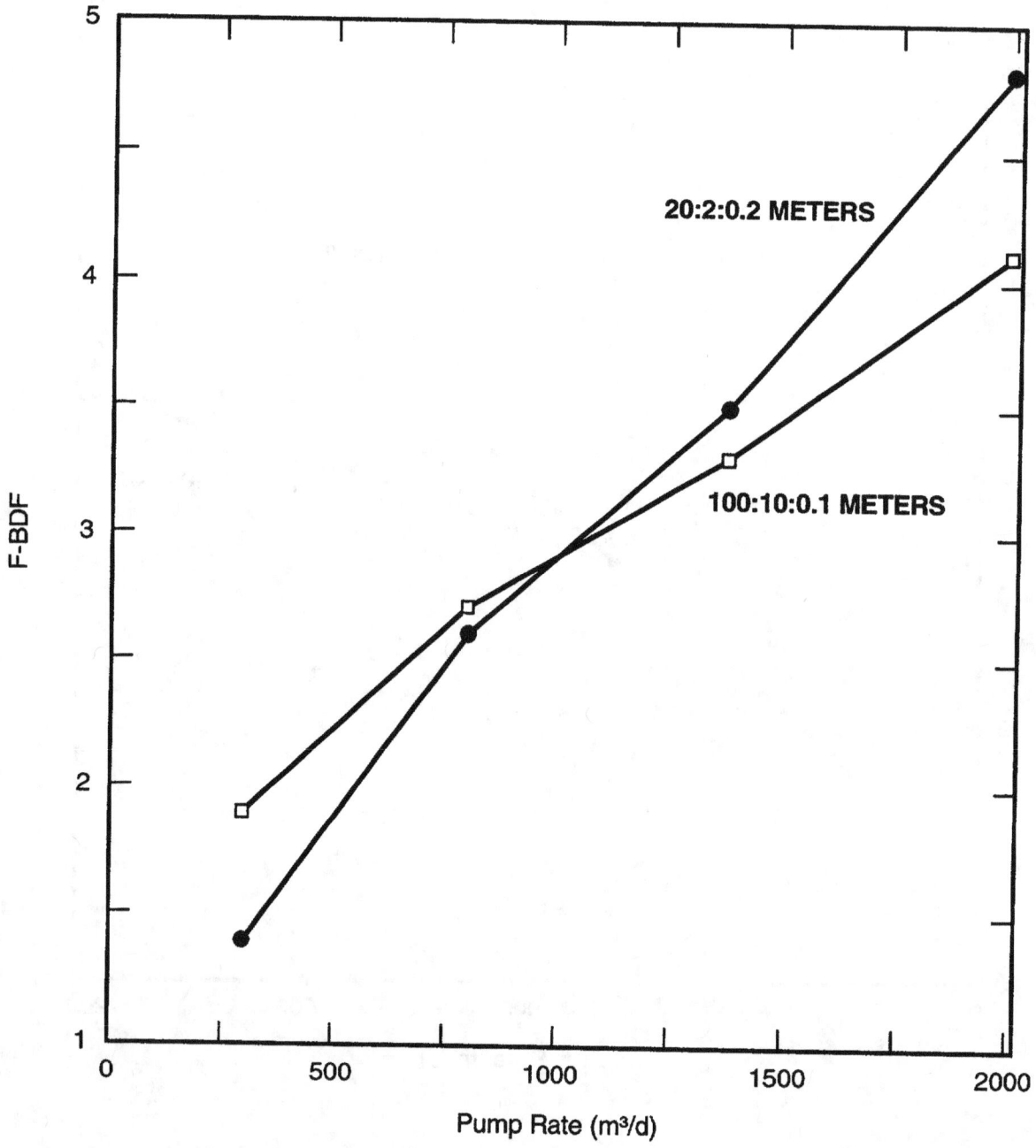

Figure 3–25. **Effect of pumping rate on borehole dilution factors for irrigation-sized wells and a plume with 3–D dispersion.** Curves are plotted for two sets of dispersivity values.

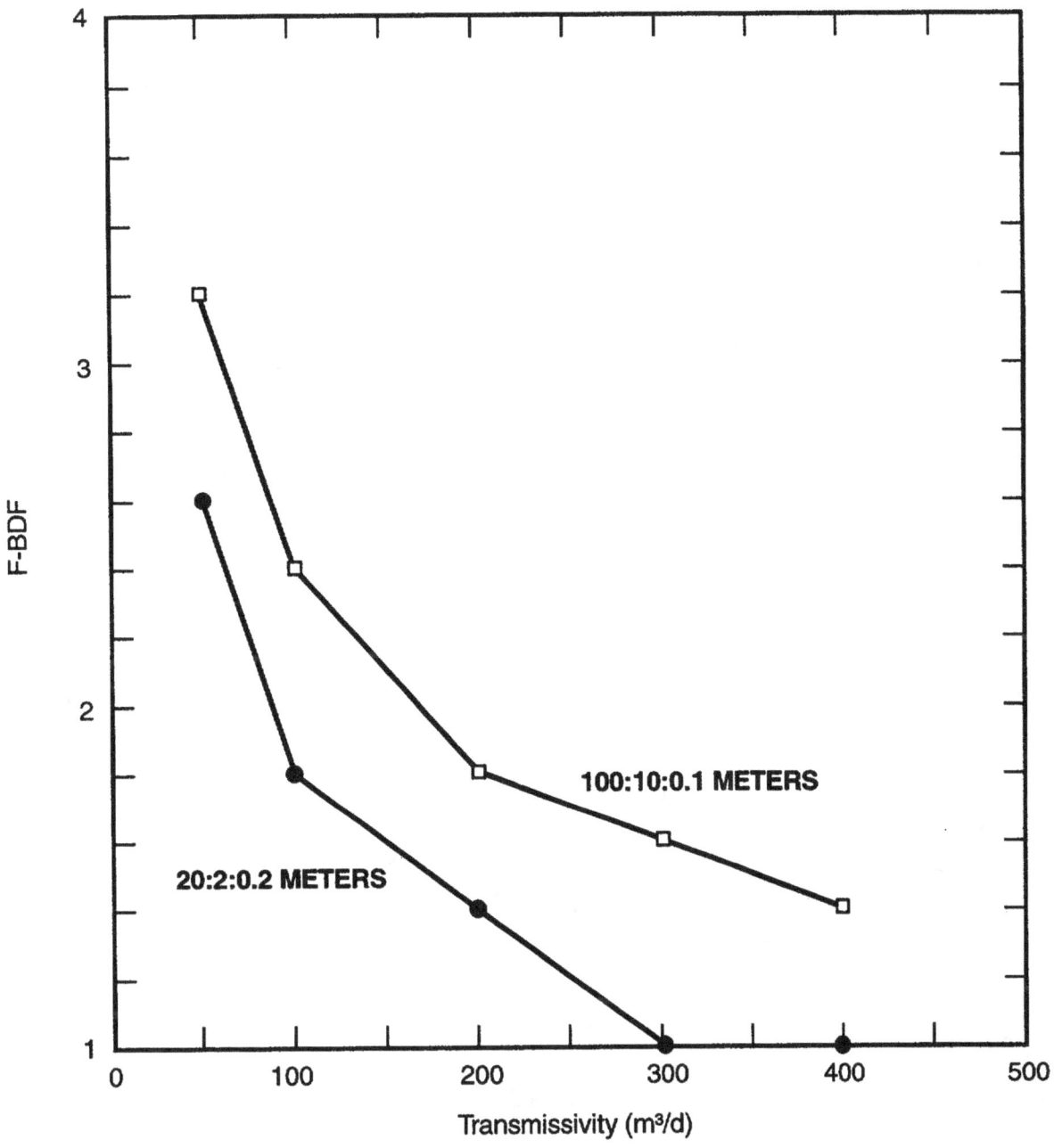

Figure 3–26. **Effect of transmissivity (range: 50 to 400 square meters/day) on borehole dilution factors for irrigation-sized wells and a plume with 3–D dispersion.** Curves are plotted for two sets of dispersivity values.

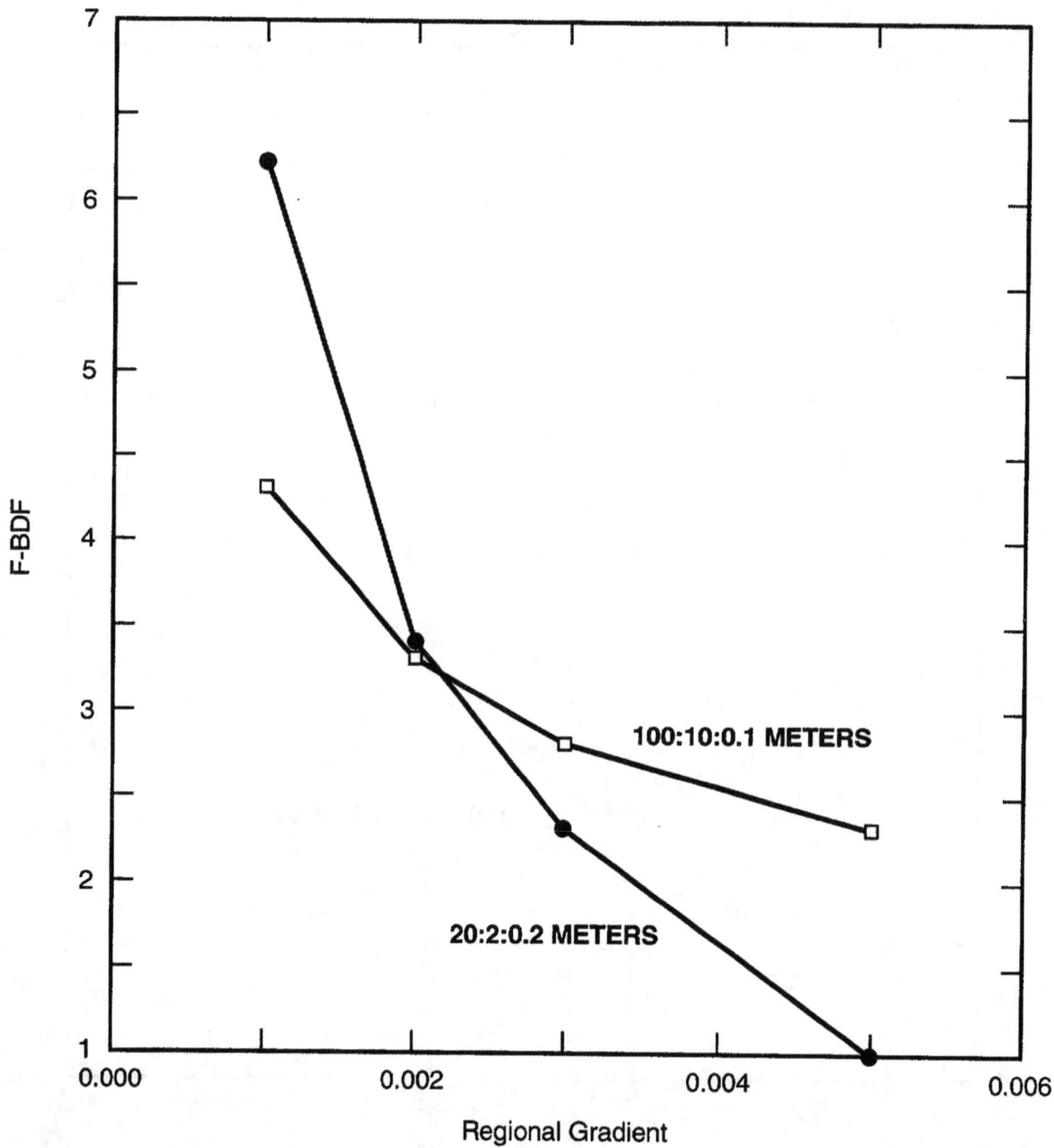

Figure 3–27. **Effect of regional hydraulic gradient (range: 0.001 to 0.0005) on borehole dilution factors for irrigation-sized wells and a plume with 3–D dispersion.** Curves are plotted for two sets of dispersivity values.

In summary, the effect of the plume size has the largest effect on the F–BDF. The values of the dilution factors are tabulated in Appendix F.

The plume width may increase or decrease for diverging/converging flow fields, respectively, but the volumetric flux does not change.

3.2.4.4 Borehole Dilution Factors Based on Dispersive Transport

The F–BDFs estimated in the previous section do not account for the concentration distribution of a migrating plume. Kessler and McGuire (1996) accounted for dispersion during plume migration by assuming the dilution factor was the ratio of the source concentration to the centerline concentration. Implicit in their assumption is that the plume has a uniform concentration equal to the centerline value that they justify as a conservative choice in terms of eventual dose to a receptor group. This section will address the effect on borehole dilution of a concentration distribution within a plume.

The *transport dispersion-based borehole dilution factor* (T–BDF) was calculated by integrating the concentration distribution across the area of the portion of the plume that is captured by a pumping well. Portions of the plume not captured by the well do not contribute radionuclide mass to the well. The T–BDF was estimated by numerical integration of the concentration distribution in the area of the plume that was captured. The total borehole dilution factor can be estimated by linear combination of the F–BDF and T–BDF. The effect of domestic and irrigation wells on T–BDFs varies significantly because of the thickness of the capture area, and will be presented separately.

3.2.4.4.1 Domestic Wells

Figures 3–27 and 3–28 illustrate the effect of the concentration distribution within a plume on the T–BDF for two different plume configurations; a thin plume (25 meters) with no vertical dispersion and a 3–D dispersion plume. The T–BDF for the thin plume is nearly constant and its value is close to that of the P–DF (1.8) for pumping rates in the range of domestic and quasi-municipal wells (Figure 3–27). The T–BDF for the plume with 3–D dispersion vary from 9 to 18, increasing as the pumping rate increases. The larger values of T–BDF indicate the significance of pumping from less concentrated portions of the plume as compared with the centerline. T–BDF is inversely proportional to the transmissivity (Figure 3–28) with values ranging from 12 to 9 as transmissivity increases for the 3–D dispersion plume. Smaller transmissivity values lead to larger capture areas thus drawing water from portions of the plume with lower concentration. The effect of hydraulic gradient is similar to that of transmissivity.

3.2.4.4.2 Irrigation Wells

Figures 3–29 and 3–30 illustrate the effect of the concentration distribution on borehole dilution for irrigation wells. For the plume configuration with 3–D dispersion, the T–BDFs are as much as 5 times larger (Figures 3–29 and 3–31) than those for the domestic wells, because of the large thickness of the irrigation capture area drawing in portions of the plume with low concentrations. Unlike a domestic well, the T–BDF, for a thin plume (i.e., 25 meters) increases as the pumping rate increases. The straight line increase in T–BDF for the plume with 3–D dispersion and dispersivity ratio of 100:10:0.1 meters reflects the large size of the plume relative to the capture areas (Figure 3–31). The plateau in the curve for the 3–D plume with dispersivity ratio of 20:2:0.2 meters at the larger pumping rates is caused by the entire plume being captured.

For transmissivity increases from 50 to 400 square meters/day, the T–BDF decreases from 48 to 18 for the 3–D plume with dispersivity ratio of 20:2:0.2 meters, and from 43 to 30, for the 3–D plume with dispersivity ratio of 100:10:0.1 meters. Effects caused by hydraulic gradient are similar to those of the transmissivity (see Appendix F).

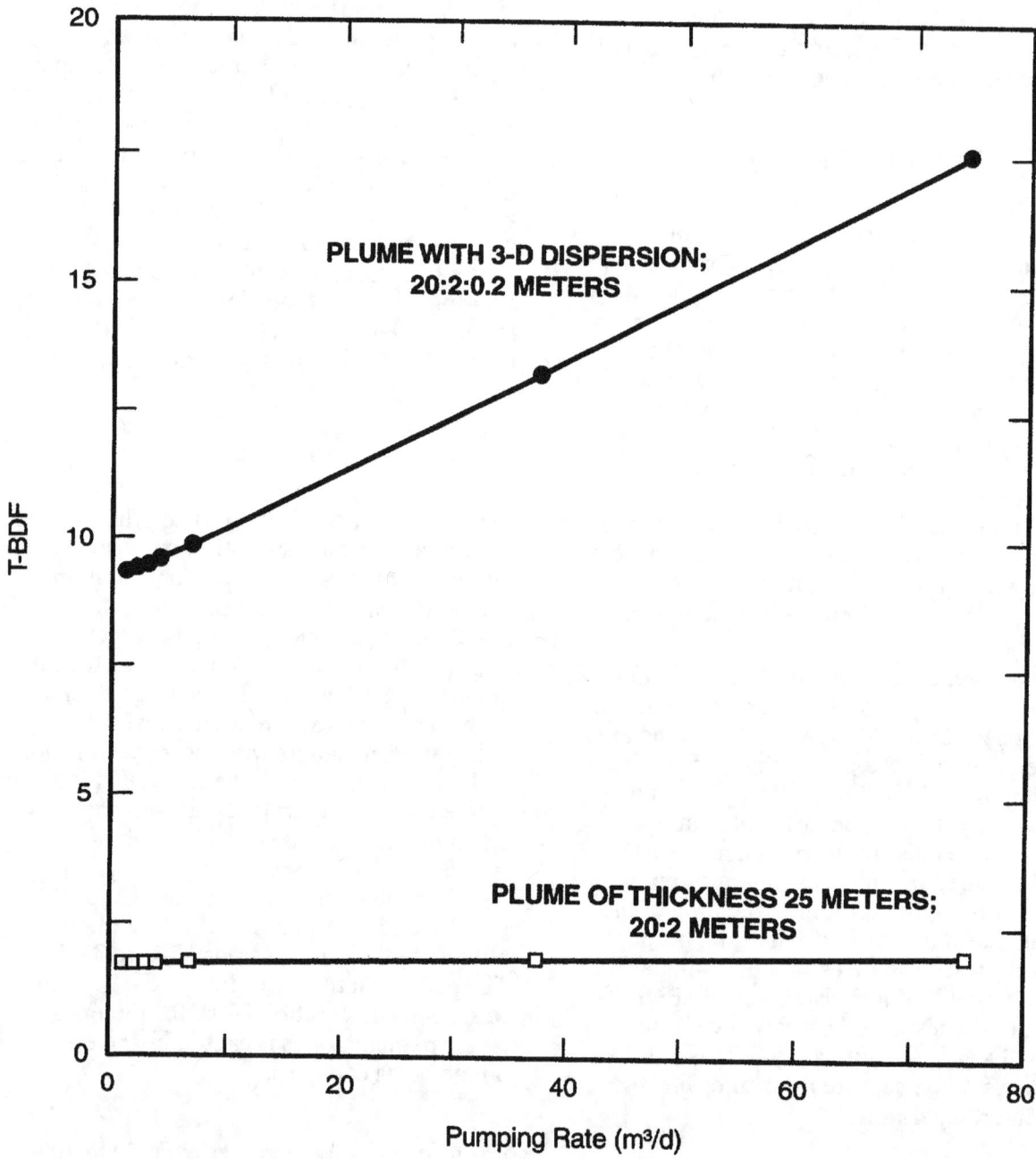

Figure 3–28. **Effect of pumping rate (range: 1 to 75 cubic meters/day) for domestic wells on transport dispersion-based borehole dilution factors for two different plume configurations. A thin plume with no vertical dispersion and a 3–D dispersion plume both with dispersivity ratios as noted in the plot.**

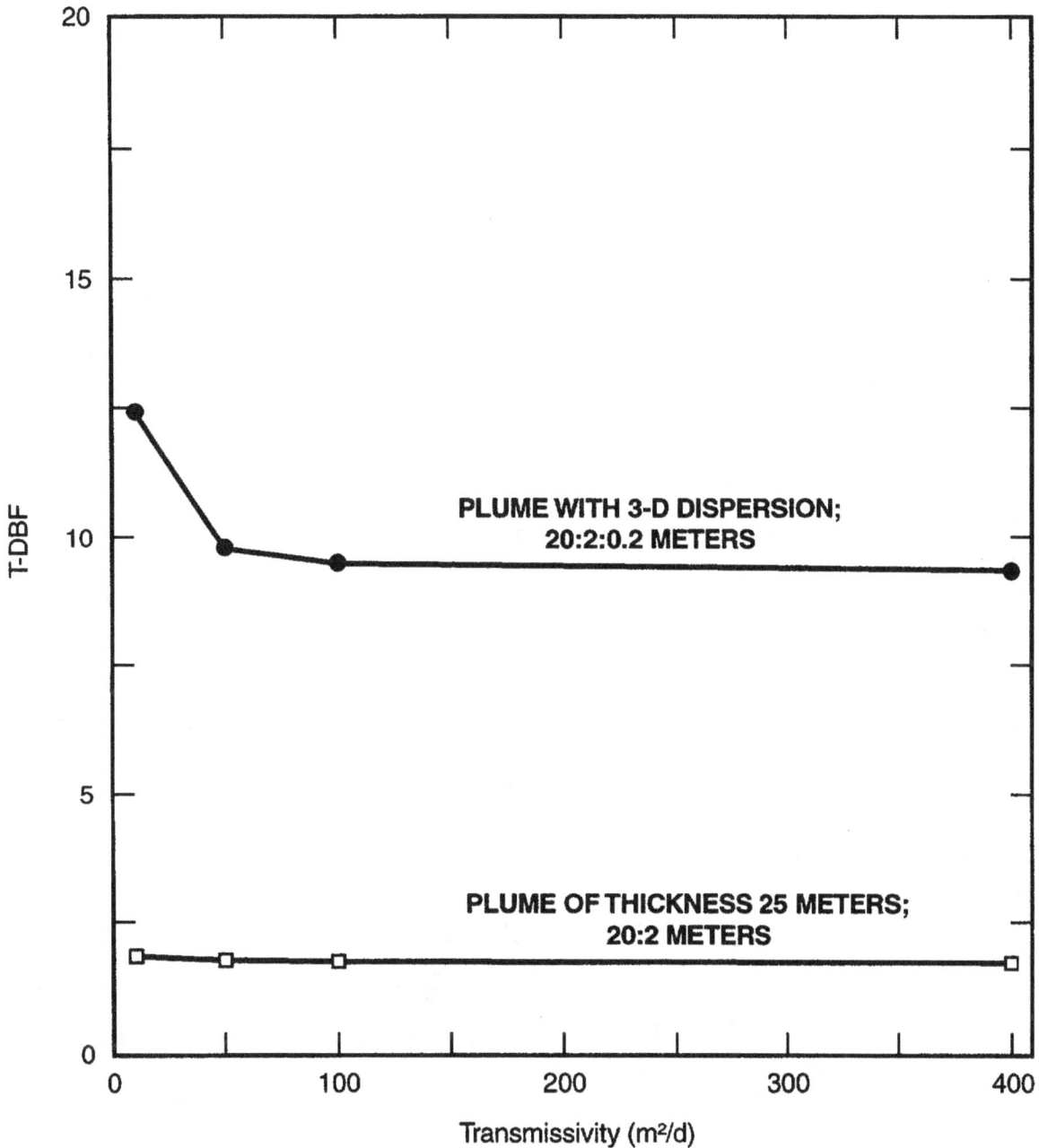

Figure 3–29. **Effect of transmissivity (range: 10 to 400 square meters/day) for domestic wells (Q = 3 cubic meters/day) on transport dispersion-based borehole dilution factors for two different plume configurations.** A thin plume configuration with no vertical dispersion and a 3–D dispersion plume, both with dispersivity ratios as noted in the plot.

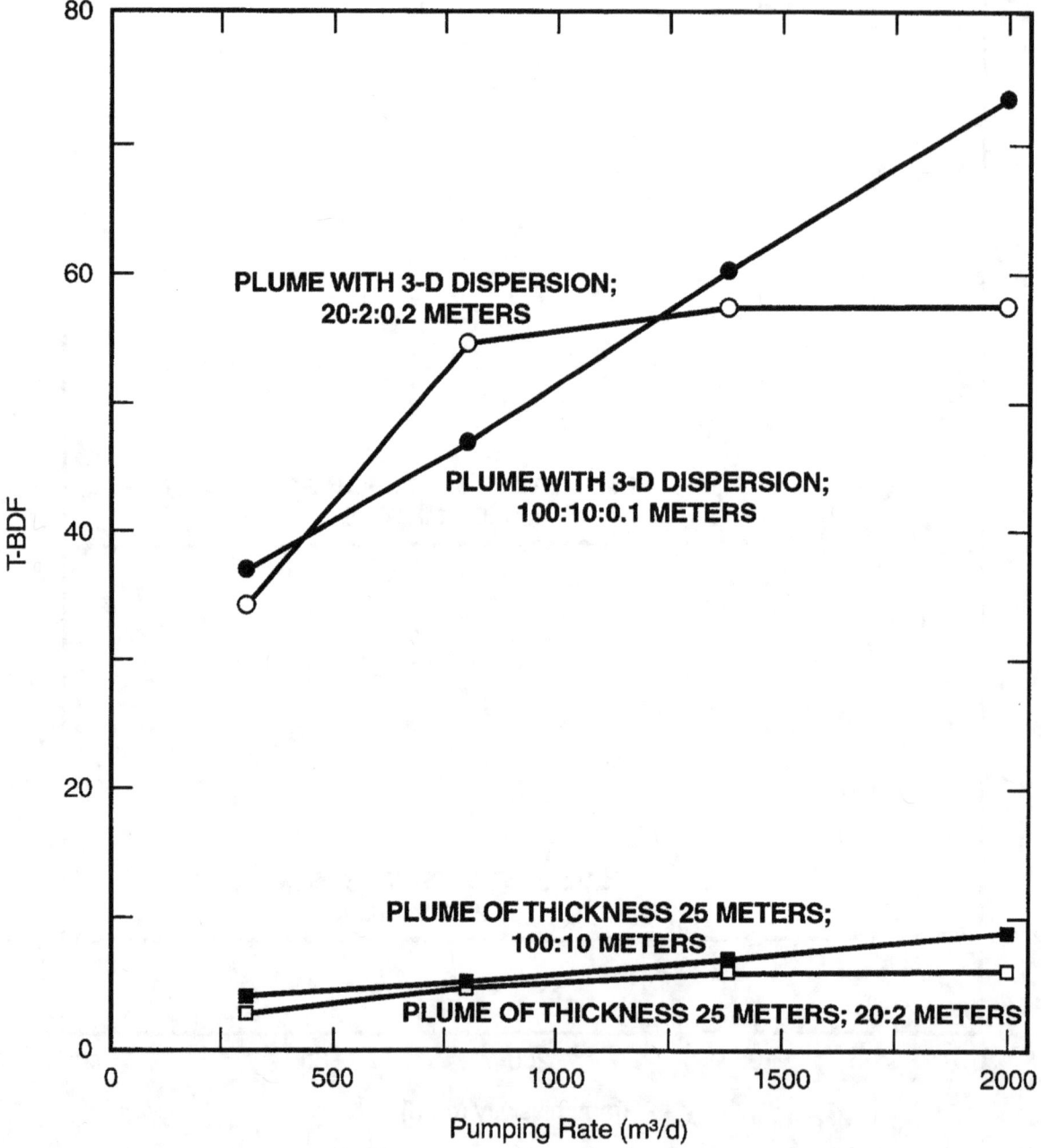

Figure 3–30. **Effect of pumping rate (range: 300 to 2000 cubic meters/day) for irrigation wells on transport dispersion-based borehole dilution factors for four different plume configurations.** Two thin plume configurations with no vertical dispersion and two 3–D dispersion plumes, all with dispersivity ratios as noted in the plot.

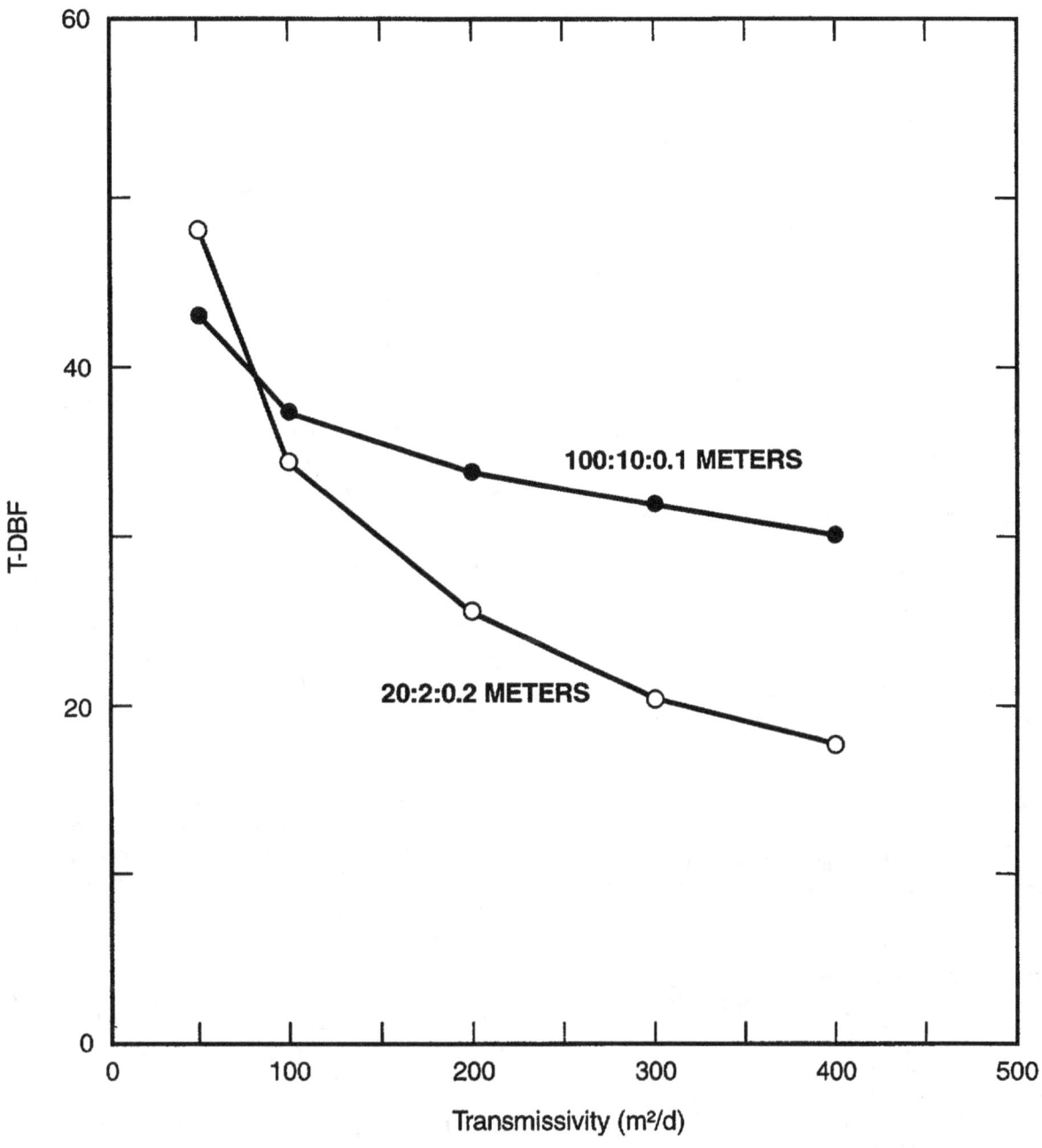

Figure 3–31. **Effect of transmissivity (range: 50 to 400 square meters/day) for large irrigation wells (Q = 2116 cubic meters/day) on transport dispersion-based borehole dilution factors for two different plume configurations.** Two 3–D dispersion plumes with dispersivity ratios as noted in the plot.

3.2.5 References

Akindunni, F.F., *et al.*, "Modeling of Contaminant Movement Near Pumping Wells: Saturated-Unsaturated Flow with Particle Tracking," *Ground Water*, 33(2):264–274 [1995].

Bair, E.S., and T.D. Lahm, "Variations in Capture-Zone Geometry of a Partially Penetrating Pumping Well in an Unconfined Aquifer," *Ground Water*, 34(5): 842–852 [1996].

Bauer, E.M., and K.D. Cartier, "Reference Manual for Data Base on Nevada Well Logs," U.S. Geological Survey, Open-File Report 95–460, 1995.

Bedient, P.B., H.S. Rifai, and C.J. Newell, *Ground Water Contamination Transport and Remediation*, Englewood Cliffs, New Jersey, PTR Prentice Hall, 1994.

Bedinger, M.S., K.A. Sargent, and W.H. Langer (eds.), "Studies of Geology and Hydrology in the Basin and Range Province, Southwestern United States, for Isolation of High-Level Radioactive Waste—Characterization of the Death Valley Region, Nevada and California, U.S. Geological Survey Professional Paper 1370–F, 1989.

Bellin, A., G. Dagan, and Y. Rubin, "The Impact of Head Gradient Transients on Transport in Heterogeneous Formations: Applications to the Borden Site," *Water Resources Research*, 32(9): 2705–2713 [1996].

Buqo, T.S., "Baseline Water Supply and Demand Evaluation of Southern Nye County, Nevada," Blue Diamond, Nevada, [1997].

Burchfiel, B.C., "Reconnaissance Geologic Map of the Lathrop Wells 15-Minute Quadrangle, Nye County, Nevada," U.S. Geological Survey, Miscellaneous Geological Investigations Map I–474, 1996.

Chiang, C., G. Raven, and C. Dawson, "The Relationship Between Monitoring Well and Aquifer Solute Concentration," *Ground Water*, 33(5):718–726 [1995].

D'Agnese, F.A., "Using Scientific Information Systems for Three-Dimensional Modeling of Regional ground-water Flow Systems, Death Valley Region, Nevada and California," Golden, Colorado, Colorado School of Mines, Ph.D. Dissertation, 1994.

D'Agnese, F.A., *et al.*, "Hydrogeologic Evaluation and Numerical Simulation of the Death Valley Regional Ground-Water Flow System, Nevada and California, Using Geoscientific Information Systems," U.S. Geological Survey, Open-File Report 96–4300, 1997.

Denny, C.S., and H. Drewes, " Geology of the Ash Meadows Quadrangle, Nevada–California," U.S. Geological Survey Bulletin 1181–L, 1965.

Faybishenko, B.A., I. Javandel, and P.A. Witherspoon, "Hydrodynamics of the Capture Zone of a Partially Penetrating Well in a Confined Aquifer," *Water Resources Research*, 31(4): 859–866 [1995].

Fedors, R.W., and G.W. Wittmeyer, "Initial Assessment of Dilution Effects Induced by Water Well Pumping in the Amargosa Farms Area," San Antonio, Texas, Center for Nuclear Waste Regulatory Analyses, letter report (revised), January 1998.

Fischer, J.M., "Sediment Properties and Water Movement through Shallow Unsaturated Alluvium at an Arid Site for Disposal of Low-Level Radioactive Waste Near Beatty, Nye County, Nevada," U.S. Geological Survey, Water-Resources Investigations Report 92–4032, 1992.

Gelhar, L.W., C. Welty, and K.R. Rehfeldt, "A Critical Review of Data on Field-Scale Dispersion in Aquifers," *Water Resources Research*, 28(7):1955–1974 [1992].

Grubb, S., "Analytical Model for Estimation of Steady-State Capture Zones of Pumping Wells in Confined and Unconfined Aquifers," *Ground Water*, 31(1):27–32 [1993].

Haitjema, H.M., *Analytic Element Modeling of Groundwater Flow*, New York, Academic Press, 1995.

Hoover, D.L., W.C. Swadley, and A.J. Gordon, "Correlation Characteristics of Surficial Deposits with a Description of Surficial Stratigraphy in the Nevada Test Site Region," U.S Geological Survey, Open-File Report 81–512, 1981.

Kessler, J., and R. McGuire, " Yucca Mountain Total System Performance Assessment, Phase 3 [Final Report]," Palo Alto, California, Electric Power Research Institute, EPRI TR–107191, December 1996. [Prepared by Risk Engineering (Boulder, Colorado).]

Kilroy, K.C., "Ground-Water Conditions in Amargosa Desert, Nevada-California, 1952–87," U.S. Geological Survey, Water-Resources Investigations Report 89–4101, 1991.

Laczniak, R.J., *et al.*, "Summary of Hydrogeologic Controls on Ground-Water Flow at the Nevada Test Site, Nye County, Nevada," U.S. Geological Survey, Water-Resources Investigations Report 96–4109, 1996.

Mathey, S.B. (ed.), "National Water Information System User's Manual: Volume 2, Chapter 4—Ground-Water Site Inventory System," U.S. Geological Survey, Open-File Report 89–587, 1989.

Mohanty, S., *et al.*, "Engineered Barrier System Performance Assessment Code: EBSPAC Version 1.1—Technical Description and User's Manual," San Antonio, Texas Center for Nuclear Waste Regulatory Analyses, CNWRA 97–006, June 1997. [Prepared for NRC.]

Mohanty, S. and McCartin, T.J. (coordinators), "Sensitivity and Uncertainty Analyses for a Proposed HLW Repository at Yucca Mountain, Nevada, Using TPA Computer Code Version 3.1–Volume 1: Conceptual Models and Data," U.S. Nuclear Regulatory Commission, NUREG–1668, February 2001.

Naff, R.L., "Hydrogeology of the Southern Part of the Amargosa Desert in Nevada," Reno, Nevada, University of Nevada, Master's Thesis, 1973.

Nichols W.D., and J.P. Akers, "Water-Level Declines in the Amargosa Valley Area, Nye County, Nevada, 1962–84," U.S. Geological Survey, Water-Resources Investigations Report, WRI–85–4273, 1985.

Oatfield, W.J., and J.B. Czarnecki, "Hydrogeologic Inferences from Drillers' Logs and from Gravity and Resistivity Surveys in the Amargosa Desert, Southern Nevada," *Journal of Hydrology*, 124:131–158 [1991].

Osterkamp, W.R., L.J. Lane, and C.S. Savard, "Recharge Estimates Using a Geomorphic/ Distributed-Parameter Simulation Approach, Amargosa River Basin," *Water Resources Bulletin*, 30(3):493–507 [1994].

Plume, R.W., "Hydrogeologic Framework of the Great Basin Region of Nevada, Utah, and Adjacent States," U.S. Geological Survey, Professional Paper 1409–B, 1996.

Reilly, T.E., O.L. Franke, and G.D. Bennett, "Bias in Groundwater Samples Caused by Wellbore Flow," *Journal of Hydraulic Engineering*, 115(2):270–276 [1989].

Savard, C.S., "Selected Hydrologic Data from Forty Mile Wash in the Yucca Mountain Area, Nevada, Water Year 1992," U.S. Geological Survey, Open-File Report 94–317, 1995.

Schafer, D.C., "Determining 3D Capture Zones in Homogeneous, Anisotropic Aquifers," *Ground Water*, 34(4):628–639 [1996].

State of Nevada, "Well Drillers' Logs for Amargosa Desert Townships 15, 16, 17 S. and Ranges 47, 48, 49, and 50 E. from Nevada Division of Water Resources," Carson City, Department of Conservation and Natural Resources/Division of Water Resources, 1997a.

State of Nevada, "Annual Estimates of Water Use for Hydrographic Basin 230, Amargosa

Desert," Carson City, Department of Conservation and Natural Resources/Division of Water Resources, 1997b.

State of Nevada, "Well Permit Database for Hydrographic Basin 230, Amargosa Desert," Carson City, Department of Conservation and Natural Resources/Division of Water Resources, 1997c.

Strack, O.D.L., *Groundwater Mechanics*, Englewood Cliffs, New Jersey, Prentice-Hall, 1989.

Swadley, W.C., "Map Showing Surficial Geology of the Lathrop Wells Quadrangle, Nye County, Nevada," U.S. Geological Survey, Miscellaneous Investigations Series Map I–1361, 1983.

Swadley, W.C., and W.J. Carr, "Geologic Map of the Quaternary and Tertiary Deposits of the Big Dune Quadrangle, Nye County, Nevada, and Inyo County, California," U.S. Geological Survey, Miscellaneous Investigations Series Map I–1361, 1980.

TRW Environmental Safety Systems Inc., "Total System Performance Assessment— 1995: An Evaluation of the Potential Yucca Mountain Repository," Las Vegas, Nevada, Document No. B00000000–01717–2200– 00136 (Rev. 01), November 1995.

U.S. Department of Energy, "Chapter 3, Hydrology" in "Site Characterization Plan, Yucca Mountain Site, Nevada Research and Development Area, Nevada," Office of Civilian Radioactive Waste Management, Nevada, DOE/RW–0199, Vol. II, Part A, December 1988.

Walker, G.E., and T.E. Eakin, "Geology and Ground-Water of Amargosa Desert, Nevada– California," Carson City, Nevada, State of Nevada Department of Conservation and Natural Resources, Ground-Water Resources Reconnaissance Series Report 14, 1963.

Wescott, R.G., *et al.* (eds.), "NRC Iterative Performance Assessment Phase 2: Development of Capabilities for Review of a Performance Assessment for a High-Level Waste Repository," U.S. Nuclear Regulatory Commission, NUREG–1464, October 1995.

Wexler, E.J., "Analytical Solutions for One-, Two-, and Three-Dimensional Solute Transport in Ground-Water Systems with Uniform Flow," in "Techniques of Water-Resources Investigations of the U.S. Geological Survey," U.S. Geological Survey, Chapter B7, Book 3 (*Applications of Hydraulics*), 1992.

Wilson, M.L., *et al.*, "Total-System Performance Assessment for Yucca Mountain— SNL Second Iteration (TSPA–1993)," Albuquerque, New Mexico, Sandia National Laboratory, SAND93–2675, 2 vols., April 1994.

Winograd I. J. and W. Thordarson, "Hydrogeologic and Hydrochemical Framework, South-Central Great Basin, Nevada-California, with Special Reference to the Nevada Test Site (Hydrology of Nuclear Test Sites)," U.S. Geological Survey, Professional Paper 712–C, 1975.

3.3   Annual Individual Dose Estimates

3.3.1   Introduction

In its 1995 report, the NAS recommended that future standards for Yucca Mountain limit individual risk to the average member of the exposed critical group and that compliance should be evaluated at the time and place where greatest risk occurs (up to the limit of geologic predictability of the site, which NAS asserts to be 1 million years) following repository closure. Moreover, no scientific basis was found for limiting the compliance period to 10,000 years as done under existing regulations. Thus, to gain some insight into potential implementation issues associated with this particular recommendation, as well as to better understand the relative importance of site-specific assumptions and parameters in dose-based calculations at the Yucca Mountain site, the staff performed some preliminary calculations to estimate annual individual dose.

3.3.2 Simulation Approach

Evaluation of annual individual dose requires specification of an exposure scenario that defines the geosphere and biosphere pathways for the transport of radionuclides released from a geologic repository to a human receptor in the biosphere. Simulation of radionuclide release and transport in the geosphere were conducted based on models developed within NRC's IPA program. Some modifications to the computational modules[11] were necessary to allow investigation of sensitivities of the dose calculation, improve calculational efficiencies, and allow the calculation to go beyond a 10,000-year performance period, to the time of peak dose. Two exposure pathways were developed for release of radionuclides to ground water. The first exposure pathway is consistent with the distance used for integrated release calculations performed in previous IPA efforts (Wescott *et al.*, 1995). It assumes that a hypothetical receptor group exists at a distance of 5 kilometers down-gradient of the proposed repository. Radioactive exposure results from ingestion of contaminated water (water withdrawal by a well for a residential community intercepts radionuclides in the saturated zone). The second exposure pathway assumes a hypothetical farming/ranching-type receptor group is located approximately 30 kilometers downgradient from Yucca Mountain (based on the conclusions reached in Section 2.3). Radioactive exposure pathways at this location are: ingestion (of contaminated water, crops and animal products); inhalation (from resuspension of contaminated soil); and direct exposure.

To better understand and quantify the variation in dose estimates caused by uncertainties in the geosphere models (i.e., source-term release, hydrologic flow, and radionuclide transport), the NRC staff performed probabilistic analyses for the two hypothetical receptor locations. Important

attributes and assumptions of these analyses were as follows.

- Simplifications of the flow and transport models include a steady-state flow system; no thermal effects; fracture retardation assumed to be a fraction of the matrix retardation (a range of 0 to 10 percent was used for the uncertainty analyses); assumed waste package container lifetime of 1000 years; disruptive scenarios not considered; and a source term based on leach rate, solubility, and amount of water contacting the waste.

- A continuous transport path is assumed to exist from the saturated zone, below the proposed repository footprint, to the two hypothetical receptor locations—5 kilometers (in fractured tuff) and 30 kilometers (27 kilometers in the fractured tuff and 3 kilometers in porous alluvium).

- All releases from the proposed repository eventually pass the 5-kilometer receptor location and are uniformly mixed in the annual volume of water pumped by the hypothetical receptor group at the 30-kilometer location (at a rate of 3800 cubic meters/day for the 5-kilometer location and 30,400 cubic meters/day for the 30-kilometer location).[12] Water usage was based on broad assumptions regarding pumping rates required to intercept the entire contaminant plume (applied to the 5-kilometer location) and water usage consistent with a farming community (applied to the 30-kilometer location).

- The hypothetical receptor group at 5 kilometers uses untreated ground water for drinking water only.

- The hypothetical receptor group at 30 kilometers uses untreated ground water for drinking water, the irrigation of agricultural crops, and the watering of livestock. [The average member of this

---

[11]The modifications in question were performed principally to the FLOWMOD (McCartin *et al.*, 1995) and the SOTEC (Sagar *et al.*, 1992) computational modules. These codes model the leaching and dissolution of radionuclides within a waste package and determine their concentrations at a distant receptor location.

[12]These production estimates are consistent with the IPA Phase 2 analysis and are believed to be sufficient pumping rates, at the two respective locations, to entrain all radionuclides in a contaminant plume that might emanate from a potential geologic repository at Yucca Mountain.

group is assumed to supply half (50 percent) of his/her food needs and all his/her water (including milk) from his/her farm/ranch.[13]]

For both hypothetical receptor group locations, certain parameters were sampled independently for each of the seven repository sub-areas,[14] whereas others were sampled only once and applied to the seven sub-areas. Parameters sampled for each repository sub-area were: (a) the assumed capture area to convert infiltration rate to a water flux for each waste package; (b) the fraction of the fuel that is wetted by the infiltrating water at any given time; and (c) the leach rate of the waste form. Parameters sampled only once, that applied to all the seven repository sub-areas, were: (a) radionuclide solubilities; (b) infiltration; (c) matrix distribution coefficients for each hydrostratigraphic unit; (d) matrix permeabilities for each hydrostratigraphic layer; and (e) fraction of matrix retardation applied to fracture. Parameter ranges for the parameters sampled in the uncertainty analysis are presented in Appendix H.

3.3.3 Results and Conclusions

The annual individual dose (expressed as TEDE—*total effective dose equivalent*), as a function of time, is presented in Figures 3–32 and 3–33 for the 5- and the 30-kilometer locations, respectively. Doses for 100 sampled vectors were calculated versus time, and the results were grouped into 100-year intervals. The values in each interval were then ranked, and the 10th, 50th, and 90th values in the rank (100 being the largest) were plotted to provide the curves denoted as 10th percentile, median, and 90th percentile, respectively. The curve marked mean is the arithmetic average of all

the values in each interval. Note that over a large range of time for both curves, the 10th percentile value was essentially zero, and is coincident with the time axis (ordinate). Although the maximum annual individual dose estimates for both locations occur at different times, the time of the maximum dose occurs shortly after initial arrival of radionuclides at the two sample locations. This result is primarily because of the (conservative) assumption that all waste package containers fail at 1000 years, which results in large releases of long-lived, soluble, and mobile radionuclides (e.g., ^{99}Tc, ^{237}Np, and ^{129}I) arriving at the receptor location at generally overlapping times. After the initial peak, the dose-versus-time curve is complicated by both short-duration spikes (e.g., spikes that appear between 3000 and 8000 years in Figure 3–32) and secondary peaks that are significantly less than the initial peak (e.g., secondary peaks at 50,000 and 700,000 years in Figure 3–32, and 700,000 years in Figure 3–33). This variation in dose is a result of varying arrival times for individual radionuclides caused by: (a) varying flow velocities and retardation; (b) representation of the unsaturated zone stratigraphy (i.e., the repository was divided into seven sub-areas, each with unique stratigraphy, and thus a distinct travel time); and (c) differences in transport velocities used for the fracture flow component versus the matrix flow component of flow within a specific stratigraphic sequence (e.g., releases that are transported through the porous matrix will arrive at the receptor location after releases that move through the fractures).

Deterministic simulations, using mean values of the parameter ranges used in the uncertainty analysis, were performed for the two hypothetical receptor locations, to identify the contribution of individual radionuclides to dose.[15] Figures 3–34 and 3–35 present the doses for specific radionuclides for the two receptor locations as well as the total dose

---

[13]The reader is referred to Appendix A, in which it is noted that the magnitude of personal, home-garden consumption could be as high as 30 percent, compared with 50 percent assumed for this particular analysis.

[14]For the purposes of the IPA Phase 2 analysis, the proposed geologic repository was divided into seven sub-areas, based on their proximity to individual boreholes. The hydrogeologic units below each of the seven sub-areas were assumed to correspond to the associated borehole stratigraphy at those points, thus producing seven different hydrogeologic sequences over the entire repository (see McCartin *et al.*, 1995; p. 4–15).

---

[15]The deterministic simulation was used for identifying the contribution of individual radionuclides because of limitations in NRC's IPA computer code. A better representation of overall performance is presented by the probabilistic results presented in Figures 3–32 and 3–33.

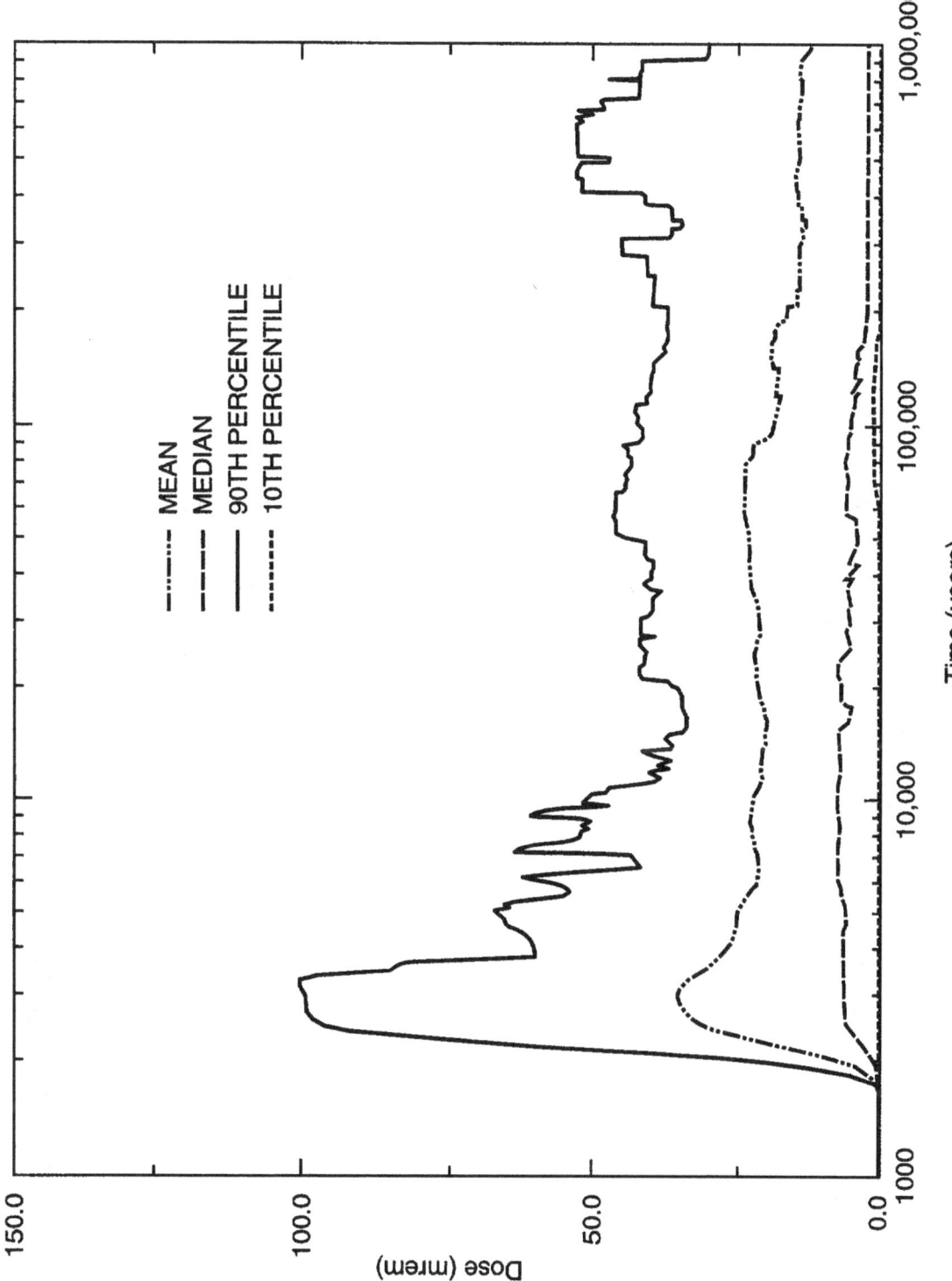

Figure 3–32. Uncertainty analysis of dose for 100 vectors at a point 5 kilometers down-gradient from the proposed geologic repository at Yucca Mountain

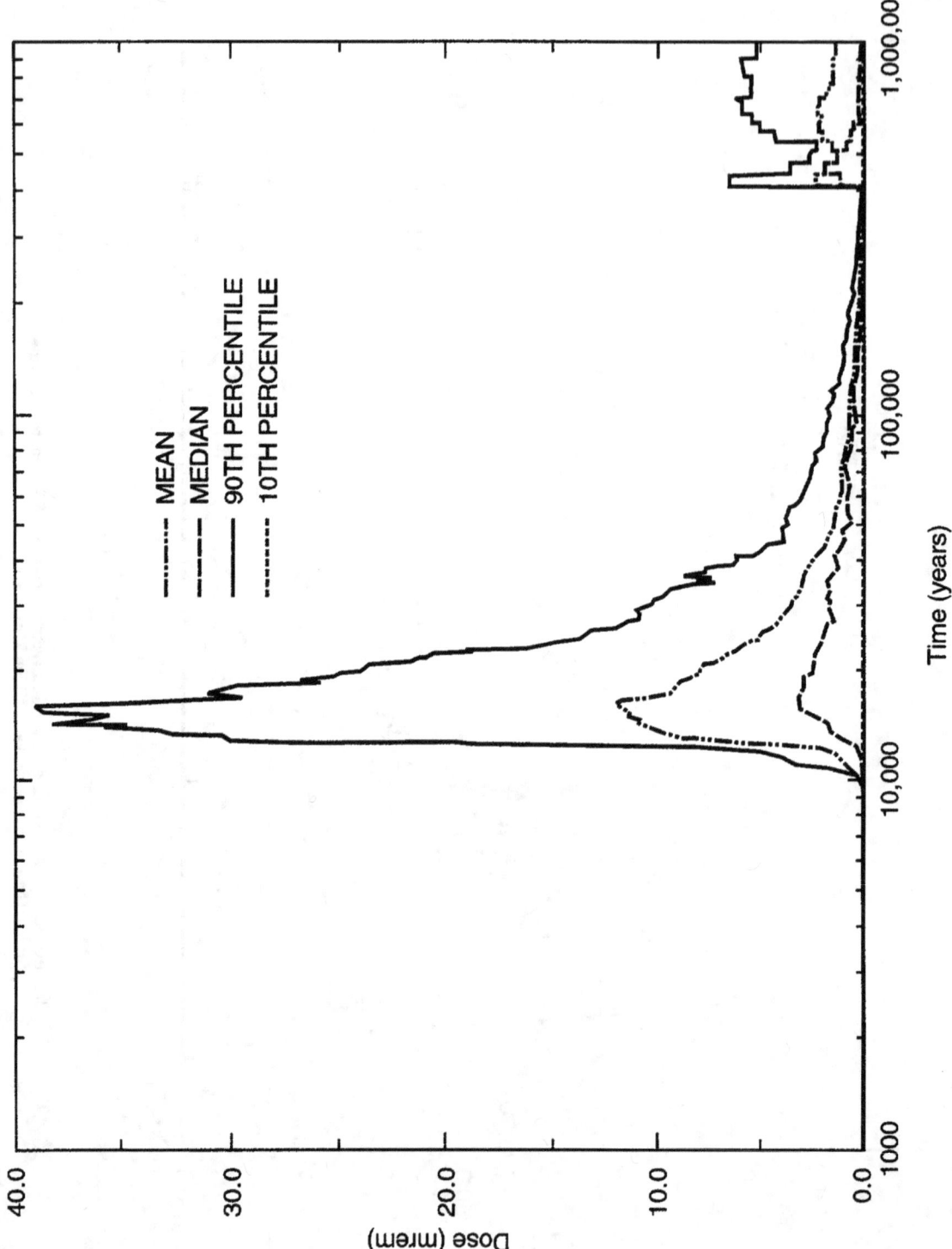

Figure 3–33. Uncertainty analysis of dose for 100 vectors (all dose pathways) at a point 30 kilometers down-gradient from the proposed geologic repository at Yucca Mountain.

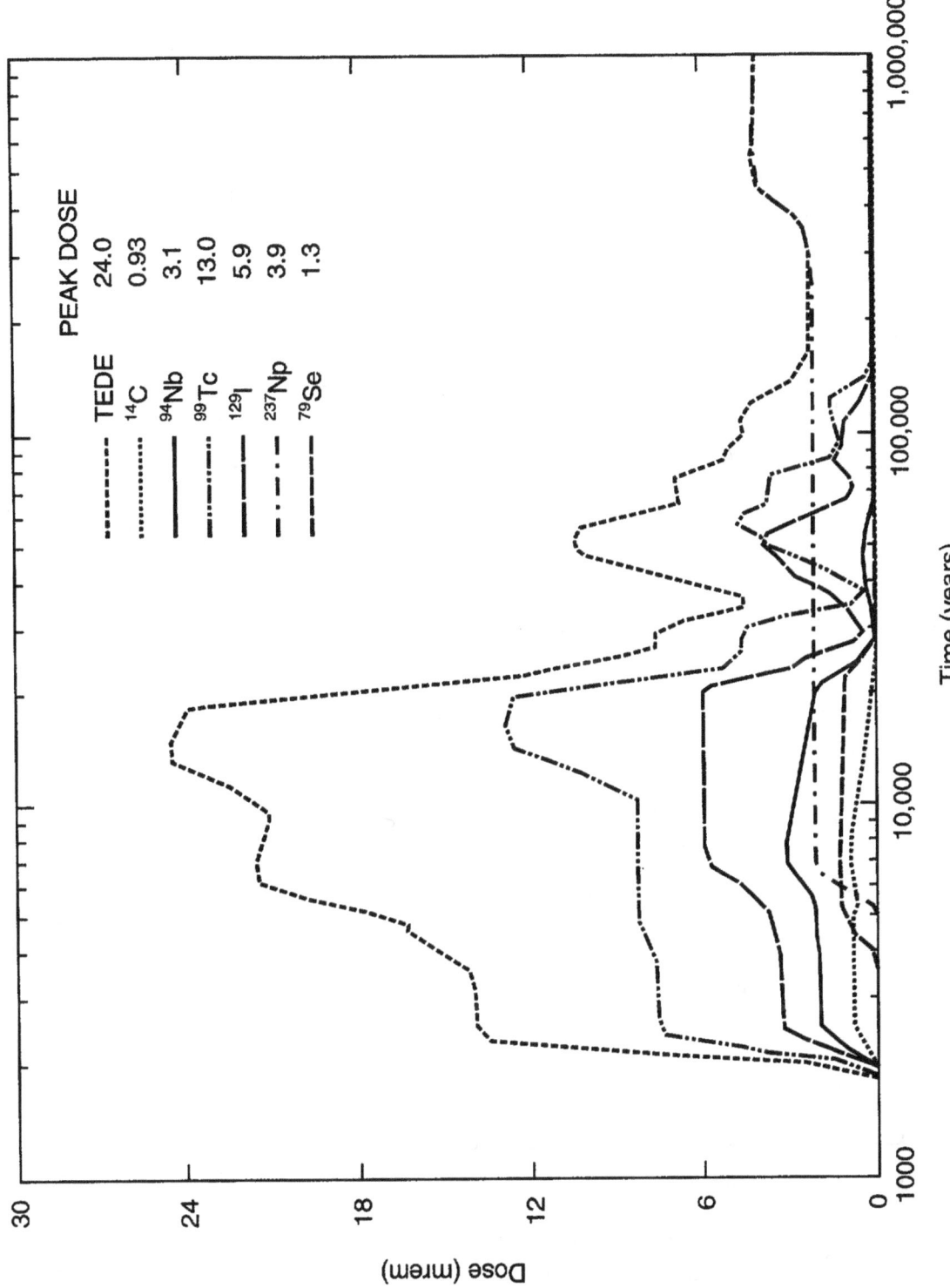

Figure 3–34. Annual individual dose from all radionuclides TEDE and for selected radionuclides for the drinking water pathway at a point 5 kilometers down-gradient from the proposed geologic repository at Yucca Mountain. Mean parameter values were used, including fracture retardation. Time of peak dose is 17,196 years.

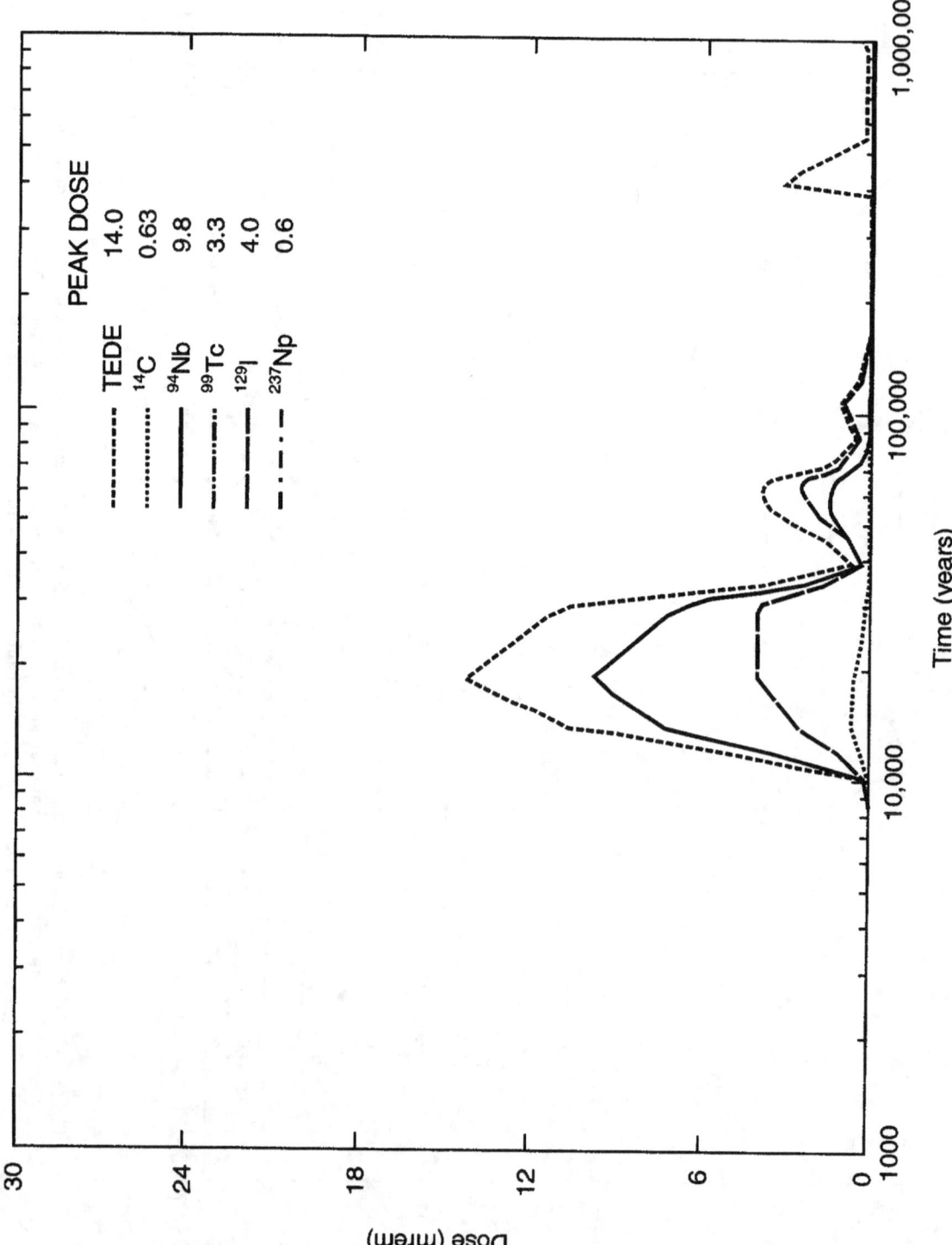

Figure 3–35. Annual individual dose from all radionuclides TEDE and for selected radionuclides for the drinking water pathway at a point 30 kilometers down-gradient from the proposed geologic repository at Yucca Mountain. Mean parameter values were used, including fracture retardation. Time of peak dose is 19,370 years.

from all radionuclides for the pathways considered, which is denoted in the legend as TEDE. A cursory examination of Figures 3–34 and 3–35 reveals that the magnitudes for the peak dose for the two receptor locations are quite similar [14 millirem (mrem) versus 24 mrem]. This similarity in results is caused by several significant differences in key assumptions (cited above) that have counterbalancing effects on the results. For example, the dose at the 5-kilometer location should be larger than the dose at the 30-kilometer location because of differences in the assumed dilution volumes (about 3800 cubic meters/day versus 30,400 cubic meters/day), which reduce concentrations at the location farther away. If drinking water dose were the only ingestion pathway, then the dose at the 30-kilometer location might have been an order of magnitude or more lower than the dose at the 5-kilometer location.

However, the hypothetical farming community, at the 30-kilometer location includes, additional ingestion pathways from animal products and crops that counterbalance the decrease in dose caused by the larger dilution volume associated with agricultural activity. Additionally, the difference in ingestion pathways result in different contributions from specific radionuclides responsible for the peak. At the 5-kilometer location, the peak dose is significantly influenced by arrival of ^{99}Tc and ^{129}I from more than one sub-area, as evidenced by the multiple peaks for ^{99}Tc. At the 30-kilometer location, the peak dose is influenced more by arrival of Niobium-94. However, at both locations, it is long-lived, soluble, and mobile radionuclides that are the key contributors to dose.

3.3.4 References

McCartin T.J., *et al.*, "Flow and Transport Module [FLOWMOD]," in R.G. Wescott *et al.* (eds.), "NRC Iterative Performance Assessment Phase 2: Development of Capabilities for Review of a Performance Assessment for a High-Level Waste Repository," U.S. Nuclear Regulatory Commission, NUREG–1464, October 1995.

Sagar, B., *et al.*, "SOTEC: A Source Term Code for High-Level Geologic Repositories— Users' Manual (Version 1.0)," San Antonio, Texas, Center for Nuclear Waste Regulatory Analyses, CNWRA 92–009, July 1992. [Prepared for NRC.]

Wescott, R.G. *et al.* (eds.), "NRC Iterative Performance Assessment Phase 2: Development of Capabilities for Review of a Performance Assessment for a High-Level Waste Repository," U.S. Nuclear Regulatory Commission, NUREG–1464, October 1995.

3.4 Overall Observations and Implications

In summary, the radionuclides released from a potential repository at Yucca Mountain can be expected to migrate to the water table and be carried down-gradient toward discharge areas, most likely, at some point, in the Amargosa-Death Valley area. The ground-water pathway is the most likely exposure pathway. Exposure to humans is assumed to occur through the use of well water that is contaminated with radionuclides. Determination of the concentration of radionuclides in well water depends on: (a) the degree of plume dispersion; (b) pumping of the well itself; and (c) the location of the discharge point.

3.4.1 Dilution Resulting from Natural Mixing

Ground-water flow beneath Yucca Mountain would initially be in volcanic tuff, generally dipping down-gradient toward the Amargosa-Death Valley area. Several tens of kilometers from the proposed repository site, the water table laterally intersects valley-fill alluvial deposits. Because the volume of water recharging the Death Valley ground-water basin is small relative to the volume of ground water already within the saturated zone of the ground-water basin, the radioactive discharges from the repository would be expected to consist initially of a shallow, laminar-like layer on the surface of the water table, as shown in Figure 3–36. The thickness of the radionuclide plume would increase with distance from the repository because of processes of molecular diffusion and mechanical mixing, especially where the water table crossed bedding planes,

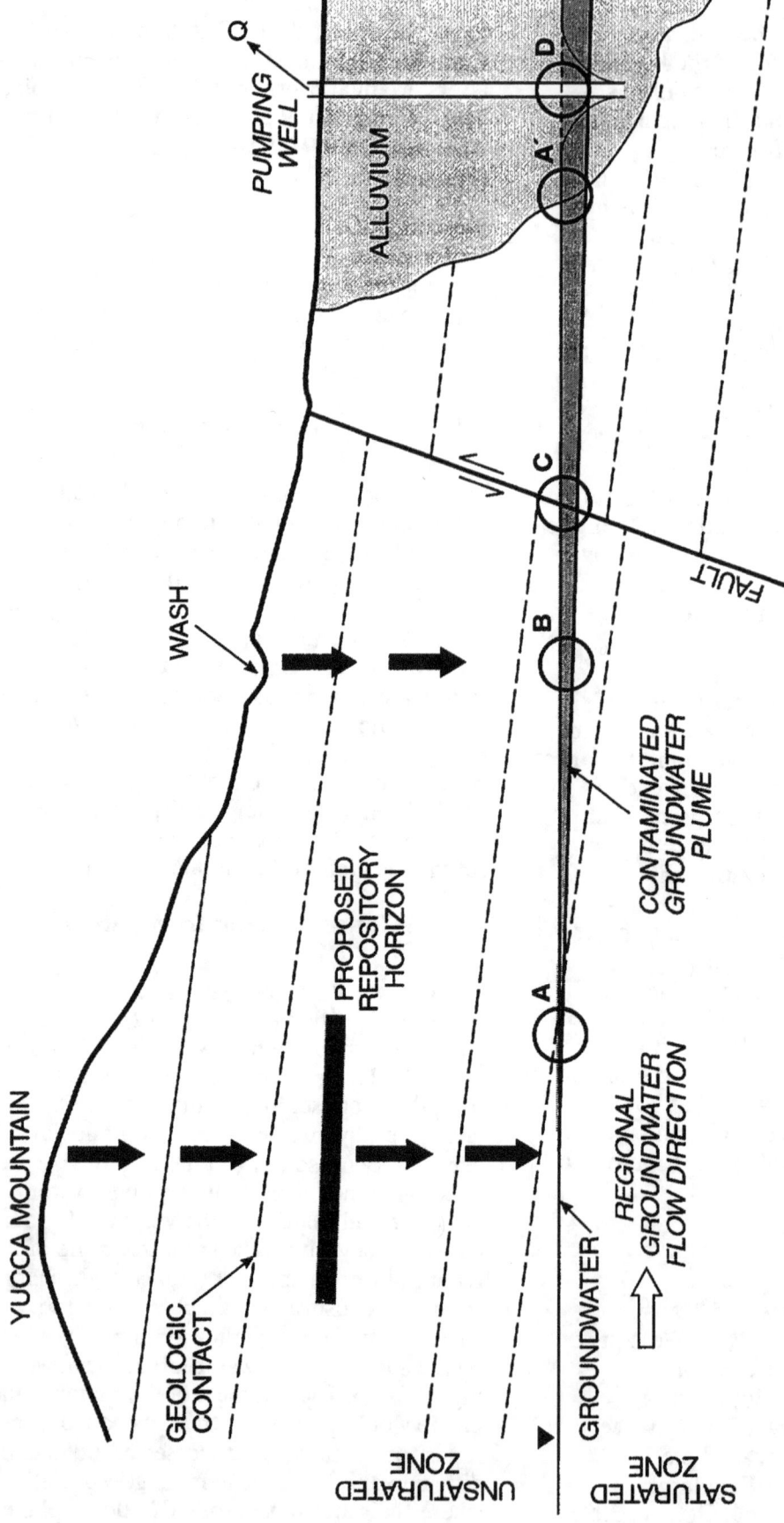

Figure 3–36. Plume dispersion between repository footprint and pumping well. Illustration shows rainwater percolating through the unsaturated zone to the repository horizon. Water seeps into emplacement drifts, accelerating corrosion of waste package canisters and exposing their radioactive contents. This water now becomes the vehicle for dissolving and transporting exposed radionuclides out of the repository horizon into the unsaturated zone below and, finally, to the water table, where it forms a plume. Regional ground-water flow in the saturated zone initially dilutes the concentration of radionuclides forming the plume through processes of advection, dispersion, and diffusion. Between the proposed repository and possible receptor locations, plume dilution within the water table is achieved principally through advective and dispersive transport. (Diffusion can be important, but only with low Darcy velocities.) Illustration shows plume dispersion can be achieved as the water table passes over bedding planes (**A**) or between different geologic media (**A´**). Percolating ground water from intermittent streams can also contribute to plume dilution owing to the increased influx of water reaching the water table (**B**). Mechanical mixing of the plume can occur within fractured or porous materials found along faults or joint sets (**C**). Lastly, additional dilution of the contaminant plume is achieved when ground water is drawn from a pumping well (**D**) that intercepts the plume and mixes it with fresh water held in storage by the aquifer.

faults, joint systems, or breccia zones, since the water table is much more horizontally aligned than are the dipping stratigraphy and structure at the site. Local recharge along ephemeral streams, like Fortymile Wash, would also affect the position and shape of the initial thin plume.

The overall finding of this analysis is that passive ground-water mixing at the Yucca Mountain site is not likely to produce very large dilution factors. In the immediate vicinity of the proposed repository, dilution is limited because of the directional characteristics of the flow and magnitudes of the Darcy fluxes (i.e., tendency for contaminant plumes to remain on or close to the water table surface). As the radionuclide plumes travel away from the proposed repository, they tend to have a greater chance of spreading and becoming diluted both laterally and vertically as a result of movement through or around large-scale structural features such as faults. Depending on their large-scale hydraulic properties, faults in the tuff aquifer could play a major role in determining the rate and direction of plume spread. At substantial distances, radionuclide plumes traveling through the alluvium are expected to be further mixed with uncontaminated waters, but the dilution at locations such as the Amargosa Desert, is unlikely to increase by many orders of magnitude. However, mixing resulting from well pumping becomes a more significant dilution process as natural mixing decreases.

3.4.2 Well Head Pumping

The effect of borehole dilution was examined by separating the overall dilution factor into two components: volumetric flux-based dilution in the borehole and dispersion transport-based components. The method used to estimate F–BDF—the *flux-based dilution factor*—in the Amargosa Farms region is to compare the capture area of a pumping well to the cross-sectional area of the portion of the plume that is captured. Borehole dilution factors presented in this NUREG are calculated using the cross-sectional areas normal to the principal direction of regional

flow. The method used to estimate the component of borehole dilution caused by dispersion during transport is to calculate an average concentration for the portion of the plume captured by a pumping well. The F–BDF and T–BDF have been kept separate to better understand the influence of well pumping on concentration estimates.

Different configurations for the plume and the capture area were evaluated. For domestic residential wells, the capture area is generally much smaller than the cross-sectional area of a plume that has undergone horizontal and vertical transverse spreading caused by macro-dispersion during transport along a 20- to 30-kilometer pathway as shown in Figure 3–15. Thus, as expected, F–BDF was minimal when the domestic well was aligned with the center of the plume. Any borehole dilution that might occur would be solely caused by vertical gradients in the plume concentration and would be reflected in the T–BDF. For irrigation wells, or any high-discharge wells, the capture area is generally thicker than the plume and could also be wider than the plume, depending on the specifics of the pumping scenario.

Several conclusions can be drawn from this analysis. First, as defined in this study, F–BDFs for individual wells are relatively small, ranging from 1 to 5 for an irrigation well extracting contaminant from a plume that exhibits 3–D dispersion; from 19 to 49 for an irrigation well extracting contaminant from a thin plume that does not disperse vertically; and from 4 to 10 for a domestic well [i.e., 6.8 cubic meters/day (1800 gallons/day or 2 acre-feet/year)], extracting contaminant from a thin plume that does not disperse vertically. However, care should be taken when comparing F–BDF for different contaminant plume configurations, since actual borehole concentrations depend on the mass of radionuclides captured and the volume of water pumped, not just the area of the plume that is captured. On the one hand, a high-capacity (agricultural) well may capture the entire mass of radionuclides in a large plume, have an apparent dilution factor of only 1, yet still produce a low borehole concentration because the large plume would have a corresponding low mean resident concentration. On the other hand, a low-capacity domestic well may capture the entire mass of radionuclides in a small plume, have a dilution factor of 10, yet produce a high borehole concentration because the plume has a very high mean resident concentration.

A second, and perhaps obvious, conclusion can be drawn from this study. Specifically, for a thin/wide plume of specified dimensions, a low-capacity well, screened over a thick section of the aquifer, may produce a higher dilution factor than a larger-capacity well screened over a shorter vertical interval. Indeed, extremes in the individual borehole concentrations within a receptor group will be greater if the contaminant plume is thin and borehole construction practices are varied, than if the plume is very thick and borehole construction practices are uniform. These results suggest that attention should be paid to understanding vertical spreading in the saturated zone along the presumed transport pathway. Indirect field evidence (Gelhar *et al.*, 1992; Bedient *et al.*, 1994) suggests minimal vertical spreading in alluvial aquifers; however, vertical spreading may be substantial in the fractured tuff aquifer, especially where flow crosses normal faults across which there is significant offset in the conductive and non-conductive strata.

Further work on borehole dilution would benefit from better delineation of the plume entering the alluvial aquifer and from large-scale modeling of the effects of multiple-well systems. This analysis has shown that the plume configuration is an important component. Additionally, modeling multiple-well systems would better define the pumping effect on ground-water flow patterns in the Amargosa Farms area.

3.4.3 Peak Dose

In summary, the NAS recommendation for an individual risk standard appears implementable because: (a) estimating dose for long time-periods (i.e., tens to hundreds of thousands of years) and a variety of exposure pathways (e.g., ingestion of contaminated water, crops, and animal products) is computationally feasible; (b) preliminary indications are that a relatively small number of long-lived, soluble, and mobile radionuclides will be most important to performance; and (c) although assumptions concerning the receptor group location and lifestyle are important in determining appropriate exposure pathways and dilution volumes used in the performance calculation, peak doses did not vary significantly between the two hypothetical receptor groups analyzed.

3.4.4 References

Bedient, P.B., H.S. Rifai, and C.J. Newell, *Ground Water Contamination Transport and Remediation*, Englewood Cliffs, New Jersey, PTR Prentice Hall, 1994.

Gelhar, L.W., C. Welty, and K.R. Rehfeldt, "A Critical Review of Data on Field-Scale Dispersion in Aquifers," *Water Resources Research*, 28(7):1955–1974 [1992].

4. CONSEQUENCES OF HUMAN INTRUSION[1]

4.1 Introduction

In Chapter 4, "Human Intrusion and Institutional Control," of its findings and recommendations, the NAS concluded that: "... (i) active institutional controls cannot be relied on to prevent breaching of the repository's engineered or geologic barriers by human activity such as exploratory drilling; and (ii) it is not possible to make scientifically supportable predictions of the probability of such breaches...." The NAS recommended that the repository developer be required to provide a reasonable system of active and passive controls to reduce the risk of inadvertent intrusion (e.g., Tolan, 1993; and Jensen, 1993). The NAS further recommended that a stylized calculation be used to analyze the impact of a hypothetical intrusion scenario on the performance of the repository. Because the probability of such a scenario would be highly speculative, the NAS recommended that the calculation not be included in the TSPA, but be considered separately, using the same critical group assumptions as in the TSPA, to provide insights on the resiliency of the repository to human intrusion.

Human intrusion has been analyzed (determinstically) as a disruptive scenario in prior TSPAs for Yucca Mountain (e.g., Codell *et al.*, 1992; Barnard *et al.*, 1992; Wilson *et al.*, 1994; Wescott *et al.*, 1995), as well as internationally, for other HLW disposal concepts.[2] Each of these analyses relied on certain basic assumptions regarding human behavior and future technology. As noted above, and in Section 1, the NAS concluded that there was no scientific basis for predicting the occurrence of human intrusion subsequent to permanent closure of a geologic repository. Consequently, the staff performed a scoping analysis to better understand the limitations,

requirements, and implementation issues associated with a stylized calculation of human intrusion caused by exploratory drilling. As part of its analysis, the staff used its IPA ability to perform some relatively simple calculations of the effect of human intrusion for the purposes of:

- Determining the relationship between the estimated dose and the human intrusion scenario assumptions;

- Determining what intrusion-related parameters (caused by drilling) appeared to be most important to dose; and

- Evaluating the time dependence of the occurrence of the drilling event on the magnitude of dose.

4.2 Specification of Intrusion Scenarios

Consistent with the NAS recommendations, the human intrusion scenario considered for analysis was that of a single borehole, drilled from the surface using conventional rotary drilling technology,[3] on top along the crest of Yucca Mountain. Such an intrusion event could have a number of possible outcomes: (a) passage between repository drifts or outside of emplacement areas (no damage to a waste package or overall repository integrity); (b) passage through a repository emplacement drift (missing a waste package) to the water table; (c) intersecting an emplacement drift, hitting and damaging a waste package, without continuation of drilling below the drift; and (d) intersecting an emplacement drift, hitting and penetrating a waste package, and continuation of drilling to the water table. The ability of a rotary drill bit to damage the waste package will depend on the state (integrity) of the waste package—i.e., a drill bit can only be expected to damage or penetrate an already

---

[1]The tables shown in this section present the results from the demonstration of the continuing staff capability to review a TSPA. These tables, like the demonstration, are limited by the use of simplifying assumptions and sparse data.

[2]Also see summaries in Nuclear Energy Agency (1995).

[3]Although a number of advanced drilling technologies and methods are under evaluation and/or development (National Research Council, 1994), based on the NAS' concerns about the difficulty in predicting future human activity, no attempt was made by the staff to speculate as to which one of these emerging technologies might become practicable in the future and then integrate this information into the analysis.

(severely) corroded waste package.[4] Thus, the extent of drilling damage to a waste package is related to the time of the intrusion, given that degradation of the waste package is anticipated to occur gradually over hundreds to thousands of years. The effects of these issues are evaluated by considering two different times for the intrusion event itself and two specific intrusion scenarios that are expected to bound the consequences.

The first human intrusion scenario analyzed is specified as a single borehole intersecting the emplacement drift and damaging the waste package. A breach of the waste package is assumed to form in the upper half of the waste package (horizontal emplacement assumed) either through direct penetration by the drill bit or through enhanced corrosion from ground water dripping from the borehole onto the surface of the damaged, but not penetrated, waste package. Once breached, the excavated borehole (annulus) provides a pathway for dripping water to enter the waste package. After the waste package is filled with water, it is assumed any additional water would result in dissolved radionuclides leaving the waste package in the water that leaves the waste package at the same rate as the additional water is entering (i.e., once the waste package is filled with water, it is conservatively assumed that all the subsequent infiltrating water displaces contaminated water from inside the waste package). The second human intrusion scenario analyzed specifies a single borehole intersecting the emplacement drift horizon, intersecting a waste package as well, and then fully penetrating (or perforating) it,[5] followed by a continuation of the drilling down to the water table. In this second scenario, infiltrating

water is assumed to enter the waste package, filling the lower half of the waste package up to the lower penetration hole (which would occur somewhere in the bottom half of the waste package), and subsequent release of radionuclides similar to the previous scenario. For the penetration scenario, the consequences of HLW entrained in the drill/borehole cuttings, which could be brought to the surface (e.g., Berglund, 1992), is not evaluated because the effect on doses to any hypothetical receptor group at 20 kilometers is assumed to be insignificant.

4.3 Description of Modeling Approach

Evaluation of annual individual dose requires specification of an exposure scenario that defines the geosphere and biosphere pathways for transport of radionuclides released from a geologic repository to a human receptor in the biosphere. Simulation of radionuclide release, transport in the geosphere, and definition of the biosphere pathways was substantially based on models and parameter ranges recently developed within NRC's performance assessment program (see Mohanty and McCartin, 2000). However, modification of a few parameter ranges was needed to represent the amount of water entering a borehole and transport of radionuclides in the borehole. Important attributes of the analysis of the human intrusion scenario were as follows:

- Conventional rotary drilling technology is assumed. The borehole diameter is 15.24 centimeters (6 inches).[6]

- The intrusion event occurs at either 100 or 1000 years after permanent repository closure.

- Ground-water inflow down the borehole is limited to a 1-square-meter catchment area or a 10-square-meter catchment area. The different catchment areas account for the possibility of borehole degradation at or below the land surface and the existence or formation of a

---

[4]It could be argued that latest waste package designs may be robust enough to withstand the effects of conventional rotary dril bits using diamond, tungsten, or carbide cutting elements. However, the purpose of this scoping analysis was not to evaluate likely failure modes for the waste package canisters nor speculate on the range of different human intrustion modes. Rather, consistent with the NAS recommendations, this analysis assumes the structural integrity of the waste package canister has been degraded, for whatever reason, and thus can be inadvertently breached by rotary drilling assuming a specific (drilling) scenario.

[5]That is to say the drilling process creates both an entrance (upper half) and exit (lower half) breach or hole within the waste package canister.

[6]This diameter size is consistent with reported information on past drilling practices in the Yucca Mountain area (see Thordarson and Robinson, 1971) as well as what is believed to be current drilling practice overall. See LeRoy *et al.,* (1977), Driscoll (1986), and American Water Works Association (1991).

depression, at the surface, around the borehole, caused by drilling activity.

- Horizontal emplacement of the waste package is assumed. Damage to the waste package results in a breach in the upper half of the waste package (location of the breach is varied between 0.5 and 1.0 of the waste package diameter). Penetration of the waste package results in a breach in both the lower and upper halves of the waste package (the location of the lower breach, which defines the exit location for radionuclides, is varied between 0.0 and 0.5 of the waste package diameter). For both conditions, the location of the lowest breach or hole in the waste package defines what fraction of HLW is contacted by water and thus contributes to release.

- When the waste package is perforated by a drill bit, the borehole extends to the water table and provides a continuous path, for radionuclide transport, from the repository emplacement depth to the water table, which is unaltered by any retardation processes.

- A continuous transport path is assumed to exist from the saturated zone, below the repository footprint, to the receptor location 20 kilometers down-gradient from Yucca Mountain. The saturated zone path is comprised of fractured tuff (approximately two-thirds of the total path length) and porous alluvium (approximately one-third of the total path length).

- All releases from the proposed repository eventually pass the receptor location and are uniformly mixed in the annual volume of water pumped by the receptor group (assumed to be a hypothetical farming community in a semi-arid environment). Water usage is based on the water demands for irrigating 13 to 27 quarter-section plots with 0.94 to 1.33 meters/year (3.1 to 4.38 feet/year)— or 0.016 to 0.049 cubic meters/year (4.4 to 13 million gallons/day).

- The hypothetical receptor group uses untreated ground water for both household purposes and irrigation of agricultural crops. The farmer is assumed to grow alfalfa for feed (for beef and dairy stock, including egg-laying hens), and vegetables, fruits, and grains for personal consumption. For the average member of the hypothetical farming community, the magnitude of personal consumption from local sources is conservatively assumed as follows: 50 percent for food needs; and 100 percent for drinking water and milk. The local sources of food, milk, and potable water are assumed to be contaminated because of the use of contaminated ground water.

4.4 Assumptions and Limitations

As stated above, the analysis was limited to consideration of only a "direct" intrusion scenario—that of a 15.24-centimeter drill bit damaging or penetrating a waste package container. An "indirect" intrusion scenario, in which a borehole misses a waste container, but penetrates contaminated portions of the repository floor and proceeds to the water table, was not considered. To calculate any consequences from the indirect scenario, it would have to be assumed that at least some waste packages, nearby, are degraded and leaking (the number and rate of leakage would either be arbitrary or need to be determined probabilistically) and the contaminated water is diverted to the borehole. The staff considers the second type of intrusion analyzed (i.e., penetration of a waste package and subsequent water inflow leading to radionuclide release down a borehole to the water table) a reasonably conservative approximation for an indirect scenario (i.e., exploratory drilling misses the waste package but provides an alternative pathway for radionuclides). In addition, for the differential in consequences to be significant, the unsaturated zone underlying the repository footprint would have to favor *matrix flow*, such that the borehole represents a significant fast conduit to the water table. If *fracture flow* predominates, the borehole could have limited additional effect on transport of radionuclides to the water table, compared with transport in fractures.

4.5 Results and Conclusions

Estimates of the annual individual dose are uncertain due to variation and uncertainty in the parameters and assumptions associated with the intrusion scenario, as well as other key aspects of the analysis (e.g., infiltration, release rate from the waste form, retardation, etc.). To better understand and quantify the variation in dose estimates caused by uncertainties in the geosphere models (i.e., source-term, hydrologic flow, and radionuclide transport) and the human intrusion scenarios, the staff performed probabilistic analyses. This uncertainty results in a distribution, of the annual individual dose, the estimates for which the staff has elected to represent with a mean value and 95th percentile of the distribution for each of the cases analyzed. Tables 4.1 and 4.2 present the annual individual dose (expressed as TEDE) for the damaged waste package scenario and the perforated waste package scenario, respectively. Additionally, these results represent the dose consequence from only the intrusion event; therefore, the results represent the increase in dose caused by the intrusion event (e.g., this result would be added to the performance results for the remaining waste packages of the repository to determine the total performance).

In regard to the initial review objectives, the staff concludes that the most likely range of doses from a reasonably credible human intrusion drilling event is up to tens of microrems (μ rem).[7] Certain drilling-related parameters (i.e., borehole diameter, catchment area, and timing of the drilling event) have varying degrees of effect on the dose estimates; however, all doses are estimated to be well below 1 millirem (mrem). Although the length of the time of the performance period (e.g., 10,000 versus 50,000 years after repository closure) had the largest

impact on the consequences, the doses from the longer period were still well below 1 mrem.

The staff agrees with the NAS finding that it is highly speculative to predict the consequences of future human activity from exploratory drilling for natural resources. However, at this time (and for the foreseeable future), the staff considers exploratory drilling for energy and mineral resources at the Yucca Mountain site to be an extremely unlikely event based on available information.[8] As discussed in Section 2.1, a more likely scenario in the foreseeable future might be exploratory drilling for ground water in one of the intermontane basins (valleys) that lie beyond the site. In the unlikely event that exploratory drilling should take place at or near the repository footprint, the chances are remote that it would intersect a waste

---

[7]The reader is reminded that the NAS' recommendations apply only to the critical group. Potential doses to the drilling crew, due to inadvertent exploratory drilling, can be expected to be higher than the values reported elsewhere in this NUREG for hypothetical receptor groups. See Charles and McEwen (1991) for an example of this type of calculation.

[8]Because exploratory drilling for natural resources is believed to be the most likely manner in which the geologic repository may be breached, the purpose of this calculation was to assess the resilience of the repository to drilling (using the surrogate of dose), not the likelihood of the drilling event itself taking place. There are many factors that contribute to decisions to explore for energy and mineral resources (see Anderson, 1982; and Harris, 1990). One of these factors certainly would be the existence of known energy, mineral, or ground-water resources at the Yucca Mountain site. In this regard, the staff's review of available natural resource information was intended to provide some simple insights regarding how this information might affect the prospect of future exploratory drilling.

The Yucca Mountain area lies in the southern Great Basin, an area that has been extensively investigated and reported in the literature. DOE provided a preliminary assessment of the potential for natural resources at the site in its 1988 SCP. Although the Yucca Mountain site contains areas of mineralization, these areas don't occur in concentrations or amounts sufficient for exploitation (see DOE, 1988; pp. 1–256 — 1–313). Moreover, experts do not believe that hydrocarbon resources exist in the area (*Op cit.*, pp. 1–313—1–323). Based on recent reports (Raines *et al.*, 1991; Schalla and Johnson, 1994; Sherlock *et al.*, 1996), it is not clear if any mineral resources (including prospects and occurrences) exist beyond those that have been previously identified.

Because a majority of the mineral resources exposed at the surface are believed to have already been discovered, a study was conducted by the USGS, in cooperation with the Nevada Bureau of Mines and Geology (Singer, 1996), to evaluate the metallic mineral resource potential below the cover (within 1 kilometer of the surface). As part of the study, geologic environments that were believed to be permissive for the occurrence of certain types of mineral deposits were identified (i.e., broad resource tracts) where deposits could hypothetically occur (see Cox *et al.*, 1996). No specific mineral deposits, prospects, or occurrences were identified at Yucca Mountain, although some potential (mineral) resource tracts were identified within the boundary of NTS. Thus, based on the information cited, it is not apparent that Yucca Mountain, or the area immediately around it, would represent an attractive candidate for either random or systematic exploratory drilling at this time. The staff believes that a more likely scenario might be drilling for ground water in one of the basins that lie beyond the site.

Table 4–1. Peak Annual Dose Resulting from a Damaged Waste Package.

Time of Intrusion (Years after Repository Closure)	*Mean and (95th percentile) for TEDE over a 10,000-year Performance Period*		*Mean and (95th percentile) for TEDE over a 50,000-year Performance Period*	
	1 m² Catchment Area (μ rem)	*10 m² Catchment Area (μ rem)*	*1 m² Catchment Area (μ rem)*	*10 m² Catchment Area (μ rem)*
100 years	1.2 (1.5)	1.9 (1.7)	3.6 (24)	3.8 (33)
1000 years	0.9 (1.1)	1.2 (1.1)	2.8 (20)	2.8 (20)

Table 4–2. Peak Annual Dose Resulting from a Perforated Waste Package.

Time of Intrusion (Years after Repository Closure)	*Mean and (95th percentile) for TEDE over a 10,000-year Performance Period*		*Mean and (95th percentile) for TEDE over a 50,000-year Performance Period*	
	1 m² Catchment Area (μ rem)	*10 m² Catchment Area (μ rem)*	*1 m² Catchment Area (μ rem)*	*10 m² Catchment Area (μ rem)*
100 years	0.4 (0.5)	0.4 (0.5)	1.1 (6.8)	1.1 (7.8)
1000 years	0.3 (0.4)	0.3 (0.4)	0.8 (5.2)	0.9 (6.1)

package; rather, exploratory drilling would most likely intersect emplacement tunnels or drifts of the repository or the geologic unit comprising the waste emplacement horizon.

Nonetheless, should a borehole intersect a waste package, the staff believes that it would be a low-consequence event for the types of hypothetical receptor groups considered in this NUREG, when limited to reasonable assumptions. Moreover, the use of active institutional controls, to delay the intrusion event for 1000 years after permanent repository closure, would not significantly affect the resulting, based on the calculations presented in this analysis.

4.6 References

American Water Works Association [AWWA], "AWWA Standard for Water Wells," Denver, Colorado, ANSI/AWWA A100–90, February 1991.

Anderson, J., "Gold—Its History and Role in the U.S. Economy, and the U.S. Exploration

of [the] Homestake Mining Company," *Mining Congress Journal*, pp. 51–58, [January] 1982.

Barnard, R.W., *et al.*, TSPA 1991: A[n] Initial-Total System Performance Assessment for Yucca Mountain," Albuquerque, New Mexico, Sandia National Laboratories, SAND91–2795, September 1992. [Prepared for DOE.]

Berglund, J.W., "Mechanisms Governing the Direct Removal of Wastes from the Waste Isolation Pilot Plant Repository Caused by Exploratory Drilling," Albuquerque, New Mexico, Sandia National Laboratories, SAND92–7295, December 1992. [Prepared by the New Mexico Engineering Institute for DOE.]

Charles, D., and T.J. McEwen, "Radiological Consequences of Drilling Intrusion into a Deep Repository for High Level Waste," United Kingdom, Intera Sciences, [Report] I244–1, January 1991. [Prepared for the

Swedish National Institute of Radiation Protection.]

Codell, R.B., *et al.*, "Initial Demonstration of the NRC's Capability to Conduct a Performance Assessment for a High-Level Waste Repository," U.S. Nuclear Regulatory Commission, NUREG–1327, May 1992.

Cox, D.P., *et al.*, Delineation of Mineral Resource Assessment Tracts and Estimates of Numbers of Undiscovered Deposits in Nevada (Chapter 12)," in D.A. Singer (ed.), "An Analysis of Nevada's Metal-Bearing Mineral Resources," Reno, Nevada, Nevada Bureau of Mines and Geology, Open File Report 96–2, 1996. [Prepared in cooperation with the USGS.]

Driscoll, F.G., *Groundwater and Wells (2nd Edition)*, St. Paul, Minnesota, Johnson Screens, 1986.

Harris, D.P., *Mineral Exploration Decisions—A Guide to Economic Analysis and Modeling*, New York, John Wiley and Sons Intersciences, 1990.

Jensen, M., "Conservation and Retrieval of Information: Elements of a Strategy to Inform Future Societies about Nuclear Waste Repositories (Final Report of the Nordic Nuclear Safety Research Project KAN – 1.3)," Copenhagen, Denmark, The Nordic Council of Ministers/The Nordic Committee for Nuclear Safety Research, Nordiske Seminar-og Arbejdsrapporter 1993:356, August 1993.

LeRoy, L.W., D.O. LeRoy, and J.W. Raese (eds.), *Subsurface Geology—Petroleum, Mining, and Construction (4th Edition)*, Golden, Colorado, Colorado School of Mines, 1977.

Mohanty, S. and McCartin, T.J. (coordinators), "NRC Sensitivity and Uncertainty Analyses for a Proposed HLW Repository at Yucca Mountain, Nevada, Using TPA Computer Code Version 3.1 – Volume 1: Conceptual Models and Data," U.S. Nuclear Regulatory Commission, NUREG–1668, February 2001.

National Research Council, *Drilling and Excavation Technologies in the Future*, Washington, D.C., National Academy Press, Committee on Advanced Drilling Technologies, 1994.

Nuclear Energy Agency [NEA], "Future Human Actions at Disposal Sites," Paris, France, NEA Working Group on Assessment of Future Human Actions at Radioactive Waste Disposal Sites, Safety Assessment of Radioactive Waste Repositories Series, Organisation for Economic Co-Operation and Development, 1991.

Raines, G.L., *et al.* (eds.), "Geology and Ore Deposits of the Great Basin," Geological Society of Nevada/U.S. Geological Survey, *Symposium Proceedings, April 1–5, 1990, Reno/Sparks, Nevada,* 2 vols. [1991].

Schalla, R.A., and E.H. Johnson (eds.), *Oil Fields of the Great Basin*, Reno, Nevada, Geological Society of Nevada, 1994.

Singer, D.A. (ed.), "An Analysis of Nevada's Metal-Bearing Mineral Resources," Reno, Nevada, Nevada Bureau of Mines and Geology, Open File Report 96–2, 1996.

Sherlock, M.G., D.P. Cox, and D.F. Huber, "Known Mineral Deposits and Occurrences in Nevada (Chapter 2)," in D.A. Singer (ed.), "An Analysis of Nevada's Metal-Bearing Mineral Resources," Reno, Nevada, Nevada Bureau of Mines and Geology, Open File Report 96–2, 1996.

Thordarson, W. and B.P. Robinson, "Wells and Springs in California and Nevada within 100 Miles of the Point 37 Deg. 15 Min. N., 116 Deg. 25 Min. W., on Nevada Test Site," U.S. Geological Survey, USGS–474–85, 1971. [Prepared for the AEC.]

Tolan, T.L., "The Use of Protective Barriers to Deter Inadvertent Human Intrusion into a Mined Geologic Facility for the Disposal of Radioactive Waste: A Review of Previous Investigations and Potential Concepts," Albuquerque, New Mexico, Sandia National Laboratories, SAND91–7097, June 1993.

U.S. Department of Energy, "Site Characterization Plan, Yucca Mountain Site,

Nevada Research and Development Area, Nevada," Office of Civilian Radioactive Waste Management, Nevada, DOE/RW–0199, 9 vols., December 1988.

Wescott, R.G., *et al.* (eds.), "NRC Iterative Performance Assessment Phase 2: Development of Capabilities for Review of a Performance Assessment for a High-Level Waste Repository," U.S. Nuclear Regulatory Commission, NUREG–1464, October 1995.

Wilson, M.L., *et al.*, "Total-System Performance Assessment for Yucca Mountain-SNL Second Iteration (TSPA–1993)," Albuquerque, New Mexico, Sandia National Laboratory, SAND93–2675, 2 vols., April 1994.

5. EXAMPLE CALCULATION OF EXPECTED ANNUAL DOSE, AS A FUNCTION OF TIME, FROM EXTRUSIVE VOLCANIC EVENTS AT YUCCA MOUNTAIN[1]

5.1 Introduction

As discussed in previous sections of this NUREG, the 1995 NAS report recommended that future standards for Yucca Mountain limit individual risk (dose) to the average member of a critical group and performance could be assessed over timeframes during which the geologic system is relatively stable (i.e., on the order of 10^6 years). Implementation of this NAS recommendation for an individual risk standard was evaluated earlier, in Section 3.3, by estimating annual doses for the ground-water pathway. Analysis of the risk of an extrusive volcanic (igneous) event is described in this section to gain insight into implementation issues with respect to estimating radiological exposures from low-probability events. Specifically, this (example) scoping analysis was undertaken to provide insights on the ability to estimate exposures for low-probability events and the relationship, if any, between the time period of the analysis and the estimate of dose.

5.2 Approach

Evaluation of the expected annual dose from an extrusive volcanic scenario at the proposed Yucca Mountain repository requires specification of an exposure scenario that defines the transport and fate of radionuclides released in such an event. The exposure scenario modeled in these analyses is depicted in Figure 5–1 and consists of four major components, in the following progression:

Event	Description
I	Magma enters the repository and becomes contaminated with only SNF[2] particles.
II	Tephra[3] forms from the contaminated magma and is released from the repository.
III	An eruption column, and plume, form and transport contaminated tephra to locations downwind from the event.
IV	Radionuclide contamination collects on the earth's surface, potentially exposing hypothetical receptor groups.

Each of these four components is discussed in greater detail in the following paragraphs. A more detailed discussion of the models and parameter sampling mechanisms is also provided in Jarzemba *et al.* (1999). The amount of SNF that is incorporated into magma and eventually extruded in the volcanic event is estimated by probabilistically determining the diameter of the volcanic conduit and then determining the amount of SNF overlapped by that area. See Doubik and Hill (1998).

For example, a conduit 50 meters in diameter (1963 square meters in area), occurring within the proposed repository boundary, would extrude 40.8 MTU of SNF assuming an areal mass loading of 85 MTU/acre (0.02079 MTU/square meter)[4] for the current reference repository design (see DOE, 1998; p. 3–23). The range of volcanic conduit diameters used in these analyses is from 24.6 to 77.9 meters.

Once SNF has been incorporated into magma and released from the cone, estimations of the downwind transport and deposition of contaminants must be made. These estimations are performed using the *ASHPLUME* computer code (Jarzemba and LaPlante,

---

[1]The figures shown in this section present the results from the demonstration of the continuing staff capability to review a TSPA. These figures, like the demonstration, are limited by the use of simplifying assumptions and sparse data.

[2]The principal waste forms to be disposed of at Yucca Mountain will be either SNF or vitrified waste. Other waste forms that may possibly be disposed of include low-level, greater-than-class-C (GTCC), or transuranic wastes. Only SNF was considered for this analysis.

[3]A general term for all pyroclastic rock material ejected from an erupting volcano.

[4]Thermal loading units are expressed in terms of MTU/acre for easy comparison with DOE's recently published 5-volume *Viability Assessment* (DOE, 1999).

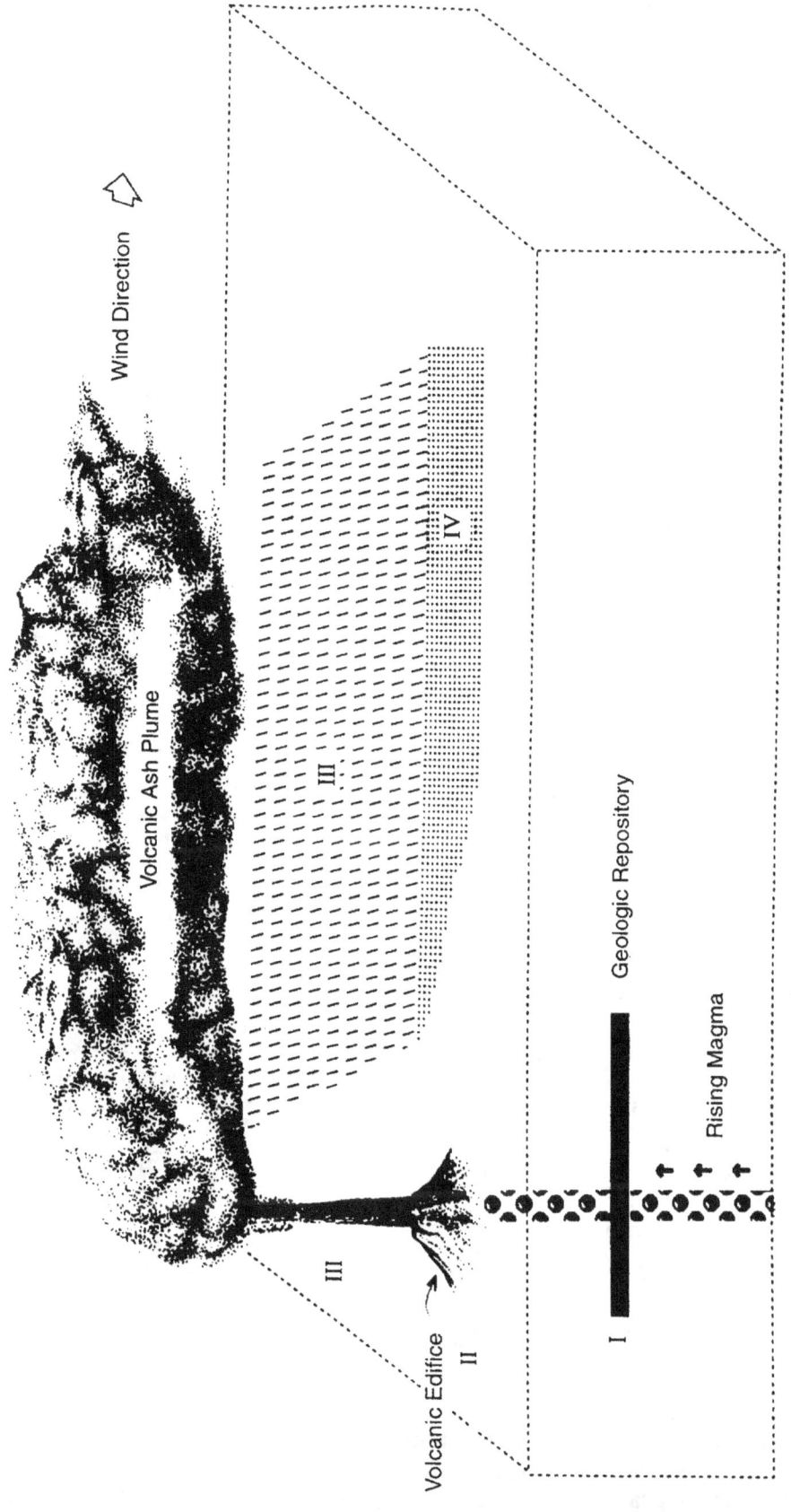

Figure 5–1. **Diagram showing the exposure scenario selected for the extrusive volcanic event calculation.** Processes depicted by numbers are described in Section 5.2 of the text.

1996; Jarzemba, 1997) which uses probabilistically-determined parameter values to describe the magnitude of the event in order to calculate the downwind deposition of contaminants. Once parameter values have been chosen, the computer code calculates downwind deposition based on a model modified from that of Suzuki (1983). Such parameters include (but are not limited to): wind speed and direction; volcanic event power and duration; eddy diffusivity; and parameters characterizing the fuel and ash particulate size distribution and density after incorporation. For a more complete description of transport and deposition parameters, the reader is referred to Jarzemba and LaPlante (1996). For the most recent information on the parameter sampling mechanisms, the reader is referred to Jarzemba *et al.* (1999).

Since these analyses require the estimation of expected dose as a function of time, and since *ASHPLUME* only determines the radionuclide deposition at the receptor location immediately following the volcanic event, the radionuclide areal concentration at the receptor location as a function of time after the event must be determined. These simulations use a semi-analytical model that accounts for radionuclide ingrowth/decay, leaching of contaminants from the radioactive ash blanket, and bulk erosion of the ash blanket (Jarzemba and Manteufel, 1997). The model uses quantities such as: radionuclide distribution coefficients—K_ds; the relative rate of ash blanket erosion λ^B; amount of water ingress into the ash blanket from irrigation and rainfall; and radioactive decay constants to estimate the radionuclide areal concentration of the ash blanket at times after the event. [For a description of these parameters and their numerical values the reader is referred to Jarzemba and Manteufel (1997).]

Once the radionuclide areal concentrations at times after the event have been estimated, conversion of these contamination levels to dose must be performed. For the purposes of this analysis, there are four possible dose pathways that can cause exposures to members of the hypothetical receptor group (assumed to be located 20 kilometers downwind from the proposed repository):

- Ingestion of crops grown on the contaminated ash blanket;

- Ingestion of contaminated animal products from stock that were raised on agricultural products grown on the contaminated ash blanket;

- Direct exposure from radionuclides in the ash blanket itself; and

- Inhalation from resuspended contamination.

Ingestion of ground water contaminated by radionuclides leaching from the ash blanket is not included in the model. For all pathways except inhalation, biosphere dose conversion factors (DCFs), which are simply multiplicative factors that convert areal contamination levels to dose, are used to estimate radiation doses (LaPlante and Poor, 1997). Because of the large fraction of the total dose from the inhalation pathway, a more mechanistic dose conversion process is used herein. Equation $(5-1)$ describes how doses are estimated for the inhalation pathway:

$$\dot{D}_i = BI_i S\eta_i f_e \, \frac{T_{B-0}\exp[-\lambda^B(t - t_{event})]}{T_R} \qquad (5-1)$$

where:

$\dot{D}_i$ = Dose rate due to inhalation from radionuclide i of resuspended contamination (rem/year);

B = Breathing rate (1.05×10^4 m³/year);

I_i = Inhalation-to-dose conversion factor for radionuclide *i* [rem/Ci; see Eckerman *et al.* (1988)];

S = Airborne mass load (loguniform distribution from 1×10^{-4} to 1×10^{-2} g/m³);

η_i = contamination level of the ash in radionuclide *i* (Ci/g); or the areal density of radionuclide *i* (Ci/cm^2) divided by the areal density of ash (g/cm^2) at the hypothetical receptor location;

f_e = fraction of year receptor individual is exposed to contaminated air (0.24);

T_{B-0} = thickness of ash blanket immediately after the event;

t_{event} = time of the volcanic event; and

T_R = thickness of the resuspendable layer (0.3 cm).

Important assumptions and conservatisms used to model the four major components of this exposure scenario are described as follows:

• All waste consumed by the conduit is conservatively assumed to be available for incorporation into the magma and subsequent ejection during the extrusive volcanic event.

• The volcanic cone is assumed to form at the center of the hypothetical repository block with an annual probability of 10^{-7}.

• The size distribution of tephra particles is undisturbed by the incorporation of SNF particles.

• The wind duration remains constant throughout the duration of the event.

• Only contamination within the top 15 centimeters of the ash blanket (soil) contributes to dose.

• Contamination of ground water from radionuclides leached out of the ash blanket is not considered.

• The inhalation-to-dose conversion factors found in Eckerman *et al.* (1988) are applicable to the hypothetical receptor (individual) modeled in these analyses.

5.3 Calculation of the Expected Dose to a Hypothetical Receptor Group

The "average risk" or expected annual dose is the product of the consequence (i.e., dose) and the probability that the dose has occurred. Estimates of dose are uncertain because the models and their input parameters are uncertain, as are the times of occurrence of the disruptive events such as volcanic activity. Monte Carlo analysis is used to account for the uncertainty in the parameters used for estimating doses resulting from volcanic events, similar to the approach used in Section 3.3. The Monte Carlo analysis propagates the uncertainty in model inputs through the conceptual models. A Monte Carlo simulation evaluates a model repeatedly using input values that have been randomly selected from the probability distributions for the input variables. The output of the Monte Carlo analysis is a set of results such as dose versus time, for each of the randomly chosen input sets of values. Each dose curve has an associated probability based on the probability of the model inputs selected. Generally, each Monte Carlo output result has equal probability. Thus, each dose curve from the Monte Carlo analysis has a probability of occurring that is the product of the probability associated with the parameter uncertainty (i.e., *1/N*, where *N* is the number of Monte Carlo samples) and the probability associated with event uncertainty. The overall expected annual dose curve is developed by combining each of the dose curves, with their associated probabilities, into a single dose curve that represents the "average risk" or expected annual dose.

For volcanic activity, dose consequences depend on when the event occurs and the length of time between the occurrence of the event and the exposure. Events that occur soon after repository closure produce larger consequences because the relatively short-lived but high-activity radionuclides like americium-241 (^{241}Am) are still present in significant quantities. Radionuclides can reach the affected population in short times (hours to days), but persist in the environment and also cause lower levels of exposure long after the event (hundreds to thousands of years).

After the event occurs, doses diminish over time because of radioactive decay and erosion of the radioactive ash blanket. The time of occurrence of the event is very important to the dose consequences, and is therefore included in the probabilistic analysis as one of the sampled parameters. The fact that there are short-term variations in the consequences from volcanic events complicates the probabilistic analysis by requiring a large number of Monte Carlo samples to resolve the overall expected dose on both the short- and long-term time scales. For example, if 100 samples are needed to properly represent the parameter uncertainty (e.g., volcanic event power and duration, wind speed, and direction), then theoretically 1 million samples would be required for a 10,000-year simulation [i.e., (100 samples per/year) × (10,000 years)] to ensure that the sampling procedure produced a sufficient number of samples at individual years. Such a large number of Monte Carlo simulations is impractical with the present TPA code.

A more efficient approach to developing the expected annual dose curve is to develop average dose curves for volcanic events at a few and discrete event times. Specific times of occurrence of volcanic activity are selected for the evaluation rather than randomly selecting occurrence times in a Monte Carlo approach. In the present analysis, the event times were 100, 500, and 1000 to 10,000 years in 1000-year time steps. Each specific event time has a distinct probabilistic analysis and associated family of dose curves. The probabilistic analysis is used to develop an average dose curve for each of the distinct times (see Figure 5−2). Linear interpolation, between the times of conditional expected dose curves, was used to consider events at other times. Equation (5−2) describes how the expected annual dose to the receptor individual is estimated in this approach:

$$R(t) = \sum_{n=1}^{E} \Delta Tp \, D_n(t) \qquad (5-2)$$

where:

$R(t)$ = the expected annual dose to the hypothetical receptor as a function of time;

$D_n(t)$ = the average dose rate as a function of time for specific event time n;

p = the annual probability of an event;

ΔT = increment of time associated with the event time n (if events are evaluated on a per-year basis, this would be 1 year); and

E = the number of specific event times used to represent variation in event uncertainty (interpolation between events can be used to generate dose curves for each year).

5.4 Results and Conclusions

The expected annual dose as a function of time is presented in Figure 5−3. The expected dose curve reaches a peak dose of approximately 1 mrem around 1000 years after repository closure. The time of the peak of the expected annual dose curve is a direct result of time-dependent processes (radiation decay and soil erosion) that decrease consequences over time. Figure 5−2 displays this reduction in consequence for volcanic events by showing the variation in consequences for volcanic events over specific occurrence times for the events. The reduction in consequence is largest during the first 1000 years, when short-lived radionuclides have their largest effect. Americium-241, which has a radioactive half-life of 432 years, is the largest contributor to dose over the 10,000-year time period. The direct release of radionuclides occurring in the first 100 years was not considered in this analysis because active institutional controls are assumed to be used to mitigate any potential exposure consequences by restricting human activity in areas with contaminated ash.

Four general conclusions may be drawn from the present analysis:

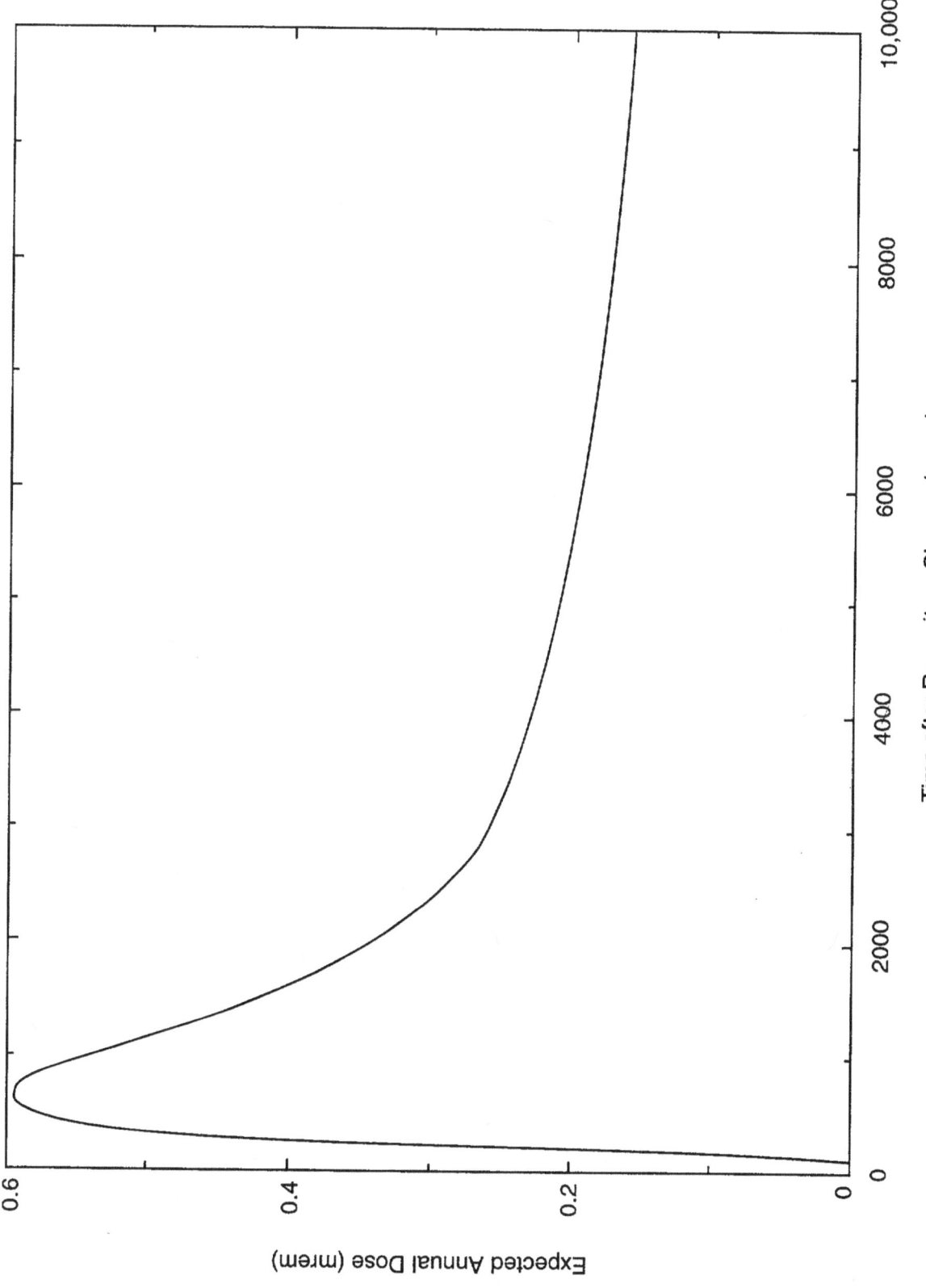

Figure 5–2. Average annual conditional dose resulting from extrusive volcanic events occurring at specific times. Calculation of conditional dose assumes the event probability is one (1). Initiating times, following repository closure, are as indicated.

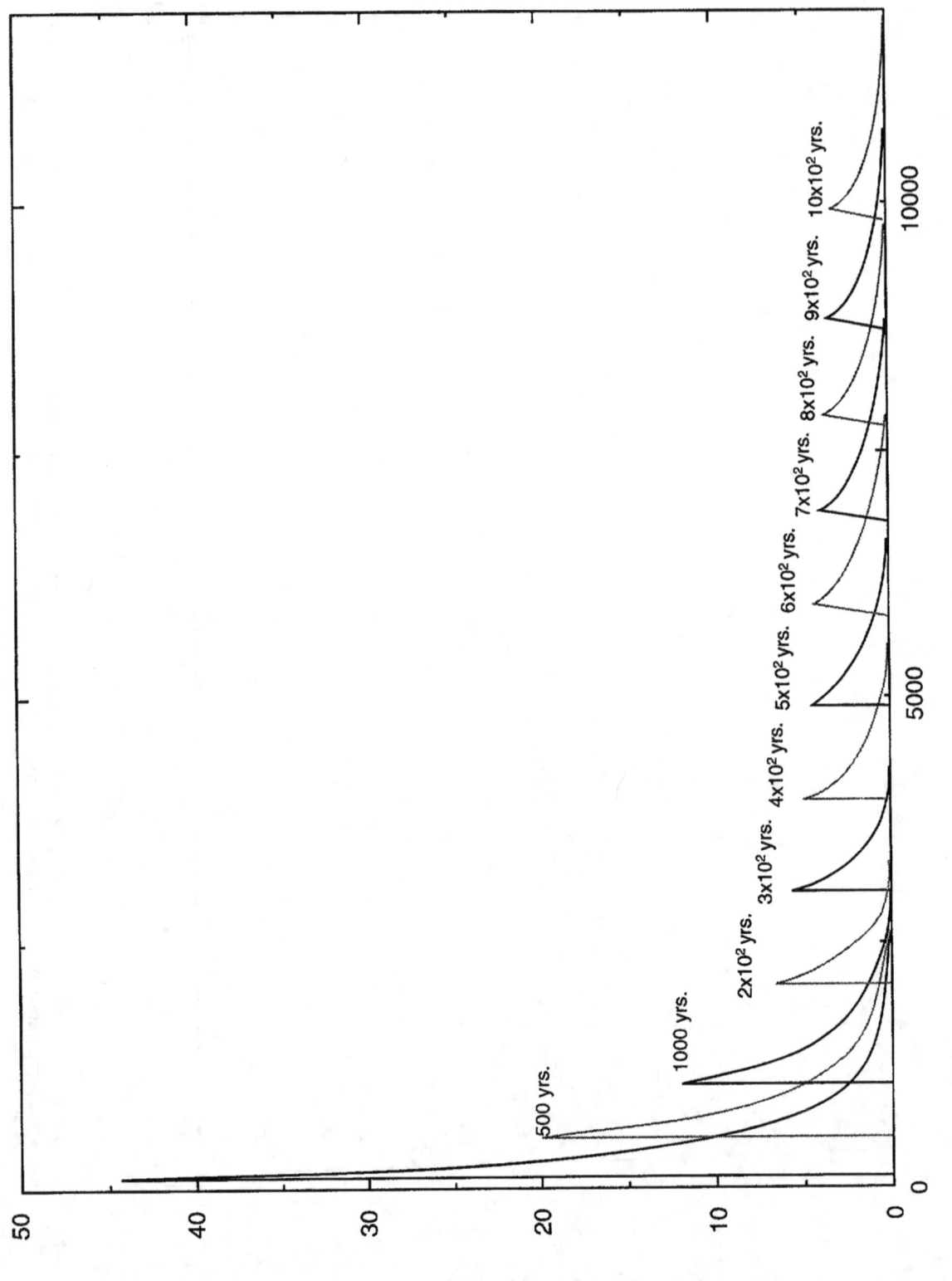

Figure 5–3. Expected annual dose as a function of time from extrusive volcanic events.

- A capability for estimating the annual individual dose, from direct release of radionuclides from an volcanic event, can be incorporated into performance assessments, assuming the concentrations of radionuclides can be estimated in contaminated tephra that collects on the earth's surface;

- The time of occurrence of the volcanic event has a significant effect on the annual individual dose estimate;

- The length of time between when the volcanic event occurs and when the exposure takes place has a significant effect on the annual individual dose estimate; and

- The peak expected annual dose for a direct release of radionuclides occurs during the initial 10,000 years, and is estimated to be on the order of 1 mrem.

5.5 References

Doubik, P. Yu., and B.E. Hill, "Xenolith Formation and the Development of Basaltic Volcanic Conduits During the 1975 Tolbachik Eruptions, Kamchatka [U.S.S.R.], with the Implications for Volcanic Hazards Assessments at Yucca Mountain, Nevada," San Antonio, Texas, Center for Nuclear Waste Regulatory Analyses, Intermediate Milestone Deliverable 20–1402–461–860, October 1998.

Eckerman, K.F., A.B. Wolbarst, and A.C.B. Richardson, "Limiting Values of Radionuclide Intake and Air Concentration and Dose Conversion Factors for Inhalation, Submersion, and Ingestion," U.S. Environmental Protection Agency, EPA 520/1–88–020, September 1988.

Jarzemba, M.S., and P.A. LaPlante, "Preliminary Calculations of Expected Dose from Extrusive Volcanic Events at Yucca Mountain," San Antonio, Texas, Center for Nuclear Waste Regulatory Analyses, Intermediate Milestone Letter Report 5708–771–610, May 17, 1996.

Jarzemba, M.S., "Stochastic Radionuclide Distributions after a Basaltic Eruption for Performance Assessments of Yucca Mountain," *Nuclear Technology*, 118(2):132–141 [May 1997].

Jarzemba, M.S., P.A. LaPlante, and K.J. Poor, "ASHPLUME Version 1.0—A Code for Contaminated Ash Dispersal and Deposition: Technical Description and User's Guide," San Antonio, Texas, Center for Nuclear Waste Regulatory Analyses, CNWRA 97–004, Revision 1, June 1997.

Jarzemba, M.S., and R.D. Manteufel, "An Analytically Based Model for the Simultaneous Leaching-Chain Decay of Radionuclides from Contaminated Ground Surface Soil Layers," *Health Physics,* 73(6): 919–927 [December 1997].

Jarzemba, M.S., B.E. Hill, and C.B. Connor, "ASHPLUMO Module Description [Section 3.12]" in S. Mohanty and T.J. McCartin (coordinators), "Sensitivity and Uncertainty Analyses for a Proposed HLW Repository at Yucca Mountain, Nevada, Using TPA Computer Code Version 3.1—Volume 1: Conceptual Models and Data," U.S. Nuclear Regulatory Commission, NUREG–1668, February 2001.

LaPlante, P.A., and K.J. Poor, "Information and Analyses to Support Selection of Critical Groups and Reference Biospheres for Yucca Mountain Exposure Scenarios," San Antonio, Texas, Center for Nuclear Waste Regulatory Analyses, CNWRA 97–009, August 1997.

Suzuki, T., "A Theoretical Model for Dispersion of Tephra," in D. Shimozuru and I. Yokoyama (eds.), *Arc Volcanism: Physics and Tectonics, 1981 IAVCEI Symposium Proceedings, August 31–September 5, 1981, Tokyo, Hakone, Japan,* pp. 95–113 [1983].

U.S. Department of Energy, "Viability Assessment of a Repository at Yucca Mountain—Total System Performance Assessment, Volume 3," Las Vegas, Nevada, Office of Civilian Radioactive Waste Management/Yucca Mountain Site Characterization Office, DOE/RW–0508/V3, December 1998.

6. ANALYSIS OF RELATIVE HAZARD OF HLW OVER LONG TIME PERIODS[1]

6.1 Introduction

An issue raised by the NAS in its findings and recommendations concerned the time period over which compliance with HLW standards should be of regulatory concern. In its 1995 report, the NAS recommended (National Research Council, 1995; pp. 71–72) that:

> "... [the] calculation of the maximum risks of radiation releases **whenever** they occur as long as the geologic characteristics of the repository environment do not change significantly (emphasis added). The time scale for long-term geologic processes at Yucca Mountain is on the order of approximately one million years."

The purpose of this particular recommendation was to focus on the time at which future populations might be at maximum risk. With time, the radionuclides in a potential geologic repository will decay, and the radiological hazard associated with the waste will decrease (see DOE, 1980; pp. 1.3–1.4). Thus, at some particular point in the future, the hazard associated with the HLW repository will become comparable to the hazard of naturally occurring radioactive sources, such that the disposal facility hazard becomes similar to that of uranium naturally concentrated in an ore body.

6.2 Discussion

The NAS has stated that probably the most significant difference between its findings and recommendations and the existing HLW standards is the time period of regulatory interest (*Op cit.*, p. 119). As noted in Section 1, current regulations at Part 191 recognize a 10,000-year time period of regulatory concern, whereas the NAS has suggested that this time frame be longer—whenever the peak risk occurs (e.g., on the order of up to 1 million

years after permanent closure of the repository). Because both EPA and NRC are re-evaluating this time period, the following analysis was conducted to determine when the radioactivity and more importantly, the radiological hazard associated with SNF (the dominant waste constituent in the proposed geologic repository) might become comparable to that of naturally occurring radioactive materials.

The health hazard of radioactive waste depends on two primary factors: (a) the inherent radiotoxicity of the material; and (b) the accessibility of the material to possible human intake or exposure. This scoping analysis compares the hazard associated with a HLW repository with that of a hypothetical ore body at the same location in the unsaturated zone at Yucca Mountain. Specifically, this analysis considers the amount of percolating water that contacts SNF, solubility limits for radionuclides, and radionuclide release rates to account for the accessibility of radionuclides for exposures through the ground-water pathway. Contributions from other characteristics of engineered and geologic barriers will be neglected.

The approach used in this study was to compare the variations in total radioactivity and radiological hazard for a geologic repository containing **only** SNF (hereafter referred to as the "spent fuel repository") and a hypothetical uranium ore body, over a 100-million-year time period. The hypothetical ore body is defined to have the same amount of uranium and occupy the same volume as the proposed geologic repository at Yucca Mountain. The hypothetical ore body is considered to contain only ^{235}U and ^{238}U and their radioactive daughters. The primary difference between a potential geologic repository and the hypothetical ore body referred to in this analysis, is that repository-destined waste has a significant man-made radionuclide inventory (through neutron irradiation and fissioning) as

---

[1]The figures and table shown in this section present the results from the demonstration of the continuing staff capability to review a TSPA. These figures and table, like the demonstration, are limited by the use of simplifying assumptions and sparse data.

compared with the ore body, which contains naturally occurring nuclides only. The major difference between this analysis and previous work[2] is that the most recently available data and characteristics of the Yucca Mountain site (e.g., solubilities, radionuclide inventories) are used.

6.3   Description of Modeling Approach

6.3.1   Ore Body and Geologic Repository

Uranium is widely distributed throughout the Earth's crust (at about 2 parts per million). It is more abundant than gold, platinum, silver, bismuth, cadmium, and antimony (Krauskopf, 1979). But because it is chemically active, it never occurs as a native element and is usually found in combinations with other minerals (about 100 different ones).[3] Certain geologic conditions (see Finch *et al.*, 1973) permit uraniferous minerals to occur in anomalous concentrations, at about 400 to 2500 times typical crustal abundance, which render these materials exploitable and, therefore, *ore*.

Figure 6−1 shows the major steps in the uranium life-cycle, where ore is extracted from the earth and transformed into SNF (and other radioactive wastes). The first step begins with the extraction of uranium-bearing minerals from an ore-bearing deposit. It takes approximately 50 kilograms of uraniferous ore (containing at least 0.08 percent U_3O_8,[4]) to yield about 1 kilogram of uranium. Uranium, in the form of U_3O_8, is recovered from ore through three primary steps: mining, mill concentration, and chemical processing (see Rahn *et al.*, 1984). Each process step also generates certain byproducts (and wastes). For example, during mining and mill processing,

uranium is extracted from ore and separated from gangue materials (the ore aggregate or matrix), thereby creating byproducts (in the form of tailings) that contain radioactive daughters of uranium-234 (^{234}U) and ^{238}U—primarily the isotopes thorium-230 (^{230}Th), radium-226 (^{226}Ra), and lead-210 (^{210}Pb) and ^{235}U—primarily the isotopes protactinium-231 (^{231}Pa) and actinide-227 (^{227}Ac). (Most of the ore's radioactivity is contained in the tailings, in the form of radon gas.) Chemical processing (e.g., refining) of the concentrated ores (now at about $0.5-0.8$ percent U_3O_8[5]) and subsequent enriching of the uranium concentrates makes it suitable as nuclear fuel. After enrichment (to about 3.5 percent of fissile ^{235}U, for light-water reactors), the uranium is fabricated into ceramic pellets and sealed into stainless steel or zirconium alloy rods. The rods are subsequently bundled into fuel assemblies, which are then used to power reactors. Over time, the fuel assemblies become inefficient for the purposes of nuclear fission because of neutron irradiation, and thus becomes "spent" (nuclear fuel).

The principal waste forms considered for disposal in a HLW repository at Yucca Mountain will be either SNF from commercial nuclear power reactors and vitrified waste (glass) from both defense and commercial sources, although other waste forms may be disposed.[6] In accordance with Section 114(d)(2) of the Nuclear Waste Policy Act of 1982 (NWPA), as amended (Public Law 97−425), no more than 70,000 metric tons equivalent of waste can be disposed of at any one geologic repository in the U.S.

6.3.2   Radioactivity as a Function of Time

In Figure 6−2, the total radioactivity of SNF is shown, along with the radioactivity of a number of the dominant radionuclides. At early times, the radioactivity is dominated primarily by fission products, whereas at later times, it is dominated by transuranics (and

---

[2]A number of reports and analyses have addressed the reduction of radioactivity, and radiological hazards of HLW with time, or made comparisons of its hazard relative to uranium ore. For example, see Cohen (1982); Cohen *et al.* (1989); Elayi and Schapira (1987); EPA (1982a, 1982b, 1985); Hamstra (1975); Levi (1980); Liljenzin and Rydberg (1996); Mehta *et al.* (1991); Tacca *et al.* (1991); Wick and Cloninger (1980); and Williams (1980).

[3]Uraninite (UO_2) and carnotite [$U(SiO_4)_{1-x}(OH)_{4x}$] are the chief ores of uranium, although other minerals have also proven to be important sources (e.g., tyuyamunite, torbernite, and autunite). See Hurlbut (1971).

[4]U_3O_8 or triuranium octoxide is a refined oxide of uraniferous ores. Sometimes referred to as *yellow cake*, it is the final product generated during the milling process.

---

[5]This process step also generates depleted uranium, which is used for kinetic-energy projectiles for the military (Adams, 1995).

[6]Other waste forms that may possibly be disposed of in a geologic repository include low-level, GTCC, or transuranic wastes.

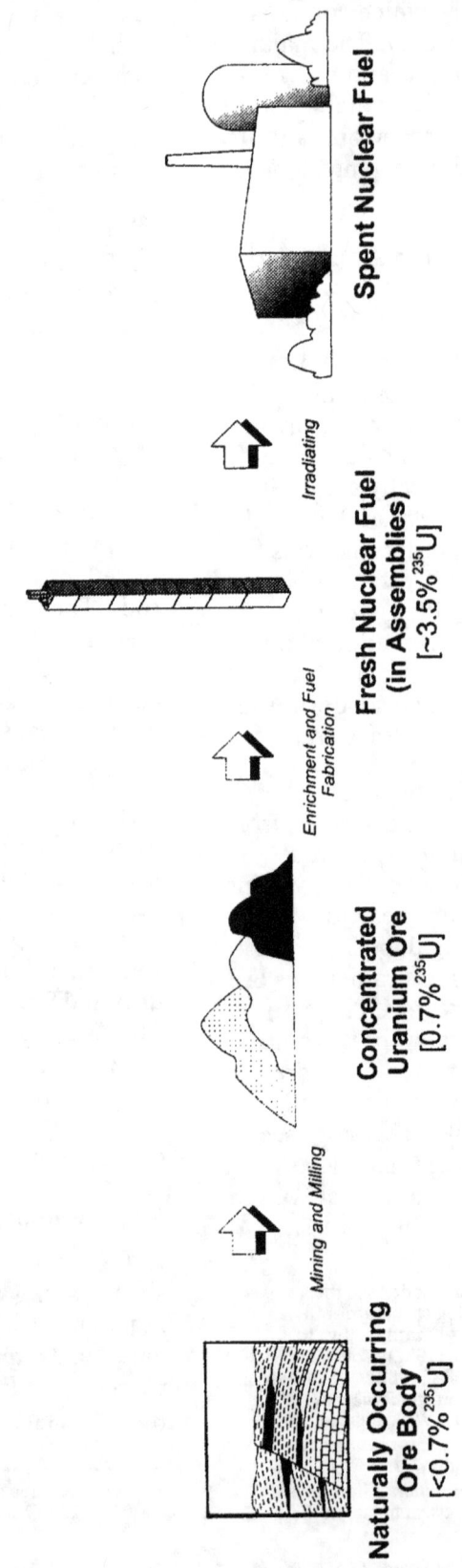

Figure 6–1. Major steps in extraction and use of uranium, along with major byproducts. (Enrichment, fuel fabrication, and irradiation can generate other radioactive waste hazards not addressed in this analysis.)

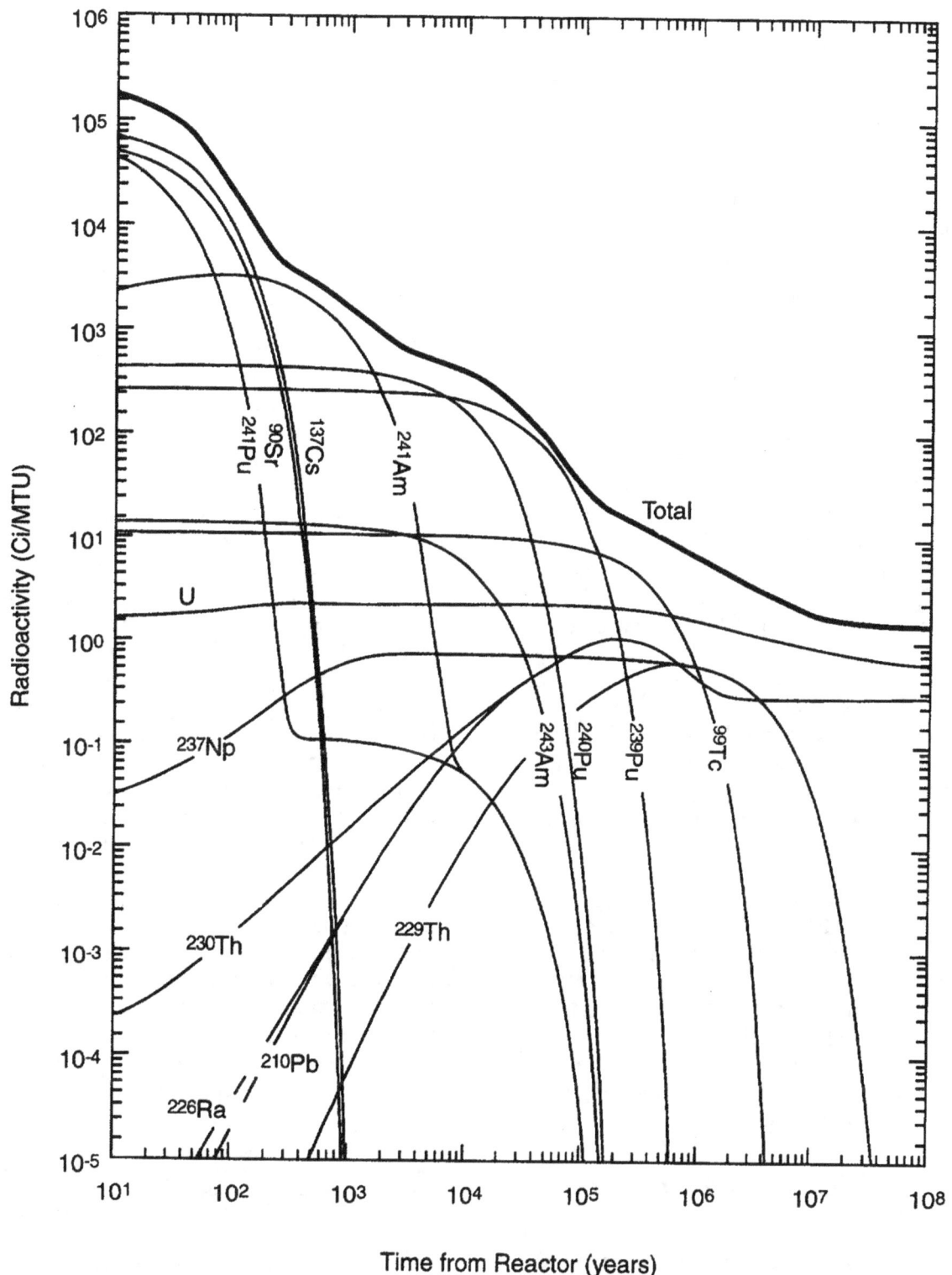

Figure 6–2. Radioactivity of SNF. Inventory based on Lozano *et al.* (1994).

their daughters). Strontium-90 and cesium-137 (^{137}Cs) dominate the activity up to 100–200 years; americium and plutonium up to 100,000 years; and technetium and uranium beyond 100,000 years. At times beyond 10 million years, the activity is dominated by ^{235}U, ^{238}U; and their daughters, which are naturally occurring radionuclides. Figure 6–2 is in agreement with a similar figure shown in a study that was performed to support the rulemaking process for Part 191 in the mid 1980s [see Figures A–4 and A–5 of EPA (1985)].

In Figure 6–3, the inventory of the hypothetical ore body used in this analysis is shown. The ore body is enriched to 3.5 percent ^{235}U to match the pre-irradiation uranium content of SNF. The inventory ranges over 9 orders of magnitude, indicating the ore is predominantly uranium. The daughters are in equilibrium and their activity is 0.318 curies per MTU of uranium (Ci/MTU) for ^{238}U, ^{234}U, ^{230}Th, ^{226}Ra, and ^{210}Pb, and is 0.085 Ci/MTU for ^{235}U, ^{231}Pa, and ^{227}Ac. The total radioactivity is 1.85 Ci/MTU for the nuclides tracked in this analysis. Because ^{235}U and ^{238}U have very long half-lives, their inventory and radioactivity remain essentially constant over 100 million years. In Figure 6–4, the total radioactivity of the spent fuel repository and the hypothetical ore body are compared. By 1000 years, the radioactivity of SNF is 1 percent of what it was at 10 years after irradiation. At 10 years from the reactor, the spent fuel radioactivity is about 182,800 Ci/MTU. The ore body radioactivity is about constant at 1.85 Ci/MTU. At approximately 10^4 years, the spent fuel radioactivity will have decreased by 99.9 percent. Beyond 10 million years, the total radioactivity is essentially equal to the hypothetical ore body.

6.3.3 Radiological Hazard as a Function of Time

Although informative, a comparison of total radioactivity of ^{241}Am is approximately 100 times more hazardous than ingesting 1 curie of ^{137}Cs (EPA, 1988; DOE, 1988). For this analysis, the staff compared the radiological hazards associated with drinking ground

water, which has been contaminated by either the spent fuel repository or the hypothetical ore body. To make such a comparison, some modeling assumptions and site-specific data are employed. The model, as illustrated in Figure 6–5, consists of steadily percolating ground water that flows through the repository and into the saturated zone. Some of the percolating ground water contacts some of the waste packages. The water that contacts the waste subsequently becomes contaminated with radionuclides. For the analyses, 43 different radionuclides are considered from 10 to 100 million years after irradiation (Lozano *et al.*, 1994). The current geologic repository design[7] is assumed to have a footprint covering an area of about 5 square kilometers (TRW Environmental Safety Systems, Inc., 1994), a 1-millimeter-per-year spatially homogeneous percolation rate [based on Wilson *et al.* (1994) and Wescott *et al.* (1995)]; a cross-sectional area, perpendicular to the infiltration path, of approximately 10 square meters/waste package; a payload of 10 MTU/waste package (TRW Environmental Safety Systems, Inc., 1994); and a package areal density of one waste package per 500 square meters (corresponding to an 80-MTU/acre areal mass loading[8]). Both the spent fuel repository and the hypothetical ore body contain 63,000 MTU, which is consistent with current designs for the proposed repository (*Op cit.*). The percentage of percolating ground water available for contacting the waste is the ratio of the cross-sectional area of all the waste packages compared with the total repository footprint area (approximately 1 percent). The percentage of waste packages contacted is based on the ratio of the area of a single waste package to that surface area necessary to

---

[7]The geologic repository design described in TRW Environmental Safety Systems, Inc. (1994) and assumed for this NUREG is the reference design found in the 1988 SCP. However, in 1997, DOE announced plans to change both the size and geometry of the repository footprint (see DOE, 1997a; pp. ES–15 – ES–15). These changes were subsequently described in the *Reference Design Description for a Geologic Repository* (DOE, 1997b; p 13). The size of DOE's revised repository footprint is now reported to be 3 square kilometers (300 hectares). This change is not believed to fundamentally change the conclusions of any of the analyses described in this NUREG.

[8]80 MTU/acre are used in this NUREG for easy comparison with DOE's 1988 SCP.

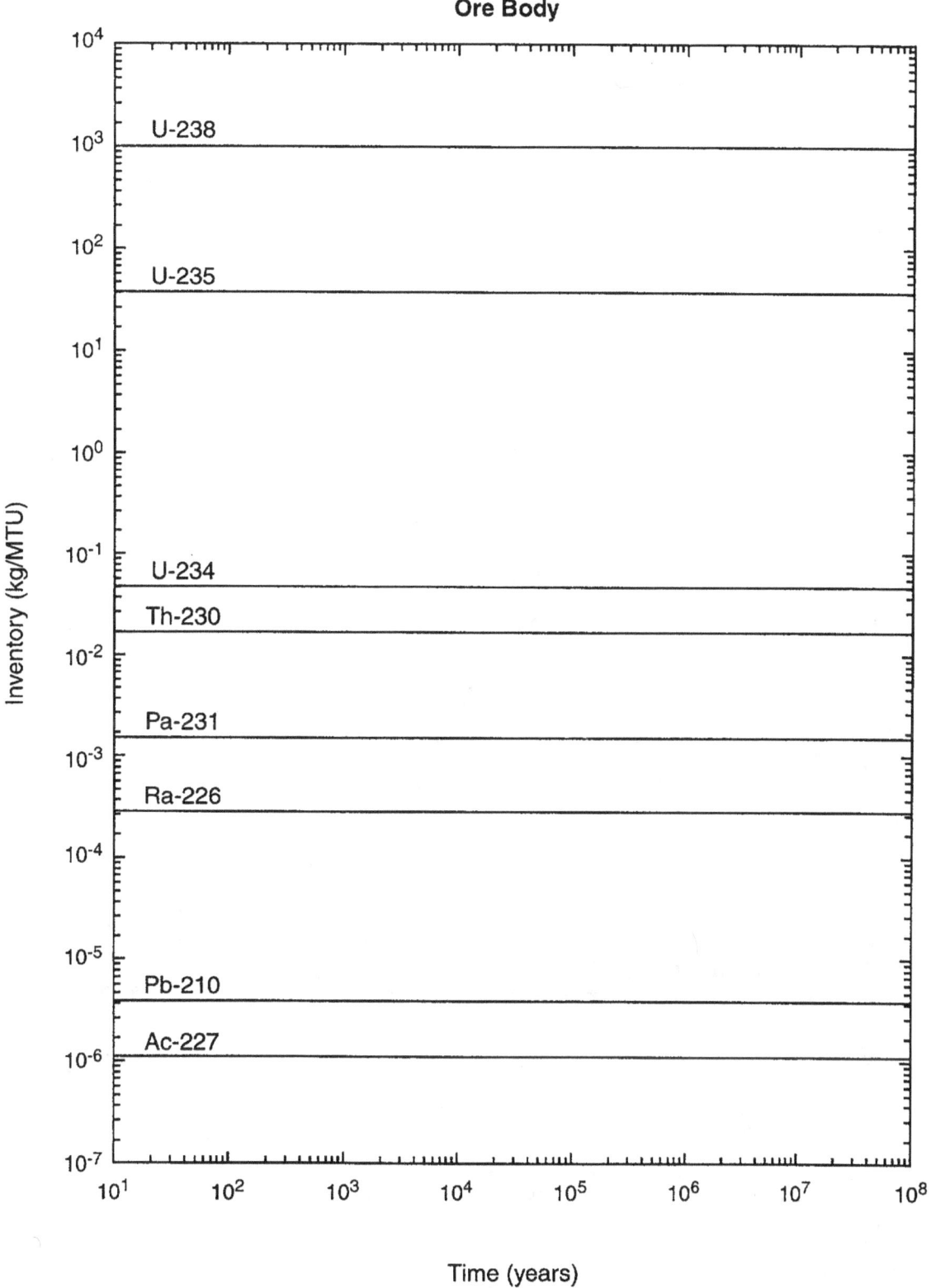

Figure 6—3.   **Radionuclide inventory of the hypothetical ore body.**

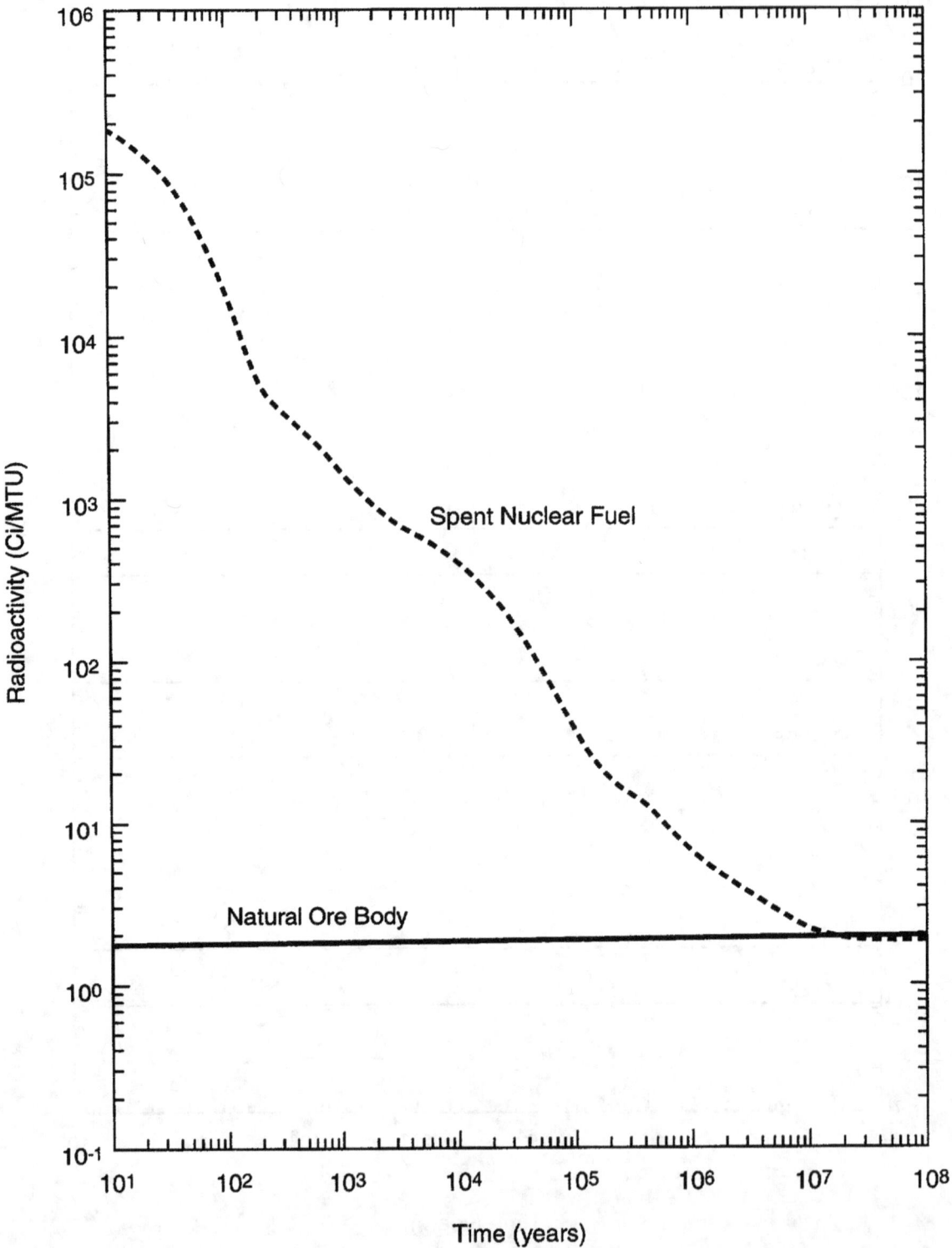

Figure 6–4. **Comparison of radioactivity between the spent fuel repository and the hypothetical ore body.**

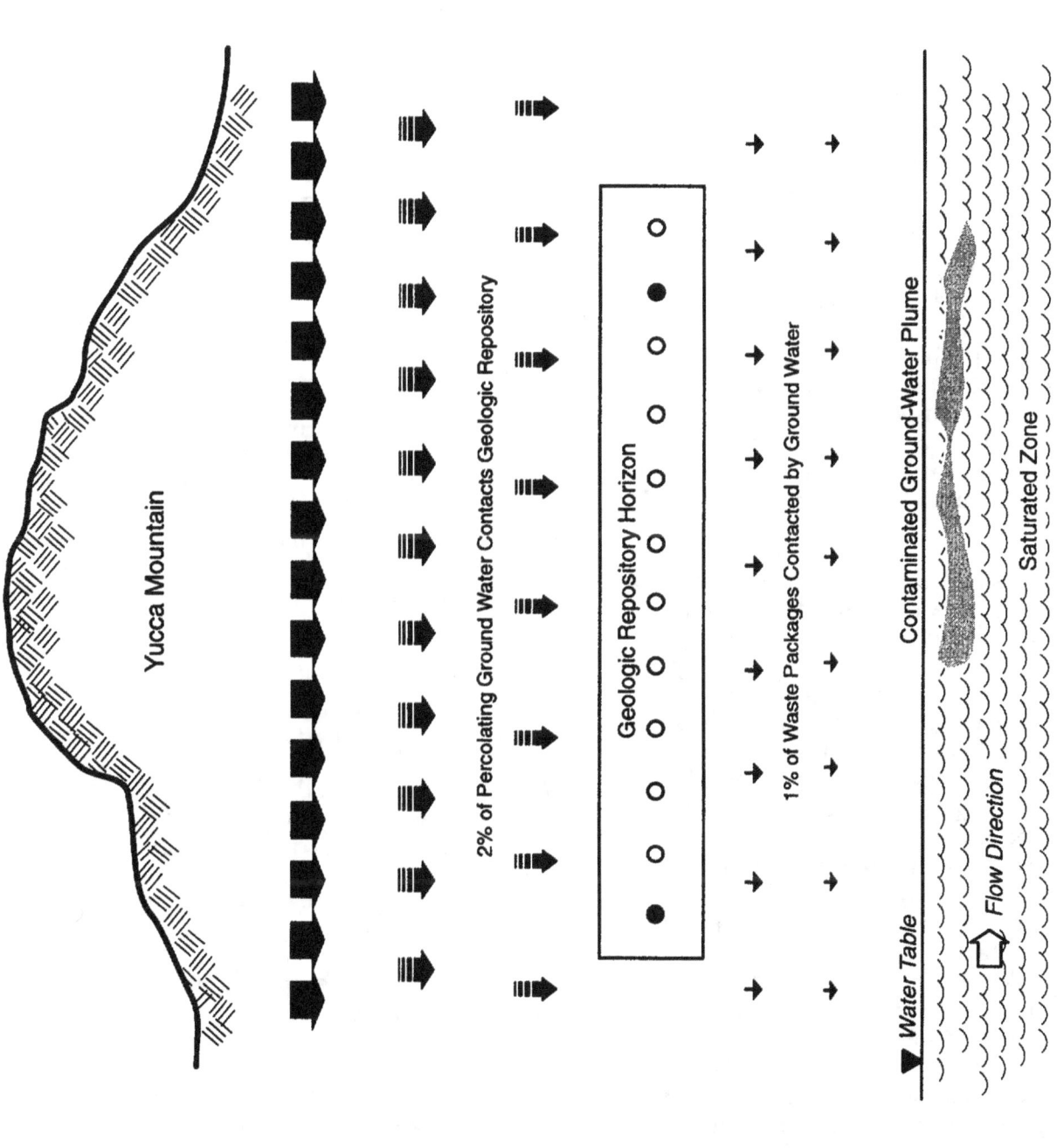

Figure 6–5. **Drinking water dose model.** Illustration shows ground water percolating through Yucca Mountain, 2 percent of which reaches waste emplacement horizon and contacts 1 percent of the waste package canisters. Subsequently, the radioactive leachate continues to percolate downward until it reaches the water table.

funnel water, to sustain dripping. Sustained dripping is estimated to require a focusing from a 1000-square-meter area above the waste package. Therefore, the ratio of the two areas results in 1 percent of the waste packages experiencing dripping. To be consistent, these same assumptions are used for the hypothetical ore body.

The *drinking water pathway dose conversion factors* (DCF$_{dw}$ s)—assuming a drinking rate of two liters per day—and solubilities of the radionuclides, with associated uncertainties, are summarized in Table 6–1. The DCF$_{dw}$ s are based on a drinking water pathway being the sole means of exposure, and the *ingestion dose conversion factors* (DCFs) used to calculate the DCF$_{dw}$ s are taken from EPA (1988) and DOE (1988). The solubilities are based largely on earlier work contained in Wilson *et al.* (1994) and Wescott *et al.* (1995), and are uncertain because of limited knowledge of the behavior of nuclides (especially actinides) and uncertain geochemical conditions. The same ranges of solubility, which include the associated uncertainties, are used for calculations of both the spent fuel repository and the hypothetical ore body.

Figure 6–6 shows the relative radiological hazard that is the ratio of the doses received by drinking ground water contaminated by the spent fuel repository, and contaminated by a hypothetical ore body. What this figure shows is that a ratio greater than one corresponds to the spent fuel repository being a greater hazard than the hypothetical ore body. The ratio of drinking water doses is not affected by dilution because the dilution volumes are the same for the spent fuel repository and the hypothetical ore body. Sorption of radionuclides is neglected, which may affect the relative hazard. Mean values for radionuclide solubilities and bulk waste dissolution (release) rate were used to generate Figure 6–6. The radiological hazard is dominated by strontium and cesium up to 100–200 years; by plutonium and americium up to 20,000 years; and by neptunium and

uranium daughter products beyond 20,000 years. The plateaus in some of the radionuclide dose curves are caused by the solubility-limited release of the radionuclide. Plutonium and americium have relatively low solubilities and hence are solubility-limited. Other radionuclides (technetium, iodine), which are highly soluble, represent a hazard that is controlled by release rate. The maximum release rate that was assumed for generating Figure 6–7 was 1 part in 100,000 of the current inventory per year based on previous staff work (Wescott *et al.*, 1995). The relative hazard is based on a ratio of doses calculated as follows:

$$\frac{D_{dw,rep}}{D_{dw,ob}} = \frac{\sum_i DCF_i \ \min(sol_{i,rep} \times F_g \times A_i, \ R_{i,rep} \times F_w \times \frac{I_{i,rep}}{Q})}{\sum_i DCF_i \ \min(sol_{i,ob} \times F_g \times A_i, \ R_{i,ob} \times F_w \times \frac{I_{i,ob}}{Q})}$$

$$(6\text{–}1)$$

where:

$D_{dw,rep}$ = dose from drinking ground water contaminated by the spent fuel repository–*rep* (rem/year);

$D_{dw,ob}$ = dose from drinking ground water contaminated by the hypothetical ore body–*ob* (rem/year);

DCF_i = DCF from drinking ground water contaminated by the ith radionuclide [(rem/year)/(Ci/liter)];

sol_i = solubility of the ith radionuclide in the spent fuel repository or the hypothetical ore body (mol/liter);

A_i = activity of the ith radionuclide (Ci/mol);

F_g = fraction of seeping ground water that becomes contaminated (2 percent);

F_w = fraction of inventory contacted by seeping ground water (1 percent);

Table 6-1. Solubilities and Dose Conversion Factors for the 43 Radionuclides Used in the Relative Hazards Scoping Calculation.

Nuclide	Common Logarithm of Solubility [a] (mol/L)	Drinking Water Dose Conversion Factors [b] (rem/year/Ci/m^3)
^{238}U	-5.3 ± 1	1.68×10^6
^{246}Cm	-5.3 ± 1	3.29×10^7
^{242}Pu	-8.5 ± 2	2.99×10^7
^{242m}Am	-10.0 ± 2	3.07×10^7
^{238}Pu	-10.0 ± 2	2.77×10^7
^{234}U	−5.3 ± 1	1.90×10^6
^{230}Th	−8.0 ± 2	3.87×10^6
^{226}Ra	−7.0 ± 2	8.03×10^6
^{210}Pb	−6.0 ± 1	3.72×10^7
^{243}Cm	−5.3 ± 1	2.12×10^7
^{243}Am	−8.5 ± 2	3.29×10^7
^{239}Pu	−10.0 ± 2	3.14×10^7
^{235}U	−5.3 ± 1	1.83×10^6
^{231}Pa	−7.0 ± 2	8.03×10^7
^{227}Ac	−10.0 ± 2	1.02×10^8
^{245}Cm	−8.5 ± 2	3.29×10^7
^{241}Pu	−10.0 ± 2	6.28×10^5
^{241}Am	−8.5 ± 2	3.29×10^7
^{237}Np	−3.7 ± 1	2.85×10^7
^{233}U	−5.3 ± 1	1.97×10^6
^{229}Th	−8.0 ± 2	2.56×10^7
^{244}Cm	−8.5 ± 2	1.68×10^7
^{240}Pu	−10.0 ± 2	3.14×10^7
^{236}U	−5.3 ± 1	1.83×10^6
^{232}U	−5.3 ± 1	9.49×10^6
^{151}Sm	−10.0 ± 2	2.48×10^3
^{137}Cs	Large [c]	3.65×10^5
^{135}Cs	Large	5.18×10^4
^{129}I	Large	2.04×10^6
^{126}Sn	−7.3 ± 2	1.24×10^5
^{121m}Sn	−7.3 ± 2	9.49×10^3
^{108m}Ag	−10.0 ± 2	5.48×10^4
^{107}Pd	−6.0 ± 1	1.02×10^3
^{99}Tc	Large	9.49×10^3
^{93}Mo	−6.0 ± 1	9.49×10^3
^{94}Nb	−8.0 ± 2	3.72×10^4
^{93}Zr	−9.0 ± 2	1.17×10^4
^{90}Sr	−3.7 ± 1	9.49×10^5
^{79}Se	Large	6.06×10^4
^{63}Ni	−2.7 ± 1	3.94×10^3
^{59}Ni	−2.7 ± 1	1.46×10^3
^{36}Cl	Large	2.19×10^4
^{14}C	Large	1.53×10^4

[a] Based on Wilson *et al.* (1994) and Wescott *et al.* (1995).
[b] Based on EPA (1988); and DOE (1988).
[c] Highly soluble radionuclides are release-rate-constrained.

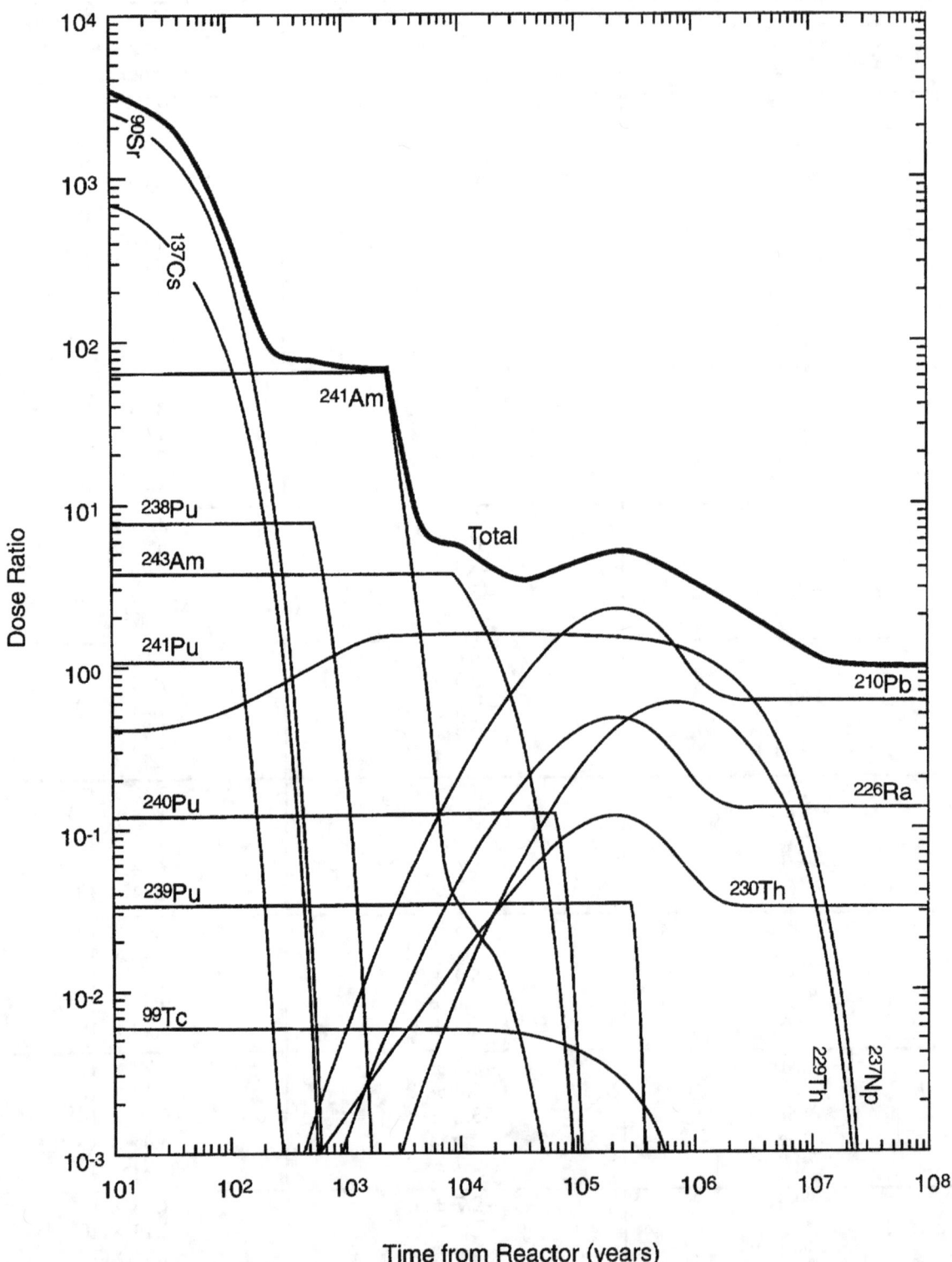

Figure 6—6.   Relative radiological hazard of SNF calculated as the ratio of doses from drinking ground water contaminated by the spent fuel repository and by the hypothetical ore body.

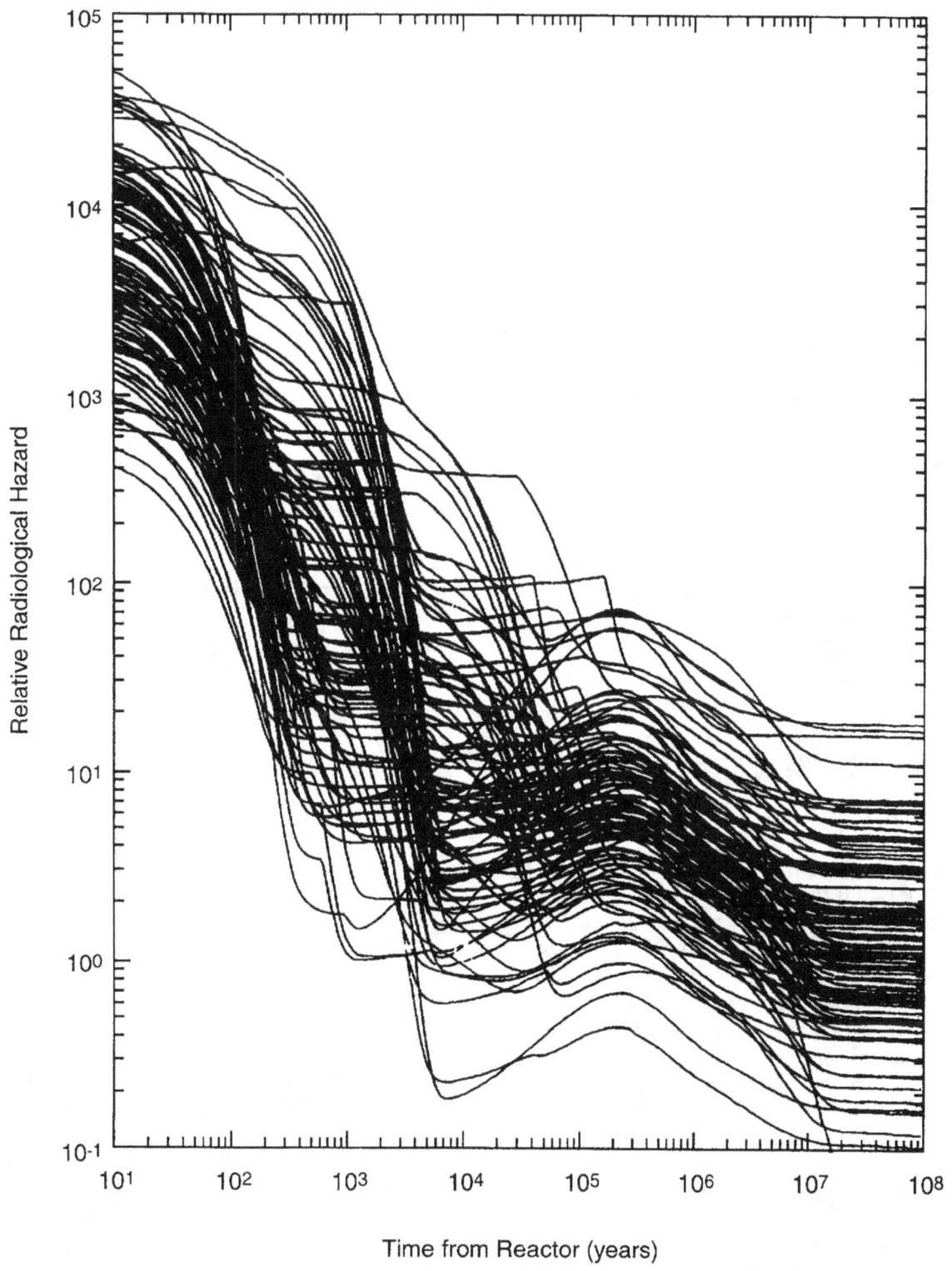

Figure 6—7. Comparison of hazards accounting for uncertainties in radionuclide solubilities and release rates.

R_i = maximum release rate for the ith radionuclide in the spent fuel repository or the hypothetical ore body (1/year);

I_i = total inventory of the ith radionuclide in 63,000 MTU of SNF or a hypothetical uranium ore body (Ci); and

Q = volumetric flow rate of ground water flowing past the repository (liters/year).

By comparing Figures 6–1 and 6–6, one concludes that total radioactivity roughly correlates with radiological hazard. The radiological hazard and total radioactivity are highest during the first 1000 years. In general, the hazard of a radionuclide is significantly diminished if it has a relatively low solubility in water or a low-ingestion DCF.

Figure 6–7 shows the range of relative radiological hazard from uncertainties in radionuclide solubilities and release rates. For both the spent fuel repository and the hypothetical ore body, 100 distinct estimates have been generated by lognormally sampling the radionuclide solubilities and release rate. [The common logarithm of the release rate was assumed to be -5 with a standard error of one-half, based on previous staff work (see Wescott *et al.*, 1995).] If one draws a horizontal line on Figure 6–7 at a relative hazard equal to 1, it can be observed that none of the 100 realizations crosses below the line before 1000 years, and half of the lines cross below, before about 10 million years. Before 1000 years, the spent fuel repository is distinctly more hazardous than the hypothetical ore body. Beyond 10 million years, there is a negligible difference between the spent fuel repository and the hypothetical ore body.

6.4 Assumptions and Limitations

The assumptions and limitations were discussed throughout this work as the analysis was described, but are summarized below for convenience:

- The only radiological hazard considered is drinking contaminated ground water.

- Ground water percolates through a 5-square-kilometer repository area at a rate of 1 millimeter/year such that 2 percent of the ground water contacts 1 percent of the waste, thereby becoming contaminated to the maximum extent reasonable (either solubility-limited or release-rate-limited).

- Radionuclide solubilities and release rates (for highly soluble elements) are assumed to be the same for the spent fuel repository and the hypothetical ore body. The geochemical conditions in and around a naturally occurring uranium ore body could be quite different from the conditions representative of Yucca Mountain assumed in this analysis. Therefore, the hypothetical ore body hazard suggested by this analysis may not be representative of the hazard posed by a naturally occurring ore body.

- The hypothetical ore body contains the same quantity of uranium as the pre-irradiation nuclear fuel, as well as the decay daughters of the uranium in equilibrium.

- The contamination of the ground water by the hypothetical ore body is the same as for the spent fuel repository. The primary difference is that SNF has radioactive fission and activation products that are not present in a naturally occurring ore body.

6.5 Summary and Conclusions

The relative radiological hazard of the spent fuel repository is initially about 4 orders of magnitude greater than that of the hypothetical ore body. The hazard diminishes most rapidly over the first few hundred to a few thousand years. Beyond about 10,000 years, the radiological hazard diminishes less rapidly. The apparent increase in hazard at 100,000 to 500,000 years is from the ingrowth of radionuclides such as ^{230}Th, ^{229}Th, ^{226}Ra, and ^{210}Pb, as observed in Figure 6–2. By 10,000 years the relative hazard will have

decreased by 99.9 percent and be within less than an order of magnitude of the hypothetical ore body. A time period of interest for regulation of a proposed repository of 10,000 years would, therefore, focus attention on the time period when the waste has a significant man-made hazard component that is readily discernable from an equivalent hypothetical ore body, after considering uncertainties associated only with solubilities and release rates.

6.6   References

Adams, J.P., "National Low-Level Waste Management Program Radionuclide Report Series: Volume 15, Uranium-238," Idaho Falls, Idaho, Idaho National Engineering Laboratory, Lockheed Idaho Technologies Company, 1995.

Cohen, B.L., "Effects of ICRP Publication 30 and the 1980 BEIR Report on Hazard Assessments of High-Level Waste," *Health Physics*, 42:133–143 [1982].

Cohen, J.J., *et al.*, "An Assessment of Issues Related to Determination of Time Periods Required for Isolation of High-Level Waste," in R.G. Post (ed.), *Waste Management '89: Proceedings of the Symposium on Waste Management, February 26–March 2, 1989, Tucson, Arizona*, 1:187– 195 [1989].

Elayi, A.G. and J.P. Schapira, "Impact of the Changes from ICRP–26 to ICRP–48 Recommendations on the Potential Radiotoxicity of the Discharged LWR, FBR and CANDU Fuels," *Radioactive Waste Management and the Nuclear Fuel Cycle*, 8(4):327–338 [1987].

Finch, W.I., *et al.*, "Uranium" (in "Nuclear Fuels") in D.A. Brobst and W.P. Pratt (eds.), "United States Mineral Resources," U.S. Geological Survey Professional Paper 820, 1973. [Provides discussion of the geology of uranium ore bodies.]

Hamstra, J., "Radiotoxic Hazard Measure for Buried Solid Radioactive Waste," *Nuclear Safety*, 16(2):180–189 [March–April 1975].

Hurlbut, C.S., *Dana's Manual of Mineralogy (18th Edition)*, New York, John Wiley and Sons, 1971.

Krauskopf, K.B., "Average Abundances of Elements in the Earth's Crust, in Three Common Rocks, and in Seawater (Appendix III)" in *Introduction to Geochemistry (Second Edition)*, New York, McGraw-Hill Book Co., 1979.

Levi, H.W., "The 'Project-Safety-Studies Entsorgung' in the Federal Republic of Germany," in IAEA/OECD Nuclear Energy Agency, *Symposium on the Underground Disposal of Radioactive Wastes Proceedings, July 2–6, 1979, Otaniemi, Finland*, International Atomic Energy Agency, IAEA–SM–243/17, 2:437–450 [1980].

Liljenzin, J-O., and J. Rydberg, "Risks from Nuclear Waste (Revised Edition)," Stockholm, Sweden, Swedish Nuclear Power Inspectorate [or Statens Kärnkraftinspektion–SKI], SKI Report 96:70, November 1996. [Includes an extensive literature review.]

Lozano, A.S., *et al.*, "INVENT: A Module for the Calculation of Radionuclide Inventories, Software Description, and User's Guide," San Antonio, Texas, Center for Nuclear Waste Regulatory Analyses, CNWRA 94–016, July 1994. [Prepared for NRC.]

Mehta, K., G.R. Sherman, and S.G. King, "Potential Health Hazard of Nuclear Fuel Waste and Uranium Ore," Pinawa, Manitoba, Whiteshell Nuclear Research Establishment, Atomic Energy of Canada, Ltd., AECL–8407, June 1991.

National Research Council, "Technical Bases for Yucca Mountain Standards," Washington, D.C., National Academy Press, Commission on Geosciences, Environment, and Resources, July 1995.

Rahn, F.J., *et al.*, "Mining and Production of Reactor Fuel Materials," in *A Guide to Nuclear Power Technology: A Resource for*

Decision-Making, New York, John Wiley and Sons, 1984.

Tacca, J.A., G.G. Wicks, and W.L. Marter, "Relative Activity of DWPF Waste Glass Compared to Natural Uranium Ore," in American Ceramic Society, *93rd Annual Meeting and Exposition of the American Ceramic Society: Annual Meeting Abstracts, April 28 – May 2, 1991, Cincinnati, Ohio*, p. 164 [1991].

TRW Environmental Safety Systems, Inc., "Initial Summary Report for Repository/Waste Package Advanced Conceptual Design," Las Vegas, Nevada, Document No. B00000000–01717–5705–00015 (Rev. 00), 2 vols., 1994.

U.S. Department of Energy, "Final Environmental Impact Statement—Management of Commercially Generated Radioactive Waste," Office of Nuclear Waste Management, DOE/EIS–0046F, Vol. 1, October 1980.

U.S. Department of Energy, "Site Characterization Plan, Yucca Mountain Site, Nevada Research and Development Area, Nevada," Office of Civilian Radioactive Waste Management, DOE/RW–0199, 9 vols., December 1988.

U.S. Department of Energy, "Internal Dose Conversion Factors for Calculation of Dose to the Public," Washington, D.C., DOE/EH–0071, September 1988.

U.S. Department of Energy, "Site Characterization Progress Report: Yucca Mountain, Nevada (April 1, 1996–September 30, 1996, Number 15)," Office of Civilian Radioactive Waste Management, DOE/RW–0498, April 1997.

U.S. Department of Energy, "Reference Design Description for a Geologic Repository," North Las Vegas, Nevada, Civilian Radioactive Waste Management System Management and Operating Contractor, B00000000–1717–5707–00002, Revision 00, June 5, 1997.

U.S. Environmental Protection Agency, "Population Risks from Disposal of High-Level Radioactive Wastes in Geologic Repositories," Washington, D.C., EPA–520/3–80–006, 1982a.

U.S. Environmental Protection Agency, "Draft Regulatory Impact Analysis for 40 CFR 191: Environmental Standards for Management and Disposal of Spent Nuclear Fuel, High-Level and Transuranic Radioactive Wastes," Washington, D.C., EPA–520/3–82–024, 1982b.

U.S. Environmental Protection Agency, "Environmental Standards for the Management of Spent Nuclear Fuel, High-Level and Transuranic Wastes [Final Rule]," *Federal Register*, vol. 50, no. 182, September 19, 1985, pp. 38066–38089. [Also see U.S. Environmental Protection Agency, "High-Level and Transuranic Radioactive Wastes: Background Information Document for Final Rule," Washington, D.C., EPA–520/1–85–023, 1985.]

U.S. Environmental Protection Agency, "High-Level and Transuranic Radioactive Wastes: Background Information Document for Final Rule," Washington, D.C., EPA–520/1–85–023, 1985.

U.S. Environmental Protection Agency, "Limiting Values of Radionuclide Intake and Air Concentration and Dose Conversion Factors for Inhalation, Submersion, and Ingestion," Washington, D.C., EPA–520/1–88–020, September 1988.

Wescott, R.G., *et al.* (eds.), "NRC Iterative Performance Assessment Phase 2: Development of Capabilities for Review of a Performance Assessment for a High-Level Waste Repository," U.S. Nuclear Regulatory Commission, NUREG–1464, October 1995.

Wick, O.J. and M.O. Cloninger, "Comparison of Potential Radiological Consequences from a Spent-Fuel Repository and Natural Uranium Deposits," Battelle Pacific Northwest National Laboratories, PNL–3540, September 1980.

Williams, W.A., "Population Risks from Uranium Ore Bodies," U.S. Environmental

Protection Agency, EPA 520/3−80−009, October 1980.

Wilson, M.L., *et al.*, "Total-System Performance Assessment for Yucca Mountain—SNL Second Iteration (TSPA−1993)," Albuquerque, New Mexico, Sandia National Laboratory, SAND93−2675, 2 vols., April 1994.

APPENDIX A

OVERVIEW OF FARMING AND RANCHING ACTIVITIES
IN THE YUCCA MOUNTAIN AREA

A-1 INTRODUCTION

In characterizing the lifestyles and habits of potential receptor groups in the Yucca Mountain area, it will be necessary to consider, among other things, the extent to which agriculture and ranching takes place down-gradient from a geologic repository because of the potential importance of the food-ingestion pathway to dose to humans [see Neel ("Dose-Assessment Module") in Wescott *et al.* (1995)].[1] As noted in Section 2.1 of the main report, the largest population centers down-gradient from the potential repository are the rural communities in the Amargosa Desert, located south of State Highway 95. Most, if not all of these communities rely on private wells for their water supply.

The first two sections of this overview briefly review the types of farming and ranching practices in this portion of the State. The principal sources for this compilation include the State of Nevada/University of Nevada (1974); the U.S. Department of Energy (DOE)(1986); TRW Environmental Safety Systems, Inc. (1995); LaPlante *et al.* (1995); Raines (1996); and Eisenberg (1996). This compilation was also supplemented through an interview and subsequent dialogs with a knowledgeable local resident (Kenneth G. Garey[2]). Because of the exclusive reliance on

ground water in these areas, the last section of this overview includes a discussion of some of the issues that affect its availability. It was prepared with the assistance of knowledgeable individuals at both the State and Federal levels.

In reviewing this information, the reader is reminded that the Yucca Mountain area is comprised of several small rural communities, some of them so-called "commuter or bedroom" communities. Most of the activities described below, therefore, do not represent the major industry of southern Nevada.[3] In the past, most farms and ranches were operated on a part-time basis, with the owner working full-time in another occupation (DOE, 1986; p. 3–103); this practice is still believed to be the case in most situations.[4] Nonetheless, farming and ranching are important to the local economy and to the diets of individual households, to varying degrees. Most of these activities rely on alluvial ground water for their water supply. Moreover, some of these activities have other linkages to each other, as discussed below.

A-2 FARMING

There are practical limitations on the types of agriculture that can take place in the Amargosa Desert and Pahrump Valley

---

[1]As discussed later in this NUREG (see Appendix B), mining played a key role in the early development of southern Nevada, including the Amargosa Desert. Although not discussed in any detail here, it should be noted that the mining of specialty clays (by IMV Floridin), calcium borate (borax—by the American Borate Company), gold (by St. Joe Bullfrog), and fluorspar (fluorite), today, in the southern reaches of the area, continues to make these companies important local employers as well as major consumers of ground water (see Table 2–7).

[2]In addition to being the operator of the *Bar-B-Q Ranch* (Amargosa Valley), Mr. Garey was also the Amargosa Center on-site representative for the Community Radiation Monitoring Program (CRMP), at the time of the first interview. The CRMP, sponsored by DOE, is a cooperative project among DOE, the U.S. Environmental Protection Agency, the Desert Research Institute (Nevada), and the University of Utah (see Black *et al.*, 1995).

[3]Moreover, today, there are a number of other commercial and recreational activities that support the local economies of these two areas. Information on most of these businesses— convenience stores, gas stations, restaurants, and the like—can be obtained from the Chamber of Commerce in the area, as well as from directories published in local newspapers such as *The Amargosa News* or *The Pahrump Valley Gazette*.

Also noteworthy in the Amargosa Desert area is the Longstreet Inn and Casino. Opened in April 1996, this 60-room hotel is located on State Highway 373 at the Nevada-California State line. This hotel has a capacity of 300 guests, as well as having a recreational-vehicle trailer park with hook-ups (spaces) for 120 vehicles. An 18-hole golf course was under construction at the time this *Overview* was being prepared.

[4]Personal communication, K. Garey, *Bar-B-Q Ranch* (Amargosa Valley), May 1996.

because of local soil conditions,[5] the length of the freeze-free season, and other meteorological factors. These factors limit the types and amounts of crops that can be grown in southern Nevada. Under irrigation, only hardy to moderately hardy crops adapted to the region are grown. The growing season is about 200 days [see Bedinger *et al.* (1985; Table 8, p. G32) and Sakamoto *et al.* (1973)]. Late frosts can be a problem. Trees usually bud in February, but there usually is a killing frost every one in four years, in March.

The principal agricultural crop in the Amargosa Desert and Pahrump Valley areas is alfalfa. The long growing season in the area permits about seven cuttings per year. Irrigation rigs are either rotary or wheel lines. However, because of its low nutritional content (e.g., total digestible nutrients or TDNs), most of the crop is destined for markets outside of southern Nevada; no more than 10 percent of the crop is believed to be used locally.[6] Some percentage of the local crop is exported to markets in Japan. Other agricultural products grown in the area include grain; barley; oats; hay (including hayfine); and cotton (about 800 hectares in Pahrump Valley, only). However, these crops are believed to represent a smaller proportion of all total agricultural output for the area. The principal irrigation methods are center-pivot or furrow. Winter temperatures are generally too low for the commercial production of winter vegetables.

Many Amargosa Desert-Pahrump Valley residents maintain "kitchen" gardens. It is estimated that at least 50 percent of the residents in the area maintain some form of garden (or orchard) that provides more than two dozen fruits, nuts, and vegetables—see Table A–1. (Some residents in Pahrump Valley are reported to maintain bee colonies for honey production.) Most of the products grown are shared, sold, or bartered among the local residents, although two households are reported to have commercial operations. Commercial operations are believed to not be more widespread owing to problems in entering the local markets—Las Vegas or Los Angeles (see McCracken, 1990; pp. 82–83). The magnitude of personal home-garden consumption in the area is difficult to estimate—it is generally believed to be about 10 percent[7]—although no resident is understood to subsist solely off of his or her garden. Most residents still purchase the majority of their food stuffs at local grocery stores and use the home-grown produce to supplement their diets.

A third type of agricultural activity reported in the area is the turf farm in the community of Amargosa Valley, adjacent to a dairy. Finally, "Bermuda grass and fescue" are grown for the landscaping market in the greater Las Vegas area.

All of the activities described above rely on some degree of pre-treatment of the soils—with manure, fertilizers, acidifiers, etc.—to allow these crops to grow. What agricultural activities do exist are confined chiefly to the centers of the valley; exposed bedrock along the margin of the basins is generally unsuitable for the practice of agriculture—because of the topography (slope), thin soil veneer, and low moisture-holding capacity. Soils within the alluvial basins are medium- to fine-textured with somewhat higher-moisture holding capacities. However, the high evapotranspiration (ET) rates[8] results in a soil chemistry that is highly alkaline. Moreover, hardpan (pedogenic carbonate or *caliché*) exists extensively throughout the area and presents an additional limitation for agricultural use. As a consequence, based on information prepared by the State Engineers Office/University of Nevada, it is estimated that at least 60 percent of the soils in the

---

[5]Most of the soils in the Yucca Mountain area are gravelly and coarse textured with low inherent fertility and low waterholding capacity. Consequently, they have been classified as having properties that "...preclude their use for irrigated agriculture..." or "...have severe limitations that reduce [the] choice of crops or require special conservation practices or both...." (State of Nevada, 1974)

[6]Personal communication, K. Garey, *Bar-B-Q Ranch* (Amargosa Valley), May 1996.

[7]Personal consumption could be as high as 30 percent [personal communication, J. Gauthier, DOE Management and Operating Contractor (SPECTRA Research Institute), July 1997].

[8]Due to low humidity (30 to 40 percent), abundant sunshine, and light to moderate winds, ET in this area may exceed 120 inches of pan evaporation (French *et al.*, 1981; p. 32).

Table A–1. Produce Grown in the Amargosa Desert-Pahrump Valley Areas.
Compiled from various sources cited in this appendix.

Fruits and Vegetables		

Beets
Broccoli
Brussel Sprouts
Cabbage
Cantaloupes
Carrots
Cauliflower
Corn
Garlic
	Kohlrabi
	Lettuce (Head and Loose
	  Leaf)
	Okra
	Onions
	Peppers (Chili, Sweet, Banana,
	  and Bell)
	Potatoes
		Pumpkins
		Radishes
		Squash (summer and winter
		  varieties)
		Tomatoes
		Turnips
		Watermelon
		Zucchini

Fruit Trees		
Apple Apricot Cherry Grapes (Vineyard)*	Fig Nectarines Peach Peanuts	Pear Plum Pomegranate

Nut Trees		
Almond	Pecan	Pistachio

* Including Zinfandel, California Red, Thompson Seedless, and Concord.

Table A–2. Area Tabulation of Soil Irrigability Class in the Amargosa Desert-Pahrump Valley Areas. Taken from the State of Nevada/University of Nevada (1974; See separate plate in back of report).

Hydrographic Basin	*Soil Irrigability Class (in hectares, described below)*					*TOTAL*
	A	*B*	*C*	*D*	*E*	
Pahrump Valley	6070	1214	4856	3844	188,364	204,348
Amargosa Valley	0	3035	64,326	23,876	140,806	232,043
AREA TOTAL	6070	4249	69,182	27,720	329,170	436,391

EXPLANATION

Class A   Soils that have slight or few limitations that restrict their use for irrigated agriculture.

Class B   Soils that have moderate limitations that reduce the choice of crops grown or require moderate conservation practices.

Class C   Soils that have severe limitations that reduce the choice of crops grown or require moderate conservation practices, or both.

Class D   Soils that have very severe limitations that restrict the choice of crops grown or require special practices and management, or both.

Class E   Soils that have properties that preclude their use for irrigated agriculture.

Amargosa Desert hydrographic subbasin are not considered irrigable; an additional 28 percent of the soils are classified "severely limited to very severely limited" in their ability to sustain some type of cultivation (see Table A–2).

A–3 RANCHING

In recent years, dairy farms have proven to be the major livestock activity in the area. Two dairy farms operate in Amargosa Desert and Pahrump Valley. The production capacity at the dairy in Pahrump Valley is about 2500 head; in the community of Amargosa Valley, there were about 3300 head in 1996, although the dairy is reported to have a capacity of about 5000 head. All raw dairy products are believed to be destined for processing facilities in southern California. Although the dairies provide local farmers with a dedicated market for a portion of their alfalfa crop, because of the need for livestock feed with a high TDN, most of the feed comes from outside of the County—principally California, Utah, and Lincoln County (Nevada).

Another activity in the area is a commercial catfish farm. Surplus catfish fry are purchased by the State's Department of Conservation and Natural Resources to stock lakes and other waterways throughout the State.

There is some beef cattle ranching in the county but it takes place principally to the north of the Nevada Test Site (NTS), where there is more (and better) natural forage. However, there are a few range cattle in the area (estimated to be less than 100), as well as some lesser numbers of pigs, goats, sheep, chickens, rabbits, and ostriches. The pig, sheep, and ostriches were introduced into the area in the early 1990s; these operations are understood to be commercial. The other stock is raised for local/private consumption. Almost all of these activities rely on the locally produced alfalfa and grains to feed the stock.

A–4 GROUND WATER

Because of the arid climate, there appears to have been an early interest in both the development and conservation of ground

water within the State (Maxey and Jamison, 1948; pp. 4–12). The only reliable sources of water historically have been the numerous springs, weeps, and seeps (*Op cit.*) and ground water, to the extent it was accessible. Rapid growth and unregulated use of ground water in the 1920s and 1930s in the greater Las Vegas area resulted in increased withdrawal of water from local aquifers and decreased yields from wells and springs. In 1938, the State Engineer's office became actively involved in the evaluation of ground-water resources (*Op cit.*, pp. 7–8), which resulted in a comprehensive and systematic evaluation of ground water within the State. In an effort to conserve the resource, curtail wasteful practices, and protect legitimate water rights, the Nevada State Legislature approved the *Comprehensive Underground Water Act of 1939* (see Shamberger, 1991; pp. 57–58). This act declares that all underground (ground water) water within the boundaries of the State belongs to the public. To ensure beneficial use of the resource, the Office of the State Engineer was empowered with the authority to regulate ground-water use, through "appropriation" or permitting [see Morros (1982, p. 20545); and State of Nevada (1982, pp. 79–83)]. (Also see French *et al.* (1981) for more discussion of this history.)

Walker and Eakin (1963, pp. 37–38) provide a brief history of the development of ground water in the area. The first reported water well in the area was dug 1852, to support the boundary survey of the California- Nevada State line (Mendenhall, 1909; pp. 36–37). Other wells were subsequently developed around the turn-of-the century to support railroad construction and operation (the *Tonopah and Tidewater,* and *Las Vegas and Tonopah* lines) and mining activities (see Myrick, 1992). The first reported irrigation well in the Amargosa Desert area was reported to have been drilled in 1917 (Walker and Eakin, 1963; p. 37).

Before electrification of the Amargosa Desert area in the early 1960s, the ground-water potential was generally under-developed and as a consequence, there was limited farming and ranching. For example, the number of pre-electrification wells in the Amargosa

Desert area was about 160 (Walker and Eakin, 1963; Table 3). (Before electrification, electric power was typically provided by diesel generators.) Since then, the number of wells has grown by about 25 percent. In DOE's *1986 Environmental Assessment* for NTS, 207 domestic wells were reported, citing State of Nevada data (DOE, 1986; p. 3–85).

The maximum amount of ground water that can be appropriated from a given hydrogeologic basin in Nevada is limited to its perennial or *safe yield*.[9] For each of the hydrologic basins in the State, the State Engineer has estimated the perennial yield, relying on assessments prepared cooperatively by Nevada's Division of Water Resources and the U.S. Geological Survey. When ground-water withdrawals exceed recharge, overdrafting or water-mining can occur. Overdrafting of ground water produces a number of undesirable effects on ranching and farming interests; the most significant is the depletion of the existing ground-water resource because overdrafted water comes from storage. Additional undesirable effects would include deteriorating water quality, well interference, and land subsidence—each of which is problematic from a cost perspective. At present, over-appropriation is prohibited by the State (see Morros, 1982, pp. 20467–20557).

All water use in Nevada is regulated by the Office of the State Engineer in the Division of Water Resources.[10] At present, the maximum permissible water use allowed in southern Nevada, based on the State's perennial yield philosophy, is as follows: residential/domestic use—6.8 cubic meters/day (1800 gallons/day) per single-family unit (State of Nevada, 1982; p. 79) and only one well per household; and agricultural/ranching: 4900 to 6200 cubic

meters/year (4 to 5 acre-feet per year).[11] However, it is generally recognized that there is "overdrafting" (e.g., mining or over appropriation) of the aquifers, throughout a large portion of southern Nevada (Harrill, 1986; Plume, 1989; Morgan and Dittinger, 1996), which is believed to have led to some restrictions on development. In instances where it is believed that ground-water withdrawals could exceed ground-water recharge, the State Engineer may designate a ground-water basin (or any portion thereof) as a "designated basin." "Designation" is a means of protecting basins from over-use by restricting the issuance of permits in that area.

Rapid growth in southern Nevada during the last half-century has resulted in an increased demand for potable water. As a result, there have been documented overdrafts throughout the region (Maxey and Jameson, 1948; Malmberg, 1967; Nichols and Akers, 1985; Harrill, 1986; Morgan and Dettinger, 1996). These overdrafts have continued for several decades despite being prohibited by State law. Traditionally, supply-side solutions—such as dams and canals—have been used to meet the growing water needs in the West (Reisner, 1993); today, such solutions may have become prohibitively expensive (Frederick *et al.*, 1996). In a 1992 report prepared for the State of Nevada, it was noted that the greater Las Vegas area would most likely need to adopt a regional solution to its potable water problem (Water Resources Management, Inc., 1992; p. 21). Inasmuch as Nevada already relies on its full allocation from the Colorado River, such solutions may include acquiring unallocated ground water in the valleys of the greater Las Vegas region (Basse, 1990; p 24), which would include Amargosa Desert and Pahrump Valley areas. Such was the case recently in the Amargosa Desert area when a private concern petitioned the State Engineer to initiate forfeiture proceedings to acquire unused water rights (Buqo, 1997; p. 30).

Because there have been overdrafts, both the Amargosa and Pahrump Valley basins are currently listed as "designated basins" (State

---

[9]The State Engineer applies the "safe-yield" philosophy to the allocation of ground water in Nevada. "Safe yield" is a term of art and is generally regarded as the amount of water that can be pumped from an aquifer, on a sustained annual basis, without depleting the reserve or impacting existing legal rights. Any withdrawal in excess of the safe yield can be considered an "overdraft" (Freeze and Cherry, 1979; p. 364).

[10]Ground water is appropriated by the Nevada State Engineer in the manner described in *Water Supply Report 2* (State of Nevada, 1982; pp. 79–83).

[11]Personal communication, T. Gallagher, Nevada Division of Water Resources(Carson City), July 1997.

of Nevada, 1982; Table 29). One possible explanation for the overdrafts, generally, could be a limitation on the State's 1939 regulatory authority. Ground-water appropriations made before 1913, and used continuously since then, are not covered by the State Engineers 1939 authority. Thus, because there are unregulated ground-water rights in place, it is difficult to evaluate the total amount of ground water available for apportioning throughout the State (*Op cit.*, p. 80). (One of the more well-known examples of the impacts of overdrafting in southern Nevada was the incident involving the now-present Ash Meadows National Wildlife Refuge, in which reduced discharge to some springs in southern Nye County, in the late 1960s-early 1970s, resulted in the extinction of some late-Pleistocene ancestral fish and the endangering of others.[12])

For the Amargosa Desert and Pahrump Valley areas, it is believed that the initial ground-water resource assessments used for water budgeting were performed, respectively, by Walker and Eakin (1963) and Malmberg (1967), using the methodology described by Eakin *et al.* (1951). These initial assessments were limited to the first 30 meters of the aquifer. More recent assessments, relying on a greater thickness of the aquifer, may suggest more extensive ground-water resources than first thought (Harrill 1986; and Pal Consultants, 1995). However, despite years of

extensive study, it is believed that there is significant uncertainty associated in estimating the ground-water budgets of basin deposits in Southern Nevada (Harrill, 1986; D'Agnese *et al.*,1997).

A–5 REFERENCES

Basse, B., "Water Resources in Southern Nevada," Denver, Colorado, Adrian Brown Consultants, Inc., August 1990. [Prepared for the Center for Nuclear Waste Regulatory Analyses.]

Bedinger, M.S., W.H. Langer, and J.E. Reed, "Synthesis of Hydraulic Properties of Rocks in the Basin and Range Province, Southwestern United States," U.S. Geological Survey, Water-Supply Paper 2310, 1985.

Black, S.C., W.M. Glines, and Y.E. Townsend (eds.), "U.S. Department of Energy Nevada Operations Office Annual Site Environmental Report—1994," Las Vegas, Nevada, Reynolds Electrical & Engineering Co., Inc., Document No. DE–AC08–94NV11432, September 1995. [Prepared for the U.S. Department of Energy/Office of Civilian Radioactive Waste Management.]

Buqo, T.S., "Baseline Water Supply and Demand Evaluation of Southern Nye County, Nevada," Blue Diamond, Nevada [1997].

D'Agnese, F.A., *et al.*, "Hydrologic Evaluation and Numerical Simulation of the Death Valley Regional Ground-Water Flow System, Nevada and California," U.S. Geological Survey, Water-Resources Investigations Report 96–4300, 1997.

Dudley, W.W., Jr., and J.D. Larson, "Effect of Irrigation on Desert Pupfish Habitats in Ash Meadows, Nye County, Nevada," U.S. Geological Survey Professional Paper 927, 1976.

Eakin, T.E., *et al.*, "Contributions to the Hydrology of Eastern Nevada," State of Nevada, Office of the State Engineer, Water Resources Bulletin No. 12, 1951.

Eisenberg, N.A., U.S. Nuclear Regulatory Commission/Division of Waste Management,

---

[12]Incorporated by Presidential Proclamation into the Death Valley National Monument in 1952, the 8950 hectares of spring-fed wetlands and alkaline desert uplands are located in the southern tip of the Amargosa Desert. Established as a wildlife refuge in 1984 and now managed by the U.S. Fish and Wildlife Service, the location provides a habitat for 24 unique flora and fauna; four kinds of fish; and one plant are currently listed as endangered.

There are about 50 permanent fresh-water springs and seeps that discharge into the refuge. Although this discharge area is geologically and hydrologically complex, it is believed that a series of poorly connected gravel, sand, and terrestrial limestone aquifers, supplied by Paleozoic carbonate rocks to the west, provide water to the refuge (Dudley and Larson, 1976). Development of well fields adjacent to Ash Meadows resulted in water-level declines that threatened the endangered Devil's Hole pupfish (*Cyprinodon diabolis*) and other species of the genus *Cyprinodon* found at the removed Devil's Hole Unit of the Death Valley National Monument. Since a 1976 U.S. Supreme Court decision (*Cappaert v. U.S.*), pumping in the Ash Meadows area has been permanently enjoined to prevent further water-level declines. After the Supreme Court decision, continuous monitoring revealed that the water level in the Devil's Hole sink-hole recovered to pre-pumping levels [Personal communication, T. Mayer, U.S. Fish and Wildlife Service (Portland, Oregon), July 1997].

memorandum to M.V. Federline, U.S. Nuclear Regulatory Commission/Division of Waste Management, [Subject: "Staff Visit to Amargosa Valley: Trip Report"], Rockville, Maryland, May 14, 1996.

Frederick, K.D., J. Vandenberg, and T. Hanson, "Economic Values of Freshwater in the United States," Washington, D.C., Resources for the Future Discussion Paper 97−03, October 1996. [Prepared for the Electric Power Research Institute.]

Freeze, R.A., and J.H. Cherry, *Groundwater*, Englewood Cliffs, New Jersey, 1979.

French, R.H., et al., "History of Water Rights in Nevada [Appendix A]," in "Hydrology and Water Resources Overview for the Nevada Nuclear Waste Storage Investigations, Nevada Test Site, Nye County, Nevada," Las Vegas, Nevada, U.S. Department of Energy/Nevada Operations Office, NVO−284, June 1981 [issued June 1984]. [Prepared by the Desert Research Institute/Water Resources Center.]

Harrill, J.R., "Ground-Water Storage Depletion in Pahrump Valley, Nevada-California, 1962−75," U.S. Geological Survey, Water-Supply Paper 2279, 1986.

LaPlante, P.A., S.J. Maheras, and M.S. Jarzemba, "Initial Analysis of Selected Site-Specific Dose Assessment Parameters and Exposure Pathways Applicable to a Groundwater Release Scenario at Yucca Mountain," San Antonio, Texas, Center for Nuclear Waste Regulatory Analyses, CNWRA 95−018, September 1995. [Prepared for the U.S. Nuclear Regulatory Commission.]

Malmberg, G.T., "Hydrology of the Valley-Fill and Carbonate-Rock Reservoirs, Pahrump Valley, Nevada-California," U.S. Geological Survey, Water-Supply Paper 1832, 1967.

Maxey, G.B., and C.H. Jameson, "Geology and Resources of Las Vegas, Pahrump, and Indian Spring Valleys, Clark and Nye Counties, Nevada," State of Nevada, Office of the State Engineer, Water Resources Bulletin No. 5, 1948.

McCracken, R.D., *A History of Amargosa Valley Nevada*, Tonopah, Nevada, Nye County Press, 1990.

Mendenhall, W.C., "Some Desert Watering Places in Southeastern California and Southwestern Nevada," U.S. Geological Survey, Water Supply Paper 224, 1909.

Morgan, D.S., and M.D., Dettinger, "Ground-Water Conditions in Las Vegas Valley, Clark County, Nevada: Part 2, Hydrogeology and Simulation of Ground-Water Flow," U.S. Geological Survey, Water-Supply Paper 2320−B, 1996.

Morros, P.G. (compiler), "Nevada Water Laws: Title 48—Water," Carson City, State of Nevada, Department of Conservation and Natural Resources/Division of Water Resources, 1982.

Myrick, D.L., *The Railroads of Nevada and Eastern California: Part II—The Southern Railroads*, Reno, Nevada, University of Nevada Press, 1992.

Nichols W.D., and J.P. Akers, "Water-Level Declines in the Amargosa Valley Area, Nye County, Nevada, 1962−84," U.S. Geological Survey, Water-Resources Investigations Report, WRI−85−4273, 1985.

Pal Consultants, Inc., "A Conceptual Model of the Death Valley Ground-Water Flow System, Nevada and California," San Jose, California, December 1995. [Prepared for the U.S. Department of Interior/National Park Service.]

Plume, R.W., "Ground-Water Conditions in Las Vegas Valley, Clark County, Nevada: Part 1, Hydrogeologic Framework," U.S. Geological Survey, Water-Supply Paper 2320−A, 1989.

Raines, J.A., TRW Environmental Safety Systems Inc./Regional Studies Department, memorandum to M.A. Lugo, TRW Environmental Safety Systems Inc. [Subject: "Data Defining the Characteristics of a Critical Group in Amargosa Valley, Nevada"], Las Vegas, Nevada, April 18, 1996.

Reisner, M., *Cadillac Desert—The American West and Its Disappearing Water*, New York, Penguin Books, 1986 [revised 1993].

Sakamoto, C.M., *et al.*, "Freeze-Free (32°F) Seasons of the Major Basins and Plateaus of Nevada," in State of Nevada and University of Nevada of Nevada [Reno], "Water for Nevada: Report 8. Forecasts for the Future—Agriculture," Carson City, Division of Water Resources/Department of Conservation and Resources and Division and Agricultural and Resource Economics/Max C. Fleischmann College of Agriculture, January 1974. [Separate plate dated 1973.]

Shamberger, H.A., "Evolution of Nevada's Water Laws, as Related to the Development and Evaluation of the State's Water resources, from 1866 to about 1960," Carson City, Nevada, Department of Conservation and Natural Resources/Division of Water Resources, Water-Resources Bulletin 49, 1991. [Prepared by the U.S. Geological Survey.]

State of Nevada and University of Nevada of Nevada [Reno], "Water for Nevada: Report 8. Forecasts for the Future—Agriculture," Carson City, Division of Water Resources/ Department of Conservation and Resources and Division and Agricultural and Resource Economics/Max C. Fleischmann College of Agriculture, January 1974.

State of Nevada, "Water for Southern Nevada," Carson City, Division of Water Planning/Department of Conservation and Natural Resources, Water Supply Report 2, November 1982. [Prepared by URS Company

and Converse Ward Davis Dixon, with contributions by the Las Vegas Valley Water District.]

TRW Environmental Safety Systems Inc., "Summary of Socioeconomic Data Analyses Conducted in Support of Radiological Monitoring Program during Calendar Year 1994," Las Vegas, Nevada, Document No. DE–AC01–91RW001134, June 1995. [Prepared for the U.S. Department of Energy/Office of Civilian Radioactive Waste Management.]

U.S. Department of Energy, "Environmental Assessment: Yucca Mountain Site, Nevada Research and Development Area, Nevada— Volume I," Office of Civilian Radioactive Waste Management, Nevada, DOE/RW–0073, May 1986.

Walker, G.E., and T.E. Eakin, "Geology and Ground Water of Amargosa Desert, Nevada-California," Carson City, State of Nevada, Department of Conservation and Natural Resources, Ground-Water Resources— Reconnaissance Series Report 14, March 1963.

Water Resources Management, Inc. [WRMI], "WMRI Process—Water Supply Planning Process for the Las Vegas Region," Columbia, Maryland, May 1992.

Wescott, R.G., *et al.* (eds.), "NRC Iterative Performance Assessment Phase 2: Development of Capabilities for Review of a Performance Assessment for a High-Level Waste Repository," U.S. Nuclear Regulatory Commission, NUREG–1464, October 1995.

APPENDIX B

LIFESTYLES AND WATER-USE PRACTICES IN AND AROUND THE NEVADA TEST SITE BEFORE ITS ESTABLISHMENT: A PRELIMINARY EVALUATION

One of the issues that may have significant weight in defining a potential receptor group for Yucca Mountain performance assessments would be the nature of human activity within the current boundaries of the Nevada Test Site (NTS) before its withdraw from public use. Understanding what took place previously at the site may be valuable inasmuch as it may reflect the lifestyles that would be taking place today had NTS land not been withdrawn. Because of time constraints, the staff was not able to perform an extensive evaluation of the literature or conduct personal interviews to better understand what took place historically within NTS' boundaries. Based on a limited review of some literature, as well as some anecdotal staff knowledge,[1] it appears that limited mining, ranching, and homesteading took place within the current boundaries of NTS before its initial withdraw from public use by the War Department in the early 1940s and later, by the Atomic Energy Commission (AEC), in the 1950s.

As noted earlier in this NUREG, there are no perennial streams in the NTS area. Before development of the ground-water resource, the only reliable sources of water at NTS were the many springs and seeps, as well as a few *tanks*.[2] Cold springs and seeps are located sporadically but frequently throughout the area. Thordarson and Robinson (1971) reported that there were 754 springs within 161 kilometers of NTS. Most of the springs were reported to discharge 0.63 cubic meters/second (10 gallons/minute) or less (*Op cit.*, p. 16). In this portion of the arid southwest, springs are marked by an abundance of foliage (and wildlife—see Ball, 1907; pp. 23–24) when compared with their surroundings. The springs found in the area are typically of the *contact variety*—where a permeable rock overlies a rock of much lower permeability, such as a contact between the more permeable alluvial deposits and less permeable bedrock, or of the *depression variety*—in which ground water seeps into topographic depressions that are covered with a veneer of detrital material (usually gravel). The flow or discharge rate is seasonal, typically corresponding to the amount of precipitation in the previous months (*Op cit.*, p. 21) thereby suggesting that many of the weeps and springs possess juvenile, meteoric water. Tanks also occur in the Yucca Mountain area. They are impermeable, topographic depressions that form natural collection basins for precipitation and snow. The volume and quality of water in tanks typically decrease in the summer months. By August, many tanks in the area are dry and the water in others was scarcely drinkable (*Op cit.*). Playas occur within NTS (Yucca Flat, Frenchman Flat, Gold Flat, and Kawich Valley) and do collect surface-water run-off from periodic storms. Because the storms are infrequent and because the surface water typically evaporates within a few days or weeks, it has never been considered a reliable source of supply.

In historic times, the NTS area was occupied by Native Americans—the Western Shoshone and Southern Paiute. These peoples were nomadic, hunter-foragers and it is generally believed that they relied on the numerous springs for water as well as for the animals and vegetation they attracted and sustained. Ash Meadows, for example, covers approximately 163 square kilometers and contains more than 20 major springs. Ball (1907, pp. 22–23) notes that the placement of many of the early Indian trails in the area was influenced by the locations of the various springs and tanks, and

---

[1] When at the Lawrence Livermore National Laboratory, H.L. McKague was associated with the NTS from 1972 to 1993. P.T. Prestholt was the U.S. Nuclear Regulatory Commission's on-site licensing representative from 1984–92. Before that, he was stationed at Camp Desert Rock, in the 1950s, while serving in the U.S. Army Signal Corps. Mr. Prestholt later worked as an NTS geophysics contractor in the 1960s.

[2] Naturally occurring cisterns found in impervious rock.

the distance between these sites rarely exceeded 64 kilometers (40 miles—*Op cit.*).

Archeological investigation of the site shows evidence of the Southern Paiute culture in caches of artifacts (beads, pottery, etc.) at camp sites, rock shelters, or stone circles within NTS—but no architecture suggesting that the NTS area was ever permanently inhabited (see Worman, 1969). Close to Yucca Mountain itself, the terraces adjacent to Forty Mile Canyon contain abundant artifacts in the form of projectile points, blanks, and flakes (Worman, 1969; Pippin and Zerga, 1983). In general, most aboriginal groups were believed to reside in Ash Meadows, Indian Springs, Pahrump Springs, or along the Amargosa River (Steward, 1938). Ball's 1906 geologic reconnaissance map identifies an "Indian camp" within Oasis Valley, to the west of NTS. Steward does report that at least nine Shoshone family (or family groups) maintained winter camps within current NTS boundaries between 1875 and 1880 (*Op cit.*, pp. 93–99, 182–185) .

Before the 1800s, European exploration of southern Nevada appears to have been limited to along the Colorado River and to the vicinity of *Las Vegas Meadows* (with its great springs) through which passed the Old Spanish Trail, connecting Santa Fe (New Mexico) and San Gabriel (California). However, the 1849 California gold rush precipitated the great Western migration, and the search for immigration routes and natural resources. These events introduced the NTS area to the first-reported geographical survey and mapping by U.S. Army topographic engineer J.C. Frémont sometime in the mid 1840s (McCracken, 1992; pp. 6–14). Like most explorers in the southwest at that the time, Frémont followed the existing Indian and game trails, with their established sources of water supply, or looked for other recognized natural signs of water (i.e., phreatophytic vegetation and the presence of wildlife—see Ball, 1907; pp. 22–23) to maintain renewable supplies. Again, historical as well as archeological information suggests that the area was regularly traversed in the late 1840s, by emigrants in wagons on their way to

California, who took advantage of these springs (see Worman, 1969; pp. 3, 5–8; and Pippin and Zerga, 1983; pp. 51–54, 66–68).

During the first 50 years of Statehood, before the First World War, Nevada's economy depended chiefly on mining (State of Nevada, 1964; p. 273). After the discovery of placer gold at Sutter's Mill (California) in 1848, the lure of mineral wealth opened the West up to exploration. However, it wasn't until 1855, after the discovery of the gold-silver bonanzas, that mining was reported to have begun in Nevada (*Op cit.*, p. 3). The state experienced extensive prospecting and exploration after the 1859 discovery of the Comstock lode, in Virginia City, by the backwash of miners and immigrants in search of new deposits following the playing-out of the California gold fields. Examination of *U.S. Geological Survey 7½ topographic quadrangle maps* for the NTS area shows many "dog holes" in the Calico Hills area, for example. Consequently, as new ore bodies were discovered, mining camps began to spring up. In areas for which there was no artesian water, flumes, tunnels, and pipelines were built (e.g., Shamberger, 1972), or water was hauled to serve the mining communities (see Ransome, 1907).[3]

Despite extensive prospecting within the site, most of the mining activity in the area took place outside of the current NTS boundaries—e.g., the Bare Mountain, Bullfrog (Rhyolite), Goldfield, and Johnnie Districts. However, a modest level of mining took place partially or wholly within NTS boundaries, but never at Yucca Mountain itself (Castor *et al.*, 1989; p. 5).[4] In Area 26, for example, mining was conducted in the Wahmonie District 1928 (see Hewett *et al.*, 1936). The silver-gold deposits there were mined-out in about 3 months. Although the district ultimately attracted a

---

[3]In 1907, it is reported that water was hauled to the mining community of Rawhide (Mineral County, Nevada), by the *Dead Horse Wells Water Company*, from wells about 13 kilometers (8 miles) outside of town. The haulage cost per barrel was $2.50 (Batchelor and Batchelor, 1998; p. 69) (In this example, a barrel is assumed to hold 31 gallons or 117 liters of water.) Using the 1998 consumer price index to adjust for inflation, that would be about $80.00/barrel, in current dollars (Personal communication, R. Turtil, Division of Waste Management, January 1999).

[4]Between 1987 and 1988, about 30 mining claims were staked at Yucca Mountain. In 1989, DOE purchased the rights to these claims (*Op cit.*).

population of about 1500, the literature suggests that the area was essentially abandoned by 1929. In Area 15, the Oak Spring (Tungsten) District can be found. It was discovered in 1937, followed by development and production in the 1940s (Kral, 1951); significant tungsten production did not begin until the 1950s. After 10 years of co-use during the period of atmospheric bomb testing, the principal mining claims (Climax and Crystal Mines) were acquired through routine condemnation procedures and closed in the early 1960s (see Energy Research and Development Administration, 1977; p. 2–11). Ball (1907, pp. 128–130) reported prospects being developed in the district for precious metals and polymetallics in 1905. Base metals, in the Groom (Lake) District (see Humphrey, 1945), were discovered about 1864; the district was surveyed until about 1915; principal mining was at the Sheahan Groom Mine from 1918–42, with limited mining until the early 1950s (Tschanz and Pampeyan, 1970; p. 148). A mercury mine at Mine Mountain (in Area 6) is also frequently reported to have operated; claim notices indicate exploration in the area in 1928 (Cornwall, 1972; p. 39).

In southern Nevada, there are at least 23 mining districts within 145 kilometers of NTS (see Kral, 1951). The abundant springs and tanks throughout the area influenced the location of thoroughfares between the mining camps and tent towns that developed within these districts—Indian trails evolving to wagon trails and later to finished "carriage" ways (see The Clason Map Company, 1907). As stagecoach and carriage travel became more commonplace, water stops along travel routes became a necessity for both draft animals and people. Before 1900, some relay stations were constructed at several spring locations within the site (see Table B–1) for the stage, freight, and mail lines that operated between southern California and Utah along what is believed to be the so-called "Emigrant Trail" (Long, 1950). Relay station construction frequently included improvements to the spring discharge points (Worman, 1969) but the use of these facilities for their intended purpose to be short-lived (no later than 1910—Pippin and Zerga, 1983; p. 54), probably because of

fluctuations in mining activity in the area and the establishment of other more direct thoroughfares to the West. As a consequence, it is likely that some type of homesteading/ranching took place at these sites until the late 1930s, which included wild horse or mule herding, owing to the presence of corrals and barbed wire fence remnants. Mendenhall (1909, p. 21) recommended that travelers passing through the area carry adequate supplies of grain and hay for their horses because of inadequate forage at the lower elevations. It is likely that any ranching that took place occurred only at elevations above 1500 meters.[5] If ranching took place at lower elevations, it is likely that grain and hay were brought in from elsewhere because of the lack of suitable natural forage. Kit fox, mountain lion, bob cat, mule deer, pronghorn and bighorn sheep, and game birds are indigenous to the area, so it is also likely that some of the abandoned homestead sites also may have been used as lodges for hunting excursions.

Despite fluctuations in the U.S. economy through the 1920s and 1930s, the chief employer in southern Nevada continued to be mining. Several mining camps and communities continued to prosper (Beatty, Tonopah) because of the quality of the ores and the size of the deposits. However, as some mining districts became exhausted, new and richer districts were discovered. As a consequence, some mining camps and tent towns ceased to exist (e.g., Rhyolite: 1904–16; Johnnie: 1890s–1920s). These and other such locations are now regarded as ghost towns. In addition, there were a few small unrecorded prospect pits and claims located within current NTS boundaries, some of which have unreported production. They were worked or

---

[5]It should be noted that there is an extensive variety of vegetation throughout the site. However, the type of vegetation depends on elevation (temperature); slope; slope orientation; precipitation (climate); and soil properties [see Romney *et al.* (1973); and Beatley (1974, 1975).] In general, steep slopes, especially those that face south or west at NTS, generally have little or no vegetation. Desert scrub—mesquite, salt grass, greasewood, and rabbit brush—which makes poor livestock forage, can be found at elevations of less that 1500 meters. At elevations of 1500 meters and above, higher-density cover and better livestock forage—creosote bush, bur-sage, Mormon tea brush, barrel cactus, yucca, and juniper—can generally be found. At elevations of about 1800 meters and above, piñon pines, Joshua trees, and grasses begin to dominate.

staked before acquisition of the site by the government and were not economically viable. To facilitate commerce and trade among the respective mining communities as well as to haul away ore, railroad lines were introduced to the south and west of the site—the *Las Vegas and Tonopah* (Myrick, 1992; pp. 454–503) and the *Tonopah and Tidewater* (*Op cit.*, pp. 545–593); but no lines or spurs were constructed within NTS.[6] With the arrival of railroads, more abundant (and regular) sources of water had to be located and provided for steam locomotive boiler supply. The supply methods took various forms. Usually, railroad companies attempted to use surface water, from either streams or springs. When surface water wasn't available, railroad companies sometimes attempted to create springs by drilling into the sides of mountains, hoping to collect percolating surface water (Kraus, 1969), or dug or drilled wells. [See Baker *et al.* (1973) for descriptions of archetypical examples of early water supplies in several arid states.]

The increase in human activity in the area placed greater demands for water far above that which could be supplied by the natural springs and tanks. In general, water development practices were far from scientific. Overall, the intent was to discover artesian water (under hydraulic pressure or "head"). This is suggested by Mendenhall (1909), where it was noted that the location of early farming/ranching homesteads could be correlated with the occurrence of such springs. Mendenhall (1909, pp. 36–37) reports that the Franklin well was dug in 1852 for parties surveying the California-Nevada boundary line. Ball (1907, p. 21) reports that shallow wells were subsequently sunk in the gravel areas found in flats or gulches adjacent to the main travel routes and railroad alignments, to supplement the springs. Although these shallow wells were sufficient for human consumption and livestock, they were not

sufficient for irrigation. The first irrigation well was sunk in the Amargosa Desert area at the *T and T Ranch* (T. 25 S., R. 48 E.) in 1917, to produce crops for the mining communities in Bullfrog and Beatty (Walker and Eakin, 1963; p. 37).[7] Water wells drilled at the ranch ranged in depth from 22 to 25 meters (McCracken, 1990; p. 45).

It is likely that the first wells in the area were hand-dug improvements of springs, followed later by wells sunk using various boring and drilling methods, as improved technologies became available. Before 1900, it is also likely that most water wells in the area were bored by hand-operated or power-driven augers following the drilling techniques practiced in the eastern United States (U.S.—see Carlston, 1943). After 1900, following the successful use of hydraulic rotary methods of drilling in the oil and gas industries, most wells in the area were probably developed using this new technique.[8] However, the water supplies developed using rotary drilling methods were usually only sufficient for a small livestock ranch but never quite adequate for farming or serving large communities because the means for raising the sufficient quantities of water to the surface were believed to not be generally available until the 1910s.[9]

There is no archeological evidence or reports of commercial farming having taken place within the confines of NTS. For the reasons described elsewhere in this NUREG (see Section 2.1 and Appendix A), commercial

---

[6]In addition to these mining activities, the excavation of industrial minerals/materials also played an important role in the development of the area: clay and peat—Ash Meadows; marble—Carrara; calcium borate (borax)—Death Valley junction area; specialty clays—Clay Camp area and New Discovery mine; and fluorspar—Daisy Mine(Bare Mountain District). See Papke (1979), McCracken (1992), and Myrick (1992).

[7]The *T and T Ranch* was a 4.5-hectare experimental farm and dairy owned and operated by the *Tonopah and Tidewater Railroad*. The goals of the experimental farm were twofold. First, because it was located on the existing right-of-way, it was operated to increase the profitability of this particular railroad line. Second, it was reasoned that if agricultural activity could be established in the area, the products could be transported on the railroad, thereby increasing the line's volume of commercial haulage (see McCracken, 1992; pp. 44–47).

[8]See Bowman (1911) and Tainsh and Churchfield (1978) for a review of drilling technology history.

[9]Before the introduction of electric versions of the centrifugal pump (in the 1910s), a bucket and rope was probably used to lift water to the surface (Wilson, 1896). After their development in the mid-1880s, it was demonstrated that centrifugal pumps were capable of lifting water against high and low head conditions, with good efficiency (Allen, 1958; p. 524). Once such pumps were demonstrated as a practical means for pumping water, designs were soon modified for mobility, driven initially by steam-, coal gas-, or oil-powered machines, and later, by gasoline and electricity (Hood, 1898; Bruce, 1958; p. 560).

farming has been limited to discrete locations outside of the site. Farming (and ranching) was first reported in the Ash Meadows area in the early 1870s, following the example of the Ash Meadows Paiute[10] (see McCracken, 1992; pp. 15–17). As noted earlier, the location of early farming/ranching homesteads can be correlated with the locations of major springs. Before the 1950s, the only reported inhabitants in the Amargosa Desert area were located at the *T and T Ranch*, Ash Meadows, and Lathrop Wells (*Op cit*; p. 51). Wider development of the valley did not take place until amendments were passed to the *Desert Lands Act of 1877*, in the 1950s, which resulted in some additional commercial agricultural activity. However, the introduction of an electric power grid to the Lathrop Wells and Death Valley Junction areas in 1963, by the Rural Electrification Administration, permitted the use of high-capacity pumping equipment and an expansion of irrigated farming (see Walker and Eakin, 1963; pp. 37 38).

Establishment of a national system of parks in the U.S. resulted with the dedication of the Desert National Wildlife Refuge, in 1935, in which the first 6428 square kilometers adjacent to NTS were withdrawn from development and established for public use. However, it wasn't until the early 1940s that land within current NTS boundaries was withdrawn from public use. Originally, 1658 square kilometers were withdrawn to create an aerial bombing and gunnery range for the Army Air Corps (formerly the *Las Vegas Bombing and Gunnery Range*; presently the *Nellis Air Force Range*) at the outbreak of the Second World War. Brady (1975, p. 7) reports that between 300 and 400 cattle ranged at Topopah, Whiterock, and Cane Springs before the war, when the grass was taller and more plentiful. This type of activity would be consistent with the archeological information reported by Worman (1969). After the war, some cattle ranching is reported to have returned, but only at Topopah Spring,

Frenchman Flats, and Emigrant Valley (Anonymous, 1969; pp. 7–8). In the 1950s, after testing in the Pacific Ocean, the Nellis Air Force Range was selected as the site of the U.S.' continental nuclear test site because of its closed topographic basins (see Energy Research and Development Administration, 1977; pp. 2–12 – 2–13), and control of the site was assumed by the AEC. Water and grazing rights for the two remaining ranches were acquired by negotiated purchase in 1955 (*Op cit*., p. 2–12). Subsequent, additional land withdraws by the AEC to the west (in 1954) and the north (in 1964) established the current dimensions of NTS. Today, NTS is approximately 3496 square kilometers and is surrounded by a 10,671-square-kilometer buffer zone.[11]

Over the years, there have been a number of programs and activities at NTS. To support this work, an infrastructure has been created within the site to provide the necessary services. This infrastructure has been described in DOE (1996, pp. 4-10–4-17), including information on water supply (*Op cit*., pp. 4-22, 4-24). Over the years, about 17 wells supplied the freshwater needs for NTS. Most were located in Yucca Flats, Frenchman Flats, and Mercury Valley and were drilled in the mid-to-late 1950s or early 1960s [see Hood (1961); and Claassen (1973)]. Today, only 11 of these wells still supply water to NTS (see Table 2–4), and these are limited to the southern portion of the site. Construction of NTS facilities to support the weapons testing programs began in 1951. The base camp for nuclear testing operations was Mercury. Located approximately 8 kilometers (5 miles) north of state Highway 95, it served as the main administrative and industrial support center for NTS. The water supply for Mercury is provided principally from Wells 5B and 5C (Frenchman Flats) and Army Well 1 (Mercury Valley), which were drilled in the early 1950s and 1960s. Water from the Frenchman Flats area is lifted vertically about 213 meters over Checkpoint Pass by a series of pumping stations (Corchary and Dinwiddie, 1974; p. 37) and conveyed by an underground aqueduct. Camp Desert Rock, a military installation

---

10The Ash Meadows Paiute practiced aboriginal agriculture. They grew corn, squash, beans, and sunflowers, supplemented by hunting for deer, mountain sheep, small reptiles, antelope, and rabbit, and foraging for pine nuts, screw beans, Yucca, cactus leaves and fruit, and other types of desert flora.

11That includes the Nellis Air Force and Tonopah Test Ranges.

under the command of the Sixth Army (headquartered at the Presido, in San Francisco, California), was also established to house up to 6000 troops participating in military operations at NTS until 1958. Located between Mercury and the highway, the water supply for Camp Desert Rock was trucked in from a series of pre-existing wells drilled along the former *Las Vegas and Tonopah Railroad* alignment, now abandoned, and replaced by the highway.[12]

Finally, it should be noted that some limited farming and ranching took place at NTS in support of routine radiological surveillance on-site and other health physics studies (see Table B–1). Because these activities were unique forms of government-sponsored (subsidized) research, they should not be viewed as archetypical of the site without further study.

References

Allen, J., "Hydraulic Engineering (in 'Part VI. Civil Engineering')" in C. Singer, *et al.* (eds.), *A History of Technology, Volume V: The Late Nineteenth Century—c. 1850 to c. 1900*, Oxford, England, Clarendon/Oxford University Press, 1958.

Anonymous, "NTS History Steeped in Fact and Fiction," *NTS News*, 12 (16):4–8, August 8, 1969.

Anonymous, "Unique 36-Acre Experimental Farm Tested Crops, Animals," *NTS News and Views* [Special Edition], April 1993.

Baker, T.L., *et al.*, "Water for the Southwest— Historical Survey and Guide to Historic Sites," American Society of Civil Engineers (ASCE), ASCE Historical Publication No. 3, 1973.

Ball, S.H., "A Geologic Reconnaissance in Southwestern Nevada and Eastern California," U.S. Geological Survey Bulletin 308, 1907.

Batchelor, Y., and D. Batchelor, "Rawhide— Yesterday and Today," *In Focus*, 11(1): 57–77 [1997–98]. [Published by the Churchill County Museum Association (Fallon, Nevada).]

Beatley, J.C., "Effects of Rainfall and Temperature on the Distribution and Behavior of Larrea tridentata (creosote bush)," *Ecology*, 55:245–161 [1974].

Beatley, J.C., "Climates and Vegetation Patterns Across the Mojave/Great Basin Desert Transition of Southern Nevada," *American Midland National*, 93:53–70 [1975].

Bowman, I., "Well-Drilling Methods," U.S. Geological Survey, Water Supply Paper 257, 1911.

Brady, W.J., "The Early Days at NTS," *NTS News/Bicentennial Issue 1975*, 5(5):7–11, 1975.

Bruce, F.E., "Water Supply (in 'Part VI. Civil Engineering')" in C. Singer, *et al.* (eds.), *A History of Technology, Volume V: The Late Nineteenth Century—c. 1850 to c. 1900*, Oxford, England, Clarendon/Oxford University Press, 1958.

Castor, S.B., S.C. Feldman, and J.V. Tingley, "Mineral Evaluation of the Yucca Mountain Addition, Nye County, Nevada," Las Vegas, Nevada, Science Applications International Corporation, December 1989. [Prepared by the Nevada Bureau of Mines and Geology (Reno) and the Desert Research Institute (Reno).]

Carlston, C.W., "Notes on the Early History of Water-Well Drilling in the United States," *Economic Geology*, 38: 119–136 [1943].

Claassen, H.C., "Water Quality and Physical Characteristics of Nevada Test Site Water Supply Wells," Lakewood, Colorado, U.S. Geological Survey, USGS-474-158— [NTS–242], 1973. [Non-serial report prepared for the AEC.]

---

[12]This railroad line was closest to the present site. It ran from 1906 to 1918, with stations/sidings/watering stops at Indian Springs, Charleston, Point of Rocks, Johnnie siding, and Amargosa. In 1920, Nevada State Highway 5 was constructed along the dismantled rail alignment (Myrick, 1992; p. 503).

Table B-1. Historic and Recent Nevada Test Site (NTS) Locations.
Table summarizes preliminary evaluation by the staff. Approximate locations are shown in brackets [ ].

Location	Latitude	Longitude	Water Supply Source	Comments	Reference
Pre-NTS Development					
Big Georges's cave	37° 04' 52" N.	116° 21' 08" W.	Unknown	Indian artifacts and prospecting material; occupied no later than 1937. Elevation 1478 meters	Worman (1969, pp. 25-28)
Captain Jack Spring Corral	37° 10' 06" N.	116° 10' 12" W.	Captain Jack Spring	Small corral. Elevation 1737 meters	Worman (1969, p. 40)
Cane Spring Ranch	36° 47' 56" N.	116° 05' 45" W.	Cane Spring	1 stone and 2 frame cabins, corrals; occupied no later than 1922. Elevation 1241 meters	Worman (1969, pp. 12-15)
Las Vegas and Tonopah Railroad	See Figure B-1.		Wells reported to have been dug/drilled at *Rose's Well* and *Amargosa* stations. Also, Pavit's Spring (?) shown on 1906 geologic map [a] close to *Charleston* station.	Concrete tanks known to have been erected at some station stops [b]	The Clason Map Company (1907); Myrick (1992, pp. 454-503); Walker and Eakin (1963, pp. 46, 47)
Fortymile Canyon Relay Stations	Unknown		Not reported: Black Spring (?) and Belted Mountain Spring shown on 1907 map [c]	Site(s) never located along the *Emigrant Trail*	Anonymous (1969); Pippin and Zerga (1983, p. 54)

Location	Latitude	Longitude	Water Supply Source	Comments	Reference
Groom District	37° 21' N.	115° 46' W.	Cane Spring reported 1.8 kilometers southwest of Groom mine	Polymetallic replacement deposits mined periodically from 1864 to 1955; largest mine is the Groom mine (T. 7 S., R. 55 E.), first acquired by the *Sheahan Family* in 1885	Humphrey (1945, pp. 13, 35-45);Tschanz and Pampeyan (1970, pp. 148-149)
George Lathrop Ranch	Jackass Flats (NTS Area 25)		Concrete water tank at *Lathrop's Well* (located at intersection of State Highway 95 and State Road 373)	Before Second World War, water hauled by wagon from Fairbanks Spring (36°29'20" N., 115°20' 30"W.) to concrete water tank used in earlier construction of *Las Vegas and Tonopah Railroad*	K. Garey (personal comm., Nov. 1998)
Mine Mountain District	[37° 00' N.]	[16° 07' W.]	Not reported.	Mercury retort associated with adits and shafts in T. 11 S., R. 52 E.	Cornwall (1972, p. 39); Worman (1969, p. 8); Brady (1975, p. 10)
Oak Spring District	37° 14' N.	116° 13' W.	Local springs – Oak and Tub Springs – (?) provided sufficient water for domestic use; 107- meter well 11 kilometers east of mine; water lifted 262 meters.	Climax mine worked tungsten skarn deposit until the early 1960s; other polymetallic claims reported to be worked in district before Second World War	Kral (1951); Cornwall (1972, p. 39)
Sheahan (or Sheehan) Ranch	[37° 26' 45" N.]	[116° 53' 24" W.]	Exact supply of water not reported; Cattle Springs closest water supply (?)	Emigrant Valley horse/cattle ranch operated until 1955. Elevation ≈ 1951 meters	Worman (1969, p. 8); Solnit (1994)
Tippipah Spring Ranch	37° 02' 34" N.	116° 12' 13" W.	Tippipah Spring	2 stone cabins, stable, corrals, and barbed-wire pasture fence. Elevation 1583 meters	Worman (1969, pp. 10-11)

Location	Latitude	Longitude	Water Supply Source	Comments	Reference
Topopah Spring Ranch	36° 59' 19" N.	116° 16' 17" W.	Topopah Spring	Ranch debris from fire (ca. 1951) – NaQuinta Ranch (?) Elevation 1737 meters	Anonymous (1969, pp. 7-8); Worman (1969, pp. 15-16); Brady (1975, p. 9)
Sterling Mine	Crater Flat		Water trucked-in from Beatty	240,000 gallons/day	French et al. (1981, p. 28)
White Rock Springs Ranch	37° 12' 04" N.	116° 07' 04" W.	White Rock Springs	Cabin and corral occupied no later than the 1930s. Elevation 1530 meters	Worman (1969, pp. 36-40)
Wahmonie District	36° 49' N.	116° 49' W.	Cane Spring	Comstock vein-type of deposits – Horn Silver Mine, ca. 1905 (in T. 5 S., R. 47 E.)	Kral (1951); Brady (1975, pp. 8-9)
Post-NTS Development					
Camp Desert Rock (NTS Area 22)	36° 37' N.	116° 03' W.	Pre-existing *Las Vegas and Tonopah Railroad* wells and/or Army Well 1 (Mercury Valley)	ca. 1951-58	Anonymous (1993, pp. 2, 4); DOE (1996, pp. 4-15 – 4-16)
Mercury (NTS Area 23)	36° 39' 30" N.	115° 59' 45" W.	Wells 5B and 5C (Frenchman Flats) and Army Well 1, on a rotating basis	1951- present	French et al. (1981, p. 18); DOE (1996, p. 4-16)
Animal Investigation Program in NTS Area 17	Timber Mountain Moat area[d]		Water pond at Test Well 8	Small herds of beef cattle (75 to 100 head) used for on-site radiological surveillance from 1955 through 1970s. Elevation 1736 meters	ERDA (1977, pp. 2-135 – 2-137)
Rock Valley Study Area (NTS Area 25)	36° 40' N.	116° 12' W.	None	Controlled-study area selected in 1960 for desert ecosystem studies	DOE (1996, p. 4-17)

Location	Latitude	Longitude	Water Supply Source	Comments	Reference
U.S. Environmental Protection Agency experimental farm (NTS Area 15)	37° 12' 30" N.	116° 02' 30" W.	Rehabilitated well UE-15d (and 3800-cubic-meter reservoir)	11-hectare farm and dairy operated from 1964-81. 30 Holstein cows, 100 Hereford beef cattle, and other horses, pigs, goats, and chickens raised on farm-grown forage and vegetables. Site included 6 hectares agricultural plots and 0.8 hectares microplots and greenhouse irrigated. Elevation ≈ 1372 meters	Anonymous (1993, p. 26); ERDA (1977, pp. 2-17, 2-137); DOE (1996, p. 4-15)

a See Ball (1907).
b Charleston, Point of Rocks, Johnnie siding, and Amargosa.
c See The Clason Map Company (1907).
d And possibly other areas in which there had been nuclear testing activities.

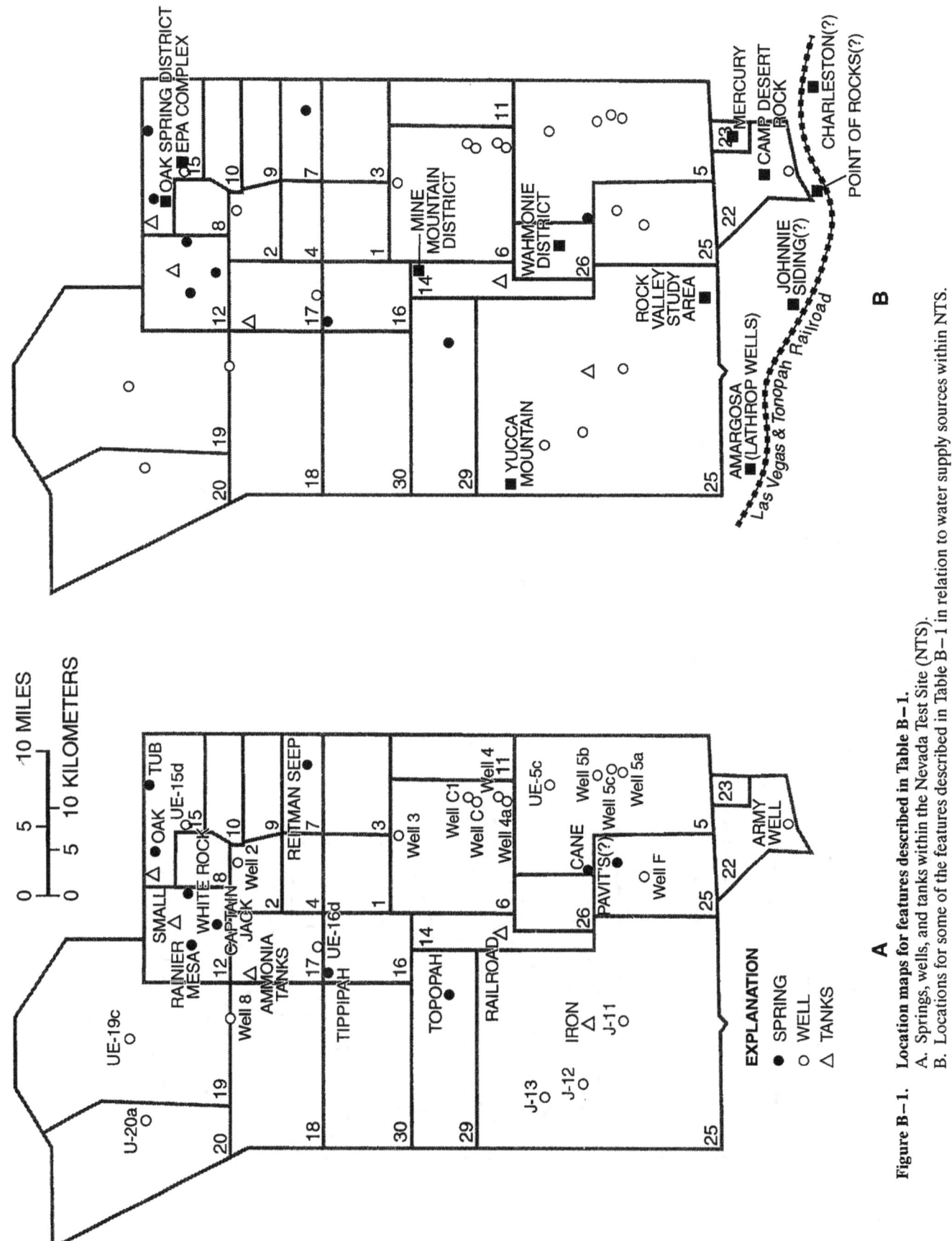

Figure B–1. **Location maps for features described in Table B–1.**
A. Springs, wells, and tanks within the Nevada Test Site (NTS).
B. Locations for some of the features described in Table B–1 in relation to water supply sources within NTS.

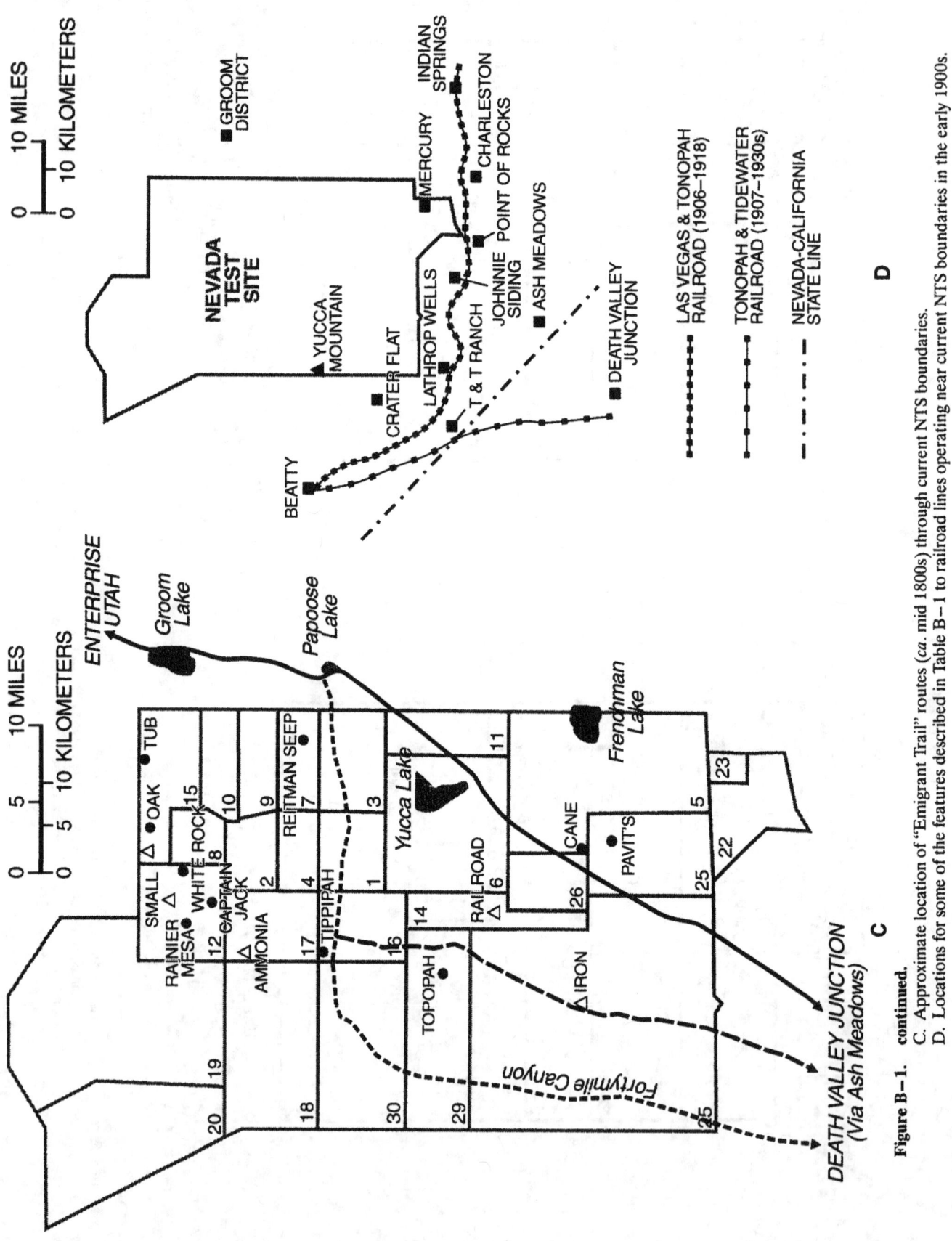

Figure B–1. continued.
C. Approximate location of "Emigrant Trail" routes (*ca.* mid 1800s) through current NTS boundaries.
D. Locations for some of the features described in Table B–1 to railroad lines operating near current NTS boundaries in the early 1900s.

Corchary, G.S., and G.A. Dinwiddie, "Field Trip to [the] Nevada Test Site," Denver, Colorado, U.S. Geological Survey [1974]. [Limited circulation NTS field guide prepared for the AEC.]

Cornwall, H.R., "Geology and Mineral Deposits of Southern Nye County, Nevada," Reno, University of Nevada/Mackay School of Mines, Nevada Bureau of Mines and Geology Bulletin 77, 1972.

Energy Research & Development Administration [ERDA], "Final Environmental Impact Statement: Nevada Test Site, Nye County, Nevada," Washington, D.C., ERDA–1551, September 1977.

French, R.H., *et al.*,"Hydrology and Water Resources Overview for the Nevada Nuclear Waste Storage Investigations, Nevada Test Site, Nye County, Nevada," Las Vegas, Nevada, U.S. Department of Energy/Nevada Operations Office, NVO–284, June 1981 [issued June 1984].

Hewett, D.F., *et al.*, "Mineral Resources around the Region of Boulder Dam," U.S. Geological Survey Bulletin 871, 1936.

Hood, O.P., "New Tests of Certain Pumps and Water Lifts Used in Irrigation," U.S. Geological Survey, Water-Supply and Irrigation Paper No. 14, 1898.

Hood, J.W., "Water Wells in Frenchman and Yucca Valleys, Nevada Test Site, Nye County, Nevada," U.S. Geological Survey, Open File Report, TEI–788, 1961. [Prepared for the AEC.]

Humphrey, F.L., "Geology of the Groom District, Lincoln County, Nevada," *Nevada University Bulletin*, Vol. 39, No. 5, Geology and Mining Series, No. 42, June 1945.

Kral, V.E., "Mineral Resources of Nye County," *Nevada University Bulletin*, Vol. 45, No. 3, Geology and Mining Series, No. 50, January 1951.

Kraus, G., *High Road to Promontory*, Palo Alto, California, American West Publishing Company, 1969.

Long, M., *The Shadow of the Arrows*, Caldwell, Idaho, Caxton Printers, 1950.

McCracken, R.D., *A History of Amargosa Valley Nevada*, Tonopah, Nevada, Nye County Press, 1990.

McCracken, R.D., *The Modern Pioneers of the Amargosa Valley*, Tonopah, Nevada, Nye County Press, 1992.

Mendenhall, W.C., "Some Desert Watering Places in Southeastern California and Southwestern Nevada," U.S. Geological Survey, Water Supply Paper 224, 1909.

Myrick, D.L., *The Railroads of Nevada and Eastern California: Part II—The Southern Railroads*, Reno, Nevada, University of Nevada Press, 1992.

Papke, K.G., "Fluorspar in Nevada," Reno, University of Nevada/Mackay School of Mines, Nevada Bureau of Mines and Geology Bulletin 93, 1979.

Pippin, L.C., and D.L. Zerga, "Cultural Resources Overview for the Nevada Nuclear Waste Storage Investigations, Nevada Test Site, Nye County, Nevada," University of Nevada System, Desert Research Institute, NVO–266, November 1983. [Prepared for the U.S. Department of Energy.]

Ransome, F.L., "Preliminary Account of Goldfield, Bullfrog, and other Mining Districts in Southern Nevada, with notes on the Manhattan District (by G.H. Garrey and W.H. Emmons)," U.S. Geological Survey Bulletin 303, 1907.

Romney, E.M., *et al.*, "Some Characteristics of Soil and Perennial Vegetation in Northern Mojave Desert Areas of the Nevada Test Site," Los Angeles, University of California, USAEC Report UCLA12–916, 1973. [Available through the National Technical Information Service.]

Shamberger, H.A., "The Story of the Water Supply for The Comstock—Including the

Towns of Virginia City, Gold Hill, and Silver City, Nevada (Together with Other Water-Related Events for the Period 1859–1969), U.S. Geological Survey Professional Paper 779, 1972.

State of Nevada, "Mineral and Water Resources of Nevada," Reno, University of Nevada/Mackay School of Mines, Nevada Bureau of Mines and Geology Bulletin 65, 1964. [Prepared by the U.S. Geological Survey and the Nevada Bureau of Mines.]

Steward, J.H., "Basin-Plateau Aboriginal Sociopolitical Groups," *Smithsonian Institution Bureau of American Ethnology Bulletin*, Vol. 120, 1938. [Reprinted by the University of Utah Press (1970).]

Solnit, R., *Savage Dreams: A Journey into the Hidden Wars of the West*, San Francisco, Sierra Club Books, 1994.

Tainsh, H.R., and S.E. Churchfield, "Production of Petroleum Oil and Natural Gas," in T.I. Williams (ed.), *A History of Technology, Volume VI: The Twentieth Century—c. 1900 to c. 1950, Part I*, Oxford, England, Clarendon/Oxford University Press, 1978.

The Clason Map Company, "[Map of] Nevada and the Southern Portion of California," Denver, Colorado, Third Edition, 1907.

Thordarson, W., and B.P. Robinson, "Wells and Springs in California and Nevada within 100 Miles of the Point 37 Deg. 15 Min. N., 116 Deg. 25 Min. W., on Nevada Test Site," U.S. Geological Survey, USGS–474–85, 1971. [Prepared for the AEC.]

Tschanz, C.M., and E.H. Pampeyan, "Geology and Mineral Deposits of Lincoln County, Nevada," Reno, University of Nevada/Mackay School of Mines, Nevada Bureau of Mines and Geology Bulletin 72, 1970.

U.S. Department of Energy, "Final Environmental Impact Statement for the Nevada Test Site and Off-Site Locations in the State of Nevada," Nevada Operations Office, DOE/EIS 0243, 3 vols. (and appendices), August 1996.

Walker, G.E., and T.E. Eakin, "Geology and Ground-Water of Amargosa Desert, Nevada-California," Carson City, Nevada, State of Nevada Department of Conservation and Natural Resources, Ground-Water Resources Reconnaissance Series Report 14, 1963.

Worman, F.C.V., "Archeological Investigations at the U.S. Atomic Energy Commission's Nevada Test Site and Nuclear Rocket Development Station," Los Alamos, New Mexico, Los Alamos Scientific Laboratory, LA–4125, August 1969. [Prepared for the AEC.]

Wilson, H.M., "Pumping Water for Irrigation," U.S. Geological Survey, Water-Supply and Irrigation Paper No. 1, 1896.

APPENDIX C

DETAILED DESCRIPTIONS OF DEEP WELLS

In some portions of the arid U.S., individuals and communities rely on deep wells (i.e., depths to the water table exceed 240 meters) for their fresh water supply. Because this issue could have weight in the definition of a potential receptor group in any Yucca Mountain performance assessment, the staff performed an evaluation to determine the prevalence of deep well drilling practices in areas of the country somewhat comparable to the Yucca Mountain area— specifically in Arizona, Nevada, New Mexico, and the Trans-Pecos region of Texas. The discussion in this appendix documents the results of this evaluation.

C-1 DEEP WELLS IN ARIZONA

The City of Flagstaff in Coconino County has developed two well fields that pump from the Coconino Sandstone aquifer. Five municipal wells in the vicinity of Woody Mountain southwest of Flagstaff have depths to water that range from 337 to 433 meters, whereas a second well field in the vicinity of Lake Mary, southeast of Flagstaff, has depths to water that range from 100 to over 300 meters. Although the Coconino Sandstone can be quite productive where extensively fractured, most of the Flagstaff municipal wells produce 0.006 cubic meters/second or less.[1] Analysis of electronic maps constructed from U.S. Geological Survey (USGS) data indicates two other clusters of wells, northeast of Flagstaff, with depths to water ranging from 388 to 458 meters, which, based on the relatively small diameters of the casings (20 centimeters), appear to be water supply wells for mountain subdivisions.[2] Well head elevations in the Flagstaff area range from 1940 to 2195 meters mean sea level (msl). The average annual precipitation at the Flagstaff meteorological station is 53 centimeters (Sellers *et al.*, 1985). Using the Köppen-Geiger climatological

classification system, the climate of Flagstaff is *Dfa*, or humid temperate. According to Fairbridge (1967), Flagstaff is in the special highland climate category.

Two wells in the vicinity of the towns of Twin Arrows and Angell in Coconino County have depths to water of 280 and 287 meters. One of these wells is used for domestic supply; at the other well, water use is not specified. Well head elevations are 1760 and 1790 meters msl. Twin Arrows lies approximately 35 kilometers east of Flagstaff on Interstate 40. The nearest meteorological stations to Twin Arrows are those at Walnut Canyon National Monument, 20 kilometers to the west, and Meteor Crater, 35 kilometers to the east-southeast, with measured mean annual precipitation of 45 and 21 centimeters, respectively (Sellers *et al.*, 1985). Because of the extreme variation in precipitation between the nearest meteorological stations, it is difficult to classify the local climate; however, it is estimated that the area has a cool to cold semi-arid climate (*BWk* to *BWk'*).

In the vicinity of Gray Mountain in Coconino County are two wells, with depths to water of 360 and 377 meters, that are used for domestic and public water supplies. Gray Mountain is located about 65 kilometers north of Flagstaff on U.S. Interstate 89 near the southern boundary of the Navajo Indian Reservation. Well head elevations are approximately 1500 meters msl. Gray Mountain meteorological station recorded mean annual precipitation of 13 centimeters; however, this station only recorded data from August 1956 to April 1962, during which time Arizona experienced two prolonged droughts (*Op cit.*). Wupatki National Monument, approximately 20 kilometers south of Gray Mountain, has a record of 34 years and mean annual precipitation of 20 centimeters, whereas Cameron, lying about 16 kilometers to the north, has a record of 20 years and mean annual precipitation of 14 centimeters (*Op*

---

[1]Personal communication, R. Wilson, U.S. Geological Survey (Arizona), June 1996.

[2]*Ibid.*

cit.). Gray Mountain probably has a *BWk* to *BWk'* climate.

In the northeastern end of the Sacramento Valley, approximately 15 kilometers west of Kingman in Mohave County, there are three public water supply wells with depths to water that range from 309 to 321 meters. Seven other wells in the Sacramento Valley have depths to water ranging from 265 to 406 meters; all lie within three adjacent townships (T. 21 N., R. 18 W.; T. 22 N., R.18 W.; and T. 23 N. 18 W.). Of these seven wells, two are for industrial use, one is for domestic use, and the remaining four are now unused. Well head elevations in this area range from 800 to 1030 meters msl. The average annual precipitation in Kingman is approximately 26 centimeters (*Op cit.*). Köppen-Geiger's climatological classification for Kingman is *BSh*, or tropical steppe.

Four wells in the eastern part of the Detrital Valley near Dolan Springs in Mohave County have depths to water that range from 215 to 240 meters. Although the depth to water in these wells does not equal or exceed 240 meters, a detailed description was provided because the climate may be similar to that of Yucca Mountain under pluvial conditions. Two of these wells are unused, and the remaining two wells appear to be pumped for domestic use. Elevations of the well heads range from 900 to 920 meters msl. According to a description of the pedology of this region, the soils and climate support native vegetation consisting of blackbrush, creosote bush, Mohave yucca, rayless goldenhead, big galleta, and desert needlegrass.[3] The same source states that the rangeland is suited for wildlife habitat and grazing livestock. Dolan Springs is approximately 40 kilometers northwest of the Kingman meteorological station (elevation 1050 meters).

Within a 1100-square-kilometer area of northwest Yavapai County, including the 12

townships from T. 22. N., R. 10 W. to T. 25 N., R. 8 W., are two clusters of three wells each, and four additional isolated wells that have depths to water which range from 244 to 406 meters. Nine of the 10 wells have depths to water between 244 and 290 meters. One cluster lies within a 14-kilometer radius of the town of Yampai, whereas the second cluster lies within a 5-kilometer radius of the town of Pica—a rail stop on the *Atchison, Topeka, and Santa Fe Railroad*. The three wells near Yampai are currently unused, whereas two of the three wells near Pica are for stock water, and the third for public supply. Elevations of the well heads range from 1570 to 1720 meters msl. Peach Springs meteorological station lies approximately 25 northwest of Yampai and Pica, along Route 66, at an elevation of 1510 meters, and has an average annual precipitation of 28 centimeters (*Op cit.*). Based on the Arizona isohyet map (National Oceanic and Atmospheric Administration, 1974), it seems reasonable to assume that the average annual precipitation in the general area is less than 30 centimeters. Meteorological data from Peach Springs are incomplete so data from nearby Truxton Canyon were used to estimate the region's climate. Using Köppen-Geiger's climatological system, the climate of the region is *BSh*.

On the Paria Plateau, north of the east end of Grand Canyon National Park, there are four stock wells and one domestic well with depths to water that range from 262 to 457 meters. Well head elevations for these wells range from 1875 to 1950 meters msl. The Paria Plateau appears to have an average elevation of approximately 1850 meters msl, some 300 meters lower than the Kaibab Plateau to the west, where the average annual precipitation at the Jacob Lake meteorological station is 52 centimeters (*Op cit.*). House Rock, Arizona, which lies 16 kilometers west of Jacob Lake at an elevation of 1640 meters msl, has an average annual precipitation of 18 centimeters (*Op cit.*). Based on the magnitude of local orogenic effects, it is estimated that the mean annual precipitation on the Paria Plateau ranges from 30 to 40 centimeters. Because meteorological data for House Rock are incomplete, it is difficult to accurately

---

[3]Information found on the *World Wide Web* (location, as of August 7, 1996: http://www.statlab.iastate. edu/soils-info/osd) for Nealy series soil. The web page describes the Nealy series soil, type, location about 14 kilometers southwest of Dolan Springs, Mohave County, Arizona. Server located at Iowa State University.

determine the climate of the Paria Plateau. The Paria Plateau is approximately 580 meters lower in elevation than the meteorological station at Jacob Lake, which has a climate similar to Flagstaff. Hence, the plateau probably has a cool semi-arid to highland climate.

At the extreme north central part of the State is a cluster of three wells located in the vicinity of Wahweap and Glen Canyon Dam State Park, with depth to water that ranges from 259 to 268 meters. Two of the wells are pumped for public water supply, whereas the use of the third well is unknown. Well head elevations are approximately 1250 meters msl. Average annual precipitation in Wahweap is only 15 centimeters (*Op cit.*). The Wahweap area has a climate that is similar to that of Las Vegas, which is classified as cool arid or as mid-latitude desert (Fairbridge, 1967).

The city of Williams, Coconino County, Arizona, is considering constructing a municipal supply well that would pump water from the Redwall unit where the depth to water is approximately 600 meters.[4] Williams is located about 45 kilometers west of Flagstaff on Interstate 40, and appears to have a similar highland climate.

C–2 DEEP WELLS IN NEVADA

Of the six wells in Nye and Lincoln Counties with depths to water in excess of 240 meters, five are unused test boreholes, associated with the mobile Inter-Continental Ballistic Missile siting study (the so-called *MX/Peacekeeper Program*), that were constructed by the USGS for the U.S. Department of Defense during the late 1970s and early 1980s. Depths to water in these test boreholes range from 245 to 263 meters. Well head elevations for three of the test boreholes in Coal Valley range from 1550 to 1710 meters msl. Because these boreholes were constructed for national defense, it seems that few inferences can be drawn from their existence regarding water well develop- ment near Yucca Mountain. The

use of the sixth deep well (265 meters) is unspecified.

There are seven wells in Clark County, with depths to water that range from 250 to 407 meters. Four of these wells are scattered from west to east across a wide area north of Las Vegas extending from 12 kilometers southeast of Mercury (256 meters) to the southeastern terminus of the Desert Range (407 meters), to a narrow valley between the Dry Lake Range and Muddy Mountains in far eastern Clark County (251 and 251 meters). The well southeast of Mercury has a well head elevation of 1087 meters msl, and pumps water for unspecified use from the Bonanza King formation. The very deep well southeast of the Desert Range has a well head elevation of 1272 meters msl, and is currently unused. The two wells in far eastern Clark County have well head elevations of 789 and 791 meters msl; one well is currently unused, the other supplies stock water. Three other deep wells are located south of Las Vegas. One currently unused well is located in the south end of Hidden Valley directly to the west of the McCullough range at an elevation of 924 meters and has a depth to water of 290 meters msl. South of Boulder City near the northwestern terminus of the Black Hills at an elevation of 707 meters is a domestic well with a depth to water of 250 meters. Approximately 16 kilometers north of Searchlight, along U.S. Interstate 95, there is a stock well, at an elevation of 925 meters, that has a depth to water of 262 meters msl. It is assumed the climate for most of this area is similar to that of Las Vegas or mid-latitude desert.

C–3 DEEP WELLS IN NEW MEXICO

In Bernalillo County, to the west of Albuquerque, there are three wells, that pump at depths to water of 237,[5] 263, and 270 meters, which are located on top of a north-trending mesa some 60 to 70 kilometers in length. Two of the wells are located approximately 10 kilometers west of Albuquerque. Two of the wells on the mesa are currently unused and one is a commercial well. Two other wells with depths to water of

---

[4]Personal communication, S. Leake, U.S. Geological Survey (Tucson), July 1996.

[5]Included because of association with other wells deeper than 240 meters.

256 and 281 meters are located east of Albuquerque near the town of Sedillo and near Bear Canyon, respectively. The deep well located near Sedillo is also a commercial well; however, Bear Canyon well water use is not specified.

In south central Sandoval County near the county line with Bernalillo County, there are three public supply wells with depths to water of 276, 307, and 342 meters. All three wells are located in or near the town of Alameda, approximately 20 kilometers north-northwest of Albuquerque on a mesa rising about 300 meters above the Rio Grande Valley. Alameda is primarily an upper middle-class residential community. The elevation of Alameda is approximately 1800 meters msl. Alameda probably has a cool semi-arid to arid climate similar to Albuquerque.

Within Santa Fe County (east of Sandoval County) there are three wells with depths to water of 276, 299, and 318 meters. The two deeper wells are located in the Santa Fe National Forest near Pankey Peak, which has an elevation of 2200 meters msl. Both of these wells are powered by windmills and used to supply stock water. The shallowest well is located on Glorieta Mesa approximately 13 kilometers southwest of Pecos, New Mexico. This well also supplies stock water; however, it is pumped by a gasoline-powered pump jack. This region's climate would probably be classified as highland.

Within Taos County, which is north-northeast of Santa Fe County, there are two wells with depths to water of 247 and 329 meters. The deeper of the two wells is located about 10 kilometers south-southeast of Tres Piedras near State Highway 285. This well is used for domestic supply and is pumped by a gasoline-powered pump jack. The shallower well is located about 14 kilometers north of Tres Piedras and appears to be operated by the Johns Mansville Perlite Corporation, for industrial purposes.

West of Albuquerque, in McKinley and Cibola Counties, there are a number of deep wells located on or near Indian reservations.

Fourteen kilometers north-northeast of Cebolleta (Seboyeta), Cibola County, near Canon de Marques, in far southeastern McKinley County, there is an unused well with a depth to water of 314 meters. Eight kilometers east-southeast of Cebolleta in Cibola County there are two deep industrial wells located along Meyer Draw, each with a depth to water of 258 meters. Elsewhere in McKinley County there are two unused wells located 21 and 23 kilometers south of the Chaco Culture National Monument, with depths to water of 288 and 314 meters, respectively. A fourth deep well in McKinley County is located 5 kilometers west of Borrego Pass Trading Post, has a depth to water of 240 meters, and is pumped for domestic use. On the Ramah Navajo Indian Reservation located in west central Cibola County approximately 13 kilometers south of the community center, there is a well with depth to water of 298 meters. Orr (1987) designates this as the Ramah-2 well and notes that it pumps from the Glorieta-San Andres aquifer. The Ramah-1 well is located within the same quarter-section as Ramah-2 and pumps from the Glorieta-San Andres aquifer at a depth to water of 291 meters (*Op cit.*). Well head elevations for Ramah-1 and Ramah-2 are 2269 and 2279 meters msl, respectively. The Cheechilgeetho School in Cheechilgeetho, Cibola County, approximately 35 kilometers south-southwest of Gallup, New Mexico, at an altitude of 2076 meters msl, had a well that pumped from the Glorieta-San Andres aquifer with a depth to water of 339 meters, before it was plugged (*Op cit.*).

In southwestern New Mexico near Silver City, Grant County, there are two wells with depths to water of 299 and 594 meters. The shallower well is located about 4 kilometers east of the mining town of Turnerville and is used for public supply. The deep well is located about 3 kilometers south of Turnerville and is used for industrial supply. The extreme depth to water recorded in this latter well may reflect pumpage to dewater underground copper mine adits.

C–4 DEEP WELLS IN TEXAS

In the Trans-Pecos region there are 38 wells with depths to water that equal or exceed 240 meters. Twenty-two of these deep wells are located in Hudspeth County, with 20 being in the general vicinity of the town of Sierra Blanca. Diamondhead Corporation owns seven wells, to the northwest of Sierra Blanca, that have depths to water ranging from 287 to 339. Two of Diamondhead wells are used for public water supply, one for stock, one for industrial supply, one for domestic supply, and one former public supply well is currently unused. All Diamondhead wells pump from the Cretaceous aquifer and produce from 0.00019 cubic meters/second, for stock water, to 0.032 cubic meters/second, for public supply. Well head elevations for the Diamondhead wells range from 1393 to 1522 meters msl. Sierra Blanca Corporation owns two wells near Sierra Blanca with depths to water of 271 and 275 meters. One of Sierra Blanca Corporation deep wells is unused, whereas the other is used for stock water. Nine other wells near Sierra Blanca have depths to water ranging from 240 to 341 meters and are primarily used to supply stock. In northern Hudspeth County, approximately 40 kilometers south of Dell City, there are two wells that pump from a Paleozoic aquifer at depths to water of 244 and 347 meters.

In Culberson County, which lies immediately east of Hudspeth County, there are seven wells with depths to water in excess of 240 meters. Five of these wells are located in a cluster northwest of the town of Kent near the Apache Mountains. Two of these five wells are owned by the Foster Ranch and used to supply domestic and stock water. One of the Foster Ranch wells is a converted oil test well and pumps from a depth to water of 463 meters. The second Foster Ranch well pumps from a depth to water of 276 meters. The other three wells of this cluster are owned by the Apache Ranch and are abandoned industrial wells originally owned by Elcor Chemical Corporation. These three wells have depths to water that range from 307 to 323 meters; two wells are used to provide water for stock tanks, the third is unused. In northern Culberson County south of the city of Pine Springs, which lies at the southern end of the Guadalupe Mountains, the Six-Bar Cattle Company operates a well for stock

water that has a depth to water of 244 meters. In the immediate vicinity of Kent, Reynolds Cattle Company pumps stock water from a well with a depth to water of 293 meters. The five wells in the Apache Mountains area and the one well near Kent pump from the Permian Capitan Reef Complex aquifer. The well near Pine Springs pumps from the Paleozoic Bone Spring limestone aquifer. Well head elevations for the Apache Mountains cluster range from 1350 to 1543 meters msl. The Reynolds Cattle Company well head elevation is 1359 meters and the Six-Bar Cattle Company well head elevation is 1391 meters msl.

Scattered along the Rio Grande River in southeastern Brewster County are three wells, used by local ranches for domestic and stock water, that have depths to water ranging from 245 to 328 meters. This area is significantly lower in elevation than most of the Trans-Pecos region, with well head elevations ranging from 745 to 804 meters msl. Two of these wells pump from the Edwards-Trinity Plateau aquifer.

Other deep wells in the Trans-Pecos region include: (i) one in Jeff Davis County near the town of Valentine; (ii) one in Terrell County south of the town of Dryden; and (iii) one in southwestern Val Verde County. The depths to water in these very widely scattered wells range from 241 to 293 meters.

C–5 REFERENCES

Fairbridge, R.W., *The Encyclopedia of Atmospheric Sciences and Astrogeology: Encyclopedia of Earth Sciences Series, Volume II*, New York, New York, Reinhold Publishing Corporation, 1967.

National Oceanic and Atmospheric Administration, "Climates of the States: A Practical Reference Containing Basic Climatological Data of the United States, Volume II—Western States, Including Alaska and Hawaii," Port Washington, New York, Water Information Center, 1974.

Orr, B.R., "Water Resources of the Zuni Tribal Lands, McKinley and Cibola Counties,

New Mexico," U.S. Geological Survey Water Supply Paper 2227, 1987.

Sellers, W.D., R.H. Hill, and M. Sanderson-Rae, *Arizona Climate: The First Hundred Years,* Tucson, Arizona, University of Arizona Press, 1985.

APPENDIX D

WELL CONSTRUCTION COSTS

D–1 DESCRIPTION OF WELLS[1]

Drilling and installation costs for five separate wells were estimated. The completion details for four of the five wells were based on existing wells; the fifth well was a non-specific, low-cost well for supplying a stock pond. Also, not all well completion details were available for the four existing wells; therefore, some standard well installation practices were assumed.

All drilling costs are for air-rotary drilling. All casing costs are for low-carbon steel casing. Replacement wells for the four known wells were completed as gravel packed wells. For consistency, all wells used the same screen—a louvered Johnson Irrigator screen.

The five wells are described in the following paragraphs, below.

Well 1: Well 1 is a 3385-foot-deep well, completed in welded and bedded tuffs. Completion details of Well 1 are described in Table D–1 and shown in Figure D–1, and include the following:

Total borehole depth . . . . *3500 feet*
Well depth . . . . *3385 feet*
Borehole diameter . . . . *26 inches*
Casing diameter . . . . *14 inches*
Total Screen length . . . . *2162 feet*

The well that Well 1 replaced was a telescoped well, with casing diameters of 18, 13 3/8, 11 3/4, and 6 inches. The original Well 1 was completed as a telescoped well because of problems encountered during drilling. Well 1 is simpler to install as a single casing diameter well.

Well 1 is outfitted with a submersible pump that was sized to produce 700 gallons/minute against a static head of 1000 feet.

Well 2: Well 2 is an 887-foot-deep well, completed in welded and bedded tuffs. Completion details of Well 2 are described in Table D–2 and shown in Figure D–2, and include the following:

Total borehole depth . . . . *900 feet*
Well depth . . . . *887 feet*
Borehole diameter . . . . *22 inches*
Casing diameter . . . . *12 inches*
Total screen length . . . . *75 feet*

Well 2 is outfitted with a submersible pump that was sized to produce 800 gallons/minute against a static head of 800 feet.

Well 3: Well 3 is a 320-foot-deep well, completed in alluvial deposits consisting of medium to fine-grained sand interbedded with silt. Well 3 is an irrigation well that provides water to a quarter-section center-pivot irrigation system. Completion details of Well 3 are described in Table D–3 and shown in Figure D–3, and include the following:

Total borehole depth . . . . *320 feet*
Well depth . . . . *320 feet*
Borehole diameter . . . . *28 inches*
Casing diameter . . . . *16 inches*
Total screen length . . . . *150 feet*

Pump requirements for Well 3 were estimated based on conversations with a local knowledgeable expert, who noted that most center-pivot irrigation systems in southern and eastern Nevada are fitted with 100-horsepower motors and pump against 150 feet of head.[2] Flow rates from these wells are known. Theoretical calculations for flow rates indicate a 100-horsepower motor produces 2637 gallons/minute against 150 feet of static head. Depending on the size and make of the

---

[1]Most drilling engineers in the United States still prefer the use of inch-pound units (the so-called English system), when describing water well characteristics. Therefore, for ease of comparison with engineering existing practice, in this regard, the English system will be used in this appendix. Conversion factors can be found in the front of this NUREG.

[2]Personal communication, B. Wilson, Nevada Agricultural Extension (Ely), July 1996.

discharge pipe, this flow rate will be reduced by friction, but will likely remain above 2400 gallons/minute.

In accordance with irrigation practices in other parts of Nevada, Well 3 is outfitted with a 100-horsepower turbine shaft pump.

Well 4: Well 4 is a 600-foot deep well, completed in alluvial deposits consisting of coarse sand interbedded with gravel and silt. Well 4 is a domestic well, providing water to one or two dwellings. Completion details of Well 4 are described in Table D–4 and shown in Figure D–4, and include the following:

Total borehole depth . . . . *600 feet*
Well depth . . . . *600 feet*
Borehole diameter . . . . *19 inches*
Casing diameter . . . . *8 inches*
Total screen length . . . . *200 feet*

Well 4 is outfitted with a 5-horsepower submersible pump, set at 450 feet below the ground surface. The pump was sized to produce at least 10 gallons/minute against a static head of 300 feet.

Well 5: Well 5 is a 1500-foot-deep well, completed in welded and bedded tuff. Well 5 provides water to a stock tank and Well 5 is cased to a depth of 150 feet. Between 150 feet and 1500 feet, Well 5 is completed as an open hole in fractured tuff. This well is designed to be drilled and completed in a single pass with minimal completion details. Completion details of Well 5 are described in Table D–5 and shown in Figure D–5, and include the following:

Total borehole depth . . . . *1500 feet*
Well depth . . . . *1500 feet*
Borehole diameter . . . . *8 inches*

Casing diameter . . . . *Not Applicable*
Total screen length . . . . *Not Applicable*

Well 5 is outfitted with a 5-horsepower submersible pump set at 1250 feet below the ground surface. The pump was sized to produce 2 gallons/minute against a static head of 1000 feet.

D–2 WELL COSTS

Estimated capital costs for Wells 1 through 5 are included on Tables D–1 through D–5. These cost estimates are in 1996 dollars.

D–3 OPTIONAL PUMP COSTS

Costs for two optional pumping systems were estimated. The two pumping systems include a windmill and a pump jack. Each optional pumping system was designed to produce 2 to 3 gallons per minute against a static head of 1000 feet.

Windmill: Lifting a column of water 1000 feet requires a 20-foot-diameter windmill. The only available windmills of this size are reconditioned Aermotor windmills. The standard tower for these windmills is 40 feet high. The purchase cost for this tower is unknown. Any other tower over 40 feet high would be custom-built.

Costs for a 20-foot-diameter windmill mounted on a 40-foot tower are included in Table D–6. The total cost is estimated at $25,700.

Pump Jack: A pump jack capable of producing approximately 3 gallons/minute against a head of 1000 feet costs around $5000. This cost does not include the electric motor for powering the pump jack.

Table D−1. Well 1 Estimated Costs				
ITEM	*UNITS*	*QUANTITY*	*UNIT COST ($)*	*COST ($)*
Install 30" Conductor Casing	feet	50	175	8750
Drill Pilot Hole	feet	3450	45	155,250
E-log	line item	1	7000	7000
Ream Pilot Hole to 26"	feet	3450	60	207,000
Caliper Log	line item	1	4000	4000
Install Blank Casing	feet	1223	120	146,760
Install Screen	feet	2162	160	345,920
Install Gravel Pack	feet	2515	45	113,175
Gravel Tube	feet	990	6	5940
Grout Seal	feet	985	55	54,175
Plumbness & Alignment Test	line item	1	5500	5500
Surge/Airlift Development	hours	24	275	6600
Pumping Development	hours	24	150	3600
Step Test	hours	10	150	1500
Constant Q Test	hours	40	150	6000
Pump Cost	line item	1	20,000	20,000
Install Pump	line item	1	6500	6500
Electrical & Wellhead Finish	line item	1	20,000	20,000
TOTAL COST				$ 1,117,670

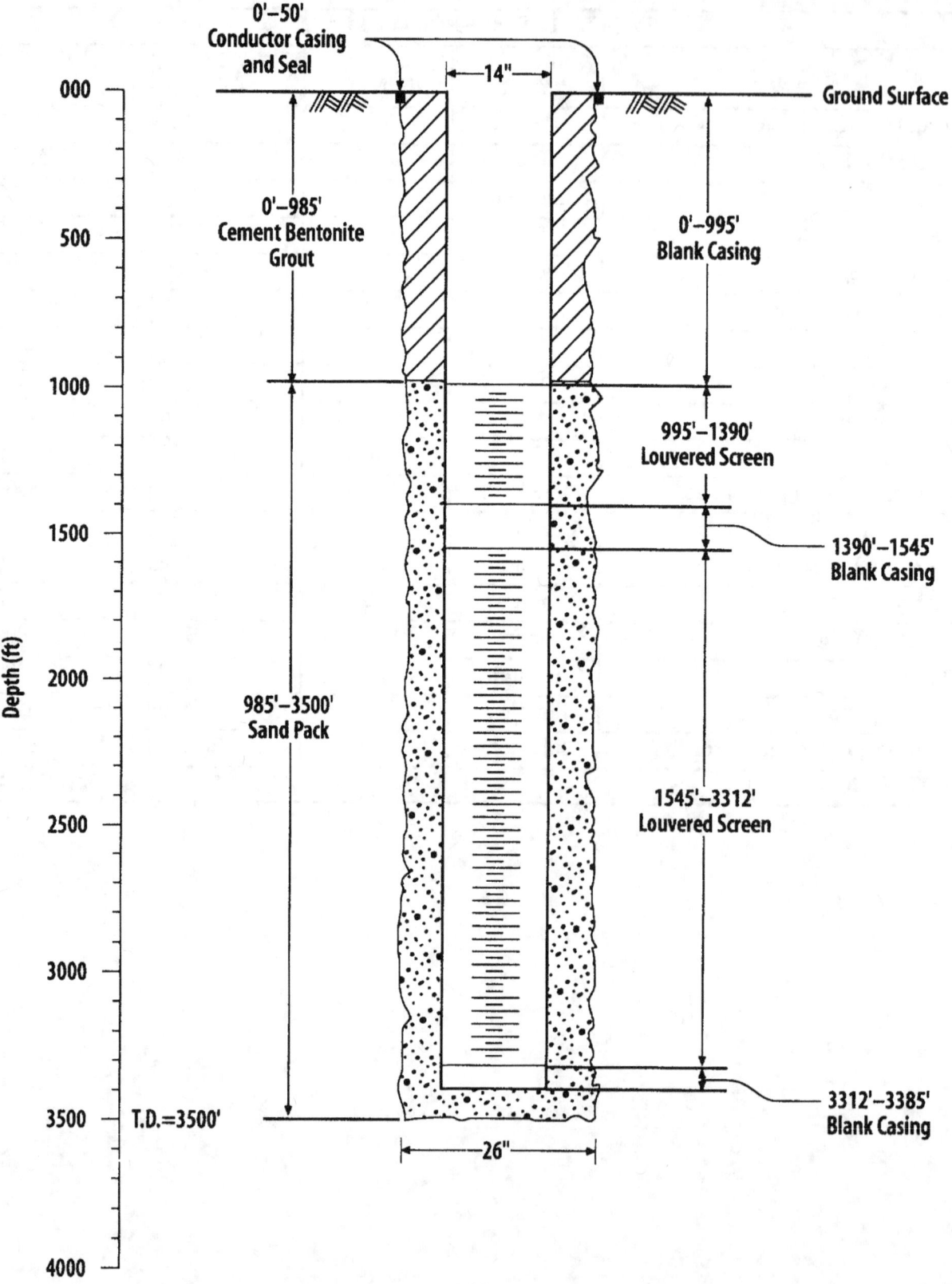

Figure D–1. Completion details for Well 1.

ITEM	UNITS	QUANTITY	UNIT COST ($)	COST ($)
Install 22" Conductor Casing	feet	50	125	6250
Drill Pilot Hole	feet	400	40	16,000
E-log	line item	1	4000	4000
Ream Pilot Hole to 22"	feet	900	50	45,000
Caliper Log	line item	1	2000	2000
Install Blank Casing	feet	812	55	44,660
Install Screen	feet	75	75	5625
Install Gravel Pack	feet	117	25	2925
Gravel Tube	feet	125	6	750
Grout Seal	feet	783	45	35,235
Plumbness & Alignment Test	line item	1	2500	2500
Surge/Airlift Development	hours	24	275	6600
Pumping Development	hours	24	150	3600
Step Test	hours	10	150	1500
Constant Q Test	hours	40	150	6000
Pump Cost	line item	1	20,000	20,000
Install Pump	line item	1	6500	6500
Electrical & Wellhead Finish	line item	1	20,000	20,000
TOTAL COST				$ 229,145

Table D–2. Well 2 Estimated Costs

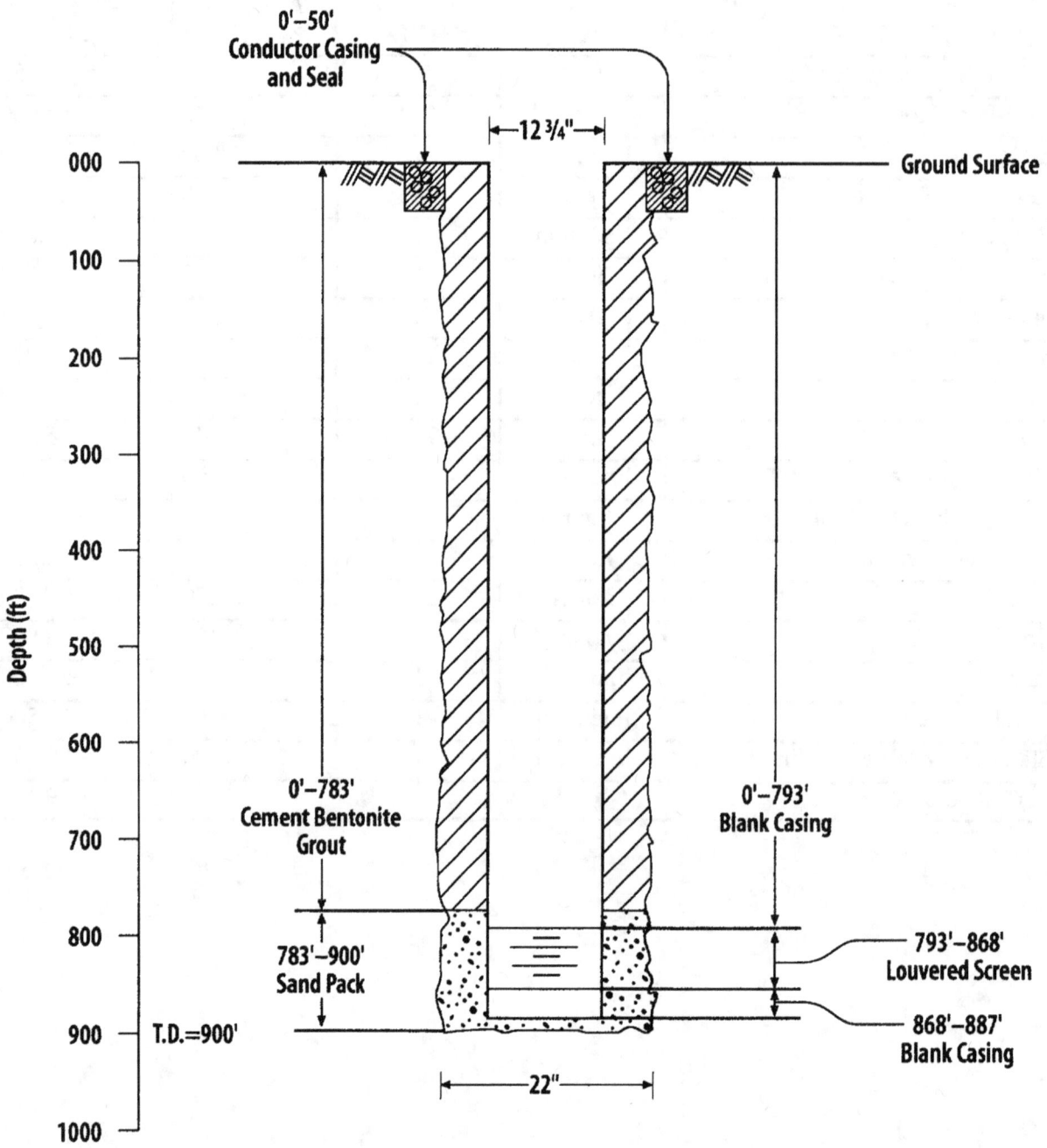

Figure D–2.   Completion details for Well 2.

Table D−3. Well 3 Estimated Costs				
ITEM	*UNITS*	*QUANTITY*	*UNIT COST ($)*	*COST ($)*
Install 30" Conductor Casing	feet	50	175	8750
Drill Pilot Hole	feet	320	40	12,800
E-log	line item	1	3000	3000
Ream Pilot Hole to 28"	feet	320	50	16,000
Caliper Log	line item	1	2000	2000
Install Blank Casing	feet	175	65	11,375
Install Screen	feet	150	85	12,750
Install Gravel Pack	feet	180	35	6300
Gravel Tube	feet	145	6	870
Grout Seal	feet	140	55	7700
Plumbness & Alignment Test	line item	1	2500	2500
Surge/Airlift Development	hours	24	275	6600
Pumping Development	hours	24	150	3600
Step Test	hours	10	150	1500
Constant Q Test	hours	40	150	6000
Pump Cost	line item	1	40,000	40,000
Install Pump	line item	1	6000	6000
Electrical & Wellhead Finish	line item	1	20,000	20,000
TOTAL COST				$ 167,745

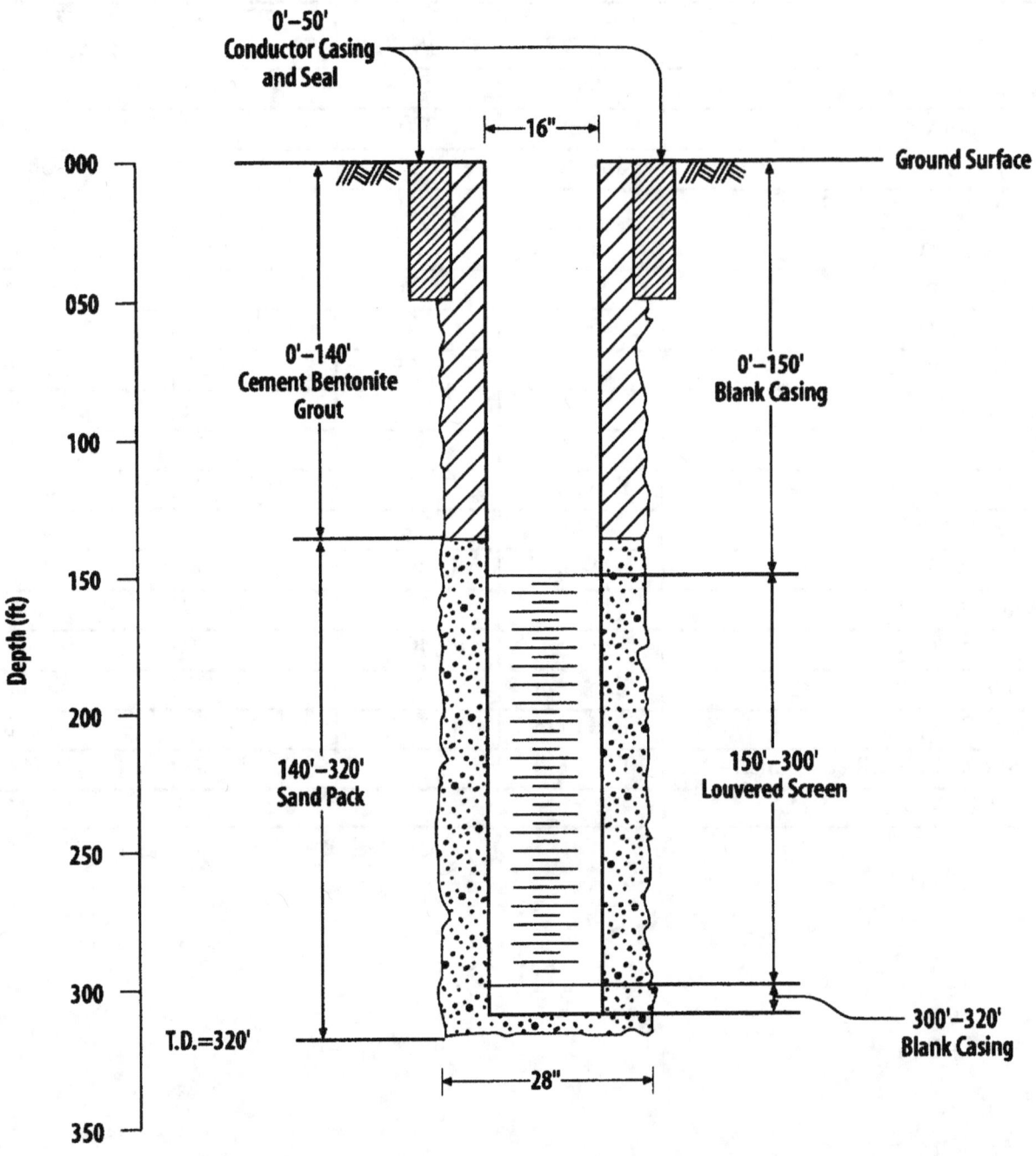

Figure D–3. Completion details for Well 3.

Table D—4. Well 4 Estimated Costs				
ITEM	*UNITS*	*QUANTITY*	*UNIT COST ($)*	*COST ($)*
Install 16" Conductor Casing	feet	50	100	5000
Drill Pilot Hole	feet	600	35	21,000
E-log	line item	1	3000	3000
Ream Pilot Hole to 19"	feet	600	45	27,000
Caliper Log	line item	1	2000	2000
Install Blank Casing	feet	400	41	16,400
Install Screen	feet	200	60	12,000
Install Gravel Pack	feet	260	20	5200
Gravel Tube	feet	345	6	2070
Grout Seal	feet	340	40	13,600
Plumbness & Alignment Test	line item	1	2500	2500
Surge/Airlift Development	hours	24	275	6600
Pumping Development	hours	24	150	3600
Step Test	hours	10	150	1500
Constant Q Test	hours	40	150	6000
Pump Cost	line item	1	8000	8000
Install Pump	line item	1	6000	6000
Electrical & Wellhead Finish	line item	1	20,000	20,000
TOTAL COST				$ 161,470

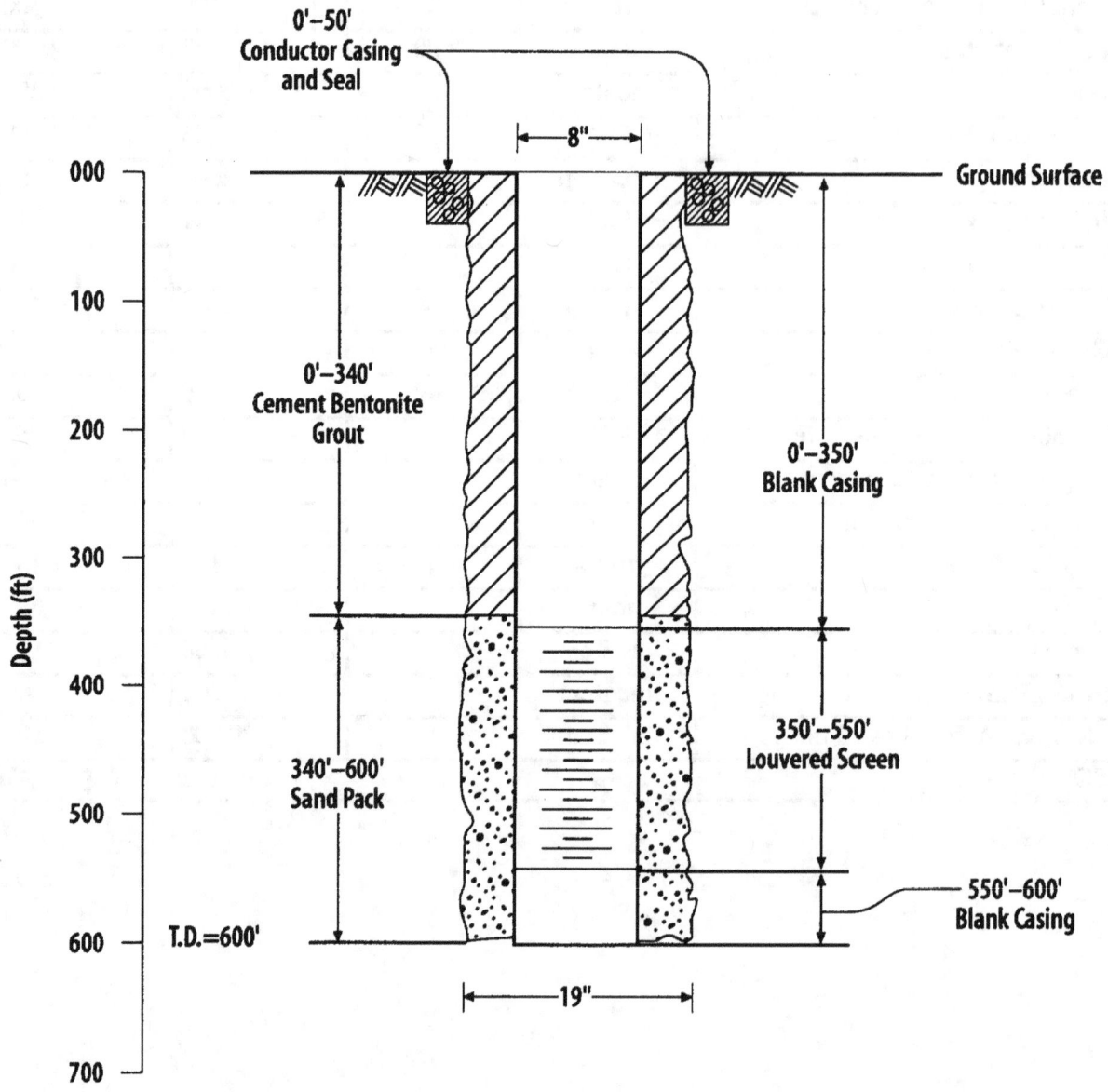

Figure D–4.   Completion details for Well 4.

Table D–5. Well 5 Estimated Costs				
ITEM	*UNITS*	*QUANTITY*	*UNIT COST ($)*	*COST ($)*
Install 16" Conductor Casing	feet	50	100	5000
Drill Pilot Hole	feet	1500	45	67,500
E-log	line item	1	5000	5000
Ream Pilot Hole to 26"	feet		N/A	N/A
Caliper Log	line item	1	3000	3000
Install Blank Casing	feet	150	41	6150
Install Screen	feet		N/A	N/A
Install Gravel Pack	feet		N/A	N/A
Gravel Tube	feet		N/A	N/A
Grout Seal	feet		N/A	N/A
Plumbness & Alignment Test	line item	1	N/A	N/A
Surge/Airlift Development	hours	24	275	6600
Pumping Development	hours	24	150	3600
Step Test	hours	10	150	1500
Constant Q Test	hours	40	150	6000
Pump Cost	line item	1	15,000	15,000
Install Pump	line item	1	6000	6000
Electrical & Wellhead Finish	line item	1	20,000	20,000
TOTAL COST				$ 145,350

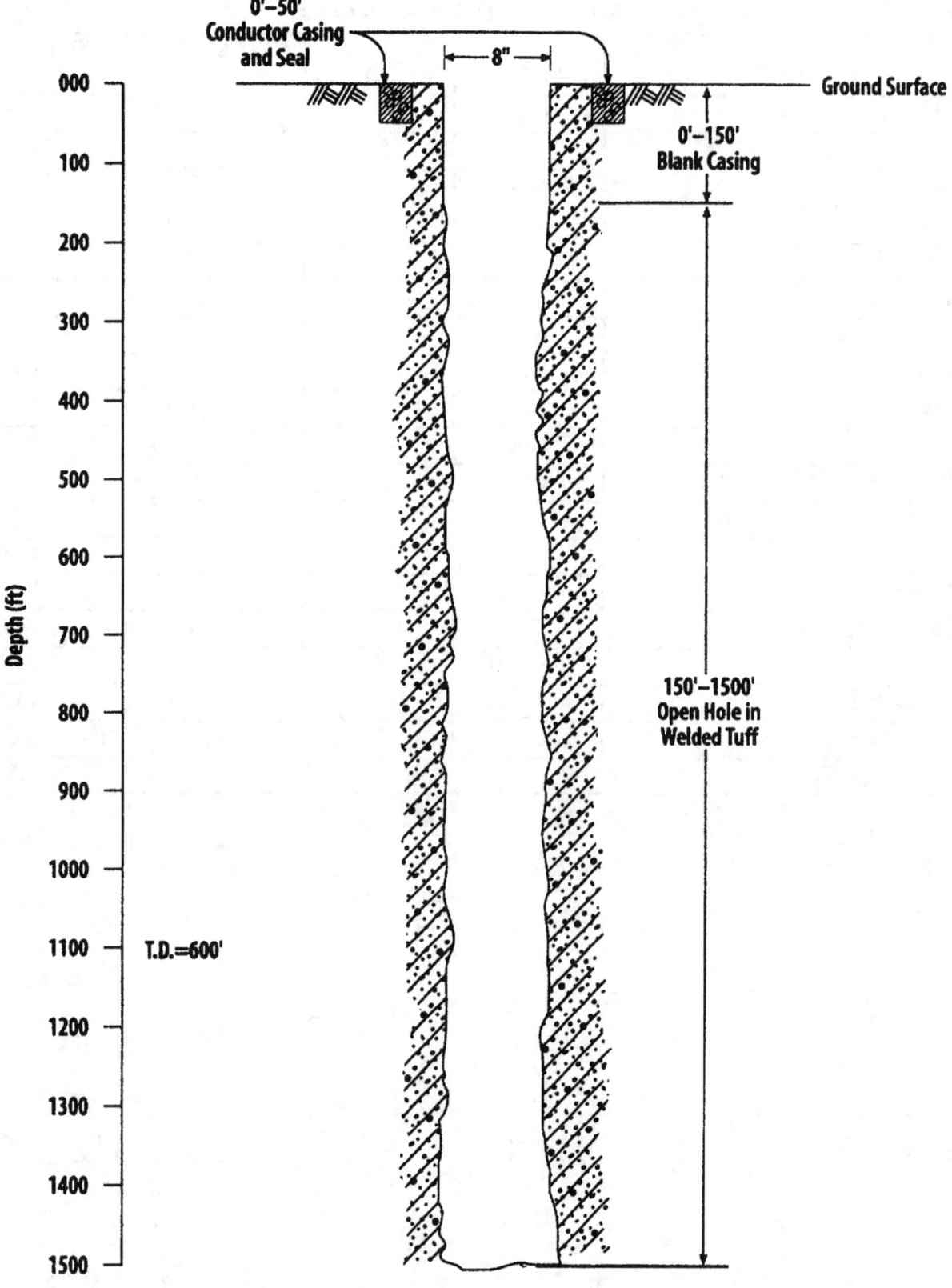

Figure D–5 Completion details for Well 5.

Table D−6. Estimated Windmill Costs				
ITEM	*UNITS*	*QUANTITY*	*UNIT COST ($)*	*COST ($)*
20' Diameter Windmill on a 40' Tower	Lump Sum	1	18,000.00	18,000.00
3/4" Sucker Rod	21' Rod	72	65.94	4747.68
2" Threaded Black Steel Drop Pipe	21' Pipe	72	37.99	2735.28
Pump Cylinder	Lump Sum	1	225.00	225.00
TOTAL COST				$ 25,707.96

APPENDIX E
DETAILED WATER USE TABLE FOR THE YEARS 1983 AND 1985-96

Annual water use estimates (cubic meters) from the U.S. Geological Survey's *Ground-Water Site Inventory* (Mathey, 1989). Location: quarter-quarter section – *QQ* ; quarter section – *QTR* ; section – *SEC* ; township – *TWN* ; and range – *RNG* . Water use types: commercial – *COM* ; mining – *MM* ; irrigation – *IRR* ; and quasi-municipal – *QM* .

Location:[a] QQ QTR SEC TWN RNG	Use	1983	1985	1986	1987	1988	1989	1990	1991	1992	1993	1994	1995	1996
SE SE 13 15 49	COM	–	–	–	–	–	–	–	–	–	–	–	–	617
SE NE 16 16 48	COM	–	–	–	–	–	–	–	–	–	–	–	–	2468
NE NE 14 16 49	COM	–	–	–	–	–	–	–	–	–	–	–	–	123.4
NE NW 12 17 48	MM	314670	135740	350456	367732	702146	647850	472622	413390	428815	286288	419560	430666	335648
NE NW 25 18 50	COM	–	–	740.4	617	617	–	–	–	–	–	–	–	–
XX SE 35 16 49	COM	–	–	–	–	–	–	–	–	–	–	–	–	1234
XX SW 36 17 49	COM	–	1e+06	328244	4936	526918	1e+06	620825	141910	377604	631808	465218	531854	921181
NW NE 10 17 49	COM	–	–	–	–	–	–	–	–	–	–	–	–	61700
NE NW 10 16 48	IRR	493600	462750	475090	475090	475090	–	–	–	–	–	74040	370200	–
NE NW 8 16 48	IRR	185100	–	–	–	–	–	–	–	–	–	–	–	–
NE NE 16 16 48	IRR	–	493600	740400	123400	863800	61700	493600	493600	740400	357860	345520	493600	154250
SW NW 7 16 48	IRR	–	–	–	–	–	–	–	45658	45658	228290	228290	228290	114145
XX XX 36 16 48	IRR	771250	1e+06	–	1061240	–	–	30850	1e+06	1e+06	1e+06	1443780	1e+06	986583
NW NW 18 16 48	IRR	–	370200	–	–	246800	–	–	–	–	246800	592320	493600	493600
NE SE 14 16 48	IRR	–	–	–	–	–	–	–	–	–	215950	215950	215950	215950
NE NE 23 16 48	IRR	771250	401050	–	–	–	–	–	987200	771250	825299	771250	771250	771250

NUREG–1538

Location:[a] QQ QTR SEC TWN RNG	Use	Year												
		1983	1985	1986	1987	1988	1989	1990	1991	1992	1993	1994	1995	1996
NE SW 25 16 48	IRR	771250	771250	—	—	—	—	—	—	771250	—	—	—	—
NW NE 17 16 48	IRR	92550	159063	—	—	—	—	—	—	—	—	61700	—	—
NE NW 15 16 48	IRR	—	—	—	—	—	—	—	—	2468	2468	18510	15425	6170
NE NW 15 16 48	IRR	—	—	—	—	7774.2	—	12340	—	4936	1234	3085	3085	9255
NE NE 8 16 48	IRR	—	—	240630	—	61700	—	—	—	—	111060	92550	111060	6170
SW NW 20 16 48	IRR	370200	—	—	—	—	—	—	24680	49360	24680	12340	21595	21595
NE NE 24 16 48	IRR	—	—	—	215950	215950	215950	185100	215950	215950	215950	246800	370200	280735
NE SE 24 16 48	IRR	—	—	—	—	—	—	—	246800	246800	—	771250	771250	771250
NE NE 36 16 48	IRR	—	—	—	—	—	30850	30850	—	19744	234460	61700	61700	30850
SE SW 10 16 48	IRR	—	—	—	—	—	—	—	—	—	246800	—	493600	—
SE NW 18 16 48	IRR	—	656.25	777.25	—	58245	—	27765	—	—	405369	667347	842822	811355
SE SW 10 16 48	IRR	—	—	—	—	—	—	—	—	—	—	—	6170	6170
NW SW 10 16 48	IRR	—	—	3085	3085	3085	6170	6170	—	21595	21595	21595	21595	21595
NW SW 10 16 48	IRR	—	—	—	—	—	—	—	—	—	—	—	—	13882.5
NW SW 10 16 48	IRR	—	—	—	—	—	—	—	—	1234	—	—	—	—
SW SE 8 16	IRR	74040	—	—	—	6170	—	—	—	7404	66636	122166	122166	29616
NW NW 15 16 48	IRR	24680	—	—	—	—	—	—	—	—	2468	12340	12340	15425
SE NW 26 16 481	IRR	720656	720039	720039	720039	—	—	308500	—	—	308500	275602	720039	720039
SE NE 26 16 48	IRR	720656	720039	720039	720039	—	—	720039	—	—	—	—	288016	288016
SW SE 8 16 48	IRR	—	—	—	—	—	—	—	—	—	37020	74040	92550	87243.8
SW NW 24 16 48	IRR	—	719854	719854	719854	—	—	719854	—	—	719916	720039	720039	720039
SW NW 15 16 48	IRR	—	30850	—	—	42450	—	—	—	7404	7404	25482.1	12340	12340
NW NW 15 16 48	IRR	—	—	—	—	—	—	—	—	—	—	—	—	15425

Location:ᵃ QQ QTR SEC TWN RNG	Use	Year												
		1983	1985	1986	1987	1988	1989	1990	1991	1992	1993	1994	1995	1996
NE NW 15 16 48	IRR	—	—	—	—	—	—	—	—	—	—	—	—	6170
NE NW 15 16 48	IRR	—	—	—	—	—	—	—	—	—	—	—	—	1234
NW NW 15 16 48	IRR	—	—	—	—	—	—	—	—	—	—	—	—	6170
NE NW 15 16 48	IRR	—	—	—	—	—	—	—	—	—	—	—	—	1234
NE NE 28 16 49	IRR	259140	135617	226316	226316	226316	92550	92550	—	226316	226316	226316	226316	226316
NE SW 9 16 49	IRR	6170	—	—	—	—	—	—	—	—	—	—	—	—
NE SE 32 16 49	IRR	—	—	—	—	—	—	172143	—	—	—	—	—	—
NE NE 14 16 49	IRR	—	—	—	—	—	—	—	—	67870	67870	—	—	—
NE NE 30 16 49	IRR	—	—	—	328244	—	—	836035	—	—	820610	820610	820610	820610
NE NW 35 16 49	IRR	—	—	—	—	—	—	—	—	2468	2468	—	2468	—
NE SE 19 16 49	IRR	—	—	—	—	—	308500	493600	771250	771250	771250	771250	771250	771250
SE SW 9 16 49	IRR	146599	61700	92550	92550	92550	146599	146538	—	146538	145982	61700	146538	129570
NE NE 8 16 49	IRR	121549	—	—	—	—	30850	30850	—	12340	12340	18510	111060	33935
SW SE 5 16 49	IRR	—	—	—	—	—	—	—	—	—	—	1234	—	—
NE SE 8 16 49	IRR	—	—	—	—	—	—	—	—	4936	4936	—	2468	6170
SE NW 35 16 49	IRR	—	—	—	—	—	—	—	—	22508	22459	22458.8	32331	32429.5
SE SW 9 16 49	IRR	30850	30850	30850	30850	30850	30850	30850	30850	30850	30850	30850	30850	30850
NE SE 23 16 49	IRR	771250	—	—	—	—	—	—	771250	771250	771250	771250	771250	771250
NW NE 8 16 49	IRR	—	—	—	—	—	—	—	—	—	16906	—	—	—
SE SW 9 16 49	IRR	30850	30850	30850	30850	30850	30850	30850	30850	30850	30850	30850	30850	30850
SE SE 22 16 49	IRR	—	28012	—	12340	12340	18510	18510	—	—	58862	43190	—	6170
SE NE 12 17 48	IRR	30850	—	—	—	—	—	—	—	—	—	—	—	—
SE NW 12 17 48	IRR	—	92550	55530	55530	55530	80210	80210	80210	80210	80210	80210	80210	80210

Location:[a] QQ QTR SEC TWN RNG	Use	1983	1985	1986	1987	1988	1989	1990	1991	1992	1993	1994	1995	1996
NE NW 9 17 49	IRR	—	—	—	246800	370200	493600	974860	678700	666360	851460	—	—	—
NE NE 9 17 49	IRR	—	—	—	—	—	—	—	—	—	—	863800	863800	863800
NE NW 15 17 49	IRR	—	30850	—	14808	14808	14808	14808	—	19744	19744	24680	30850	30850
SE SE 8 17 49	IRR	—	—	—	—	—	—	223477	—	—	—	—	146229	—
NE NE 9 17 49	IRR	—	—	—	—	—	—	—	—	—	—	—	209780	209780
NE NE 9 17 49	IRR	—	—	—	—	—	—	—	—	—	774952	385625	774952	774952
XX SW 4 16 48	IRR	—	—	—	—	462750	—	—	—	—	—	—	—	—
XX NW 23 16 48	IRR	771250	—	—	—	—	—	—	—	—	—	—	—	—
XX NW 25 16 48	IRR	771250	—	—	—	—	—	—	—	—	—	—	—	—
NW NW 15 16 48	IRR	—	—	—	—	—	—	—	—	—	—	—	—	9255
XX NW 25 16 48	IRR	—	771250	—	—	—	—	—	—	—	—	771250	771250	771250
XX NW 25 16 48	IRR	—	—	—	—	—	—	—	—	—	—	—	771250	771250
NE NW 17 16 48	IRR	—	296160	—	—	—	—	—	—	—	—	74040	74040	—
SW SE 32 16 49	IRR	—	—	—	—	—	215950	215950	215950	—	123400	123400	—	—
NE NE 28 16 49	IRR	—	123400	—	—	—	—	—	—	—	—	—	—	—
NW SE 1 17 48	IRR	771250	—	—	—	—	—	—	—	—	—	—	—	—
SE NW 12 17 48	IRR	370200	—	—	—	—	—	—	—	—	—	—	—	—
NE SE 12 17 48	IRR	—	—	—	—	—	154250	154250	61700	61700	61700	61700	61700	61700
XX SE 1 17 48	IRR	—	—	462750	462750	—	—	—	—	—	—	—	49360	49360
SW NE 9 17 49	IRR	—	462750	462750	—	—	—	—	—	—	—	—	49360	49360
SE NE 9 17 49	IRR	—	771250	—	246800	—	—	61700	—	—	—	—	49360	49360
XX SE 7 17 49	IRR	—	771250	771250	771250	—	—	—	—	—	—	—	771250	771250
XX SW 7 17 49	IRR	—	318372	—	—	385625	—	—	—	—	—	—	—	—

Location:[a] QQ QTR SEC TWN RNG	Use	Year												
		1996	1995	1994	1993	1992	1991	1990	1989	1988	1987	1986	1985	1983
NE SW 9 17 49	IRR	246800	246800	–	–	–	–	–	–	–	–	–	–	–
NW SW 9 17 49	IRR	246800	246800	61700	–	–	–	–	–	–	–	–	–	–
NW SE 7 17 49	IRR	–	–											771250
NW SW 7 17 49	IRR	–	–										–	385625
NW NE 24 15 49	QM	9872	–	–	–	–	–	–	–	–	–	–	–	–
NE NW 27 16 49	QM	4195.6	–	–	–	–	–	–	–	–	–	–	–	–
SW SE 31 16 49	QM	12957	–	–	–	–	–	–	–	–	–	–	–	–
SE SE 26 16 49	QM	123.4	–	–	–	–	–	–	–	–	–	–	–	–
NW NE 16 16 49	QM	24680	–	–	–	–	–	–	–	–	–	–	–	–
SE SW 1 17 48	QM	9255	–	–	–	–	–	–	–	–	–	–	–	–
SE SW 2 17 49	QM	12340	–	–	–	–	–	–	–	–	–	–	–	–
SE SW 2 18 49	QM	19744	–	–	–	–	–	–	–	–	–	–	–	–
SW SW 2 18 49	QM	61700	–	–	–	–	–	–	–	–	–	–	–	–
SW NE 3 18 50	QM	2468	–	–	–	–	–	–	–	–	–	–	–	–

a Note that *NE* means north-east, *SE* means south-east, *NW* means north-west, *SW* means south-west, and *XX* means that the location was not reported.

Reference

Mathey, S.B. (ed.), "National Water Information System User's Manual: Volume 2, Chapter 4– Ground-Water Site Inventory System," U.S. Geological Survey, Open-File Report 89-587, 1989.

NUREG–1538

APPENDIX F
TABLE OF BOREHOLE DILUTION FACTORS

Calculated dilution factors for combinations of plume scenarios and capture zones at 25 kilometers used in the analyses described in Section 3.2 of this NUREG. *Capture identification number,* in the second column, is in reference to the *Capture Zone Delineation Table* found in Appendix G; pumping rate (m^3/day) – Q ; transmissivity (m^2/day) – T ; and regional gradient – *grad* . The dilution factors are: volumetric flux-based borehole dilution factor – *F-BDF*; point dilution factor based on centerline concentration – *P-DF* ; and dispersion during transport-based borehole dilution factor – *T-BDF* . Additional significant figures are reported to illustrate relative differences, only.

Plume Description	*Capture Zone Description*	*F-BDF*	*P-DF*	*T-BDF*
3-Dimensional (3-D) Plume 1				
20:2:0.2 m	#8, Q = 300	1.4	9.1	34
20:2:0.2 m	#9, Q = 800	2.6	9.1	55
20:2:0.2 m	#10, Q = 1,380	3.5	9.1	57
20:2:0.2 m	#11, Q = 2,000	4.8	9.1	57
Small Irrigation Well, 3-D Plume 1				
20:2:0.2 m	#31, T = 50	2.6	9.1	48
20:2:0.2 m	#32, T = 100	1.8	9.1	34
20:2:0.2 m	#33, T = 200	1.4	9.1	26
20:2:0.2 m	#34, T = 300	1.0	9.1	20
20:2:0.2 m	#35, T = 400	1.0	9.1	18
Large Irrigation Well, 3-D Plume 1				
20:2:0.2 m	#36, T = 200	2.8	9.1	57
20:2:0.2 m	#37, T = 300	3.0	9.1	52
20:2:0.2 m	#38, T = 400	2.4	9.1	45
20:2:0.2 m	#39, grad = 0.001	6.2	9.1	57.5
20:2:0.2 m	#40, grad = 0.002	3.4	9.1	57.5
20:2:0.2 m	#41, grad = 0.003	2.3	9.1	56.6
20:2:0.2 m	#42, grad = 0.005	1.0	9.1	45

Plume Description	*Capture Zone Description*	*F-BDF*	*P-DF*	*T-BDF*
Domestic Wells, 3-D Plume 1				
20:2:0.2m	#21, 940–1,000	9.1	1	9.5
20:2:0.2 m	#22, 930–990	9.1	1	9.7
20:2:0.2 m	#23, 920–980	9.1	1	9.9
20:2:0.2 m	#24, 900–960	9.1	1	10.4
20:2:0.2 m	#1, Q = 1	9.1	1	9.36
20:2:0.2 m	#2, Q = 2	9.1	1	9.44
20:2:0.2 m	#3, Q = 3	9.1	1	9.5
20:2:0.2 m	#4, Q = 4	9.1	1	9.6
20:2:0.2 m	#5, Q = 6.8	9.1	1	9.9
20:2:0.2 m	#6, Q = 37.5	9.1	1	13
20:2:0.2 m	#7, Q = 75	9.1	1	18
20:2:0.2 m	#12, T = 10	9.1	1	12
20:2:0.2 m	#13, T = 50	9.1	1	9.8
20:2:0.2 m	#14, T = 100	9.1	1	9.5
20:2:0.2 m	#15, T = 400	9.1	1	9.3
20:2:0.2 m	#16, grad = 0.001	9.1	1	11
20:2:0.2 m	#17, grad = 0.0025	9.1	1	9.8
20:2:0.2 m	#18, grad = 0.005	9.1	1	9.5
20:2:0.2 m	#19, grad = 0.01	9.1	1	9.4
3-D Plume 2				
100:10:0.1 m	#8, Q = 300	1.9	14	37
100:10:0.1 m	#9, Q = 800	2.7	14	47
100:10:0.1 m	#10, Q = 1,380	3.3	14	60
100:10:0.1 m	#11, Q = 2,000	4.1	14	73

Plume Description	Capture Zone Description	F-BDF	P-DF	T-BDF
\multicolumn{5}{c}{Small Irrigation Well, 3-D Plume 2}
100:10:0.1 m	#31, T = 50	3.2	14	43
100:10:0.1 m	#32, T = 100	2.4	14	37
100:10:0.1 m	#33, T = 200	1.8	14	34
100:10:0.1 m	#34, T = 300	1.6	14	32
100:10:0.1 m	#35, T = 400	1.5	14	30
\multicolumn{5}{c}{Large Irrigation Well, Plume 2}
100:10:0.1 m	#36, T = 200	3.0	14	53
100:10:0.1 m	#37, T = 300	2.6	14	45
100:10:0.1 m	#38, T = 400	2.3	14	41
100:10:0.1 m	#39, grad = 0.001	4.3	14	—
100:10:0.1 m	#40, grad = 0.002	3.3	14	59
100:10:0.1 m	#41, grad = 0.003	2.8	14	49
100:10:0.1 m	#42, grad = 0.005	2.3	14	41
\multicolumn{5}{c}{Thin Plumes, Domestic Wells at 25 Kilometers, 20:2 Meter Dispersivity Ratio}
25-m-thick; 20:2 m	#21, 940-1,000	3.3	1.8	1.78
25-m-thick; 20:2 m	#22, 930-990	4.3	1.8	1.77
25-m-thick; 20:2 m	#23, 920-980	5.4	1.8	1.77
25-m-thick; 20:2 m	#24, 900-960	43	1.8	1.76
10-m-thick; 20:2 m	#21, S = 940-1,000	8.2	1.8	1.78
10-m-thick; 20:2 m	#22, S = 930-990	10.3	1.8	1.77
10-m-thick; 20:2 m	#23, S = 920-980	26	1.8	1.70
10-m-thick; 20:2 m	#24, S = 900-960	N/A	1.8	N/A
25-m-thick; 20:2 m	#1, Q = 1	2.8	1.8	1.76
25-m-thick; 20:2 m	#2, Q = 2	3.1	1.8	1.77
25-m-thick; 20:2 m	#3, Q = 3	3.3	1.8	1.78
25-m-thick; 20:2 m	#4, Q = 4	3.5	1.8	1.78

Plume Description	Capture Zone Description	F-BDF	P-DF	T-BDF
25-m-thick; 20:2 m	#5, Q = 6.8	4.0	1.8	1.80
25-m-thick; 20:2 m	#6, Q = 37.5	7.6	1.8	1.90
25-m-thick; 20:2 m	#7, Q = 75	10.2	1.8	2.01
10-m-thick; 20:2 m	#1, Q = 1	7.0	1.8	1.76
10-m-thick; 20:2 m	#2, Q = 2	7.7	1.8	1.77
10-m-thick; 20:2 m	#3, Q = 3	8.2	1.8	1.78
10-m-thick; 20:2 m	#4, Q = 4	8.8	1.8	1.78
10-m-thick; 20:2 m	#5, Q = 6.8	10.1	1.8	1.80
10-m-thick; 20:2 m	#6, Q = 37.5	19	1.8	1.90
10-m-thick; 20:2 m	#7, Q = 75	26	1.8	2.01
25-m-thick; 20:2 m	#12, T = 10	6.9	1.8	1.88
25-m-thick; 20:2 m	#13, T = 50	3.9	1.8	1.80
25-m-thick; 20:2 m	#14, T = 100	3.3	1.8	1.78
25-m-thick; 20:2 m	#15, T = 400	2.7	1.8	1.76
25-m-thick; 20:2 m	#16, grad = 0.001	5.3	1.8	1.84
25-m-thick; 20:2 m	#17, grad = 0.0025	3.9	1.8	1.80
25-m-thick; 20:2 m	#18, grad = 0.005	3.3	1.8	1.78
25-m-thick; 20:2 m	#19, grad = 0.01	2.9	1.8	1.77
10-m-thick; 20:2 m	#12, T = 10	17	1.8	1.88
10-m-thick; 20:2 m	#13, T = 50	9.8	1.8	1.80
10-m-thick; 20:2 m	#14, T = 100	8.2	1.8	1.78
10-m-thick; 20:2 m	#15, T = 400	6.8	1.8	1.76
10-m-thick; 20:2 m	#16, grad = 0.001	13.2	1.8	1.84
10-m-thick; 20:2 m	#17, grad = 0.0025	9.8	1.8	1.80
10-m-thick; 20:2 m	#18, grad = 0.005	8.2	1.8	1.78
10-m-thick; 20:2 m	#19, grad = 0.01	7.4	1.8	1.77

Plume Description	Capture Zone Description	F-BDF	P-DF	T-BDF
Thin Plumes Irrigation Wells at 25 Kilometers				
25-m-thick; 20:2 m	#8, Q = 300	19	1.8	2.8
25-m-thick; 20:2 m	#9, Q = 800	26	1.8	4.8
25-m-thick; 20:2 m	#10, Q = 1,380	36	1.8	5.9
25-m-thick; 20:2 m	#11, Q = 2,000	49	1.8	5.9
25-m-thick; 50:5 m	#8, Q = 300	19	2.6	3.3
25-m-thick; 50:5 m	#9, Q = 800	26	2.6	4.8
25-m-thick; 50:5 m	#10, Q = 1,380	30	2.6	6.8
25-m-thick; 50:5 m	#11, Q = 2,000	33	2.6	8.8
25-m-thick; 100:10 m	#8, Q = 300	19	3.6	4.1
25-m-thick; 100:10 m	#9, Q = 800	26	3.6	5.2
25-m-thick; 100:10 m	#10, Q = 1,380	30	3.6	6.9
25-m-thick; 100:10 m	#11, Q = 2,000	32	3.6	8.9

APPENDIX G
CAPTURE ZONE DELINEATION TABLE

Calculated capture zone widths and thicknesses used in the analyses described in Section 3.2 of this NUREG. Screen elevation based on 1000-meter-thick aquifer.

Identification Number	Screen Elevation (m)	Pump Rate (m³/day)	Gradient	Transmissivity (m²/day)	Width (m)	Thickness (m)	Not Captured on Top (m)
1	940 – 1000	1	0.005	100	29	73	—
2	940 – 1000	2	0.005	100	54	82	—
3	940 – 1000	3	0.005	100	76	88	—
4	940 – 1000	4	0.005	100	97	96	—
5	940 – 1000	6.815	0.005	100	146	113	—
6	940 – 1000	37.5	0.005	100	418	224	—
7	940 – 1000	75	0.005	100	607	309	—
8	940 – 1000	300	0.005	100	1292	575	—
9	940 – 1000	800	0.005	100	2330	825	—
10	940 – 1000	1380	0.005	100	3382	941	—
11	940 – 1000	2000	0.005	100	4450	985	—
12	940 – 1000	3	0.005	10	369	203	—
13	940 – 1000	3	0.005	50	133	108	—
14	940 – 1000	3	0.005	100	76	88	—
15	940 – 1000	3	0.005	400	22	70	—
16	940 – 1000	3	0.001	100	248	151	—

Identification Number	Screen Elevation (m)	Pump Rate (m³/day)	Gradient	Transmissivity (m²/day)	Width (m)	Thickness (m)	Not Captured on Top (m)
17	940 – 1000	3	0.0025	100	133	108	–
18	940 – 1000	3	0.005	100	76	88	–
19	940 – 1000	3	0.05	100	41	78	–
20	940 – 1000	3	0.005	100	76	88	–
21	930-990	3	0.005	100	69	98	0.2
22	920-980	3	0.005	100	67	107	5
23	900-960	3	0.005	100	68	127	21
24	980 – 1000	3	0.005	100	115	65	–
25	940 – 1000	3	0.005	100	76	88	–
26	900 – 1000	3	0.005	100	51	122	–
27	0 – 1000	300	0.005	100	574	1000	–
28	500 – 1000	300	0.005	100	940	752	–
29	810 – 1000	300	0.005	100	1238	601	–
30	940 – 1000	300	0.005	100	1292	575	–
31	940 – 1000	300	0.005	50	1944	751	–
32	940 – 1000	300	0.005	100	1292	575	–
33	940 – 1000	300	0.005	200	876	424	–
34	940 – 1000	300	0.005	300	705	352	–
35	940 – 1000	300	0.005	400	607	309	–
36	940 – 1000	2116	0.005	200	2810	890	–

Identification Number	Screen Elevation (m)	Pump Rate (m³/day)	Gradient	Transmissivity (m²/day)	Width (m)	Thickness (m)	Not Captured on Top (m)
37	940 – 1000	2116	0.005	300	2146	793	—
38	940 – 1000	2116	0.005	400	1798	719	—
39	940 – 1000	2116	0.001	100	5596	1000	—
40	940 – 1000	2116	0.002	100	3282	934	—
41	940 – 1000	2116	0.003	100	2486	850	—
42	940 – 1000	2116	0.005	100	1798	719	—

APPENDIX H
LATIN HYPERCUBE SAMPLED INPUT PARAMETERS USED IN THE ANALYSIS OF DOSE

The following is a list of important parameters used in the analysis of dose described in Section 3.3 of this NUREG. The reader is referred to Wescott et al.(1995) for a description of how these parameters (shown in brackets [ ]) were used in the U.S. Nuclear Regulatory Commission's Iterative Performance Assessment Phase 2 computer code.

Parameter	Range in Value		Distribution	Basis for Parameter Assignment
	High	Low		
Matrix Permeability (m^2) [permm]				
Topopah Spring	3.6×10^{-19}	1.2×10^{-18}	Lognormal	Peters et al. (1984) [a]
Calico Hills, vitric	3.9×10^{-15}	2.0×10^{-14}	Lognormal	Peters et al. (1984) [a]
Calico Hills, zeolitic	1.3×10^{-20}	6.7×10^{-19}	Lognormal	Peters et al. (1984) [a]
Prow Pass	1.9×10^{-16}	9.6×10^{-16}	Lognormal	Peters et al. (1984) [a]
Upper Crater Flat	5.1×10^{-18}	1.5×10^{-17}	Lognormal	Peters et al. (1984) [a]
Bullfrog	3.5×10^{-16}	4.4×10^{-16}	Lognormal	Peters et al. (1984) [a]
Middle Crater Flat	4.1×10^{-18}	1.6×10^{-17}	Lognormal	Assumed same as Upper Crater Flat
alluvium	—	1.6×10^{-12}	Constant	Assumed for this analysis
Undisturbed Infiltration (m/yr) [infiltration]				
repository footprint	0.0001	0.005	Loguniform	Assumed same as Codell et al. (1992) and Wescott et al. (1995)

Distribution Coefficient (m^3/kg) [kdm]

Parameter	Range in Value		Distribution	Basis for Parameter Assignment
	High	Low		
Curium				
Topopah Spring	0.045	4.5	Lognormal	Codell et al. (1992)[b]
Calico Hills, vitric	0.328	32.0	Lognormal	Codell et al. (1992)[b]
Calico Hills, zeolitic	0.166	16.6	Lognormal	Codell et al. (1992)[b]
Prow Pass	0.116	11.6	Lognormal	Codell et al. (1992)[b]
Upper Crater Flat	0.132	13.2	Lognormal	Codell et al. (1992)[b]
Bullfrog	0.12	12.0	Lognormal	Codell et al. (1992)[b]
Middle Crater Flat	0.132	13.2	Lognormal	Codell et al. (1992)[b]
alluvium	—	32.8	Constant	Assumed for this analysis
Plutonium				
Topopah Spring	0.017	1.7	Lognormal	Meijer (1990)[c]
Calico Hills, vitric	0.017	1.7	Lognormal	Assumed same as Topopah Spring
Calico Hills, zeolitic	0.0066	0.66	Lognormal	Meijer (1990)[c]
Prow Pass	0.013	1.3	Lognormal	Meijer (1990)[c]
Upper Crater Flat	0.0053	0.0053	Lognormal	Derived from Calico Hills, zeolitic[e]
Bullfrog	0.0094	0.94	Lognormal	Derived from Prow Pass[f]
Middle Crater Flat	0.0053	0.53	Lognormal	Same as Upper Crater Flat[e]
alluvium	—	1.7	Constant	Assumed for this analysis

Parameter	Range in Value		Distribution	Basis for Parameter Assignment
	High	Low		
Uranium				
Topopah Spring	0.00002	0.002	Lognormal	Meijer (1990) [c]
Calico Hills, vitric	0.002	0.2	Lognormal	Meijer (1990) [c]
Calico Hills, zeolitic	0.0001	0.01	Lognormal	Meijer (1990) [c]
Prow Pass	0.0	0.00001	Uniform	Assumed to be quite small
Upper Crater Flat	0.00008	0.008	Lognormal	Derived from Calico Hills, zeolitic [c]
Bullfrog	0.0002	0.02	Lognormal	Meijer (1990) [i]
Middle Crater Flat	0.00008	0.008	Lognormal	Derived from Calico Hills, zeolitic [c]
alluvium	—	0.2	Constant	Assumed for this analysis
Thorium				
Topopah Spring	0.0048	0.48	Lognormal	Codell et al. (1992) [h]
Calico Hills, vitric	0.034	3.4	Lognormal	Codell et al. (1992) [h]
Calico Hills, zeolitic	0.017	1.7	Lognormal	Codell et al. (1992) [h]
Prow Pass	0.012	1.2	Lognormal	Codell et al. (1992) [h]
Upper Crater Flat	0.014	1.4	Lognormal	Codell et al. (1992) [h]
Bullfrog	0.013	1.3	Lognormal	Codell et al. (1992) [h]
Middle Crater Flat	0.014	1.4	Lognormal	Codell et al. (1992) [h]
alluvium	—	3.4	Constant	Assumed for this analysis
Radium				
Topopah Spring	0.15	15.0	Lognormal	Meijer (1990) [j]
Calico Hills, vitric	0.15	15.0	Lognormal	Same as Topopah Spring
Calico Hills, zeolitic	0.15	15.0	Lognormal	Same as Topopah Spring
Prow Pass	0.15	15.0	Lognormal	Same as Topopah Spring
Upper Crater Flat	0.12	12.0	Lognormal	Derived from Calico Hills, zeolitic [c]
Bullfrog	0.5	50.0	Lognormal	Meijer (1990) [j]
Middle Crater Flat	0.12	12.0	Lognormal	Derived from Calico Hills, zeolitic [c]
alluvium	—	50.0	Constant	Assumed for this analysis

Parameter	Range in Value		Distribution	Basis for Parameter Assignment
	High	Low		
Lead				
Topopah Spring	0.00068	0.068	Lognormal	Codell et al. (1992) [b]
Calico Hills, vitric	0.0049	0.49	Lognormal	Codell et al. (1992) [b]
Calico Hills, zeolitic	0.0025	0.25	Lognormal	Codell et al. (1992) [b]
Prow Pass	0.0017	0.17	Lognormal	Codell et al. (1992) [b]
Upper Crater Flat	0.0020	0.20	Lognormal	Codell et al. (1992) [b]
Bullfrog	0.0018	0.18	Lognormal	Codell et al. (1992) [b]
Middle Crater Flat	0.0020	0.20	Lognormal	Codell et al. (1992) [b]
alluvium	—	0.49	Constant	Assumed for this analysis
Americium				
Topopah Spring	0.081	8.1	Loguniform	Meijer (1990) [c]
Calico Hills, vitric	0.081	8.1	Loguniform	Same as Topopah Spring
Calico Hills, zeolitic	0.17	17.0	Loguniform	Meijer (1990) [d]
Prow Pass	0.45	45.0	Loguniform	Meijer (1990) [f]
Upper Crater Flat	0.136	13.6	Loguniform	Derived from Calico Hills, zeolitic [e]
Bullfrog	0.014	1.4	Loguniform	Meijer (1990) [i]
Middle Crater Flat	0.136	13.6	Loguniform	Derived from Calico Hills, zeolitic [e]
alluvium	—	45.0	Constant	Assumed for this analysis
Neptunium				
Topopah Spring	0.00045	0.045	Loguniform	Meijer (1990) [k]
Calico Hills, vitric	0.00045	0.045	Loguniform	Same as Topopah Spring
Calico Hills, zeolitic	0.00027	0.027	Loguniform	Meijer (1990) [j]
Prow Pass	0.00051	0.051	Loguniform	Meijer (1990) [i]
Upper Crater Flat	0.00022	0.022	Loguniform	Derived from Calico Hills, zeolitic [e]
Bullfrog	0.00051	0.05	Loguniform	Same as Prow Pass
Middle Crater Flat	0.00022	0.022	Loguniform	Derived from Calico Hills, zeolitic [e]
alluvium	—	0.051	Constant	Assumed for this analysis

Parameter	Range in Value		Distribution	Basis for Parameter Assignment
	High	Low		
Cesium				
Topopah Spring	0.036	3.6	Loguniform	Meijer (1990) [f]
Calico Hills, vitric	0.024	2.4	Loguniform	Meijer (1990) [g]
Calico Hills, zeolitic	2.2	220.0	Loguniform	Meijer (1990) [h]
Prow Pass	0.22	22.0	Loguniform	Meijer (1990) [i]
Upper Crater Flat	1.76	176.0	Loguniform	Meijer (1990) [e]
Bullfrog	0.32	32.0	Loguniform	Meijer (1990) [i]
Middle Crater Flat	1.76	176.0	Loguniform	Derived from Calico Hills, zeolitic [e]
alluvium	—	220.0	Constant	Assumed for this analysis
Iodine				
Topopah Spring	0.0	0.0001	Uniform	Assumed to be quite small.
Calico Hills, vitric	0.0	0.0001	Uniform	Assumed to be quite small.
Calico Hills, zeolitic	0.0	0.0001	Uniform	Assumed to be quite small.
Prow Pass	0.0	0.0001	Uniform	Assumed to be quite small.
Upper Crater Flat	0.0	0.0001	Uniform	Assumed to be quite small.
Bullfrog	0.0	0.0001	Uniform	Assumed to be quite small.
Middle Crater Flat	0.0	0.0001	Uniform	Assumed to be quite small.
alluvium	—	0.0	Constant	Assumed for this analysis
Tin				
Topopah Spring	0.0134	1.34	Loguniform	Codell *et al.* (1992) [b]
Calico Hills, vitric	0.097	9.7	Loguniform	Codell *et al.* (1992) [b]
Calico Hills, zeolitic	0.049	4.9	Loguniform	Codell *et al.* (1992) [b]
Prow Pass	0.034	3.4	Loguniform	Codell *et al.* (1992) [b]
Upper Crater Flat	0.039	3.9	Loguniform	Codell *et al.* (1992) [b]
Bullfrog	0.035	3.5	Loguniform	Codell *et al.* (1992) [b]
Middle Crater Flat	0.039	3.9	Loguniform	Codell *et al.* (1992) [b]
alluvium	—	9.7	Constant	Assumed for this analysis

Parameter	Range in Value		Distribution	Basis for Parameter Assignment
	High	Low		
Technetium				
Topopah Spring	0.000001	0.0001	Loguniform	Meijer (1990) [k]
Calico Hills, vitric	0.0	0.0001	Uniform	Assumed to be quite small.
Calico Hills, zeolitic	0.0	0.0001	Uniform	Assumed to be quite small.
Prow Pass	0.000017	0.0017	Loguniform	Meijer (1990) [m]
Upper Crater Flat	0.0	0.0001	Uniform	Derived from Calico Hills, zeolitic
Bullfrog	0.00042	0.042	Loguniform	Meijer (1990) [m]
Middle Crater Flat	0.0	0.0001	Uniform	Derived from Calico Hills, zeolitic
alluvium	—	0.042	Constant	Assumed for this analysis
Zirconium				
Topopah Spring	0.00048	0.048	Loguniform	Codell *et al.* (1992) [h]
Calico Hills, vitric	0.0034	0.34	Loguniform	Codell *et al.* (1992) [h]
Calico Hills, zeolitic	0.0017	0.17	Loguniform	Codell *et al.* (1992) [h]
Prow Pass	0.0012	0.12	Loguniform	Codell *et al.* (1992) [h]
Upper Crater Flat	0.0014	0.14	Loguniform	Codell *et al.* (1992) [h]
Bullfrog	0.0013	0.13	Loguniform	Codell *et al.* (1992) [h]
Middle Crater Flat	0.0014	0.14	Loguniform	Codell *et al.* (1992) [h]
alluvium	—	0.34	Constant	Assumed for this analysis
Strontium				
Topopah Spring	0.008	0.8	Loguniform	Meijer (1990) [l]
Calico Hills, vitric	0.0034	0.34	Loguniform	Meijer (1990) [g]
Calico Hills, zeolitic	0.89	89.0	Loguniform	Meijer (1990) [h]
Prow Pass	0.045	4.5	Loguniform	Meijer (1990) [i]
Upper Crater Flat	0.71	71.0	Loguniform	Derived from Calico Hills, zeolitic [e]
Bullfrog	0.028	2.8	Loguniform	Meijer (1990) [i]
Middle Crater Flat	0.71	71.0	Loguniform	Derived from Calico Hills, zeolitic [e]
alluvium	—	89.0	Constant	Assumed for this analysis

Parameter	Range in Value		Distribution	Basis for Parameter Assignment
	High	Low		
Nickel				
Topopah Spring	0.00037	0.037	Loguniform	Codell *et al.* (1992) [b]
Calico Hills, vitric	0.0027	0.27	Loguniform	Codell *et al.* (1992) [b]
Calico Hills, zeolitic	0.0014	0.14	Loguniform	Codell *et al.* (1992) [b]
Prow Pass	0.0009	0.09	Loguniform	Codell *et al.* (1992) [b]
Upper Crater Flat	0.0011	0.11	Loguniform	Codell *et al.* (1992) [b]
Bullfrog	0.001	0.1	Loguniform	Codell *et al.* (1992) [b]
Middle Crater Flat	0.0011	0.11	Loguniform	Codell *et al.* (1992) [b]
alluvium	—	0.27	Constant	Assumed for this analysis
Carbon				
Topopah Spring	0.0	0.0001	Uniform	Assumed to be quite small.
Calico Hills, vitric	0.0	0.0001	Uniform	Assumed to be quite small.
Calico Hills, zeolitic	0.0	0.0001	Uniform	Assumed to be quite small.
Prow Pass	0.0	0.0001	Uniform	Assumed to be quite small.
Upper Crater Flat	0.0	0.0001	Uniform	Assumed to be quite small.
Bullfrog	0.0	0.0001	Uniform	Assumed to be quite small.
Middle Crater Flat	0.0	0.0001	Uniform	Assumed to be quite small.
alluvium	—	0.0	Constant	Assumed for this analysis
Selenium				
Topopah Spring	0.00026	0.026	Loguniform	Meijer (1990) [g]
Calico Hills, vitric	0.0003	0.03	Loguniform	Meijer (1990) [g]
Calico Hills, zeolitic	0.00045	0.045	Loguniform	Meijer (1990) [h]
Prow Pass	0.00025	0.025	Loguniform	Meijer (1990) [j]
Upper Crater Flat	0.00036	0.036	Loguniform	Derived from Calico Hills, zeolitic [e]
Bullfrog	0.0013	0.13	Loguniform	Meijer (1990) [j]
Middle Crater Flat	0.00036	0.036	Loguniform	Derived from Calico Hills, zeolitic [e]
alluvium	—	0.13	Constant	Assumed for this analysis

Parameter	Range in Value		Distribution	Basis for Parameter Assignment
	High	Low		
Niobium				
Topopah Spring	0.0	0.0001	Uniform	Assumed to be quite small.
Calico Hills, vitric	0.0	0.0001	Uniform	Assumed to be quite small.
Calico Hills, zeolitic	0.0	0.0001	Uniform	Assumed to be quite small.
Prow Pass	0.0	0.0001	Uniform	Assumed to be quite small.
Upper Crater Flat	0.0	0.0001	Uniform	Assumed to be quite small.
Bullfrog	0.0	0.0001	Uniform	Assumed to be quite small.
Middle Crater Flat	0.0	0.0001	Uniform	Assumed to be quite small.
alluvium	—	0.0	Constant	Assumed for this analysis
Fraction of Matrix k_d (percent)				
each of the seven hydrostratigraphic units	0.0	0.1	Uniform	Assumed for this analysis
UO_2 Alteration/Leach Rate (yr^{-1}), by Repository Sub-area [forwar]				
Subarea 1	0.000011	0.001	Loguniform	Estimate based on Grambow (1989)
Subarea 2	0.000021	0.001	Loguniform	Estimate based on Grambow (1989)
Subarea 3	0.000031	0.001	Loguniform	Estimate based on Grambow (1989)
Subarea 4	0.000041	0.001	Loguniform	Estimate based on Grambow (1989)
Subarea 5	0.000051	0.001	Loguniform	Estimate based on Grambow (1989)
Subarea 6	0.000061	0.001	Loguniform	Estimate based on Grambow (1989)
Subarea 7	0.000071	0.001	Loguniform	Estimate based on Grambow (1989)
Fraction of Waste Packages Contacted by Water (percent), by Repository Sub-area [warea]				
Subarea 1	0.0	1.0	Uniform	Assumed [based on Wescott et al. (1994)]
Subarea 2	0.0	1.0	Uniform	Assumed [based on Wescott et al. (1994)]
Subarea 3	0.0	1.0	Uniform	Assumed [based on Wescott et al. (1994)]
Subarea 4	0.0	1.0	Uniform	Assumed [based on Wescott et al. (1994)]
Subarea 5	0.0	1.0	Uniform	Assumed [based on Wescott et al. (1994)]
Subarea 6	0.0	1.0	Uniform	Assumed [based on Wescott et al. (1994)]
Subarea 7	0.0	1.0	Uniform	Assumed [based on Wescott et al. (1994)]

Parameter	Range in Value		Distribution	Basis for Parameter Assignment
	High	Low		
	Radionclide Solubility (Kg/m³) [sol]			
Curium	2.56×10^{-7}	0.0005	Loguniform	Assumed [based on Wescott *et al.* (1994)]
Plutonium	2.0×10^{-7}	0.0005	Loguniform	Assumed [based on Wescott *et al.* (1994)]
Uranium	4.0×10^{-8}	0.00003	Loguniform	Assumed [based on Wescott *et al.* (1994)]
Thorium	2×10^{-12}	0.0001	Loguniform	Assumed [based on Wescott *et al.* (1994)]
Radium	0.000009	0.00009	Loguniform	Assumed [based on Wescott *et al.* (1994)]
Lead	0.0000021	0.00063	Loguniform	Assumed [based on Wescott *et al.* (1994)]
Americium	0.000001	0.0003	Loguniform	Assumed [based on Wescott *et al.* (1994)]
Neptunium	0.00014	0.0237	Loguniform	Assumed [based on Wescott *et al.* (1994)]
Cesium	1000.0	1001.0	Uniform	Assumed [based on Wescott *et al.* (1994)]
Iodine	1000.0	1001.0	Uniform	Assumed [based on Wescott *et al.* (1994)]
Tin	5.0×10^{-9}	5.01×10^{-9}	Uniform	Assumed [based on Wescott *et al.* (1994)]
Technectium	1000.0	1001.0	Uniform	Assumed [based on Wescott *et al.* (1994)]
Zirconium	4.0×10^{-9}	4.01×10^{-9}	Uniform	Assumed [based on Wescott *et al.* (1994)]
Strontium	0.08	0.0801	Uniform	Assumed [based on Wescott *et al.* (1994)]
Nickel	2.8×10^{-7}	0.0017	Uniform	Assumed [based on Wescott *et al.* (1994)]
Carbon	1000.0	1001.0	Uniform	Assumed [based on Wescott *et al.* (1994)]
Selenium	1000.0	1001.0	Uniform	Assumed [based on Wescott *et al.* (1994)]
Niobium	1000.0	1001.0	Uniform	Assumed [based on Wescott *et al.* (1994)]

Parameter	Range in Value		Distribution	Basis for Parameter Assignment
	High	Low		
Fluid Capture Area of Waste Package Canister (m^2) [funnel]				
Subarea 1	0.0	0.4	Uniform	Upper limit based on twice the cross-sectional area of SCP emplacement hole (see DOE, 1988)
Subarea 2	0.0	0.4	Uniform	Upper limit based on twice the cross-sectional area of SCP emplacement hole (see DOE, 1988)
Subarea 3	0.0	0.4	Uniform	Upper limit based on twice the cross-sectional area of SCP emplacement hole (see DOE, 1988)
Subarea 4	0.0	0.4	Uniform	Upper limit based on twice the cross-sectional area of SCP emplacement hole (see DOE, 1988)
Subarea 5	0.0	0.4	Uniform	Upper limit based on twice the cross-sectional area of SCP emplacement hole (see DOE, 1988)
Subarea 6	0.0	0.4	Uniform	Upper limit based on twice the cross-sectional area of SCP emplacement hole (see DOE, 1988)
Subarea 7	0.0	0.4	Uniform	Upper limit based on twice the cross-sectional area of SCP emplacement hole (see DOE, 1988)

Parameter	Range in Value		Distribution	Basis for Parameter Assignment
	High	Low		

a   Reported range and correlation-length consideration.

b   ± one order of magnitude of the mean of the log of retardation factors cited in Codell *et al.* (1992).

c   ± one order of magnitude of the mean of the log of the reported values for Wells G3, J13, and UE25a1.

d   ± one order of magnitude of the mean of the log of the reported value for Well G2.

e   Allowances made for density and porosity.

f   ± one order of magnitude of the mean of the log of the reported values for Wells G1 and UE25a1.

g   ± one order of magnitude of the mean of the log of the reported value for Well G3.

h   ± one order of magnitude of the mean of the log of the reported values for Wells G1 and G3.

i   ± one order of magnitude of the mean of the log of the reported values for Wells G1, J13, and UE25a1.

j   ± one order of magnitude of the mean of the log of the reported value for Well G1.

k   ± one order of magnitude of the mean of the log of the reported values for Wells G3 and UE25a1.

l   ± one order of magnitude of the mean of the log of the reported values for Wells G1, G3, and UE25a1.

m   ± one order of magnitude of the mean of the log of the reported value for Well J13.

n   ± one order of magnitude of the mean of the log of the reported values for Well UE25a1.

References

Codell, R.B., *et al.*, "Initial Demonstration of the NRC's Capability to Conduct a Performance Assessment for a High-Level Waste Repository," U.S. Nuclear Regulatory Commission, NUREG-1327, May 1992.

Grambow, B., "Spent Fuel Dissolution and Oxidation: An Evaluation of Literature Data," Stockholm, Sweden, Statens Kärnkraftinspektion [SKI – Swedish Nuclear Power Inspectorate], SKI Technical Report 89:13, March 1989.

Meijer, A., "Yucca Mountain Project Far-Field Sorption Studies and Data Needs," Los Alamos, New Mexico, Los Alamos National Laboratory, LA-11671-MS, September 1990.

Peters, R.R., *et al.*, "Fracture and Matrix Hydrologic Characteristics of Tuffaceous Materials from Yucca Mountain, Nye County, Nevada," Albuquerque, New Mexico, Sandia National Laboratories, SAND84-1471, December 1984.

U.S. Department of Energy, "Chapter 6, Conceptual Design of a Repository," in "Site Characterization Plan, Yucca Mountain Site, Nevada Research and Development Area, Nevada," Nevada Operations Office/Yucca Mountain Project Office, Nevada, DOE/RW-0199, vol. III, Part A, December 1988.

Wescott, R.G., *et al.* (eds.), "NRC Iterative Performance Assessment Phase 2: Development of Capabilities for Review of a Performance Assessment for a High-Level Waste Repository," U.S. Nuclear Regulatory Commission, NUREG-1464, October 1995.

APPENDIX I
STAFF PARTICIPATING IN THE PRELIMINARY
PERFORMANCE-BASED ANALYSES

Staff members from the U.S. Nuclear Regulatory Commission Offices of Nuclear Material Safety and Safeguards (NMSS); and Nuclear Regulatory Research (RES), as well as Center for Nuclear Waste Regulatory Analyses (CNWRA) staff members, have contributed to this NUREG. Each of the eight divisions of technical activity was assigned to a working group with a designated task leader(s). The task leaders proposed plans for the various technical activities and staffing. The staff cited below were responsible for conducting the respective analyses and documenting the results.

Scoping Analysis Topic Area	*Analysis Team[a]/Organization*
Receptor Group	**M. Lee/NMSS** **G. Wittmeyer/CNWRA** N. Eisenberg/NMSS[b] R. Codell/NMSS N. Coleman/NMSS C. Glenn/NMSS P. LaPlante/CNWRA L. McKague/CNWRA P. Prestholt/NMSS[b]
Human Intrusion	**R. Wescott/NMSS** **T. McCartin/NMSS** M. Lee/NMSS
Hazards Comparison	**R. Mantuefel/CNWRA** R. Baca/CNWRA M. Jarzemba/CNWRA
Volcanism	**M. Jarzemba/CNWRA** **T. McCartin/NMSS** R. Codell/NMSS B. Hill/CNWRA C. McKenny/NMSS J. Trapp/NMSS R. Wescott/NMSS
Saturated Zone Heterogeneity	**R. Baca/CNWRA** S. McDuffie/NMSS[b] R. Rice[c] G. Wittmeyer/CNWRA
Dose	**T. McCartin/NMSS** R. Codell/NMSS M. Jarzemba/CNWRA P. LaPlante/CNWRA R. Mantuefel/CNWRA R. Neel/NMSS[b]

NUREG-1538

Scoping Analysis Topic Area	*Analysis Team [a]/Organization*
Arid Site Well Practices	**G. Wittmeyer/CNWRA** M. Miklas/CNWRA R. Klar/CNWRA D. Williams[c] D. Balin[c]
Dilution Analysis	**R. Fedors/CNWRA** **G. Wittmeyer/CNWRA** C. Glenn/NMSS R. Martin/CNWRA
Analysis Team Members at-Large	J. Bradbury/NMSS M. Byrne/NMSS[b] R. Cady/RES J. Davis/NMSS J. Firth/NMSS J. Kotra/NMSS P. Mackin/CNWRA R. Abu-Eid/NMSS

[a] Bold type designates principal investigators.
[b] Retired.
[c] Independent consultants.

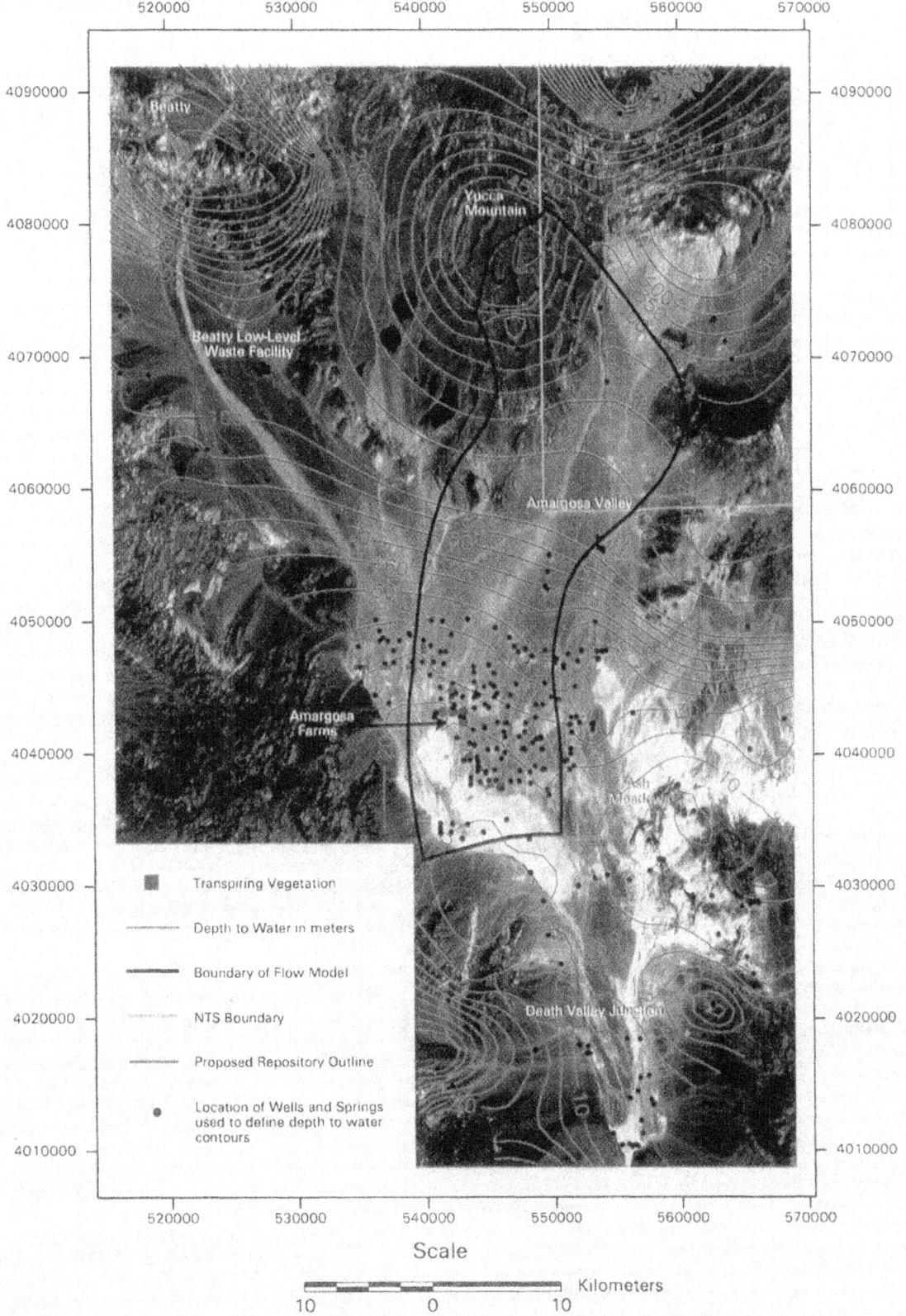

Figure 2–5. **Landsat Image of the Yucca Mountain and the Amargosa Desert Region.** In the Amargosa Farms area, red circular forms are quarter-section, center-pivot irrigation plots. These contrast with flood-irrigation plots shown as rectangular-shaped forms. Irregular red patches correspond to areas in Ash Meadows containing wetland/riparian vegetation. Blue contour lines showing the depth to the water table are in the equivalent of meters. Thematic sensor data from the Landsat satellite were used to produce the background image. Satellite altitude was approximately 185 kilometers (115 miles).

CO1

NRC FORM 335
(2-89)
NRCM 1102,
3201, 3202

U.S. NUCLEAR REGULATORY COMMISSION

BIBLIOGRAPHIC DATA SHEET

(See instructions on the reverse)

1. REPORT NUMBER (Assigned by NRC, Add Vol., Supp., Rev., and Addendum Numbers, if any.)
NUREG-1538

2. TITLE AND SUBTITLE

PRELIMINARY PERFORMANCE-BASED ANALYSES RELEVANT TO DOSE-BASED PERFORMANCE MEASURES FOR A PROPOSED GEOLOGIC REPOSITORY AT YUCCA MOUNTAIN

3. DATE REPORT PUBLISHED

MONTH	YEAR
October	2001

4. FIN OR GRANT NUMBER

5. AUTHOR(S)

T.J. McCartin and M.P. Lee (editors)

6. TYPE OF REPORT

Technical

7. PERIOD COVERED *(Inclusive Dates)*

8. PERFORMING ORGANIZATION - NAME AND ADDRESS *(If NRC, provide Division, Office or Region, U.S. Nuclear Regulatory Commission, and mailing address; if contractor, provide name and mailing address.)*

Division of Waste Management, Office of Nuclear Material Safety and Safeguards,
U.S. Nuclear Regulatory Commission, Washington, D.C. 20555-0001
Center for Nuclear Waste Regulatory Analyses,
6220 Culebra Road, San Antonio, Texas 78228-5155

9. SPONSORING ORGANIZATION - NAME AND ADDRESS *(If NRC, type "Same as above"; if contractor, provide NRC Division, Office or Region, U.S. Nuclear Regulatory Commission, and mailing address.)*

Division of Waste Management, Office of Nuclear Material Safety and Safeguards,
U.S. Nuclear Regulatory Commission, Washington, D.C. 20555-0001

10. SUPPLEMENTARY NOTES

11. ABSTRACT *(200 words or less)*

The NAS recommended that standards for HLW disposal at Yucca Mountain should: (1) set a limit on individual risk; (2) use the ICRP critical group approach; (3) define the critical group using present knowledge and cautious, reasonable assumptions; (4) use a time period for conducting compliance assessment that includes the period of greatest risk; and (5) use a stylized calculation to assess whether the repository's performance would be substantially degraded as a consequence of a postulated intrusion. The staff was able to: (1) tentatively identify characteristics for two potential receptor groups using information for lifestyles and water-use practices presently occurring in the Yucca Mountain area and in other, similar environments; (2) ascertain the potential for reducing radionuclide concentrations in ground water caused by dispersive transport processes and borehole mixing in a pumping water well; (3) describe an approach to implement a dose calculation for the residential and farming receptor groups; (4) describe an approach to implement a dose calculation for direct disruption of the repository from volcanic activity; (5) describe an approach to a stylized calculation for human intrusion; and (6) evaluate the time dependence of radiological hazard of HLW by comparison with naturally concentrated uranium in an ore body.

12. KEY WORDS/DESCRIPTORS *(List words or phrases that will assist researchers in locating the report.)*

Amargosa Valley
critical group
dilution
disruptive events
dose
exploratory drilling
geologic repository
ground water
high-level radioactive waste
human intrusion

Iterative performance assessment
National Academy of Sciences
radionuclides
radiological hazards
total system performance assessment
transport
Yucca Mountain
volcanism

13. AVAILABILITY STATEMENT

unlimited

14. SECURITY CLASSIFICATION

(This Page)

unclassified

(This Report)

unclassified

15. NUMBER OF PAGES

16. PRICE

NRC FORM 335 (2-89)